Geopolitics of the South China Sea:

Power Struggle in Asia

Ferdi Güçyetmez
Independent Researcher, Switzerland

Aybala Lale Kahraman
Bursa Technical University, Turkey

IGI Global
Scientific Publishing
Publishing Tomorrow's Research Today

Vice President of Editorial	Melissa Wagner
Managing Editor of Acquisitions	Mikaela Felty
Managing Editor of Book Development	Jocelynn Hessler
Production Manager	Mike Brehm
Cover Design	Phillip Shickler

Published in the United States of America by
IGI Global Scientific Publishing
701 East Chocolate Avenue
Hershey, PA, 17033, USA
Tel: 717-533-8845
Fax: 717-533-8661
Website: https://www.igi-global.com E-mail: cust@igi-global.com

Library of Congress Cataloging-in-Publication Data

Names: Güçyetmez, Ferdi, 1991- editor. | Lale Kahraman, Aybala, 1993- editor.
Title: Geopolitics of the South China Sea : power struggle in Asia / edited by Ferdi Güçyetmez, Aybala Lale Kahraman.
Description: Hershey, PA : IGI Global Scientific Publishing, [2025] | Includes bibliographical references. | Summary: "By unravelling the complex web of relations in the South China Sea, we aim to help readers understand the tensions in the region through geopolitical concepts. This book aims to fill the knowledge gap on the geopolitics of the South China Sea and provide readers with a comprehensive perspective"-- Provided by publisher.
Identifiers: LCCN 2024050855 (print) | LCCN 2024050856 (ebook) | ISBN 9798369381090 (h/c) | ISBN 9798369381106 (s/c) | ISBN 9798369381113 (ebook)
Subjects: LCSH: Geopolitics--South China Sea. | South China Sea--Strategic aspects. | South China Sea--International status. | South China Sea Region--Politics and govenment.
Classification: LCC DS525.8 .G46 2025 (print) | LCC DS525.8 (ebook) | DDC 327.09164/72--dc23/eng/20241231
LC record available at https://lccn.loc.gov/2024050855
LC ebook record available at https://lccn.loc.gov/2024050856

British Cataloguing in Publication Data
A Cataloguing in Publication record for this book is available from the British Library.

Table of Contents

Detailed Table of Contents

Conflicts have shifted in the 21st century from claimed territories to extraterritorial places. The disputes among states were based on territorial claims up to the previous century. The demarcation of territorial boundaries has effectively resolved land conflicts as a spatial concept. Because some states have unsettled land boundaries that serve as the basis for interstate conflict, the establishment and maintenance of land borders therefore continues to be a critical problem for state sovereignty. But in the maritime realm, the same clarity that is required to control state behaviour has not been attained. The states' perception of South China Sea (SCS) as per nautical area will dictate whether they cooperate or compete in the region. Individual maritime and territorial claims have the potential to cause regional instability. This paper aimed to analyse the energy geopolitics of the SCS by taking into account its potential, territorial disputes, the basic dynamics and the approaches of the regional states, especially in line with Beijing's claims and aggressive stance.

In recent years, India has made concerted efforts to expand its power and influence in South Asia. Asia. With the sharp increase in population, economy, and technology, India is expected to be more involved in both regional and global affairs in the future. India is unlikely to want China or any regional country or countries to assume the leadership of the region on its own. India aims to present a profile of cooperating with regional or global actors in terms of either ruling the region alone or jointly shaping the region. Any alternative policy of eliminating India from South Asia is likely to have a profound impact on the development and stability of the region. Although India is not yet a leading economy in South Asia, its economic and strategic position in the region is increasing significantly. As a growing power, India's new regional and global policy, especially its pioneering role in establishing new initiatives, demonstrates its intention to increase its power and influence both in South Asia and the world.

This study analyzes India's position in South China Sea policies. The policies followed by New Delhi are examined within the framework of the question of which actors defend which theses in the conflicts in the region. As a rising actor that creates significant impact in its own geography, India also plays a policy-determining role in the South China Sea issues with the relations it has developed with various countries. On this basis, India's steps are especially important for the strategic interests of China, with which it is in competition. The South China Sea (SCS) dispute has become an issue in which other actors in the region have been involved in recent years. Territorial conflicts and disputes over maritime jurisdictions are increasing tensions among Vietnam, the Philippines, Taiwan, Malaysia and Brunei, and China. The aforementioned countries claim that China is trying to increase its sovereign territory and Exclusive Economic Zones (EEZ) through various activities.

This chapter analyzes Malaysia's orientations within the context of strategic competition, mainly between the US and China. Since the Cold War, Malaysia has been mindful of the negative repercussions of power competition in Southeast Asia and has consistently insisted on maintaining strategic independence from this rivalry. Therefore, Malaysia often seeks to de-escalate tensions in the South China Sea and prioritizes peaceful solutions. Instead of playing a role in drawing larger alliance partners into conflict, Malaysia exemplifies the opposite: the role of an asymmetrically smaller state in alleviating regional tensions, particularly by maintaining a strategic distance from the main rival states, even though its room for maneuver is limited.

This paper delves into Taiwan's strategic use of its territorial claims in the South China Sea as a means of constructing a narrative that asserts its sovereignty and enhances its international visibility. Amidst the complex geopolitical landscape of the region, Taiwan's involvement serves not only to maintain its territorial interests but also to affirm its identity as a sovereign state independent of the PRC, which

This study examines Vietnam's strategic partnership role in India's policy to counter China's hegemonic ambitions in the East Sea. Through a qualitative analysis combining policy analysis, historical methods, and document synthesis, the research explores three key factors defining this partnership: Vietnam's geostrategic position, the impact of historical conflicts with China, and Vietnam's emergence as a middle power. The findings reveal that Vietnam's critical location at the nexus of Southeast Asian maritime routes, coupled with its direct involvement in East Sea disputes, positions it as a pivotal player in regional geopolitics. The historical context of Sino-Vietnamese conflicts has profoundly shaped Vietnamese leadership perspectives, fostering a cautious yet resilient approach to regional power dynamics. Vietnam's remarkable economic growth and increasing diplomatic clout have elevated it to the status of an emerging middle power, enhancing its capacity to engage in strategic partnerships.

This chapter analyzes Taiwan's SCS policies by examining their historical, legal, security, economic, and diplomatic dimensions. The historical context will explore the origins and evolution of Taiwan's territorial claims, while the legal section will analyze how international law influences its maritime strategy. The security section will focus on Taiwan's asymmetric defense measures and their implications for regional stability. The economic section will highlight Taiwan's reliance on the SCS for trade and resource security, illustrating how its economic strategy aligns with its broader policy objectives. Finally, the diplomatic section will evaluate Taiwan's efforts to overcome international isolation through soft power initiatives and strategic partnerships. By integrating these perspectives, this chapter aims to

Preface

The South China Sea (SCS) stands as one of the most geopolitically significant maritime regions in the world today, with its rich natural resources, critical trade routes, and overlapping territorial claims. This volume, *Geopolitics of the South China Sea: Power Struggle in Asia*, offers an in-depth examination of the complex and often contentious geopolitical landscape surrounding this vital body of water. The contributions of scholars from various parts of the world highlight the multi-dimensional nature of the SCS disputes, exploring not only the territorial and maritime claims but also the broader implications for regional and global power dynamics.

The book brings together a diverse range of perspectives, from ASEAN's diplomatic efforts to regional powers like India, Australia, and Vietnam, and the legal dimensions surrounding the territorial claims. The essays contained in this collection provide critical insights into the intersection of historical grievances, strategic alliances, and economic interests that shape the SCS conflict. As the region continues to experience rising tensions, the volume seeks to understand how local actors and global powers engage with these disputes, either through cooperation or confrontation, and the potential for both escalation and de-escalation.

We, the editors, have endeavored to compile a comprehensive resource for scholars, policymakers, and practitioners interested in understanding the complexity of the South China Sea disputes. The work presented here is intended not only to reflect the current state of affairs but also to offer forward-looking analyses that can inform future discussions and decisions regarding peace and stability in the region.

INTRODUCTION

The South China Sea disputes have captured the attention of international relations scholars, regional experts, and global policymakers for decades. As the gateway to vital maritime trade routes, this region is central to the economic interests of many countries, including China, the United States, ASEAN members, and other regional actors. Beyond economic concerns, the SCS is a stage for geopolitical competition, where nations vie for control over territorial waters, undersea resources, and strategic positioning.

In this context, ASEAN (the Association of Southeast Asian Nations) plays a crucial role as a regional organization in managing tensions. The organization's policies and strategies regarding the South China Sea are shaped by a delicate balance of national interests and collective goals. While ASEAN member states have differing views on how best to handle the dispute, they share a common desire to preserve regional stability and prevent the escalation of conflicts that could lead to wider confrontations. This volume's first chapter explores ASEAN's role in navigating these challenges, offering an analysis of its diplomatic efforts and the difficulties it faces in uniting diverse member states under a common agenda.

The competition for dominance in the South China Sea is also heavily influenced by external actors such as the United States, India, and Australia. These powers have vital interests in maintaining freedom of navigation in the region and countering China's growing assertiveness. The chapters addressing Australia's policies and India's emerging influence in the SCS demonstrate how these countries are shaping their responses to China's territorial claims and regional ambitions. Through strategic partnerships and military alliances, India and Australia seek to balance China's influence and assert their presence in this critical geopolitical space.

CHAPTER OVERVIEWS

Chapter 1. ASEAN in The South China Sea Disputes

Author: Bahar Köse

This chapter critically analyzes the role of ASEAN in managing the South China Sea disputes, examining its policies, strategies, and the organization's effectiveness in maintaining regional peace and security. It explores ASEAN's founding principles and its mechanisms for dispute resolution, focusing on how it deals with sovereignty claims, maritime jurisdiction conflicts, and external pressures. The study aims to provide a comprehensive understanding of ASEAN's contributions to regional stability and its influence on international relations in the SCS.

Chapter 2. Australia's Policy in the South China Sea

Author: Cenk Tamer

Australia's policies regarding the South China Sea are critically examined in this chapter, focusing on the impact of US-China competition. The study discusses Australia's relationships with both China and the US, its core vision for the South China Sea, and the influence of China's territorial claims on its policies. By analyzing Australia's strategic positioning in the region, the chapter offers insight into how Australia navigates its alliances while addressing its own interests in the maritime dispute.

Chapter 3. Energy Geopolitics of the South China Sea: Can The Prevailing And Prospective Hydrocarbons Within The Region Further Escalate Or De-Escalate Tensions?

Authors: Murat Yorulmaz & Sina Kısacık

This chapter delves into the energy geopolitics of the South China Sea, emphasizing the potential for hydrocarbons to exacerbate or alleviate regional tensions. The authors analyze the region's energy potential, territorial disputes, and the dynamics of regional states, particularly Beijing's aggressive stance. By examining how energy resources shape the behavior of states, the chapter provides a nuanced understanding of how energy geopolitics influences the broader geopolitical competition in the region.

Chapter 4. India's Power Struggle in South Asia

Author: Emrah Yıldırımçakar

India's growing influence in South Asia is the focus of this chapter, which examines how India is expanding its power and strategic presence in the region. The study discusses India's efforts to prevent China from assuming regional leadership and its emerging role in both regional and global affairs. By analyzing India's economic, technological, and military advancements, this chapter explores how India is positioning itself as a key player in shaping the future of South Asia and its global role.

Chapter 5. India's Policies in the South China Sea

Author: Şeyma Kızılay

This chapter analyzes India's approach to the South China Sea and its role in the broader regional dynamics. By examining the conflicting territorial claims and maritime jurisdiction disputes, the author explores India's strategic interests in the region. India's relationships with other regional actors, particularly its rivalry with China, are central to understanding its policies in the South China Sea, which have become increasingly significant as India seeks to assert itself in global geopolitics.

Chapter 6. Malaysia's South China Sea Policy: The Role of Small States in Peacebuilding?

Author: Halil Deligöz

Malaysia's strategy in navigating the South China Sea disputes is analyzed in this chapter, particularly its role as a small state attempting to de-escalate tensions between larger powers. Malaysia has maintained a policy of strategic independence, advocating for peaceful solutions and avoiding becoming entangled in the power competition between China and the US. This chapter examines how Malaysia's diplomatic efforts and its position in the region have influenced regional peacebuilding initiatives.

Chapter 7. Narrative Power: Taiwan's South China Sea Claim as a Strategy in Securing Its International Visibility

Authors: Eva Ermylina & Ali Demir

This chapter explores Taiwan's use of its territorial claims in the South China Sea as a means of asserting its sovereignty and increasing its international visibility. By applying Strategic Narrative theory, the authors analyze Taiwan's narrative construction in the SCS, which helps counter its diplomatic isolation and positions Taiwan as a responsible actor in regional security. The chapter examines Taiwan's approach to regional geopolitics, emphasizing its strategic goals in the context of its ongoing disputes with China.

Chapter 8. Navigating The Geopolitics of the South China Sea: Re-Emerging Maritime Dynamics in the Systemic World Order

Author: Bilal Elikoğlu

This chapter offers a broader, systemic perspective on the geopolitics of the South China Sea, considering the competition between continental and sea powers throughout history. The study avoids a narrow, geographically limited view of the region and instead examines the geopolitical cycles at play. The author discusses the broader global competition between powers and how the dynamics of the South China Sea reflect and influence systemic changes in the world order, highlighting the role of maritime forces in global geopolitics.

Chapter 9. The South China Sea Disputes: International Law

Author: Zeynep Fırat Erkan

This chapter focuses on the legal aspects of the South China Sea disputes, particularly the implications of the United Nations Convention on the Law of the Sea (UNCLOS). The study explores how conflicting territorial claims and interpretations of UNCLOS have complicated the resolution of the disputes. The chapter highlights the challenges in enforcing international law in the SCS due to the region's complex geopolitics and offers recommendations for legal reforms to better address the ongoing territorial disputes.

Chapter 10. The South China Sea Politics of the Philippines

Author: Sami Yıldırım

The Philippines' role in the South China Sea politics is examined in this chapter, which looks at the historical context, legal frameworks, and strategic interests of the country in relation to the maritime disputes. The chapter analyzes the Philippines' responses to China's growing influence and its efforts to protect its territorial integrity and economic interests. The Philippines' position in the SCS is central to understanding the broader regional tensions and the evolving diplomatic landscape in Southeast Asia.

Chapter 11. USA Policy in the South China Sea: An Analysis from a Geopolitical Perspective

Author: Meysune Yaşar

This chapter examines the United States' policy in the South China Sea from the perspective of critical geopolitics. The author explores the strategic, diplomatic, and historical aspects of US involvement in the region, highlighting its role in countering China's maritime claims. The study emphasizes the influence of critical geopolitics in shaping the US approach to the region and discusses the implications of US policy for global maritime security and regional stability.

Chapter 12. Vietnam's Strategic Partnership Role in India's Policy to Counter China's Hegemonic Ambitions in the East Sea

Authors: Kiet Hoang Le & Hiep Xuan Tran

This chapter explores Vietnam's critical role in India's strategy to counter China's ambitions in the South China Sea, emphasizing their strategic partnership. The authors analyze the historical context, geostrategic positioning, and evolving diplomatic relationships between India and Vietnam, and how these factors contribute to regional power dynamics. The chapter demonstrates Vietnam's growing influence as a middle power in Southeast Asia and its important role in shaping regional geopolitics in opposition to China's assertive policies.

Chapter 13. Taiwan's Policy Regarding the South China Sea

Author: Göktuğ Çalışkan

This chapter analyzes Taiwan's policies in the South China Sea from multiple perspectives: historical, legal, security, economic, and diplomatic. By examining Taiwan's territorial claims and its efforts to maintain a foothold in the region, the study sheds light on Taiwan's strategic objectives and its reliance on the South China Sea for economic and resource security. The chapter discusses Taiwan's diplomatic efforts to overcome international isolation, its asymmetric defense strategies, and its broader regional and global ambitions.

CONCLUSION

The South China Sea continues to be a flashpoint in international relations, where regional and global powers intersect in a high-stakes game of diplomacy, military posturing, and economic maneuvering. As this book demonstrates, the SCS disputes cannot be understood through a single lens; they require a comprehensive analysis of historical, legal, economic, and security dimensions. Each chapter in this volume contributes to a broader understanding of the multifaceted nature of the conflict and the various factors that influence how nations engage with the issue.

The role of international law, particularly the United Nations Convention on the Law of the Sea (UNCLOS), is central to resolving the territorial disputes in the SCS. However, as several chapters point out, the application of international legal frameworks has often been hindered by geopolitical tensions and the lack of enforcement mechanisms. The legal challenges surrounding the South China Sea highlight the difficulties in achieving a lasting and comprehensive resolution, especially when powerful nations choose to ignore or reinterpret international law to serve their interests.

Ultimately, the future of the South China Sea will depend on the ability of regional and global powers to navigate the complex web of interests and conflicts that shape the region. Cooperation and dialogue, though difficult, remain essential to de-escalating tensions and fostering a peaceful resolution. The contributions in this volume reflect the challenges and opportunities in achieving a more stable and cooperative geopolitical order in the South China Sea, and offer valuable insights for policymakers and scholars alike.

Ferdi Güçyetmez
Independent Researcher, Switzerland

Aybala Lale Kahraman
Bursa Technical University, Turkey

Chapter 1
ASEAN in the South China Sea Disputes

Bahar Köse
https://orcid.org/0000-0001-5204-7271
Karadeniz Technical University, Turkey

ABSTRACT

This study aims to critically analyze ASEAN's policies and strategies concerning the South China Sea (SCS) disputes and assess their impact on regional peace and security. By examining ASEAN's approaches to managing sovereignty claims, maritime jurisdiction conflicts, and its role in fostering dialogue and cooperation among member states, the research will shed light on the organization's effectiveness in mitigating regional tensions. The study will explore ASEAN's founding principles, its formal and informal mechanisms for dispute resolution, and the challenges it faces due to external and internal pressures. Ultimately, it seeks to provide a comprehensive understanding of ASEAN's contributions to regional stability and its influence on international relations in the context of the SCS.

INTRODUCTION

The foundation of the South China Sea disputes lies in historical and legal claims, access to natural resources, quests for strategic control, and differing interpretations of international law. Historical sovereignty claims, which began with the 'Nine-Dash Line' map published by China in 1947, have become more complex as the riparian states of the Philippines, Brunei, Malaysia, and Vietnam have also asserted rights to the same regions (Tuan, 2016). China's decision to increase its military presence in the region to bolster its claims has raised concerns among ASEAN countries, and tensions in the region have escalated as these countries have also sought to

DOI: 10.4018/979-8-3693-8109-0.ch001

strengthen their military presence (Grossman, 2020). The South China Sea has drawn the interest of both external powers and the riparian states. China's efforts to strengthen its strategic control by increasing its military presence in the area are contrary to the interests of the United States and other Western countries, which advocate for freedom of navigation and the enforcement of international law in the region (Buszynski, 2020). Similarly, other major powers, such as Japan and India, are also involved in efforts to ensure maritime security in the region and balance China's growing influence (Darmawan, 2020; Scott, 2013). The involvement of external powers in the region complicates the issue and turns the disputes into a global matter.

In the South China Sea, a competitive area for riparian states and global actors, ASEAN plays an important role in maintaining regional peace and stability. Founded on August 8, 1967, by Indonesia, the Philippines, Singapore, Thailand, and Malaysia with the Bangkok Declaration, the organization provides a platform that encourages the peaceful resolution of regional disputes and aims to enhance cooperation among its member countries (Hayton, 2014). With this declaration, the aims and objectives of the union were set forth as follows: accelerating the economic, social, and cultural development in the region; promoting regional peace and stability within the framework of justice and the rule of law; fostering cooperation in line with common interests; sharing opportunities in education and research; increasing agricultural and industrial productivity; expanding trade; improving transportation and communication infrastructure; and continuing cooperation with international and regional organizations (Association of Southeast Asian Nations [ASEAN], 1967). The establishment of ASEAN was regarded as the first serious attempt by regional states to create a mechanism for managing regional conflicts, and the organization expanded with the participation of Brunei in 1984, Vietnam in 1995, Laos and Myanmar in 1997, and Cambodia in 1999 (Caballero-Anthony, 2005).

ASEAN, since its inception, has sought to preserve the independence of Southeast Asia against foreign interference. Countries that claim rights in the South China Sea, such as Vietnam, the Philippines, Malaysia, Brunei, Indonesia, and Singapore, are also members of ASEAN. The economic growth and expansion of these countries are closely linked to the region's energy resources and trade potential (Saw, Sheng & Chin, 2005). Due to its importance, the region has become a battleground for power struggles between countries like the US, China, and India. Hence, resolving the South China Sea issue is essential for ASEAN's goal of ensuring regional stability and integration. In this context, the organization has included the issue of stability in the South China Sea in the ASEAN Political-Security Community Blueprint (APSC), which outlines its 2025 goals (ASEAN Political-Security Community Blueprint, 2009). Tensions in the region could harm ASEAN's goal of cooperation and hurt its global reputation. ASEAN resolves disputes by mediating, maintaining stability, supporting international law, and building trust, which strengthens its role in global politics.

The aim of the study is to analyze ASEAN's policies regarding the South China Sea disputes and assess their impact on the peace and stability of the region. In this context, the basic dynamics that cause disputes in the region will be discussed and ASEAN's policies to control conflicts and reduce tension in the region and the effectiveness of these policies will be analysed. An evaluation of ASEAN's founding principles and how these principles are implemented in the South China Sea context will pave the way for understanding the organization's role and effectiveness in solving this complex problem. In addition, the strong and improvable aspects of the organization's policies towards the region will be emphasized and suggestions will be presented for the organization to develop more effective policies. In this way, the necessary framework will be established for ensuring peace and stability in the region and the role and strategic importance of international organizations in ensuring regional peace will be emphasized.

In the first part of the study, which is planned as three main sections, will explore the strategic importance of the South China Sea and the historical and legal context of the sovereignty claims in the region, and will reveal the basic dynamics of the disputes. Thus, the basic information required to understand the complex geopolitical situation in the region will be provided, and a basis will be prepared for how ASEAN plays a role in this context and how the relevant policies are shaped. Next, ASEAN's basic principles and the role of these principles in resolving disputes will be analysed, and ASEAN's strategies for ensuring regional peace and security will be examined. This part will address the formal and informal mechanisms used by ASEAN in resolving disputes. Hence, preliminary information will be provided on how the organization manages diplomacy, dialogue and reconciliation processes. Finally, ASEAN's diplomatic initiatives, the difficulties it has encountered and the successes it has achieved in the South China Sea will be detailed. The study will examine ASEAN's policies on the South China Sea disputes, focusing on their effectiveness, limitations, and challenges, and provide suggestions for improving strategies to ensure regional peace and stability.

1. THE NATURE OF SOUTH CHINA SEA DISPUTES

The South China Sea, spanning approximately 3.5 million square kilometers, has great importance in regional and international politics due to its strategic location, rich natural resources and biodiversity (Buszynski & Roberts, 2013). The fact that one-third of global trade passes through the region's sea routes and that the energy resources in the region have immense potential directly affects the economic and security interests of many Asian countries (Raymond & Welch, 2022). Hence, the region is a complex geography where coastal countries make claims in terms of sovereignty and resource rights. The historical and legal claims of coastal states, access to the region's energy resources, countries' quest for strategic control and different interpretations of international law combine to make the South China Sea a complex geopolitical node in the Asia-Pacific region. In this context, understanding the geopolitical dynamics of the South China Sea and the interests of regional actors is of great importance for maintaining stability in the region.

The South China Sea, which is home to more than 250 terrestrial features, is divided into six main groups: the Paracel Islands, Spratly Islands, Pratas Islands, Scarborough Shoal, Macclesfield Bank, and the Natuna Islands (Sacks, 2022). Although the Paracel Islands are under the control of the People's Republic of China, Vietnam and Taiwan also claim these islands (Raine & Mière, 2013). China, Taiwan, and Vietnam claim the entire Spratly Islands, which are occupied by China, Vietnam, Taiwan, Malaysia, and the Philippines, while Malaysia, the Philippines, and Brunei claim rights in various parts of the Spratlys (Mitchell, 2016). Both China and Taiwan claim Macclesfield Bank, Pratas Islands, and Scarborough Shoal, with Scarborough Shoal also claimed by the Philippines (Kipgen, 2020). The Natuna Islands are entirely under the control of Indonesia. The overlapping rights claims of these countries, along with conflicting sovereignty claims and strategic interests, deepen geopolitical tensions in the region and create complexities in the context of maritime law. Thus, it is important to understand the basis of the claims made by all claimant countries.

All parties to the disputes have valid reasons to assert their claims to all or part of the region. For example, China claims rights over a large part of the sea, citing ancient archives and records dating back to the Song Dynasty (Li, 2018). It claims almost the entire region with the "U"-shaped "Nine-Dash Line," which it first expressed in 1914, and the legal meaning of the borders of this line remains unclear (Senkyr & Merkle, 2023). Taiwan also refers to ancient records, such as the nine-dash map, which are important documents supporting its historical claims to these regions (Storey, 2016). Likewise, other countries, such as Vietnam and the Philippines, argue that they historically have rights to this region. This indicates that assertions in the South China Sea are linked not only to international law and regional strategy but also national history and culture. These intricate sovereignty disputes must be addressed in their historical, legal, and strategic dimensions.

The legal challenge of the South China Sea dispute is that the general status and sovereignty of most features in the region are unclear and contested (Groten, 2019). In simpler terms, the heart of the issue revolves around the ambiguity surrounding the ownership of the islands, islets, and landmasses in the region, along with the territorial waters, continental shelves, and exclusive economic zones (EEZ) associated with these areas, and the ongoing discussions about how these rights should be clearly established. The United Nations Convention on the Law of the Sea (UNCLOS) stands out as the most fundamental and comprehensive document regarding the determination and delimitation of sea areas. While the convention limits territorial waters to 12 nautical miles, it extends the continental shelf up to 200 nautical miles and grants rights to research and utilize resources on the seabed (United Nations, 1982). The EEZ provides the right to explore and use both living and non-living resources in areas beyond territorial waters, but artificial islands have a security zone of only 500 meters and do not grant rights to an EEZ or continental shelf (United Nations, 1982). Thus, China's construction of military bases in the region and making these islands suitable for human habitation complicates legal and political issues and exacerbates the conflicts in the region.

The history of conflict and disputes in the South China Sea is not limited to regional coastal states. States' attempts to interpret international law and maritime conventions in ways that support their own interests not only create ongoing tension between countries in the region but also draw the international community into a complex diplomatic struggle. South China Sea is of interest not only to regional countries but also to external powers. The main reasons for this situation include the region's economic and strategic importance, its role in understanding and counter-balancing China's rising power, its potential impact on the relations between major powers like the USA and Asia-Pacific countries, and the interests of countries such as India, Australia, Japan, and some European Union member states in developing and maintaining relations with the countries in the region (Till, 2016). Although external actors do not claim any land or sea in the region, they seek to establish a balance of power for reasons such as the security of maritime routes, the continuity of international trade, and the preservation of strategic balances.

It is often thought that issues of authority and sovereignty should be handled solely by the states directly involved in the dispute. However, in the South China Sea disputes, which are both a regional and global issue, the complex interactions between sovereignty claims, international law, and strategic interests complicate efforts to ensure stability in the region and encourage various international actors to intervene. In fact, all actors have an interest in stopping illegal fishing activities in these waters and preventing or reducing the illegal trade of species under threat of extinction (Severino, 2016). For this reason, states that do not claim rights in the region also voice their concerns about the disputes and contribute to developing effective solutions. While some states support China, others support the Philippines and other ASEAN countries, and some prefer to remain neutral and uphold international law (Kipgen, 2020). Ultimately, international cooperation and multilateral negotiations are crucial for solving this global problem; in this context, ASEAN's role in promoting regional stability and ensuring a peaceful resolution between the parties serves a strategic function.

2. ASEAN'S PEACE AND SECURITY FRAMEWORK AND THE DEVELOPMENT OF MULTILATERAL MECHANISMS

ASEAN uses both formal and informal mechanisms and actions to enhance regional peace and security. Formal mechanisms include official meetings and negotiations on issues of mutual interest, institutionalized bilateral processes and mechanisms, and legal instruments used to manage and prevent disputes (Caballero-Anthony, 2005). These mechanisms support ASEAN's effective efforts to maintain regional peace and security, while also serving as strategic tools to strengthen cooperation and harmony among member states. The informal mechanisms used by ASEAN in conflict resolution are complementary to formal processes and include friendly relations and diplomatic efforts to establish channels of communication among member states. Besides, trust-building and mediation processes play an crucial role in increasing common trust by reducing tensions. By using both formal and informal methods, ASEAN adopts a flexible and comprehensive approach to achieving its goal of promoting regional peace and security. This part will discuss the formal and informal mechanisms that ASEAN uses for conflict management.

2.1. Formal Mechanism

The foundations of ASEAN's peace and security structure were created by establishing common norms and values through a series of important documents. In the Bangkok Declaration, the founding document of the organization, it was stated that promoting regional peace and stability by respecting justice and the rule of law, and adhering to the principles of the United Nations Charter, was one of the aims and objectives of the organization (Association of Southeast Asian Nations [ASEAN], 1967). While Article 1 of the United Nations Charter aims to maintain international peace and security, resolve disputes peacefully, and promote justice and the rule of law in international relations, Article 2 requires member states to respect the territorial integrity and political independence of other states by refraining from the use or threat of force (Charter of the United Nations, 1945). The principles set out in Articles 1 and 2 of the United Nations Charter underpin the fundamental principles adopted by ASEAN in promoting regional peace and security. In this regard, ASEAN's approach to regional peace and stability aims to strengthen international law and justice while respecting the sovereignty and independence of member states.

In this way, ASEAN provides a strong normative basis for maintaining peace and stability at the regional level.

The regional cooperation and peace goals developed by ASEAN in its early years were reinforced with the Zone of Peace, Freedom, and Neutrality (ZOPFAN) Declaration announced in November 1971. With the declaration issued after the meeting of foreign ministers held in Kuala Lumpur, ASEAN countries were invited to secure Southeast Asia as a region independent from the intervention of external powers and to promote intra-ASEAN cooperation (Narine, 2018). Although it is not a legal document, it was prepared to guide and define ASEAN's relations with non-regional states (Caballero-Anthony, 2005). This statement of intent, which does not impose any legal obligations on the signatories, once again emphasizes the basic goals and ideals of ASEAN and conveys the message that the countries in the region should avoid the interventions of external powers (such as the USA, Russia, China, etc.) and maintain autonomy in their internal affairs. To summarize, ZOPFAN distinguishes itself as an important document that aims to govern the countries of the region independently of external interventions and re-emphasizes the core principles of ASEAN, as part of ASEAN's efforts to promote regional security and collaboration.

The Southeast Asia Treaty of Friendship and Cooperation (TAC), signed at the first summit meeting of the organization held on February 29, 1976, nine years after the establishment of ASEAN, is the only legal instrument that regulates the principles that member states must comply with to resolve disputes and conflicts peacefully. Therefore, the agreement is one of the basic components of the organization's conflict management model. With the agreement, it was stated that the parties would adhere to the principles of independence, respect for sovereignty and territorial integrity, non-intervention in internal affairs, peaceful resolution, non-use of force, and the maintenance of the national existence of each state free from external intervention, subversion, or coercion in their relations with each other (Treaty of Amity and Cooperation in Southeast Asia, 1976). Additionally, Articles 14 and 15 of the agreement stipulated the establishment of a Supreme Council consisting of representatives at the ministerial level to evaluate disputes, and this Council was authorized to propose solutions such as mediation, investigation, or conciliation to the parties (Caballero-Anthony, 2005). However, such a Council has never been established. As a result, TAC aimed to establish norm-based rules of conduct for relations between regional states and strengthened regional peacekeeping efforts by determining ASEAN's basic security principles.

Various meetings held regularly among ASEAN officials reflect the organization's peace and security framework at the institutional level. One of these is the ASEAN Ministerial Meeting (AMM). Defined as the highest authority in the Bangkok Declaration, the AMM has become a dialogue tool where security issues are discussed over the years (Emmers, 2003). This meeting, held annually and sometimes as needed, is ASEAN's highest-level policy-making meeting (Keling et al., 2011). Many topics, ranging from the economy and environment to health and the workforce, are regularly discussed in various meetings, including those of heads of state, foreign ministers, and ministers of economy. After the ASEAN Ministerial Meeting, the ASEAN Post-Ministerial Conference (PMC) is usually held, where the security issues of the countries are discussed, and ASEAN member countries come together with the ministers of dialogue partners such as the USA, Japan, India, and China. Therefore, an important platform is provided for ASEAN countries to express their common security concerns and develop solution proposals.

Another important mechanism of ASEAN regarding regional peace and security is the ASEAN Regional Forum (ARF). Providing a platform to address security issues in the Asia-Pacific region, the ARF was established in 1994 by China, Russia, Laos, Vietnam, and Papua New Guinea, alongside ASEAN dialogue partners, to develop confidence-building measures and promote conflict prevention mechanisms (Severino, 2006; Li, 2018). In this regard, collaborative activities within the ARF are carried out in a three-stage process: developing preventive diplomacy, promoting confidence-building measures, and elaborating conflict approaches (Weatherbee, 2009). The establishment of the ARF is a product of ASEAN's desire to play a central role in regional security issues and is shaped within the framework of an informal and consensus-oriented approach known as the "ASEAN Way" (Acharya, 2009). While this situation provides flexibility for the ARF, it also causes the forum to be criticized as a "talk shop" (Tan, 2013). However, the dialogue and cooperation platform provided by the ARF plays a valuable role in promoting mutual understanding and cooperation on regional security issues.

2.2. Informal Mechanism and "ASEAN Way"

Another important mechanism of ASEAN regarding regional peace and security is the ASEAN Regional Forum (ARF). Providing a platform to address security issues in the Asia-Pacific region, the ARF was established in 1994 by China, Russia, Laos, Vietnam, and Papua New Guinea, alongside ASEAN dialogue partners, to develop confidence-building measures and promote conflict prevention mechanisms (Severino, 2006; Li, 2018). In this regard, collaborative activities within the ARF are carried out in a three-stage process: developing preventive diplomacy, promoting confidence-building measures, and elaborating conflict approaches (Weatherbee, 2009). The establishment of the ARF is a product of ASEAN's desire to play a central role in regional security issues and is shaped within the framework of an informal and consensus-oriented approach known as the "ASEAN Way" (Acharya, 2009). While this context provides flexibility for the ARF, it also causes the forum to be criticized as a "talk shop" (Tan, 2013). Yet, the dialogue and cooperation platform provided by the ARF plays a valuable role in promoting mutual understanding and cooperation on regional security issues.

The ASEAN Way prefers a collaborative, gradual, and flexible approach based on solidarity and dialogue, rather than rigid rules, binding agreements, and rapid institutionalization (Katsumata, 2009). Four key principles are particularly important for grasping the ASEAN Way. These are (Acharya, 2009):

- Non-interference
- Non-use of force and peaceful resolution of disputes
- Avoidance of military agreements in favor of bilateral defense cooperation
- Regional autonomy and regional solutions to regional problems

The Bangkok Declaration invited Southeast Asian countries to protect themselves from all kinds of foreign intervention to ensure their stability and security (Association of Southeast Asian Nations [ASEAN], 1967). That is to say, this document emphasized that foreign interventions pose a threat to the stability and security of the countries and declared the ASEAN countries' determination to be protected from such interventions. The principle of non-intervention in internal affairs has imposed several obligations on ASEAN members, such as not interfering in the domestic policies and human rights issues of member governments, criticizing states that violate this principle, not supporting rebels who seek to destabilize neighboring states, and providing support to member states against subversive activities (Acharya, 2001). In line with this principle, which is central to ASEAN Way norms, ASEAN has preferred not to interfere in internal affairs and to seek solutions through diplomacy for many problems. For example, in incidents such as the Santa Cruz Massacre in East Timor and the Liquiça murders, where many lives were lost, ASEAN remained inactive in line with its principle of non-intervention (Severino, 2006). Therefore, while this principle is thought to contribute to avoiding military conflict between ASEAN member countries, it has also been criticized for causing ASEAN to fail to take action in cases where a member country experiences severe victimization.

Although the principle of non-use of force and peaceful resolution of disputes is one of the reasons for ASEAN's existence, its main purpose is to prevent armed conflict between member states. Article 2 of the ASEAN Charter clearly states that ASEAN member states must refrain from participating in policies or activities that threaten the sovereignty, territorial integrity, or stability of member states by any state or actor, including the use of their own territory (ASEAN Charter, 1967). Additionally, the Charter specifies that the principles of the United Nations Charter, which stipulate that states should refrain from using force or threatening force in their international relations, will be adhered to (Association of Southeast Asian Nations,

1967). Similarly, the ZOPFAN Declaration of 1971 stated that the UN principles of avoiding the use of force and peaceful resolution of disputes were taken as a reference (Zone of Peace, Freedom and Neutrality Declaration [ZOPFAN], 1976). In this context, the organization has actively pursued solutions to numerous issues through diplomatic and non-violent methods. For example, during Vietnam's intervention in Cambodia in 1978, ASEAN employed collective diplomacy; conflicts between Indonesia and Malaysia over the Sulawesi Sea and disputes between Malaysia and Singapore over the Batu Pahat and Pedra Branca Islands were resolved by referring them to the International Court of Justice (Roberts, 2012). This approach reflects ASEAN's strict adherence to the principles of non-use of force and peaceful resolution and its determination to resolve regional problems within the framework of international law.

ASEAN has preferred bilateral defense cooperation over multilateral military agreements in response to the military security challenges faced by countries in the region. This norm was established clearly at the founding of the organization. The founding members of ASEAN were determined not to transform the organization into a military pact or defense cooperation body, and therefore were cautious about military cooperation in the early years of its establishment. For instance, during the first ASEAN Summit held in 1976, Indonesia's proposal for a joint military cooperation council was rejected, and it was stated that ASEAN would continue to function as a socio-economic organization (Acharya, 2001). The ASEAN Concord, signed in 1976, supported the continuation of bilateral cooperation on security issues among member countries in line with mutual needs and interests (Association of Southeast Asian Nations [ASEAN], 1976). This policy backed the continuation of existing agreements, like the Malaysia-Thailand Border Security Agreement (1970), the Malaysia-Indonesia Border Security Agreement, and the Indonesia-Philippines Border Control Agreement (1964), which were mainly focused on border security, while also making it easier to create new agreements. As a result, ASEAN has opted to maintain regional security through bilateral relations, avoiding multilateral military agreements.

The basis for ASEAN's security relations with external powers is the desire for regional autonomy, the avoidance of great power competition, and the goal of freely pursuing its own economic and security objectives. ASEAN's underlying principle of non-intervention aims to prevent major powers from intervening in the internal affairs of the countries in the region by keeping the region free from power competition (Kraft, 2012). The strategies to mitigate external interference involve strengthening the political and economic stability of ASEAN member states, as well as enhancing regional solidarity. In this regard, many documents such as the Bangkok Declaration, ZOPFAN, TAC, Bali Concord I, Bali Concord II, and ASEAN Vision 2025 frequently emphasize goals like "strengthening the economic and social stability of the region," "protection from foreign interventions," "non-interference in the internal affairs of states," and "creating a strong ASEAN." The statements in these documents clearly demonstrate ASEAN's efforts to strengthen regional autonomy and develop protection strategies against external interventions, reflecting its determination to ensure regional solidarity, economic stability, and security.

Based on the above-mentioned principles, ASEAN employs several informal mechanisms for managing disputes and joint decision-making. These include adherence to the fundamental rules outlined in ASEAN declarations, an emphasis on self-regulation (conciliation diplomacy), networking, consultation and compromise, mediation, and agreement in disputes (Tuan, 1996). In conciliation diplomacy, states resolve disagreements by adhering to principles such as mutual respect, tolerance, and non-intervention. This mechanism was implemented in the territorial dispute between Malaysia and the Philippines over Sabah and in the Indonesia-Singapore crisis of 1968. Compromise and solidarity, on the other hand, mean that a leader, instead of imposing their own will, suggests a path that society can accept and takes into account the opinions and feelings of all participants (Feith, 1962). This mechanism ensures that sensitive issues are discussed without being made public, thereby maintaining good relations between the parties and preventing any loss of reputation. While networking facilitates interaction and strengthens close relationships, agreeing to disagree allows the parties to buy time by setting aside the issue when the dispute reaches an impasse and to eventually reach an agreement by avoiding overt conflict (Jones & Smith, 2006). Finally, third-party mediation involves resolving disputes with the help of an impartial observer.

In summary, it is the informal aspect of inclusive and equitable processes that helps resolve differences, uphold rights, and foster positive relationships (Porter, 2010). These processes, which essentially aim to reduce tension between the conflicting parties and create new communication channels, pave the way for breaking prejudices and fostering trust between them (Burgess and Burgess, 2010). ASEAN also utilizes informal mechanisms as part of its approach to dispute resolution. In this regard, private meetings during golf games, meals, silent diplomacy, and social events outside official processes contribute to the resolution of conflicts (Emmers, 2003). By offering a more flexible space for communication and negotiation, these interactions enable ASEAN members to share their views with less pressure. Moreover, these informal initiatives promote continued cooperation and trust-building by providing alternative solutions to issues that formal diplomatic channels cannot resolve.

3. ASEAN IN SOUTH CHINA SEA DISPUTES

3.1. ASEAN's Policies Towards the South China Sea

In order to maintain its advantage in negotiations, China rejects internationalization and the involvement of a regional organisation in disputes as a negotiator or mediator, instead adopting the strategy of resolving conflicts through bilateral negotiations (Valencia, 1998). Contrary to China, ASEAN member countries prefer to handle disputes multilaterally to avoid division within the organization and favor regional formations such as the ARF to address disputes. Therefore, ASEAN countries take a common stance by supporting multilateral negotiations in resolving South China Sea issues. ASEAN first became involved in the South China Sea issue by publishing the "ASEAN Declaration on the South China Sea" on July 7, 1992, after tensions between China and Vietnam escalated due to oil exploration activities in the region (Thayer, 2013). With this declaration, which aims to establish an international code of conduct for the South China Sea, ASEAN (ASEAN Declaration on the South China Sea, 1992):

- Advocated for the resolution of sovereignty and jurisdiction issues regarding the South China Sea by peaceful means without the use of force
- Urged all parties to act with restraint in pursuit of a final solution
- Promoted the exploration of cooperation opportunities regarding maritime security, environmental protection, search and rescue, anti-piracy, and drug trafficking in the South China Sea
- Emphasized the implementation of the principles of the Southeast Asia Treaty of Friendship and Cooperation for international codes of conduct in the South China Sea. Additionally, all interested parties were invited to accept this declaration

This first statement regarding ASEAN's South China Sea issue sought to prevent the escalation of the conflict between China and Vietnam by urging the disputing parties to act cautiously (Cheeppensook, 2020). China did not support this declaration because it prefers bilateral methods for resolving disputes. Additionally, the declaration is an unofficial code of conduct aimed at ensuring the peaceful management of disputes, making it more of a conflict prevention measure rather than a conflict resolution tool (Emmers, 2003). That said, this first joint initiative by ASEAN countries on the South China Sea disputes is an important step in aligning the region's issues with ASEAN's norms and principles.

China did not participate in the Manila Declaration in response to the "Territorial Waters and Contiguous Area Law" enacted by ASEAN states in 1992. Consequently, the call made to China through this declaration, urging it not to act unilaterally, was disregarded by the country. In 1994, China secretly constructed structures on Mischief Reef, which the Philippines claimed, and deployed armed ships there (Leifer, 1999). This event was a turning point for ASEAN, prompting ASEAN foreign ministers to express their concerns in official statements. They emphasized their concern, urged all relevant parties to adhere to the Manila Declaration, and called for the avoidance of actions that threaten peace and security, while encouraging the establishment of cooperation to build trust and stability (Severino, 2010). The Philippines, in reaction, condemned China's actions as unlawful and emphasized the pressing need for a binding code of conduct. Following these developments, the Philippines and China issued a joint statement affirming that the issues should be resolved through peaceful means and stressing the importance of building trust between the two countries and remaining open to multilateral cooperation proposals (Zha & Valencia, 2001). However, after China continued similar actions, ASEAN initiated efforts to draft a code of conduct for the South China Sea disputes.

The idea of a multilateral code of conduct was first raised at the 1996 ASEAN Ministerial Meeting, and as a result of ASEAN's insistence and interaction with China in various multilateral settings, China agreed in 1998 to work on the rules of a regional code of conduct to prevent the escalation of conflict in the South China Sea (Li, 2018). After several years of effort, ASEAN officials agreed on the draft rules and sent them to China for evaluation, but China resisted making the rules binding (Southgate, 2019). Hence, the "Declaration of Conduct of the Parties in the South China Sea," a non-binding declaration, was adopted at the 8th ASEAN Summit held on November 4, 2002. In this document, which represents China's acceptance of a multilateral initiative for the first time, the parties reached important agreements on (Guidelines for the Implementation of the DOC, 2011):

- Respecting freedom of navigation and overflight in the South China Sea within the framework of international law
- Resolving disputes peacefully without the use of force
- Avoiding the inhabitation of uninhabited islands, reefs, and other geographical features
- Protecting the marine environment, conducting marine scientific research, undertaking search and rescue operations, ensuring maritime navigation and communication security, and combating cross-border crimes (drug trafficking, piracy, armed robbery at sea, etc.)

Although the DOC is non-binding, it represents a political commitment that demonstrates China's willingness to comply with the principles promoted by ASEAN countries (Emmers, 2010). It is also an important step in establishing appropriate behaviour regarding South China Sea disputes, serving as a stepping stone for the creation of binding rules and testing the effectiveness of non-binding documents (Koga, 2020). In this context, the DOC represents the beginning of a long-term process aimed at ensuring peace and stability in the region.

ASEAN has continued the process of dialogue and cooperation with China to address the South China Sea issue and establish a Code of Conduct (CoC). Although the DOC provides a framework aimed at reducing tensions in the region and building trust between the parties, it was deemed necessary to develop detailed guidelines due to difficulties encountered in implementation. The Guidelines for the Implementation of the DOC determine a set of principles and rules to guide the implementation of the 2002 Declaration of Conduct signed between ASEAN and China, ensuring that cooperation activities are carried out systematically. Accordingly (Guidelines for the Implementation of the DOC, 2011):

- Implementation of the DOC should proceed step by step in accordance with its provisions
- Parties should continue dialogue and consultations in the spirit of the DOC
- Activities or projects within the scope of the DOC should be clearly defined
- Participation in activities and projects should be on a voluntary basis
- Initial activities should focus on confidence-building measures
- Concrete measures and actions should be decided by consensus between the parties and should eventually lead to the realization of a Code of Conduct
- The progress of agreed activities and projects should be reported annually to the ASEAN-China Ministerial Meeting

At the 45th ASEAN Foreign Ministers Meeting (AMM) held in July 2012, ASEAN foreign ministers agreed on the basic elements of the Code of Conduct and reaffirmed their commitment to the following articles by issuing a document titled “Six-Point Principles on the South China Sea”. These are the key points from the Statement of the ASEAN Foreign Ministers (2012):

- Full implementation of the 2002 DoC in the South China Sea
- Implementation of the Implementation Guidelines for the Declaration on the Conduct of the Parties in the South China Sea dated 2011
- Adoption of a Regional CoC in the South China Sea as soon as possible
- Full compliance with universally accepted principles of international law, including the UNCLOS

- Maintaining the principle of self-restraint and avoiding the use of force by all parties
- Settlement of disputes by peaceful means in accordance with the UNCLOS and other universal legal principles

Another important development regarding the South China Sea disputes was the decision in 2013 by the Philippines to file an arbitration case against China under Annex VII of the UNCLOS (Beckman & Dang, 2023). Both the pressure on China due to the arbitration case and the post-2013 geopolitical dynamics increased interaction with China, ASEAN, and other relevant parties, accelerating the process of establishing a common Code of Conduct for the South China Sea disputes (Li, 2018). In fact, while only five SOM meetings regarding the DOC were held between 2004 and 2012, nine meetings were held between 2013 and 2017 (Li, 2018). As a result of all these efforts, in 2017, the foreign ministers of China and ASEAN adopted the framework text of the CoC in the South China Sea, completing an important stage in the CoC negotiations. In June 2018, ASEAN and Chinese officials adopted the Single Draft CoC Negotiating Text, determining that this draft, which was kept confidential and would be read three times, would form the basis for negotiations. After the completion of the first reading in 2019, it was tentatively published in the Preamble of the SDNT in 2021. They reached an agreement (Aziz et al., 2024). While satisfaction was expressed with the completion of the second reading of the draft at the 26th ASEAN-China Summit held on 6 September 2023, the Single Draft CoC Negotiation Text was officially launched for its third reading at the 21st ASEAN-China SOM-DOC held in Beijing, China, on 26 October 2023.

Between 2014 and 2018, a series of confidence-building measures were taken to build trust between China and ASEAN. For example, at the 17th ASEAN-China Summit, leaders agreed to adopt the first list of partnerships for Comprehensive CoC consultations, establish a hotline between search and rescue agencies and foreign ministries, and support search-and-rescue exercises (17th ASEAN-China Summit Chairman's Statement, 2014). Similarly, at the 19th ASEAN-China Summit in 2016, leaders adopted the CUES implementation statement and hotline communication guidelines, which set out security and communication procedures in the South Chin Sea, and conducted a successful hotline test exercise in 2017 (Beckman & Dang, 2023). In addition, at the 20th ASEAN-China Summit held in 2017, the declaration "A Decade for the Protection of the Coastal and Marine Environment in the South China Sea" was adopted, and the parties committed to cooperation for the protection and sustainable management of the coastal and marine environment in the region (Declaration for a Decade of Coastal and Marıne Environmental Protection in the South China Sea, 2017). Furthermore, following the ASEAN-China Defense Ministers' informal meeting held in February 2018, a joint exercise was conducted on August 2-3 as part of confidence-building measures (Koh, 2018). These steps reflect the joint efforts between the two sides to strengthen cooperation on confidence-building measures, crisis management, and environmental protection, and to promote regional peace and stability.

3.2. The Effectiveness of the ASEAN Way in South China Sea Disputes

The ASEAN Way is a set of normative rules manifested by the principles of the Treaty of Friendship and Cooperation and the constant interactions of ASEAN diplomats. ASEAN's policy towards the South China Sea disputes is carried out in line with these norms. These norms are based on managing the conflict process through dialogue and consultations; mutual respect for the sovereignty of states, non-interference, peaceful resolution of disputes, avoidance of the use of force and threats, and effective regional cooperation (ASEAN, 1976). ASEAN utilizes both formal and informal processes in implementing these norms. Informal processes enable disputes to be resolved through dialogue and consultation in less formal settings. Both China and ASEAN have requested that issues regarding the South China Sea be resolved mostly in informal meetings. Since the purpose of informal meetings is to promote cooperation, sufficient attention is not given to the disputes in these meetings, and therefore they are considered inadequate in managing the South China Sea disputes (Townsend-Gault, 1998). At the same time, informal processes are praised for encouraging China's participation in ASEAN forums and providing cooperation in the monitoring and protection of marine ecosystems (Townsend-Gault, 1998).

Another of ASEAN's basic principles is that it bases decisions on consensus. These principles seek to achieve consensus among all members and maintain unity in regional cooperation. The implementation of the consensus norm is difficult because it is challenging to find common ground due to the different national interests of ASEAN countries, and the right of veto can slow down processes and neutralize decisions. At the 2012 ASEAN Foreign Ministers' Meeting, the veto of the statements proposed by Vietnam and the Philippines regarding the disputed areas in the South China Sea by Cambodia, under pressure from China, led to the failure to publish a joint declaration for the first time in ASEAN history (Hu, 2021). On the other hand, it was planned that ASEAN countries would make a joint statement regarding the disputes in the South China Sea at the Kunming Meeting held in 2016. However, this statement was blocked due to intense pressure from China. While the DOC, which was redrafted four times between 1996 and 2002, demonstrated ASEAN and Chinese diplomats' commitment to the principle of consensus, criticism of China and support for the Philippines in the original drafts was watered down and the

Philippines' request for inclusion in the UN conference was excluded (Nischalke, 2000). Similarly, the process of preparing the CoC has been continuing for more than ten years in order to achieve consensus. These examples show that ASEAN's difficulty in implementing the consensus norm limits its effectiveness in regional cooperation and dispute resolution, preventing ASEAN from making effective and rapid decisions on critical issues such as the South China Sea.

In addition to the consensus norm, the non-interference norm is also thought to cause some limitations in managing conflict processes in the region. Although the principle of non-intervention is frequently emphasized in many founding documents of ASEAN, Article 11 of the TAC stipulates that member states shall protect their national identities in economic, political, cultural, security, etc., independent of external interventions. It was stated that they would strengthen their national resilience in many areas (TAC, 1976). In this regard, ASEAN has been involved in many issues, including the coup process in Cambodia in the 1990s, the Thailand-Cambodia border conflict, the smog caused by the burning of large areas of land by Indonesian agro-industrial operators, and human rights violations in Myanmar in the 1990s. By approaching many events in line with the principles of respect for the sovereignty of states and non-intervention, it preferred to preserve regional peace and stability rather than intervening in these situations and responding to external pressures (Ramcharan, 2003).This situation has led to criticism of ASEAN for refraining from providing an effective response to emergencies such as serious human rights violations and environmental disasters by adhering strictly to the principle of non-interference, and has led to questioning of ASEAN's effectiveness. According to Emmers (2017), respect for the autonomy of states and non-interference in their internal affairs are the reasons for ASEAN's continued existence, and if ASEAN acts within the scope of its responsibility to protect in events such as the Rohingya incident, the union will disintegrate and regional harmony will disappear. Thanks to this norm, which aims to prevent foreign interventions and to prevent member states from intervening in each other's internal affairs, member states have committed themselves not to interfere with each other and have turned to cooperation.

ASEAN has developed a detailed code of conduct to handle disputes and reduce tensions in the region. With this document, adopted in 2002, an important first step was taken to ensure cooperation between the parties, reduce tension in the region, and solve problems through dialogue. However, the challenges ASEAN faces in implementing the DOC have raised concerns about the organization's effectiveness. China's construction of military facilities despite the DOC and its maintenance of sovereignty claims on the islands have made it difficult for ASEAN to achieve its regional security goals. In addition, according to many academics, the ASEAN Way forces China to accept undesirable consequences, ASEAN's moderate approach reduces China's insecurity, and ASEAN adopts an increasingly proactive and uncompromising approach in addressing problems in the region (Hu, 2021). In other words, although ASEAN has problems in implementing the determined rules of conduct, it plays an active role in softening China's attitude and facilitating conflict-free resolution of the problems. These two opposing views highlight both ASEAN's limited success in achieving regional security and cooperation goals and its effective role in reducing tensions and facilitating cooperation with China. Although the difficulties ASEAN faces in practice and China's military activities question the effectiveness of the organization, ASEAN's moderate approach and diplomatic efforts are considered an important balancer in the search for a conflict-free solution in the region.

ASEAN is also criticized for failing to find effective solutions to regional problems and for taking too long to reach a resolution. For example, a solution to the environmental damage caused by Indonesia's illegal peat burning since 1972 was attempted with the 'ASEAN Transboundary Air Pollution Agreement' in 2002, but Indonesia only ratified this agreement in 2016 (Emmerson, 2017). In other words, it took over forty years to resolve the issue. This situation shows that ASEAN's ability to respond quickly and effectively to crises is limited, supporting criticisms of bureaucratic obstacles and delays in solving regional problems. On the other hand, since the documents signed by ASEAN are not legally binding, the signatory parties do not face serious consequences for acting contrary to them (Jones & Smith, 2006). Therefore, formal negotiations had a low impact on the conflict management process, raising questions about ASEAN's ability to develop effective crisis management solutions. However, ASEAN has been successful in pushing China to draft the CoC and engage in CoC negotiations, thereby encouraging China to accept multilateralism. Since 2013, China has shown its willingness to prepare the CoC, and negotiations are still ongoing. This situation demonstrates that although ASEAN progresses slowly, it can achieve significant diplomatic successes and has the capacity to influence regional issues.

CONCLUSION

ASEAN uses both formal and informal conflict management mechanisms to resolve disputes in the South China Sea. Formal conflict management processes involve formal negotiations and agreements made by ASEAN using legal and institutional mechanisms to promote regional peace, security, stability, and cooperation. For example, official initiatives such as the Bangkok Declaration, ZOPFAN, and TAC emphasize the basic principles of developing peaceful relations among states, respecting the sovereign rights of states by avoiding external intervention, avoiding the use of force and threats, regional cooperation, and decision-making by consensus.

Similarly, through official mechanisms such as the ASEAN Summit, the ASEAN Ministerial Meeting, and the ASEAN Regional Forum, both a platform is provided for discussing security-related issues and security cooperation is encouraged among regional countries. On the other hand, informal conflict management processes are flexible and relational approaches, generally conducted in the background through social relations and diplomatic interactions, serving as a complement to formal processes. These mechanisms, which are a reflection of the ASEAN's specific diplomacy style are called the 'ASEAN Way'. This diplomacy has a gradual and informal characteristic based on peaceful methods like solidarity, dialogue and flexibility. Conciliation diplomacy, mediation, and networking are methods frequently employed by ASEAN in informal processes.

One of the most important tests that ASEAN has given as to whether it is an organization effective enough to achieve its goals of ensuring regional peace and stability and encouraging cooperation among the parties to the dispute has been the South China Sea disputes. ASEAN took its first step towards managing regional tensions and encouraging peaceful solutions with the "ASEAN Declaration on the South China Sea" published in 1992. In this context, the DOC has provided an important foundation for reducing tensions and building trust in the region. However, China's predisposition towards bilateral negotiations and regional dynamics limited the effects of ASEAN's initial initiative. However, the fact that the DOC is not binding for the parties and China's continued military activities in the region have been factors that have hampered ASEAN's diplomatic efforts. Therefore, ASEAN's policies and the effectiveness of these policies in regional crises have begun to be questioned. For this reason, COC negotiations were initiated to determine appropriate behaviors that could help resolve conflicts in the region. Although China was initially reluctant to engage in these negotiations, a more constructive approach has emerged over time due to regional tensions and international expectations. A new era has begun in the South China Sea issues with the CoC negotiations.

ASEAN's policies on the South China Sea have both strengths and weaknesses, with several aspects needing further improvement. Although the Code of Conduct established by ASEAN has created a critical infrastructure in which regional cooperation has been promoted through negotiations, difficulties in its implementation have limited the effectiveness of the organization. The reliance on informal processes, the consensus-based decision-making, and the norm of non-interference in internal affairs have all emerged as significant factors contributing to the questioning of ASEAN's effectiveness in the region. The dominant role of informal processes in resolving disputes has limited the attention these issues receive in official processes, distancing the parties from finding formal and binding solutions and causing the resolution process to progress slowly. While the consensus norm aligns differing interests, it has also caused delays and occasional indecision. For instance, this norm prevented ASEAN from making a joint statement against China. In addition, ASEAN's non-intervention principle is very important to prevent external powers such as the US, India, and Japan from interfering in regional problems. However, this principle also prevents ASEAN from effectively intervening in the region.

ASEAN adopt a proactive policy for resolving the South China Sea disputes and has tried to resolve the problems in the region through moderate approaches. Thanks to these policies, trust has been established between the parties and the peaceful resolution of problems has been contributed to. As a result, ASEAN's moderate policies have largely prevented tensions in the region from turning into hot conflict. However, these policies, which are largely implemented informally, have also caused the organization to be inadequate in taking concrete and binding steps that will ensure a permanent resolution of disputes. Because informal policies are generally advisory and not binding. This results in states not perceiving themselves as sufficiently accountable for the implementation of these policies. The trust built through informal processes should be reinforced by binding decisions through formal mechanisms. In other words, ASEAN should play a more effective role by balancing both formal and informal processes. In addition, the fact that the organization makes decisions through consensus significantly hinders reaching a common decision. Hence, the organization must develop a more effective decision-making mechanism and find a middle ground more quickly, by minimizing conflicts of interest. ASEAN's success in regional peacekeeping will depend on the speed of its decisions and the balance between informal and formal processes.

REFERENCES

Acharya, A. (2001). *Constructing a Security Community in Southeast Asia: ASEAN and the Problem of Regional Order*. Routledge.

Acharya, A. (2009). *Constructing a Security Community in Southeast Asia: ASEAN and the Problem of Regional Order*. Routledge. DOI: 10.4324/9780203939239

ASEAN. (2014). Chairman's Statement of the 17th ASEAN-China Summit. Retrieved from https://www.asean.org/wp-content/uploads/images/Chairmans_statement_of_17th_ASEAN-China_Summit.pdf

Association of Southeast Asian Nations. (1992). ASEAN Declaration on the South China Sea. Retrieved from https://asean.org/asean-declaration-south-china-sea/

Association of Southeast Asian Nations. (2002). Declaration on the conduct of parties in the South China Sea. Retrieved from https://cil.nus.edu.sg/wp-content/uploads/2017/07/2002-Declaration-on-the-Conduct-of-Parties-in-the-South-China-Sea.pdf

Association of Southeast Asian Nations. (2011). Guidelines for the Implementation of the DOC. Retrieved from https://asean.org/guidelines-implementation-doc

Association of Southeast Asian Nations. (2012). Statement of the ASEAN foreign ministers on the six-point principles on the South China Sea. Retrieved from https://www.asean.org/wpcontent/uploads/images/AFMs%20Statement%20on%206%20Principles%20on%20SCS.pdf

Association of Southeast Asian Nations. (2017). Declaration for a decade of coastal and marine environmental protection in the South China Sea (2017-2027). Retrieved from https://asean.org/wp-content/uploads/2017/11/Declaration-for-a-Decade-of-Coastal-and-Marine-Environmental-Protection-in-the-South-China-Sea-2017-2027.pdf

Association of Southeast Asian Nations (ASEAN). (1967). The ASEAN Declaration (Bangkok Declaration). Retrieved from https://agreement.asean.org/media/download/20140117154159.pdf

Association of Southeast Asian Nations (ASEAN). (1976). The Declaration of ASEAN Concord, Bali, Indonesia, 24 February 1976. ASEAN Main Portal. Retrieved from https://asean.org

Aziz, R., Ali, A., Liaqat, B. B., & Arslan, M. (2024). ASEAN's diplomatic and strategic engagement in the South China Sea dispute: An analysis. *Journal of Social & Organizational Matters*, *3*(2), 204–224. DOI: 10.56976/jsom.v3i2.82

Beckman, R., & Dang, V. H. (2023). ASEAN and peaceful management of maritime disputes in the South China Sea. In J. Kraska, R. Long, & M. H. Nordquist (Eds.), Peaceful maritime engagement in East Asia and the Pacific region (pp. 342-358). Brill | Nijhoff.

Burgess, H., & Burgess, G. (2010). *Conducting Track II peacemaking*. United States Institute of Peace.

Buszynski, L. (2013). The development of the South China Sea Maritime Dispute. In L. Buszynski & C. Roberts (Eds.), The South China Sea Security Environment (pp. 3-7). National Security College Occasional Paper No. 5.

Buszynski, L. (2020). The Development of South China Sea Disputes. In Buszynski, L., & Hai, D. T. (Eds.), *The South China Sea: From a Regional Maritime Dispute to Geo-strategic Competition* (pp. 1–8). Routledge.

Caballero-Anthony, M. (2005). *Regional security in Southeast Asia: Beyond the ASEAN way*. Institute of Southeast Asian Studies. DOI: 10.1355/9789812307095

Charter, A. S. E. A. N. (1967). The ASEAN Charter. Retrieved from https://asean.org

Cheeppensook, K. (2020). ASEAN in the South China Sea Conflict, 2012–2018: A lesson in conflict transformation from normative power Europe. *International Economics and Economic Policy*, *17*(3), 747–764. DOI: 10.1007/s10368-020-00477-z

Darmawan, A. B. (2020). Japan's Balanced Strategy to Face China's Threat in South China Sea Dispute. *Jurnal Ilmu Sosial*, *19*(2), 137–159. DOI: 10.14710/jis.19.2.2020.137-159

Emmers, R. (2003). *Cooperative Security and the Balance of Power in ASEAN and the ARF*. RoutledgeCurzon Taylor & Francis Group. DOI: 10.4324/9780203401064

Emmers, R. (2010). *Geopolitics and Maritime Territorial Disputes in East Asia*. Routledge.

Emmerson, D. K. (2017). ASEAN between China and America: Is it time to try horsing the cow? TRaNS: Trans-Regional and -National Studies of Southeast Asia, 5(1), 1–23. DOI: 10.1017/trn.2016.31

Feith, H. (1962). *The Decline of Constitutional Democracy in Indonesia*. Cornell University Press.

Grossman, D. (2020). Military Build-up in the South China Sea. In Buszynski, L., & Hai, D. T. (Eds.), *The South China Sea: From a Regional Maritime Dispute to Geo-strategic Competition* (pp. 182–200). Routledge.

Groten, D. (2019). *How Sentiment Matters in International Relations: China and the South China Sea Dispute*. Verlag Barbara Budrich. DOI: 10.2307/j.ctvmd84bx

Hayton, B. (2014). *The South China Sea: The struggle for power in Asia*. Yale University Press.

Jones, M. J., & Smith, M. L. R. (2006). *ASEAN and East Asian International Relations: Regional Delusion*. Edward Elgar Publishing. DOI: 10.4337/9781845428921

Katsumata, H. (2009). *ASEAN's cooperative security enterprise: Norms and interests in the ASEAN Regional Forum*. Palgrave Macmillan. DOI: 10.1057/9780230277038

Keling, M. F., Som, H. M., Saludin, M. N., Shuib, M. S., & Ajis, M. N. (2011). The Development of ASEAN from Historical Approach. *Asian Social Science*, *7*(7), 169–189. DOI: 10.5539/ass.v7n7p169

Kipgen, N. (2020). *The Politics of South China Sea Disputes*. Routledge. DOI: 10.4324/9781003026334

Koga, K. (2020). *Managing Great Power Politics: ASEAN, Institutional Strategy, and the South China Sea*. Palgrave Macmillan.

Koh, C. S. L. (2018). *Inaugural ASEAN-China maritime exercise: What to expect (RSIS Commentaries, No. 131). RSIS Commentaries*. Nanyang Technological University.

Kraft, H. J. S. (2012). Driving East Asian Regionalism: The Reconstruction of ASEAN's Identity. In Emmers, R. (Ed.), *ASEAN and the Institutionalization of East Asia* (pp. 61–74). Routledge.

Le, H. (2021). Examining ASEAN's effectiveness in managing South China Sea disputes. *The Pacific Review*. Advance online publication. DOI: 10.1080/09512748.2021.1934519

Leifer, M. (1999, April 24-26). Stalemate in the South China Sea. Paper presented at aWworkshop on the Conflict in the South China Sea, Oslo.

Li, L. (2018). *China's Policy Towards the South China Sea: When Geopolitics Meets the Law of the Sea*. Routledge. DOI: 10.4324/9781315158709

Mitchell, M. D. (2016). The South China Sea: A Geopolitical Analysis. *Journal of Geography and Geology*, *8*(3), 14–25. DOI: 10.5539/jgg.v8n3p14

Narine, S. (2018). *The New ASEAN in Asia Pacific and Beyond*. Lynne Rienner Publishers. DOI: 10.1515/9781626377097

Nischalke, T. I. (2000). Insights from ASEAN's Foreign Policy Cooperation: The "ASEAN Way," a Real Spirit or a Phantom? *Contemporary Southeast Asia*, *22*(1), 89–112. DOI: 10.1355/CS22-1D

Political-Security Community Blueprint, A. S. E. A. N. (2009). ASEAN Political-Security Community Blueprint 2009. ASEAN Secretariat. Retrieved from https://asean.org/wp-content/uploads/2021/03/APSC_BluePrint.pdf

Porter, E. (2010). Women, Political Decision-making, and Peace-building. *Global Change, Peace & Security*, *15*(3), 245–262. DOI: 10.1080/0951274032000124965

Prabhakar, W. L. S. (2007). The regional dimension of territorial and maritime disputes in Southeast Asia: Actors, disagreements, and dynamics. In Guan, K. C., & Skogan, J. K. (Eds.), *Maritime security in Southeast Asia* (pp. 34–47). Routledge.

Raine, S., & Mière, L. C. (2013). *Regional Disorder: The South China Sea Disputes*. Routledge.

Ramcharan, R. (2003). ASEAN and non-interference. In Siddique, S., & Kumar, S. (Eds.), *The 2nd ASEAN reader* (pp. 52–57). Institute of Southeast Asian Studies.

Raymond, M., & Welch, D. A. (2022). What's really going on in the South China Sea? *Journal of Current Southeast Asian Affairs*, *4*(2), 214–239. DOI: 10.1177/18681034221086291

Roberts, C. B. (2012). *ASEAN regionalism: Cooperation, values and institutionalization*. Routledge. DOI: 10.4324/9780203181041

Sacks, B. J. (2022). The Political Geography of the South China Sea Disputes. Perspective: Expert Insights on a Timely Policy Issue, 1-32.

Saw, S., Sheng, L., & Chin, K. W. (2005). *ASEAN-China Relations: Realities and Prospects*. ISEAS. DOI: 10.1355/9789812306364

Scott, D. (2013). India's role in the South China Sea: Geopolitics and Geoeconomics in Play. *India Review*, *12*(2), 51–69. DOI: 10.1080/14736489.2013.786965

Senkyr, J., & Merkle, D. (2023). *Geopolitics in the South China Sea. Konrad-Adenauer-Stiftung e*. V. Monitor Security.

Severino, R. C. (2006). *Southeast Asia: ASEAN community in search of an identity*. Institute of Southeast Asian Studies. DOI: 10.1355/9789812305671

Severino, R. C. (2010). ASEAN and the South China Sea. *Security Challenges*, *6*(2), 37–47.

Severino, R. C. (2016). Global Issues and National Interests in the South China Sea. In Jenner, C. J., & Thuy, T. T. (Eds.), *The South China Sea: A Crucible of Regional Cooperation or Conflict-making SovereigntyClaims?* (pp. 31–42). Cambridge University Press. DOI: 10.1017/CBO9781139963084.003

Southgate, L. (2019). *ASEAN Resistance to Sovereignty Violation: Interests, Balancing and the Role of the Vanguard State*. Bristol University Press.

Storey, I. (2016). The South China Sea dispute: Navigating diplomatic and strategic tensions. In Storey, I., & Cheng-Yi, L. (Eds.), *ASEAN and the South China Sea: Maintaining peace in the Asia-Pacific* (pp. 134–160). Routledge. DOI: 10.1355/9789814695565

Thayer, C. A. (2013). ASEAN, China and the code of conduct in the South China Sea. *SAIS Review (Paul H. Nitze School of Advanced International Studies)*, *33*(2), 75–84. DOI: 10.1353/sais.2013.0022

Till, G. (2016). The Global Gignificance of the South China Sea Disputes. In Jenner, C. J., & Thuy, T. T. (Eds.), *The South China Sea: A Crucible of Regional Cooperation or Conflict-making Sovereignty Claims?* (pp. 13–30). Cambridge University Press. DOI: 10.1017/CBO9781139963084.002

Townsend-Gault, I. (1998). Preventive Diplomacy and Pro-activity in the South China Sea. *Contemporary Southeast Asia*, *20*(2), 171–190. DOI: 10.1355/CS20-2D

Treaty of Amity and Cooperation in Southeast Asia. (1976). Treaty of Amity and Cooperation in Southeast Asia (TAC). Retrieved from https://asean-aipr.org/treaty-of-amity-and-cooperation-in-southeast-asia-1976-tac

Tuan, H. A. (1996). ASEAN Dispute Management: Implications for Vietnam and an Expanded ASEAN. *Contemporary Southeast Asia*, *18*(1), 61–80. DOI: 10.1355/CS18-1D

Tuan, H. A. (2016). The South China Sea Dispute: Navigating Diplomatic and Strategic Tensions. In Storey, I., & Cheng-Yi, L. (Eds.), *The South China Sea dispute: Navigating Diplomatic and Strategic Tensions* (pp. 186–204). Yusof Ishak Institute.

United Nations. (1945). Charter of the United Nations and Statute of the International Court of Justice. Retrieved from https://treaties.un.org/doc/publication/ctc/uncharter.pdf

United Nations. (1983). United Nations Convention on the Law of the Sea. Retrieved from https://www.un.org/depts/los/convention_agreements/texts/unclos/unclos_e.pdf

Valencia, M. (1988). Spratley Islands: Dangerous ground in the South China Sea. *The Pacific Review*, *1*(4), 443–448. DOI: 10.1080/09512748808718792

Weatherbee, D. E. (2009). *International relations in Southeast Asia: The struggle for autonomy*. Rowman & Littlefield Publishers, Inc.

Zha, D., & Valencia, M. J. (2001). Mischief Reef: Geopolitics and implications. *Journal of Contemporary Asia*, *31*(1), 86–103. DOI: 10.1080/00472330180000061

Zone of Peace, Freedom and Neutrality Declaration (ZOPFAN). (1971). Zone of Peace, Freedom and Neutrality Declaration (ZOPFAN). Retrieved from https://pmo.gov.my

Chapter 2
Australia's Policy in the South China Sea

Cenk Tamer
https://orcid.org/0000-0002-1331-7942
Gazi University, Turkey

ABSTRACT

While discussing Australia's South China Sea policies, the paper argues that the main problem is the US-China competition, and emphasizes that relations with China are an important factor here. This includes much of China's historic claims in the South China Sea and its disputes with its coastal states. Thus, Australia's South China Sea policies are critically influenced by the extent, scale and manner in which its relations with China. Based on this idea, the study first summarized the geopolitics and sovereignty claims of the South China Sea and touched upon China's historical claims in the South China Sea. Then, the study analyses Australia's relations with the US and China, also Australia's core vision for the South China Sea and finally examines the Australia's South China Sea policies.

INTRODUCTION

Australia is facing growing concerns about geopolitical developments in the South China Sea and disputes over maritime jurisdiction in the region (The Australian Government-Department of Foreign Affairs and Trade, 2023, p. 1). The region is notable for its strategic sea routes, rich natural resources and sovereignty claims by many countries. Advocating that regional stability and the free passage of goods across the sea should be protected, Australia establishes defence-security partnerships with allied countries, especially the United States of America (US),

DOI: 10.4018/979-8-3693-8109-0.ch002

conducts multilateral exercises, and carries out freedom of navigation and freedom of flight patrols in international seas.

Australia's increasing interest in developments in the South China Sea has been interpreted as a reflection of deepening US-China rivalry at the global level. Indeed, the US continues its strategy of encircling China through bilateral, tripartite, quadratic and multilateral political-security-economic partnerships with its Asia-Pacific allies. Australia is an important player in the US multilateral containment policy towards China. Australia's strategic position within the Quadrilateral Security Dialogue (QUAD) and AUKUS inevitably makes it part of the US-China competition. Furthermore, Canberra's new partnerships with Western allies in the Pacific Islands and its South China Sea policies are undermining relations with Beijing (Pascal, 2018, p. 1).

Australia's role and importance in the South China Sea dispute is closely linked to the political isolation of China in the global power competition. Countries that have problems with China in the South China Sea may find more supporters for their legal cases when they are more politically engaged with Western countries. The South China Sea disputes are not only a matter of international law, but are also at the centre of global politics and power struggles. While Australia tries to remain neutral in these disputes, it has recently tended to adopt a zero-sum game or polarisation policy towards China in its regional policies, as seen in AUKUS security alliance. China, on the other hand, has recently frequently warned Australia to stay away from the Cold War mentality. Therefore, this study is unique and valuable in that it analyses the geostrategic competition between Australia, China and the US in the South China Sea.

While discussing Australia's South China Sea policies, the paper argues that the main problem is the US-China competition, and emphasizes that relations with China are an important factor here. This includes much of China's historic claims in the South China Sea and its disputes with its coastal states. Thus, Australia's South China Sea policies are critically influenced by the extent, scale and manner in which its relations with China. Based on this idea, the study first summarized the geopolitics and sovereignty claims of the South China Sea and touched upon China's historical claims in the South China Sea. Then, the study analyses Australia's relations with the US and China, also Australia's core vision for the South China Sea and finally examines the Australia's South China Sea policies.

SOUTH CHINA SEA GEOPOLITICS AND SOVEREIGNTY CLAIMS

The South China Sea is of high strategic importance. Approximately a third of the world's crude oil exports are carried through these seas (The U.S. Energy Information Administration, 2024, p. 21-22). The most important maritime routes for the transport of goods and raw materials from Europe and Africa to Asia pass through this region. The reefs and atolls in these seas are claimed not only by China, but also by neighbouring states such as Vietnam, Malaysia, Brunei, the Philippines and Indonesia, and their exclusive economic zones are partially or entirely overlapping.

Territorial disputes in the South China Sea involve both island and maritime claims between many sovereign states in the region, such as Brunei, China, Malaysia, the Philippines and Vietnam (Peace Palace Library, 2024, p. 1). An important aspect of the territorial dispute in the South China Sea concerns China's increased presence in the region, in recent years. China is conducting large-scale land harvesting activities in seven reefs in the controversial Spratly Islands Region of the South China Sea (Fiery Cross Reef, Johnson South Reef, Cuarteron Reef, Gaven Reef, Hughes Reef, Mischief Reef and Subi Reef). These projects created seven new artificial land masses in Spratly (Peace Palace Library, 2024, p. 1).

Table 1. Sovereignty claims in the South China Sea

Island/Reef	Claimant	Characteristics
Spratly	China, Vietnam, Taiwan, Philippines, Brunei, Malaysia	More than 100 scattered reefs, atolls and small islands
Paracel	China, Vietnam, Taiwan	130 small coral islands and reefs
Pratas (Dongsha)	China, Taiwan	Group of islands consisting of atolls
Macclesfield	China, Philippines, Taiwan	Submerged atoll consisting of reefs and beaches
Scarborough	China, Philippines, Taiwan	Several small islands and rocks on the reef

Note.(Senkyr & Merkle, 2023, p. 5).

The conflicting claims of sovereignty can be summarized as follows: in the northern part of the sea, China, Taiwan and Vietnam are fighting for the Paracel Islands. China has been in the islands since 1974. In the southern part of the sea, China, Taiwan, and Vietnam claim rights in the entire Spratly Islands of about 200. Malaysia, Brunei and the Philippines are demanding some of them. Vietnam stands out as the country with the largest number of Spratly Islands (Senkyr & Merkle, 2023, p. 7-8).

In the northeast, China, Taiwan and the Philippines all claim the Scarborough Islands. China has controlled these islands since 2012. The South China Sea is also the largest and most complex water mass in which China, Vietnam, the Philippines, Malaysia, Indonesia and Brunei claim ownership over the overlapping areas. The main reason for the conflict is not military security, but the controversial region's source of seafood and other important resources. The conflict is of great importance to Southeast Asian people, as most of them live by the sea, and this proximity has economic and ecological implications for the people (Rossiana, 2022, p. 16-17).

THE ROOT CAUSE OF THE CONFLICT: CHINA'S "NINE-DASH LINE"

The Nine-Dash Line represents a controversial maritime area consisting of intersecting lines that China claimed historical rights in the South China Sea throughout the 20th century.

Figure 1. Sovereignty claims in the South China Sea

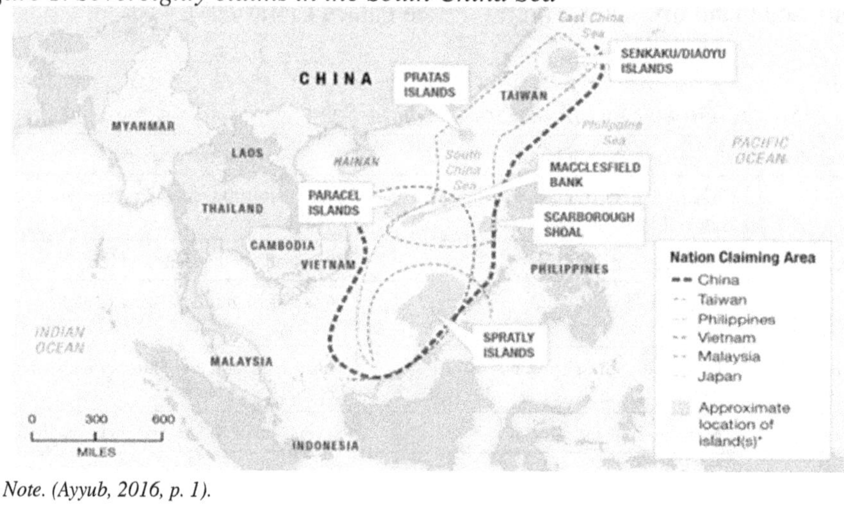

Note. (Ayyub, 2016, p. 1).

China's claim to the islands dates back to the end of World War II, when China captured these islands from Japan in 1946. A map published by the Republic of China (current Taiwan's official government) in 1947 identified the "11 Dash Line", which also covers the Gulf of Tonkin (Gragnani, 2022, p. 19). With the proclamation of the People's Republic of China in 1949, the communist government declared itself the sole legitimate representative of Taiwan and (according to China's claims) acquired all its maritime rights in the region (Pemmaraju, 2016, p. 267). Hereby,

"11 Dashed Line" map came into the official usage in the the People's Republic of China (PRC) in 1949.

Following the San Francisco Peace Agreement with Japan in 1951, China, Vietnam and the Philippines claimed rights over the archipelago (Tkachenko, 2014, p. 70). In 1953, the PRC had bilateral agreements with Vietnam and deleted the two sections of the nine-dash line between Hainan Island and the Vietnamese coast in the Beibu Gulf from the official map (Gao & Jia, 2013, p. 103). Until the 1970s, no country had raised any objection to the nine-dash line of the South China Sea, and even many countries had used this line on their maps. In 2000, China and Vietnam demarcated the boundary of the territorial sea, exclusive economic zone, and continental shelf in the Beibu Gulf (Hongbin & Ullah, 2022, p. 72).

In 2013, China began claiming a "10-dash line" by adding a new line to the coast of Taiwan in the East China Sea. Since the latest added line does not cover the South China Sea, the disputed areas in the region are referred to as the "Nine-Dash Line". (Hostetler, 2024, p. 307).

The US and the countries of the region are disturbed by the construction of military bases on the islands in the South China Sea, where China claims rights through the "Nine-Dash Line". In this context, Brunei, Indonesia, Malaysia, the Philippines, Taiwan and Vietnam view China's "Nine-Dash Line" as a violation of their sovereignty.

The Philippines has appealed to the Permanent Court of Arbitration, claiming that China's historic claim to the Nine-Dash Line violates the 1982 Convention on the Law of the Sea. In 2016, the Arbitration Court ruled that China's historical claims had no legal basis (BBC, 2016, p. 1). According to international law experts, China can only claim land sovereignty over these uninhabited islands and reefs, but cannot undertake work within the exclusive economic zone (Lee, 2023, p. 7). In response, Beijing claims that, despite being a signatory to the 1982 Convention on the Law of the Sea, the Nine-Dash Line emerged after World War II, and that after Japan's surrender, it had recovered the islands under the authority of the Allied States.

Recently, there have been severe tensions between the Philippines and China over violations of sovereign rights in the South China Sea. In this context, the US is calling on its allies in Southeast Asia to take severe measures against China's actions in these seas.

AUSTRALIA'S RELATIONS WITH THE US

One of the key factors shaping Australia's policies in the South China Sea is its relationship with the US, and the way that it reflects its relations with China. In historical terms, there is a 1951 security treaty called ANZUS, which commits the

US, Australia and New Zealand to helping each other in the war. But New Zealand suspended ANZUS in 1986 for launching a nuclear-clean zone on its national borders, including land. The Five Eyes Intelligence Network, which was established during World War II and continues to exist today, envisages co-operation between Anglo-Saxon countries in the Asia-Pacific (the US, Britain, Australia, New Zealand, and Canada). In short, the US military-security commitment in the Asia-Pacific dates back to World War II.

In addition, Australia has developed a number of defence-security co-operations with the US in recent years to ensure that the Indo-Pacific region remains free and open. The most notable of these are the QUAD, which was established in 2017 between Australia, the US, India and Japan, and the AUKUS, which was built in 2021 between the United Kingdom (UK), Australia and the US.

On March 14, 2023, the leaders of Australia, the US and the UK met to define the road map for AUKUS. Under this military plan, designed to balance China's influence in the Asia-Pacific region, nuclear submarines will be transferred to the Australian Navy, and the US and Britain will provide technological support to the country for joint production.

Australia's nuclear-powered conventional submarines are intended to contribute to security and stability in the Asia-Pacific. It should be noted that these nuclear-powered systems are only used in submarine propulsion systems. There is no risk associated with nuclear weapons. In this sense, the construction of these systems continues with permits obtained from the International Atomic Energy Agency (IAEA). The agreement under AUKUS also covers the transfer of cyber capabilities, artificial intelligence and other high-technology. Nuclear-powered submarines have a faster and longer range than conventional diesel-engine submersibles. This will enable the Australian Navy to undertake covert operations in a more remote geography and attack the enemy fleet.

Concerns about regional security are high. The Beijing administration described AUKUS as "a typical example of the Cold War mentality" and condemned it as a "threat to regional peace and stability" (Herscovitch, 2023, p. 1). China claims that the AUKUS partnership involves the illegal transfer of nuclear weapons materials. According to Beijing, the agreement is essentially an act of nuclear proliferation. The AUKUS countries emphasize that they have obtained the necessary permits from the IAEA. Indeed, if China's claim were true, the US would not be able to build a nuclear-powered aircraft carrier. China currently has two nuclear-powered submarines. So what Beijing is opposed to is that AUKUS disrupts regional security balances, leads to militarization, and serves block politics.

AUKUS is argued to serve the US's strategy of containment towards China. This platform, which envisages the UK and the US to export nuclear submarine technology to Australia, is known as a defence-security alliance, unlike QUAD. In order to free and open the region, QUAD provides for co-operation between Member States in areas such as maritime navigation and airspace security, joint exercises, the fight against piracy and the preservation of the status quo. In this respect, QUAD is seen as a joint platform aimed at contributing to regional security rather than being a defence alliance.

QUAD has also been a driving force in developing other bilateral, tripartite and quadratic dialogue mechanisms in the region. Some of the "multi-party" security dialogues, interpreted and criticized by China as "blocking" in the Asia-Pacific, include (Madan, 2022, p. 209):

- Japan-South Korea-US
- Japan-India-Italy
- Japan-UK-Australia
- Japan-Australia-US
- Japan-India-US
- Japan-Australia-India
- Australia-Indonesia-India
- Australia-India-France

China claims that actors in the Asia-Pacific are moving away from the "free and open" regional security principle, pursuing a policy of blockade with the US, conducting military exercises and thus forming defence-security coalitions. For example, South Korea, Japan, Australia and New Zealand became NATO's Indo-Pacific Partners (IP4) in 2016 and have been invited as guest to the NATO Leaders' Summit in 2022, 2023 and 2024. These partnerships have contributed to the increase in the number of military exercises in the region and their participation. For instance, 100 aircraft and 2,500 personnel from 17 countries participated in the Australian Air Force's "Pitch Black 22" exercise, while Japan, Australia, Canada, and South Korea also took part in the US-led "Pacific Vanguard 2022" naval exercise.

High-level defence and foreign affairs officials from the US and Australia met on 28 July 2023 as part of the "33rd Australia-US Ministerial Consultation (AUSMIN)". The parties agreed to enhance cooperation with India, Japan, Indonesia, the Philippines and South Korea to ensure security and stability in the region. During the talks, the two countries agreed to enhance co-operation with Asia-Pacific countries through a series of exercises. They also welcomed the first participation of Fiji, Indonesia, Papua New Guinea and Tonga in the US-Australia-led "TALISMAN SABRE 2023" exercise, as well as the deployment of observers from India, Singapore, Thailand and the Philippines (The US Department of Defense, 2023, p. 1).

Other issues agreed under the AUSMIN include reaffirming commitment to transparency, raising maritime safety and maritime awareness, cooperating to prevent illegal fishing, boosting the alliance, and starting this year, more regular visits by American submarines to Australia. A number of key priorities have been identified to strengthen their mutual alliances, partnerships, tripartite and multilateral security arrangements, according to the statement. (The Economic Times, 2023, p. 1).

Similarly, the expansion of AUKUS is on the agenda. In this context, Japan, New Zealand and Canada are expected to join the second pillar of AUKUS. The second pillar focuses on developing advanced combat capabilities such as artificial intelligence, submarine unmanned aircraft, hypersonic and electronic warfare technologies. According to US officials, countries such as Japan and New Zealand are invited to the second pillar of AUKUS because they have formed a broad network of alliances in the region.

Besides, Australia's move to extend logistics and military access agreements with its allies, including Japan, the US and the Philippines, has greatly hampered relations with China. Indeed, these agreements will facilitate Australia's access to the South China Sea. In this case, regional allies such as the Philippines, Japan and Australia are included in US military coalitions. The growing number of bilateral, tripartite and quadrilateral military coalitions in the region means that the US is accelerating its strategy of encircling China. Countries in the region are likely to see the greatest damage from this polarization. For this reason, it is essential for Australia to establish reliable and healthy channels of communication with China.

AUSTRALIA'S RELATIONS WITH CHINA

Australia's relations with Beijing are also influential in its South China Sea policy. Similarly, Australia's military-security partnerships with Western actors in recent years have negatively affected its relations with China. One of the most important factors causing the deterioration of Canberra-Beijing relations was Australia's coalition government, led by former Prime Minister Scott Morrison, taking a stance against China following US pressure. The Morrison Government failed to manage relations with China. During this process, a series of embargoes had begun to be imposed on China-Australia economic relations. The elections in May 2022 saw a change in foreign policy with the creation of the Labour Party government under the leadership of Antony Albanese, which opened a new page in relations with the states of the region, including China.

The Canberra administration, on the one hand, has continued to develop its military capacity and capabilities, while on the other, it has focused on diplomacy to improve its relations with Beijing. In this context, significant progress has been made in Australia-China relations between October and December 2022. The meeting of Chinese President Xi Jinping and Australian counterpart Antony Albenese at the G20 Summit in November marked the beginning of a period of softening and cooperation in bilateral relations.

In December 2022, Xi Jinping said his country was ready to advance relations with Australia based on mutual respect and win-win principles (China Daily, 2022, p. 1). As a result of the easing of bilateral relations, China has announced that it will resume importing coal from Australia in early January 2023. But embargoes on other pens are still ongoing. Australia, which is pleased with this opening, is working to lift the embargoes on other economic pens. The Albanian government argues that removing these barriers is in both Australia's and China's interests. So, the Canberra administration is approaching Beijing with a win-win approach. In other words, Australia is trying to show goodwill and sincerity. Because its biggest trading partner is China.

At this point, it is useful to examine the economic effects of trade embargoes on both Australia and China. To highlight, China introduced commercial embargos on many Australian exports in early 2020 in response to the Australian government's call for an investigation into the origins of Covid-19. Trade restrictions on Australian products had begun in the form of higher tariffs on wine and barley between May and November 2020. Biosafety measures against some beef and cattle, and non-tariff barriers for coal, cotton, and lobster were introduced. As a result, Australia's exports of certain goods to China fell to almost zero. Despite being China's largest trading partner, Australia has sought to mitigate the impact of trade restrictions by finding new markets in other countries.

With the inauguration of the new Australian government in early 2023, China began lifting trade restrictions, and Australia resumed exports of barley, cotton, wood, coal and copper to China. Following a meeting between Prime Minister Albanese and President Xi Jinping in October 2023, Beijing said it would resume importing lobster and review wine tariffs. In return, Australia agreed to suspend the World Trade Organization (WTO) case against China. The wine tariffs were lifted on 28 March 2024 in the hope that it would soon resume its imports (Edmonstone, 2024, p. 1). While this up-and-down trend in economic relations with China continues, Australia, on the other hand, has also developed military ties with the US.

Australia, with a recent decision, has agreed to give more bases to the US in its country. Also outlining the AUKUS road map, Australia has indicated that it will not always pursue a soft policy towards China. A meeting on 14 March 2023 between the leaders of Australia, the US and the United Kingdom (UK) to define the road map for AUKUS has also led to the disappearance of a positive atmosphere in China-Australia relations. The Beijing government has criticised AUKUS as a "threat to regional peace and stability", saying it serves the arms race and polarization (The America Times, 2023, p. 1). In this context, Chinese Foreign Affairs spokesman Wang Wenbin noted that the three countries pursued their own geopolitical interests, ignored the concerns of the international community, and, in short, followed a wrong and dangerous path (The America Times, 2023, p. 1). Australian Prime Minister Antony Albanese has argued that his country, on the one hand, has improved its military capabilities, but it can also advance its relations with China (News, 2023, p. 1).

Despite all, China wants relations with Australia to move in a positive direction, regardless of the AUKUS agreement. It is highly believed that this is because America's strategy of encircling China is moving at its last speed in the region. In this context, Australia's re-engagement in deepening the American alliance would be a major blow to China. Beijing is trying to pursue strong diplomacy to reverse this trend.

The Australian Government's paper on National Defence Strategy, issued on 17 April 2024, summarizes the nature of Australia-China relations as follows (Australian Government-Department of Defence, 2024, p. 49):

> *"While Australia and China have different values and political systems, a stable and constructive relationship is in the interest of both nations. The Government will remain patient, calibrated and deliberate in its approach to China, cooperating where we can, disagreeing where we must and engaging in Australia's national interests."*

It is estimated that Australia will not follow the US at any cost and will try to develop co-operation with China. Australian Deputy Prime Minister Richard Marles said the AUKUS agreement does not "definitely" commit to joining the US in the event of a war in Taiwan (The Guardian, 2023, p. 1). So Australia, while strengthening its military capabilities, will continue to cooperate with China based on peace and dialogue at the same time.

While Australia continues to seek dialogue with China, Prime Minister Albanese met with Chinese counterpart Li Keqiang in Jakarta, Indonesia's capital, on 7 September 2023. Albanese continued to argue that removing existing trade barriers would be in the interests of both countries. If the Canberra administration acts in its national interests, it will be able to develop positive relations with Beijing. However, under pressure from the UK and the US, Australia is positioned alongside the West in regional geopolitics.

China is working to re-establish mutual trust with every player in the region under US pressure. China, on the other hand, does not follow an entirely open-door policy towards Australia. If Canberra avoids US-led polarization, it can continue to improve its relations with Beijing.

AUSTRALIA'S FUNDAMENTAL APPROACH TO THE SOUTH CHINA SEA

The security of neighbouring oceans is a critical part of Australia's national security. In other words, Australia's national interests are closely concerned with the security of the Indo-Pacific Ocean and the Pacific Ocean, as well as the Straits of Malacca, the South China Sea and the Philippine Sea, which connect these two great oceans. Sovereignty disputes in these seas create a potential source of growing instability around Australia. Canberra therefore supports the solution of these problems in a peaceful manner and in accordance with international law.

Australia is trying to develop constructive dialogue and co-operation with each of its rival and conflicting states in the South China Sea, and is in no way a party to these disputes. Urging all rights holders to refrain from actions that would increase tensions, the Australian government is concerned about China's rapid increase in activities, as well as the potential for the use of force or pressure in the East China Sea and the Taiwan Straits. In this context, Australia argues that the Arbitration Court's ruling in 2016 on the Philippines and China is binding on both sides (Australian Government, 2017, p. 46-47).

AUSTRALIA'S POLICIES IN THE SOUTH CHINA SEA

Australia is one of the region's earliest American allies in developing South China Sea strategies. Since 2012, Australia has been incorporating the Indo-Pacific conceptualization into official documents, and since 2017, it has been focusing on security strategies in the region. Over the past 15 years, Canberra's view of the region has changed rapidly. Australia's expectations for the South China Sea have remained optimistic as global US-China competition has not deepened until the 2010s. However, the rapid deterioration of the geopolitical landscape since 2017 has led Australia to change its approach to the region. In response to China's increasing power in the seas, Australia has tightened its rhetoric against the country and has begun to redirect its policy around harsh balancing (Bisley, 2023, p. 35).

While Australia is rhetorically critical of China over the South China Sea, it is in favour of monitoring regional balances at the level of action. Indonesia and the US, in particular, have long been close to demanding joint Freedom of Navigation Operations (FONOPs) in the South China Sea. As has been seen in many other Southeast Asian countries, Australia is pursuing a strategic hedging strategy against China (Baldino & Bloomfield, 2018, p. 9).

Australia's 2024 National Security Strategy also emphasizes US-China competition in the region rather than referring directly to China. Nevertheless, the Australian government believes that China's coercive actions are effective in deteriorating the security environment in the South China Sea. In this context, Australia has developed the concept of "integrated and focused power" in order to deter China and respond to it when needed. The Australian Defence Forces has thus shifted from a balanced force capable of responding to various unexpected situations to an integrated and focused force designed to address the country's most important strategic risks (Australian Government-Department of Defence, 2024, p. 27).

This integrated and focused power strategy emphasizes co-operation with the US and other partners. The focus is on enhancing defence industry co-operation with the US, enhancing joint development, production and sustainability activities. The Australian government supports the continuation of the US-China dialogue to prevent the risk of a possible military confrontation in the region. At the same time, Australia says it will raise the issues with China if necessary, but will also continue the defence dialogue.

Australia is striving to reduce tensions and potential war risks in the South China Sea by continuously strengthening its military potential and deepening its regional partnerships. Australia is acting on the assumption that China's growing naval power will create a long-term imbalance between the US and China (Hernik, 2022, p. 1). For this reason, Canberra is in favour of Washington strengthening its position in the region and establishing a balance against Beijing. In this regard, Australia is aiming to acquire eight nuclear-powered submarines from the US and the UK under AUKUS to reach a level that can compete with China in the region. Australia's submarines under AUKUS could travel long distances thanks to its nuclear-powered. The main objective here is to enable Australia to operate in far seas, such as the South China Sea. This will also enhance Canberra's competitiveness in the Indo-Pacific.

Australia, which is surrounded by the Indian Ocean, in the east by the Pacific Ocean, and in the north by the Southeast Asian countries, is also closely concerned with the security of the South China Sea. "The Defence Strategic Update", released by the Australian Defence Ministry in 2020, mentions the expansion of "grey zone" activities in the Indo-Pacific. (Australian Government-Department of Defence, 2020, p. 5-6). These activities range from provoking conflict to another form of military and non-military pressure, the militarization of the South China Sea, active intervention, disinformation campaigns, and economic pressure.

Due to this changing security environment, Australia has taken action to reform its national strength and defence. Indeed, the security environment in these seas has much greater potential in terms of the risk of military conflict than ever before. This could also include intra-state conflicts that could occupy the Australian Defence

Forces (ADF), where Australia's interests are likely threatened. Therefore, Australia's defence needs to be more prepared for the possibility of a high-intensity conflict.

Australia's "2020 Defence Strategic Update Report" assesses the security environment in the South China Sea as follows (Australian Government-Department of Defence, 2020, p. 11-12):

"Since 2016, major powers have become more assertive in advancing their strategic preferences and seeking to exert influence, including China's active pursuit of greater influence in the Indo-Pacific. Australia is concerned by the potential for actions, such as the establishment of military bases, which could undermine stability in the Indo-Pacific and our immediate region. It is essential that countries pursue their interests in ways that are mutually respectful and supportive of stability, prosperity and security... Some countries will continue to pursue their strategic interests through a combination of coercive activities, including espionage, interference and economic levers. Tensions over territorial claims and the establishment of new military facilities are rising and are involving the use of military or para-military forces more frequently than in the past, including coercive para-military activities in the South China Sea."

Three years after the report was released, the Australian Government revised its views on South China Sea and China's activities in these seas. The "2023 National Defense-Defence Strategic Review" used the following statements on the subject (Australian Government-Department of Defence, 2023, p. 23):

"Regional countries continue to modernise their military forces. China's military build-up is now the largest and most ambitious of any country since the end of the Second World War. This has occurred alongside significant economic development, benefiting many countries in the Indo-Pacific, including Australia. This build-up is occurring without transparency or reassurance to the Indo-Pacific region of China's strategic intent. China's assertion of sovereignty over the South China Sea threatens the global rules-based order in the Indo-Pacific in a way that adversely impacts Australia's national interests. China is also engaged in strategic competition in Australia's near neighbourhood"

Australia has profound interests, in the areas of trade and security, although it does not claim rights in these controversial seas. Australia's maritime trade route with Asian countries passes through this sea. The South China Sea is strategically closely concerned with Australia's interests. The deterioration of the security environment in the South China Sea, one of the world's major trading routes, has been one of Australia's growing concerns. Thus, the South China Sea is closely linked to Australia's economy and national security. The stability, security and development of these seas are critical to Australia's national interests (Sang, 2017, p. 63).

From a security and defence perspective, sovereignty disputes between Southeast Asian countries and China negatively affect regional security, and this instability poses a direct threat to Australia's interests in the South China Sea. In the face of changing balance of power in Southeast Asia, Australia has begun to pursue a proactive policy, especially from 2020.

Australia is working with its Western allies to engage in unilateral attempts to change the rule-based order in the South China Sea. Southeast Asian states are becoming part of the competition between China and the US. The latter is pursuing activities to protect freedom of navigation and flight rights in the South China Sea to counter China's claims and provide support to countries on the coast of Southeast Asia. Australia, along with the US and other Western partners, continues to support the efforts of its Southeast Asian neighbours. For many years, the Australian government has been refrained from engaging in such military activities to avoid China's reaction (Cook, 2021, p. 3-4).

In general, Australia shares similar interests with the US in preserving the maritime rules-based order. Australia, on the other hand, is avoiding reactive approaches to disputes in these seas in order to safeguard trade relations with China. In this context, Australia is refraining from taking a stance on coastal countries' claims of sovereignty under the United Nations Convention on the Law of the Sea (UNCLOS) in the South China Sea. Australia stresses the need for greater cooperation in the South China Sea conflict as part of its bilateral and multilateral diplomacy. In this context, Canberra has consistently expressed support for ASEAN countries and Beijing's process of establishing a Code of Conduct in these seas (Strating, 2019, p. 2).

Australia is actively pursuing its military operations in the Indo-Pacific and South China Seas. For example, "Operation Gateway" is seen as one of the Australian Defence Forces' most important contributions to the maintenance of regional security and stability in Southeast Asia. As part of the operation, the Australian Army is carrying out maritime surveillance operations in the North Indian Ocean and the South China Sea. The operation, conducted from Royal Malaysian Air Force Base "Butterworth", is an important aspect of the Malaysia-Australia Joint Defence Programme.

In addition, Australia launched the Indian-Pacific Endeavour (IPE) operation in 2017, designed to "expand its regional partnerships". In this context, it has re-expanded the joint training with regional allies, port visits and inter-army cooperation. This contributes to Australia's efforts to build maritime security capabilities across the region, making Australia "a preferred partner" among Southeast Asian states. The IPE aims to make an effective contribution to humanitarian aid and security efforts through bilateral and multilateral participation, training and capacity-building activities. This is part of Australia's commitment to promoting security and stability in the surrounding region. 14 countries participated in the 2023 operation. These include Bangladesh, Brunei, Cambodia, India, Indonesia, Laos, Malaysia, the Maldives, the Philippines, Singapore, Sri Lanka, Thailand, East Timor and Vietnam.

Australia has expanded its military operations in the region to contribute more to the construction of a free, open and prosperous Indo-Pacific. For example, Operation Argos is part of the Australian Defence Forces' commitment to international efforts to implement United Nations Security Council sanctions against North Korea. But these activities also increase Australia's risk of a military confrontation with China. For example, on 26 May 2022, a Royal Australian Air Force P-8 naval surveillance aircraft was blocked by a Chinese J-16 fighter aircraft during a routine mission over the South China Sea. The prevention resulted in a dangerous manoeuvre that posed a security threat to the P-8 aircraft and its crew, and the Australian government has conveyed its concerns about the incident to the Chinese government (Mahadzir, 2022, p. 1). In this regard, China has accused Australia of "disinformation" about border violations by aircraft. Beijing has warned that if Canberra does not stop its "provocations", it could lead to "serious consequences" (The Guardian, 2022, p. 1). China's preventive intervention on an Australian plane took place near the Paracel Islands in the South China Sea. China, which claims sovereignty over the area designated as the "Nine-Dash Line", is sending "warning messages" against other states' flights or shipping there. Australia has just begun to understand China's red lines in these seas.

In addition, Australia is advancing its military relations with actors off the South China Sea. For instance, Indonesia and Singapore participated directly in the "Pitch Black 22" exercise, conducted by the Royal Australian Air Force (RAAF) from 19 August to 8 September 2022. Japan, Germany and South Korea were also noted for the first time to participate in these exercises. From the countries of the region, Malaysia, the Philippines and Thailand joined the relevant exercise by sending military personnel (Atalayar, 2022, p. 1).

Among these countries, the Philippines, in particular, is keen to cooperate with Australia in the area of security. Australian Defence Minister Richard Marles said on 25 August 2023, that his country has security interests in the South China Sea and will work closer with the Philippines on joint operations (Reuters, 2023, p. 1). In this context, more than 2,000 Australian and Philippine military personnel conducted the Alon Exercises in the South China Sea from 14 to 31 August 2023.

Australia, Japan and the Philippines had joint naval missions in the South China Sea in mid-August 2023. Besides, the Philippine and Australian navies have carried out their first joint missions in the aforementioned sea (Reuters, 2023, p. 1). Australian Prime Minister Anthony Albanese also visited the Philippines in September 2023 to discuss defence cooperation. Australia and the Philippines are seeking to expand their regional partners through maritime cooperation in response to the risk of a possible conflict in the Taiwan Strait and its surroundings.

The Philippines has shown a close interest in Australia in recent years to disperse the risks of war in Taiwan. The US and the Philippines have a 1951 Joint Defence Agreement. Australia, on the other hand, is not committed to supporting the US on Taiwan (The Guardian, 2023, p. 1). Therefore, it is expected that the Philippines will enhance bilateral defence partnerships with Australia, Japan and other allied powers.

CONCLUSION

Australia's policy in the South China Sea is based on a strategy to safeguard regional security and freedom of navigation and flight rights. Australia argues that claims of sovereignty between China and other coastal countries in the South China Sea should be handled within the framework of international law, and stresses that the UNCLOS should be complied with.

Australia's policy, in close coordination with the US and other allies on security and military co-operation in the South China Sea, is based on supporting diplomatic and international law instead of using military force, while increasing military preparedness and resilience against the potential risk of conflict in the region.

There are various agreements and strategic partnerships between Australia and the US on regional security, military co-operation and intelligence-sharing. These include strategic agreements such as ANZUS, AUSMIN, QUAD, AUKUS and Five Eyes. These agreements help the two countries common goals in the field of defence and security.

Australia remains committed to safeguarding freedom of navigation and international law-based order in the South China Sea and is seeking solutions through dialogue with all parties in the region.

The Canberra government has focused on developing a regional cooperation-support process in which the US is not involved, assuming a possible war in the South China Sea will affect them the most. In this context, Australia is showing increasing interest not only in the Philippines, but also in Japan. Australia's engagement with actors such as the Philippines, Japan and South Korea in the South China Sea has significantly damaged its relations with China.

The "anti-China" axis in the Asia-Pacific is increasingly strengthened due to tensions in the South China Sea and the Taiwan Straits. China, on the one hand, tries to develop its relations with Australia on the basis of mutual respect and win-win principles, while Australia, for the sake of American hegemony, prefers to polarize with China by pushing its own interests backwards.

As a result, Australia has begun to intervene directly in US-China competition through South China Sea geopolitics. While the blockade policy is gaining momentum in the South China Sea, the US is dragging its regional allies, such as Australia, into a "dangerous game" with China.

Consequently, the following scenarios for Australia's policies in the South China Sea can arise:

First, it seems inevitable that Australia will rapidly expand its military co-operation with the US in the South China Sea and greater Indo-Pacific. In this context, closer military partnerships - coalitions - between the US, Japan, the Philippines and Australia are expected to emerge. In this regard, it will not be surprising that regional partnerships such as QUAD and AUKUS will continue to expand in the long run. Canberra's pursuit of a policy of blockade together with its Western allies will lead to a downturn in its relations with Beijing. If Canberra expands its military alliance with Washington, it may need to be prepared for a long-term military confrontation with Beijing. In the current conjuncture, the probability of this scenario is moderate.

Secondly, while Australia is deepening its strategic partnership with the US, it will continue to explore opportunities for co-operation on common points with China. Accordingly, Canberra is well aware that the root cause of tensions in the region is US-China competition, and will try to avoid being part of that competition. Australia, which sees the risk of becoming entirely pursued by the US in regional politics, will be very careful not to disrupt its economic relations with China. Under this scenario, Australia, thanks to its ties with the US and other allies, will be able to advance its national security interests, and will also be significantly successful in its strategic hedging strategy against China. In the current conjuncture, it may be argued that this scenario is highly likely to occur.

Thirdly, Australia may think that developing military co-operation and defence partnerships with the US and other allies will eventually increase the risk of war in the region and thus start avoiding dangerous military alliances. In other words, Australia could better understand the dangers of alienating China through regional military coalitions and try to abandon that policy. In that case, Australia could open a new page in its relations with China and rapidly increase its economic gains. In the current conjuncture, it may be argued that this scenario is unlikely to happen.

REFERENCES

Australian Government. (2017). *2017 Foreign Policy White Paper.* Canberra: Australian Government. 1-124.

Australian Government-Department of Defence. (2020). *2020 Defence Strategic Update*. Department of Defence.

Australian Government-Department of Defence. (2023). *National Defence-Defence Strategic Review 2023*. Department of Defence.

Australian Government-Department of Defence. (2024). *National Defence Strategy 2024*. Department of Defence.

Ayyub, R. (2016, April 13). A primer on the complicated battle for the South China Sea. *National Public Radio-NPR*. Retrieved from https://www.npr.org/sections/parallels/2016/04/13/472711435/a-primer-on-the-complicated-battle-for-the-south-china-sea

Baldino, D. & Bloomfield, A. (2018). The rise of the 'Indo-Pacific' in Australian grand-strategic discourse. *Indo-Pacific Insight Series*, 13, Crawley: Australia: Perth USAsia Centre.

BBC. (2016, July 12). *South China Sea: Tribunal backs case against China brought by Philippines*. Retrieved from https://www.bbc.com/news/world-asia-china-36771749

Bisley, N. (2023). Australia's Indo-Pacific Strategy: From Optimism to Hard Balancing. *Asia Policy, 18*(3), 35–45. DOI: 10.1353/asp.2023.a903862

China Daily. (2022, December 21). *Xi says China ready to advance relations with Australia based on mutual respect, win-win principles*. Retrieved from http://www.chinadaily.com.cn/a/202212/21/WS63a29bb8a31057c47eba57c1.html

Cook, M. (2021). *Australia's South China Sea challenges*. Sydney: The Lowy Institute-. *Policy Brief*, •••, 1–22.

Edmonstone, G. (2024, April 2). China's trade restrictions on Australian exports. *USSC*. Retrieved from https://www.ussc.edu.au/chinas-trade-restrictions-on-australian-exports

Gao, Z., & Jia, B. B. (2013). The nine-dash line in the South China Sea: History, status, and implications. *The American Journal of International Law*, *107*(1), 98–124. DOI: 10.5305/amerjintelaw.107.1.0098

Gragnani, L. (2022). *Assessing Tsai Ying-wen's strategy in the South China Sea* (Unpublished master thesis). Charles University-Faculty of Social Sciences, Prague.

Hernik, J. (2022, April 22). Australia's Role in the Indo-Pacific Strategy of the United States. *Warsaw Institute*. Retrieved from https://warsawinstitute.org/australias-role-indo-pacific-strategy-united-states/

Herscovitch, B. (2023, March 15). China's sound and fury over Aukus will mean little for ties with Australia. *The Guardian*. Retrieved from https://t.ly/D1qT3

Hongbin, D., & Ullah, I. (2022). The South China Sea's Nine-Dash Line: Key Disputes Andchina's Historical Rights Claims. [JPCS]. *Journal of Pakistan-China Studies*, *3*(1), 67–86. DOI: 10.55733/jpcs.v3i1.53

Hostetler, L. (2024). China's Nine-Dash Line: Cartographic Science and the Adoption of New Map Languages in the Transition from Empire to Nation State. In *Reimagining the Globe and Cultural Exchange* (pp. 293–320). Brill., DOI: 10.1163/9789004684782_012

Lee, H. (2023). The legality of militarization of the South China Sea and its legal implications. *KMI International Journal of Maritime Affairs and Fisheries*, *15*(1), 1–24. DOI: 10.54007/ijmaf.2023.15.1.1

Madan, T. (2022). India and the QUAD. In T. Huxley & L. Kuok (Eds.), *Asia-Pacific regional security assessment 2022-Key developments and trends* (pp.198-221). London, UK: The International Institute for Strategic Studies (IISS).

Mahadzir, D. (2022, June 7). China denies harassing Canadian, Australian patrol aircraft in the Western Pacific. *USNİ*. Retrieved from https://news.usni.org/2022/06/07/china-denies-harassing-canadian-australian-patrol-aircraft-in-the-western-pacific

News. (2023, March 10). *Albanese defends nuclear subs plan after Beijing accuses AUKUS of stirring up an arms race*. Retrieved from https://bit.ly/3TT612e

Pascal, C. (2018, December 7). Australia and New Zealand Must Rethink Their Approach to Pacific Trade. *Chatham House*. Retrieved from https://www.chathamhouse.org/2018/10/australia-and-new-zealand-must-rethink-their-approach-pacific-trade

Peace Palace Library. (2024, June 24). *South China Sea territorial disputes*. Retrieved from https://peacepalacelibrary.nl/research-guide/south-china-sea-territorial-disputes

Pemmaraju, S. R. (2016). The South China Sea arbitration (The Philippines v. China): Assessment of the award on jurisdiction and admissibility. *Chinese Journal of International Law*, *15*(2), 265–307. DOI: 10.1093/chinesejil/jmw019

Reuters. (2023, August 25). *Australia says it will conduct more joint patrols with Philippines in South China Sea.* Retrieved from https://www.reuters.com/world/australia-says-it-will-conduct-more-joint-patrols-with-philippines-south-china-2023-08-25/

Rossiana, Y. S. (2022). The South China Sea Dispute: Code of Conduct Implementation as the Dispute Settlement. *Jurnal Diplomasi Pertahanan*, *8*(1), 15–30. DOI: 10.33172/jdp.v8i1.884

Sang, H. T. (2017). Australia's engagement in the South China Sea under the prospect theory approach and implications for Australia-Vietnam relations. *Asian Culture and History*, *9*(2), 60–70. DOI: 10.5539/ach.v9n2p60

Senkyr, J., & Merkle, D. (2023). *Geopolitics in the South China Sea.* Konrad-Adenauer-Stiftung Monitör Security.

Strating, R. (2019). *Australia's approach to the South China Sea disputes* (Number 485). Washington: East West Center-Asia Pacific Bulletin. 1-2.

The America Times. (2023, March 14). *China's reaction to AUKUS agreement.* Retrieved from https://www.america-times.com/chinas-reaction-to-aukus-agreement/

The Australian Government-Department of Foreign Affairs and Trade. (2023, December 12). *Australian Government concerns about recent actions in the South China Sea.* Retrieved from https://www.dfat.gov.au/news/media-release/australian-government-concerns-about-recent-actions-south-china-sea

The Economic Times. (2023, July 29). *US, Australia to cooperate with India to ensure security and stability of Indo-Pacific.* Retrieved from https://economictimes.indiatimes.com/news/defence/us-australia-to-cooperate-with-india-to-ensure-security-and-stability-of-indo-pacific/articleshow/102231936.cms?from=mdr

The Guardian. (2022, June 7). *China accuses Australia and Canada of 'disinformation' over jet encounters.* Retrieved from https://www.theguardian.com/world/2022/jun/07/china-accuses-australia-canada-jet-encounters

The Guardian. (2023, March 19). *Australia has 'absolutely not' committed to join US in event of war over Taiwan, Marles says.* Retrieved from https://www.theguardian.com/world/2023/mar/19/australia-has-absolutely-not-committed-to-join-us-in-event-of-war-over-taiwan-marles-says

The US Department of Defense. (2023, July 29). *Joint statement on Australia-U.S. Ministerial Consultations (AUSMIN) 2023.* Retrieved from https://www.defense.gov/News/Releases/Release/Article/3476104/joint-statement-on-australia-us-ministerial-consultations-ausmin-2023/

The U.S. Energy Information Administration. (2024). *Regional analysis brief: South China Sea*. U.S. Department of Energy.

Tkachenko, B. I. (2014). Territorial disputes in the South China Sea. The Spratly Archipelago. *Asia-Pacific Journal of Marine Science & Education*, *4*(2), 56–94.

Chapter 3
Energy Geopolitics of South China Sea:
Can the Prevailing and Prospective Hydrocarbons Within the Region Further Escalate or De-Escalate

Murat Yorulmaz
https://orcid.org/0000-0002-3664-0451
Trakya University, Turkey

Sina Kısacık
https://orcid.org/0000-0002-3603-6510
Kıbrıs İlim University, Cyprus

ABSTRACT

Conflicts have shifted in the 21st century from claimed territories to extraterritorial places. The disputes among states were based on territorial claims up to the previous century. The demarcation of territorial boundaries has effectively resolved land conflicts as a spatial concept. Because some states have unsettled land boundaries that serve as the basis for interstate conflict, the establishment and maintenance of land borders therefore continues to be a critical problem for state sovereignty. But in the maritime realm, the same clarity that is required to control state behaviour has not been attained. The states' perception of South China Sea (SCS) as per nautical area will dictate whether they cooperate or compete in the region. Individual maritime and territorial claims have the potential to cause regional instability. This paper aimed to analyse the energy geopolitics of the SCS by taking into account its potential, territorial disputes, the basic dynamics and the approaches of the regional states, especially in line with Beijing's claims and aggressive stance.

DOI: 10.4018/979-8-3693-8109-0.ch003

INTRODUCTION

Conflicts have shifted in the 21st century from claimed territories to extraterritorial places. The disputes among states were based on territorial claims up to the previous century. The demarcation of territorial boundaries has effectively resolved land conflicts as a spatial concept. Because some states have unsettled land boundaries that serve as the basis for interstate conflict, the establishment and maintenance of land borders therefore continues to be a critical problem for state sovereignty. But in the maritime realm, the same clarity that is required to control state behaviour has not been attained. Without a comprehensive governance framework with the ability to impose legally enforceable judgments on all parties, there would be no spatial certainty. The states' perception of South China Sea (SCS) as per nautical area will dictate whether they cooperate or compete in the region. Individual maritime and territorial claims have the potential to cause regional instability. In contrast, states can coordinate their ties peacefully by acknowledging it as a free and open realm and adhering to the universally recognized rule of law.

Within the context of geographical terms, SCS remains a component in terms of ocean systems. However, for geopolitical purposes, it has become an ambiguous notion for a number of reasons: China and other SCS littorals have overlapping EEZs (Exclusive Economic Zone) and territorial claims over what it considers to be a contested or disputed maritime zone. Six nations share and encircle the SCS's maritime region: China, Malaysia, Taiwan, the Philippines, Vietnam, Singapore, and Brunei Darussalam (Kim, 2015: 118). Every nation has prerogatives towards conventional deposits in the South China Sea as well as marine interests of its own. However, since the 1970s, China has made unilateral claims to a number of the region's landforms.

The SCS is one of the world's most significant seas for the reason that it is a vital maritime direction for international trade and communications and has rich marine resources and a unique biodiversity. Significant maritime positions of contacts (SLOCs) are essential issue within the framework of both the neighboring East Asian countries and the remaining globe (Singh, 2022). There is further transportation within SCS and Southeast Asia's coastal seas on account of Beijing's economic growth and area's recent trend toward more intra-Asian commerce. Another name for the SCS is ''a flashpoint for territorial and maritime disputes between and among multiple claimants.'' Conflicts with diverse national interests may arise in the complex political environment around the SCS. Because the four groups of islands are located in distinct geographic areas, their political standings are different as of each other as well. The Taiwanese government has complete authority over the Pratas Islands. Taiwan is seen as an essential part of China, hence there are no rival claims. China is in charge of the Paracel Islands; however, the Vietnamese dispute it. Because it has been going on for a long time and involves up to five states and six parties—China, Chinese Taipei, Malaysia, Vietnam, the Philippines, and Brunei—the Spratly Islands conflict is the most convoluted (Ma, 2016: 39-40; Zou, 2021: 1-2). It is anticipated that if the Spratly Islands dispute stands not resolute successfully, it may endanger and threaten the safety and security of East Asia and maybe even beyond. Having stated so, we learn that the SCS conflicts are divided into three tiers.

''Primarily, there are the overlapping claims to sovereignty over geographic features between and among littoral states; second, there are overlapping claims to maritime zones emanating from the islands or surrounding coasts of the littoral states, basically concerning sovereign rights and jurisdiction as outlined under the LOSC; and third, there are disputes pertaining to the use of the oceans, including competing uses of marine resources and development between and among littoral states, the use of sea lanes, and the conduct of military operations in the name of freedom of navigation between and among littoral states'' (Zou, 2021: 2).

On the other hand, one of the main causes of disputes in the SCS is the problem of hydrocarbon deposits within region. This stays evident that the SCS hydrocarbon deposits' question remains the tactical focal point of the struggle for pertinent parties if one accepts that the control and delineation of isles, reefs, and islands positioned at Nansha Islands as well as somewhere else epitomise the core of the existing quarrels in the SCS (Guoqiang, 2015). While continuing to forcibly hold islands and reefs that were formerly part of China, certain SCS nations have stepped up their attempts to extract oil and gas from the region in an effort to proclaim their privileges to control and prove their prerogatives since 1960s (Guoqiang, 2015). According to Rystad, the SCS has 40.3 trillion cubic feet (Tcf) of confirmed and possible natural gas deposits and around 3.6 billion barrels (bbls) of petroleum and other liquids (EIA, 2024). The SCS disputes stand further thorny since the accession question to marine energy resources is tied to concerns about national sovereignty and energy security.

By taking into account the abovementioned framework, it is within the context of this paper aimed to analyse the energy geopolitics of the SCS by taking into account its potential, territorial disputes, the basic dynamics and the approaches of the regional states, especially in line with Beijing's claims and aggressive stance.

HISTORICAL BACKGROUND OF SCS

Ships have been cruising The SCS's shores for over two millennia also known as Nanyang (South Sea) and Bi n đông (East Sea) and, more recently, West Philippine Sea (Wee, 2022; Tonnesson, 2021: 31, International Crisis Group, 2021). In order to reach Okinawa, Korea, Japan, and the northern region of the Middle

Kingdom (China), ships have entered the sea from the west through the Malacca or Sunda Straits, followed the coast of Indochina north until they can see Hainan, and then turned east toward the Chinese coast or through the Luzon or Taiwan Strait (Tonnesson, 2021: 31). From May to October, the ships travelled north, following the patterns of the monsoon and making a U-turn when the wind changed. The ships were constructed in several countries and docked in multiple ports, subject to tariffs imposed by multiple governments, some of which promoted maritime trade and others of which made an effort to keep foreigners out of their domains. *''Ships started sailing directly across The SCS in the deep-water corridor south of the Paracels and Macclesfield Bank when contemporary maps were created, accurately labelling latitudes and longitudes as well as the positions of reefs, rocks, shoals, and islands''* (Tonnesson, 2021: 32).

In the 16th, 17th and 18th centuries, in parallel with the development of trade, the trade of Western states with the region was the beginning of military and commercial rivalry with the states of the region. Maritime trade also brought along the competition of naval forces. The rivalry between the Western states (Portugal, Spain, the Netherlands, France, Britain, Germany and the United States of America) regarding maritime trade sheds light on the basis of the rivalry between the states parties in the SCS today. In other words, maritime trade and the accompanying competition in the field of naval forces are today the source of sovereignty and territorial dispute claims in the SCS.

Approximately one-third of global maritime commerce, or trade including oceans, passes via The SCS. About half of all Middle Eastern oil and gas tankers enter it en route to China, Japan, the United States, and other destinations. The Sea is strategically important from a military standpoint and important for maintaining national security. The SCS's geographical features are usually at the core of international disputes. More specifically, they argue about who is in charge of the surrounding seas. There are many fish in the sea itself. There are substantial quantities of natural gas and oil beneath the sea floor. The Sea is home to two significant land feature groupings. The Paracels are mostly made up of reefs and islands. *''Six nations actively claim parts or all of the SCS and its land features. These disputes include: Paracels (China, Taiwan, Vietnam), Spratlys (China, Taiwan, Vietnam, Brunei, Malaysia, Philippines, Malaysia, Philippines) and almost all the SCS, its land features, and resources (China)''* (BRIA, 2018: 12).

A portion of the surrounding seas and land features of the SCS are claimed by five states. The two most active claimants are Vietnam and the Philippines. Vietnam's present claims are based on maps from the 17th century. In the 1920s, troops from the French colony of Vietnam took control of a few Paracel islands. Following the Vietnam War, Vietnam acquired certain Spratly land features and took control of the western Paracels (Quyet & Nguyet, 2023: 276-277, 284-285). Vietnam proclaimed its sovereignty over the Paracels and Spratly Islands in 2009 (Buszynski, 2010: 90-91). *"1946, the Philippines took control of several Spratly land features; later, the Philippines declared all the Spratlys its territory and the Philippines also claimed sovereignty over Scarborough Shoal"* (BRIA, 2018; Chang, 1991: 400-401).

China asserts that it once controlled islands in the South China Sea. The Republic of China released a map featuring nine dashes in 1947 (Chang, 1991: 407; Caruana, 2023). The dashes join to create a U that encompasses the majority of the South China Sea and The Republic of China could not, however, provide a clear explanation of this "nine dash line" (Beech, 2016). Chinese communists pushed the anti-Communist Chinese to the large offshore island of Taiwan in 1949 after defeating the Republic of China in a civil war. The mainland was then occupied by the communist People's Republic of China. The map with the "nine dash line" was also accepted. This is the current nomenclature, albeit Taiwan was included in 2013 when China added a tenth dash. China started claiming sovereignty over several islands, reefs, and seas in the South China Sea in the 1970s, frequently using force. In 1974, it forced Vietnamese soldiers out of the western Paracels and China has complete control of the Paracels by the late 1980s. In the 1990s, China started constructing artificial islands. Despite the Philippines' prior assertion, China attempted to annex Scarborough Shoal in 2012 in an attempt to impose its "nine dash line" (Wong, 2024: 76-78).

As a marine domain, the South China Sea has played a variety of roles and meant many things in the past, present, and future. It supports a delicate environment and has served as a home to a number of biodiverse animals. The waterways and land resources of the SCS were historically significant even prior to the formation of nation-states. The villages around its waters depended on the waters for food, revenue, and livelihood, and they still do. Natural resources and energy supplies are also present in the area, which may help future generations who are energy poor. The states in this area have become increasingly competitive in their pursuit of increased energy and resources, which has resulted in the militarization of the SCS waterways and the few land resources (Caşın, 2022: 278-340). The acts of the present have the powerful ability to affect the future, even while history has a strong ability to influence the present.

ENERGY GEOPOLITICS OF SCS

China is building artificial islands to the strategic areas in the SCS and in the current circumstances, China has established naval and air bases on some of these artificial islands. The Chinese is constantly situating the waters that the confrontation on coastal security and fishery ships. Despite Philippines's acceptance of the illegality of Nine Dash Line proposed by China in terms of international law, the Philippines are unable to prevent the expansionist approaches because of the very great gaps between these countries in terms of economic as well as military power. Within that context, the U.S. has constantly been conducting freedom of seas operations on the fields claimed by China in order to protect its commercial, political together with military benefits within associated area as well as to strengthen the navigating freely in the open oceans. When it is seen from an assessment based on the open sources, Washington has organized these types of military operations 31 times in the region. When the increase in the numbers of these numbers are taken into account, it can be understood the importance attached by Washington to the region and also the escalation of tension. In addition to this factor, the U.S. has military connections with Taiwan and Philippines. The most important military connection between Philippines and U.S. is formed by 1951 Mutual Defence Pact. Within the context of this pact, two countries will support each other in case of facing an attack. In case of not finding a non-violent settlement to the military confrontation question with regard to South China Sea, the issue discussed in this pact will remain a probability. Similar to the Taiwan Question, Japan is the country that supports the U.S. most. Japan is providing economic development aid and also military equipment to Philippines and Vietnam with the intention of these countries' possessing/advancing deterrence against China (Kocadal, 2022: 119).

In contrast to these negative developments, China and ASEAN have been negotiating since 2002 towards "Code of Conduct" in order to lower tension in the SCS and to decrease the probability of war to the minimum. The talks on the agreement continuing more than the envisaged time has been deadlocked with regard to the existence of foreign powers within the region and it is continuing very slowly. The U.S. is supporting these initiatives but is not one of the negotiating parties. In case of an agreement that mostly covers the demands of Beijing, it stands unclear how will Washington behave. The freedom of navigation in the open seas which can be seen among the fundamental building stones of rules-based liberal international order is very important for the functioning of international trade. Washington has guaranteed independence of open seas in terms of liberal order that it establishes after the Second World War thanks to its sui generis military power. But in such one of the important geographies of international maritime commercial activities as the South China Sea, it is conducting a fight on dominance with China. When it is examined in terms of Thucydides Trap approach, this confrontation includes mutual lack of trust as well as the military confrontation risk in the classical dimension. The freedom of navigating seas operations or China's military engagement with the Philippines which has a defence pact with the U.S. can be considered as similar military confrontation risks. On the other hand, the regional states are searching for counterbalancing China by their increasing partnerships with the U.S. The Code of Conduct Agreement (Thao, 2003: 279-285) talks between the regional states is the most positive condition for the continuation of liberal international order. It can be stated that the fate of the negotiations in the forthcoming terms will be one of the determining factors in the escalation or de-escalation of risk of confrontation between Beijing and Washington (Kocadal, 2022: 119-120; Küçükdeğirmenci & Castro, 2020: 66-74).

In addition to passing of one third of world maritime transportation from SCS accompanied by this region's possession of rich energy resources as well as the presence of conflicting sovereignty claims, one can easily talk about a conflicting atmosphere for this region. The presence of more than half of fishery ships of the world in the SCS on top of the constant diminution of fishery deposits due to overfishing/hunting, one can easily see the fact that the hunting by the fishery ships in the conflicting sovereignty zones will continue to be a problem. The most important issue in terms of SCS which is crucially important for the regional countries ranging from many issues including sea trade, food and energy security stands the Chinese prerogatives centered over its Nine-Dash Line Map. China has been claiming sovereignty on a line that is extending 2000 kilometers from its main land. Some of the zones that China is claiming sovereignty on them are clashing with the Exclusive Economic Zones of the regional countries. Scarborough Reef known as Huangyan Island stays a problem between China and Philippines. Moreover, Spratly (Nansha) Islands Question remains another issue between China and Philippines on the conflicting sovereignty claims. China does use historical possession argument for its sovereignty claims (Kasım, 2024: 22-37).

The world's forthcoming stands in need of accessing into accompanied by obtainability of conventional deposits. Asia specially, considered the world's poorest natural deposit mainland, bearing in mind its extent besides populace, holds a passionate hunger for conventional deposits. Whether that is going to end up with enduring local fight or else collaboration on natural resources within the area stands to be observed. Is holding a richness of deposits a proposition towards quarrel? Are lessening deposits within any nation-state reinforcing the motivations intended for disagreement? Factually, it stands alleged that reaching into resources has stayed a serious aspect within the context of war as well as peace. Within the framework of the South China Sea Case, do conventional deposits stay foremost triggering factor concerning continuing row? In another sense, do other geopolitical, armed, patriotic as well as tactical fears play a focal triggering factor in terms of quarrel? Does it characterize definitely a blend of whole those aspects? The conventional deposits are described by Organization for Economic Cooperation and Development as logically happening rare elements that is able to stand benefited with the intention of commercial output otherwise usage. Conventional deposits stand characteristically regarded as inorganic as well as energy deposits, earth deposits, liquid deposits together with organic deposits. Those deposits stand bound by exhaustion via constant human use expands their standing and generates the justification for rivalry and battle amongst persons and civilisations. When it is considered in terms of natural deposits, the SCS includes abundant fishing lands which might stand useful not only to countrywide but also to home-grown economic systems. With projected figures of 11 bbls of oil, 190 Tcf of natural gas, 16.6 million tons of fish for an annual catching, and also 3,365 identified types of fish, the SCS does hold economic, military, and ecological worth. The SCS clash (Emmers, 2010: 118-131) stays thorny by the postulation that the pretender might remain permitted to the natural deposits from the SCS (Macaraig & Fenton, 2021: 43).

Most of the nation-states tangled within the nautical quarrel avow their prerogatives on the foundation of the United Nations Convention on the Law of Seas, which offers a joint lawful context for naval assets and also powers. This convention underscores that a state's Exclusive Economic Zone will stand two hundred maritime kilometres from the reference points from the extensiveness of the territorial sea stands calculated. Nevertheless, it stays in these very regions of prolongation where the allegations intersect. Some of these contradictory allegations stand defined as: allegations set forth by China and Vietnam arise concerning the Spratly & Paracel Islands (Tønnesson, 2002: 145-169; Zhang, 2021) and intersect with the precise allegations elevated by the Philippines, Malaysia and Brunei. These states hold explicit allegations to zones adjoining to their peculiar territory which similarly intersect. The Philippine allegation towards Kalayaan (Freedomland) within the framework a prolongation of Palawan Island intersects with Malaysia's allegation outspreading from Sarawak/Sabah; Brunei's allegation spreading as of its private terrain intersects with Malaysia and the Philippines. Elsewhere the clauses on Exclusive Economic Zone laid down by United Nations Convention on the Law of the Seas, China, the Philippines, Taiwan together with Vietnam stand altogether supposed to have been putting forward historic allegations within the differing boundaries, even if the latter three have changed from quarrelling on historic rights to bringing into line with the UNCLOS control (Macaraig & Fenton, 2021: 44).

Nevertheless, notwithstanding what United Nations Convention on the Law of the Seas mentions, Beijing has uninterruptedly strapped towards acknowledgement of own individual historic nine-point marking allegation, standing assumed for instigating centered over a cartographic text from Chiang Kai-shek's pro-independence rule. Nevertheless, if that thesis stands trailed, at that point the Beijing's historic allegations can stand measured whilst legal when compared with extra empires as well as domains within South(east) Asia. Darussalam has stood designated as per noiseless pretender in terms of quarrel together with it possibly will stand ascribed to the conception that it stands unnecessary for the oil-rich state to contend counter to others for natural deposits. Yet, Brunei would be negatively affected by the decrease in terms of universal oil charges within 2015 and obliged to call external investors, remarkably Beijing, with the intention of ensuring sustainable economic system. Subsequently at that time, it's remained stated that Darussalam and Beijing stand scheduling a combined search over hydrocarbons within the SCS. Brunei stays alleged to be not aggressively venturing its allegation as it would moderately concentrate on collaboration, more willingly than struggle, with China as an alternative (Putra, 2024: 1-14; Wei, 2024; Ministry of Foreign Affairs Brunei Darussalam, 2013). Beijing personally distinguishes standing of the South China Sea for its conventional deposits, on the word of Jawli, Beijing is labelling the South China Sea as per the "second Persian Sea" for having petroleum reserves. It holds 1,367,000 barrels of oil output per day. Beijing has premeditated that SCS is going to in the end produce 130 billion barrels of oil. If these estimations stand accurate at that point it encompasses additional oil when compared with any zone of the world excluding Saudi Arabia. It seems like that China stands dying to discover original energy deposits, as "Chinese oil deposits constitute solely 1.1 percent of the world in general, while it does use more than 10 percent of world oil generation and more than 20 percent of entire energy used within the world." CNOOC has capitalized $20 billion within that area accompanied by credence that it is standing massive petroleum deposits in that zone (Zhou, 2024; Paraskova, 2024), along with plentiful fishing prospects. Moreover, China has sustained to outspread its rights in the spring of 2020 by forming original administrative regions within the islands, specifying further reefs, subsidising illegitimate fishing actions, and threatening external containers (Macaraig & Fenton, 2021: 44-45).

Nautical territorial clash within the area stands not inevitably restricted towards this sea zone individually similarly covering its near terrains. To exemplify it, Jakarta stands predominantly bent over safeguarding the Natuna Islands, positioned at South China Sea's southern section, as of Chinese vessels and fishery vessels intruding within the terrain. As a portion of personal initiatives within that milieu, by 2017, Jakarta has retitled the marine round the Natuna Islands, naming this zone as the North Natuna Sea. The statement solely putting forward comparatively minor fragment of Jakarta's Exclusive Economic Zone that intersects with the nine-point marking, would be disapproved by China and stands not hitherto documented within the International Hydrographic Organization (IHO) publication on the Limits of Oceans and Seas (3rd edition of S-23). A plan established within the 1980s displays the Natuna Sea as detached from South China Sea which that would be given in to IHO Member States by 1986 nevertheless at no time acquired their consent. Along with standing the spring of income for Indonesian fishermen, the islands remain critically prominent for the forthcoming terms in terms of Indonesia's energy, due to the fact that they stand basement to the state's major untouched natural gas deposit encompassing approximately 46 trillion cubic feet of recoverable gas deposits.

Jakarta has acknowledged for missing fishery ships for working inside the isles, in addition to accommodations on land to progression fastenings. Nevertheless, the Indonesian government still trusts that in spite of these restrictions, it stays their privilege to exploit the deposits within their EEZ (Macaraig & Fenton, 2021: 44-45; Zou, 2023: 1-8; Idrus, 2024; Supriyanto, 2016: 21-28).

It stands proclaimed by Malay that the whole Islands of Spratly zone of the South China Sea remains within mainland ledge boundaries of the state. Malay springs a noteworthy portion of individual hydrocarbon deposits originating from the SCS. But, more than a few of its fields and platforms that stand benefited for exploiting hydrocarbons stand in Beijing's nine-point mark thesis. Henceforth, it ought to be seen normal that Malay has wanted after for sanctifying individual entitlement with the United Nations Secretary General, although it might in contrast with China, which holds gigantic continuing investments within the state (Macaraig & Fenton, 2021:44-45; Storey, 2024; Malaysia Ministry of Foreign Affairs, 2023; Kin & Ryan, 2023).

In the meantime, the Philippines stands looking at the SCS for natural gas with the purpose of abandoning its coal-fired power facilities. Regrettably, the state stays experiencing security dangers regarding offshore blocks owing to the fact that these are positioned at Beijing's personally-declared nine-point mark thesis within the South China Sea area. That vanished commercial chance might stand sole source of the motives why Manila keeps its allegation towards the SCS. Manila stands defined as incapable of completely achieving particular nautical capacity, in that it solely makes up 2.62% of the overall Gross National Productivity. In terms of Taiwan, the Spratly Islands does serve as assist for conventional fishery areas for own minor ships nevertheless stand documented by way of possibly abundant in hydrocarbons (Jian, 1997: 591-601). Taiwan has softly withdrawn from standing a dynamic pretender, which has to some degree to organize with Taiwan's complex association with China (Ian, 2023; Chen et al., 2024, 1-12; Kocadal, 2022: 116-118). Right now, the country stays promoting its East China Sea Peace Initiative (Taiwan Today, 2013; Ku, 2014), which appeals to parties to cancel disagreements and encourage combined exploration as well as progress. Vietnam stands a vigorous pretender within the naval row, and its purposes comprise standing capable of entirely controlling conventional deposits over and is situated at Vietnam's mainland zone along with safeguarding fish deposits for forthcoming generations (Dar, 2023: 37-59). The state has by now attempted to unearth natural deposits within the unclear zones, in the arrangement of hydrocarbon penetrating and sea bottom search, even though these have mostly been challenged by China. These reports hitherto point to how the pretenders participated within the SCS row enjoy consigned benefits within the natural deposits to stay drilled from the naval region (Macaraig & Fenton, 2021:44-45; Vu, 2024; Nguyen, 2023; Tüter, 2022).

Territorial rows within the SCS hold the prospect to turn out to be a struggle of local or even international space. Their reputation stays principally by reason of the increasing standing of this sea zone within universal commercial transactions. For this cause, not only coastal countries stand part of them, but also the U.S., assessing the South China Sea a zone of universal rivalry with China. If there remained to stand an outburst of a clear struggle amid Beijing and also Washington, it stands highly probable that this is going to commence with the help of events within the world's that area. The rows encompass both isles as well as nautical borders (Peng & Ngeow, 2022: 1-23). Within the 1970s, local players have commenced to demand islands and several districts within the SCS, for instance the Spratly Islands possessing abundant conventional deposits and also fishery zones. China, the Republic of China on Taiwan, Vietnam, the Philippines, Malaysia, Indonesia and Brunei are the conflicting sides on that issue. So far the focal countries taking part within the rows remain principally the Philippines, Vietnam and China. Furthermore, Washington contests Beijing's firm territorial demands and land repossession initiatives by exercising freedom of navigation manoeuvres and snowballing backing for Southeast Asian associates. Even though by 2016, the Permanent Court of Arbitration at the Hague would settle over a demand taken contrary to Beijing by Manila under the UN Convention of the Law of the Sea, deciding in support of Manila on practically every count, Beijing constantly rejects to admit the authority of Permanent Court of Arbitration at the Hague. On the one hand, China has constructed several armed accommodations on the Spratly and Paracel Islands (Kuşçu, 2024: 28-32). Another issue confusing the state of affairs within the area stands the persistent enlargement of non-natural isles by China, expressly the steady militarization of them, which harmfully disturbs local security. As a result of the increasing size of trade streams via the SCS, clashes might solely deepen as the time passes. China's quarrelsome posture thwarts the accomplishment of a positive resolution and positions a risk to local security. In contrast, the constant US military existence within the area can stand observed as a test to China and a justification for Chinese movements (Osiewicz, 2023: 294-295; Caşın, 2022: 278-340).

Remarkably, ASEAN and Beijing have settled on an additional agreement by 2011 that detailed the latter's re-obedience to the "Declaration of the Code of Conduct in the South China Sea," (Association of Southeast Asian Nations – ASEAN, 2012) which designated to observers that this Declaration has not been an obligatory pact and may well not stand anticipated to wholly coerce Chinese conduct relating to the row. As of 2016, the United Nations Permanent Court of Arbitration in the Hague has decided that Beijing (and definitely the added capitals holding opposing proclamations) have had not any lawful proclamation to SCS, which remained a verdict that Beijing then declined to make out. China's assertions have been reasoned to intrude upon the "United Nations Convention on the Laws of the Sea

(UNCLOS)," in that they stay in the 200 nautical mile Exclusive Economic Zones of five South East Asian countries. Notwithstanding that verdict, and insightful of the commerce, energy, regional and position fundamentals essential to Beijing's "zhoubian" international relations, accompanied by a rising decisiveness as well as self-assurance within own local international relations, Beijing's 2019 *"Defense White Paper" has clearly professed that: the South China Sea islands ... (remain an) unchallengeable component of China. China does practice its nation-wide rule to shape set-up and instal needed self-protective competences over the isles as well as reefs within the South China Sea, ... it resolutely defends navigating freely and flying over by whole states consistent with universal law and defences the safety of sea positions of contact."* By taking into account this official position, Beijing has constructed substructure over Mischief, Subi and the Fiery Cross Reefs. Those islands have today remained domesticated as of the oceans and transformed to minor human-constructed isles one-to-two square miles by magnitude. The constructed organisation comprises administrative and service buildings, military landing stage strips, naval port areas, fuel storage depots, missile launching abilities, helipads and electronic hearing arrangements. From this foundation, the islands are able to perform at the moment as military acting zones, and include defensive competences counting challenging-underwater military protections, air-guard guns, probes for satellite communiqué and complete sensor competences. Such progresses have been gone with extra recurrent sea and air patrolling within the area, and detaching admittance to islands demanded by other states (Ogden & Jones, 2023: 356-358).

The standing of the uncertain nautical zone and related islands charts onto the essential columns of Beijing's "zhoubian" international relations besides henceforth – by allowance – remain consequently revealing of its extensive worldview concerning the Indo-Pacific Region. First of all, South China Sea, accompanied by Malacca Strait stays within pivot of the Indo-Pacific area, intertwining Asia to India, Africa, the Middle East and Europe to the east and North America to the west. The United Nations Conference on Trade and Development has projected that seventy percent of the overall worth of world commerce, besides 1/3 of entire world commerce by size navigates via the SCS. This commercial activity remains treasured to occur approximately three Trillion U.S. Dollars per annum. Underscoring its vitality for Chinese economic system in addition to henceforth own transformation accompanied by progress objectives heading for re-converting into a prodigious power, greater than sixty percent of China's whole commercial activities is realized by South China Sea (China Power, n.d.; Turker, 2023). The SCS remains likewise a vigorous direction for China to hold much-required hydrocarbon supplies conveyed to it from the Middle East (Türkeş, 2018; Eco-Business, 2013; Eurasia Review, 2024). Also, the SCS and particularly its innumerable small islands stand claimed to include enormous energy deposits. Even though the exact volume of hydrocarbons stands doubtful, the forthcoming profits to Beijing with the purpose of answering its ever-mounting energy requirements – along with the lesser prices that such reservoirs possibly will make available in terms of transportation and defence, besides dropping its requirement upon unbalanced districts for instance the Middle East – stand pure. Safeguarding such deposits stand understood as vital to safeguarding its longstanding affluence and solidity (Ogden & Jones, 2023: 358).

Thirdly, China's movements within the SCS encompass an emblematic measurement which re-counts to the row holding a noteworthy standing component as of standpoint of this state. Intrinsically, various experts highlight how regional clashes within this area (and somewhere else lengthwise its boundaries) stands practised by Beijing as "diplomatic devices to show indications to other countries and to challenge their obligations and replies". Highlighting such a plan remains the profounder goal of asserting China's distinguished local location, even as restraining the existence of the U.S. within the Indo-Pacific Region. In this manner, constructing significant armed set-up intends to dissuade the existence of US maritime ships within the zone. All-encompassing entirely of these fundamentals stands the additional impetus of benefiting from the row to mark China's increasing power prognosis abilities as component of upgrading of the nation-state's military aptitude. Such demonstrations of strong point correspondingly competently perform to internal pro-independence viewers as indication of Beijing's "rising up" as well as proclaiming its historic rights, whereby Beijing's exact "ordinary situation does lay at the pivotal point of East Asia" (Ogden & Jones, 2023: 358).

CONCLUSION

The South China Sea stands single of the most significant regions for Southeast Asia (Asia-Pacific/Indo-Pacific) geography. This is in that it does include not only rich hydrocarbon resources, fish stocks as well as it represents as one of the critically momentous transportation route for the world trade. It will continue to preserve this situation in the forthcoming terms. But its sharing and also benefiting by the littoral states are very problematic. Here China has been alleging that with the presence of its historic Nine-Dash Line, most parts of this sea does possess to China. Even if this claim is rejected on the international law basis, China has not been withdrawing from historical claims (Küçükdeğirmenci, 2024: 364, 379). Within this context, it must be mentioned that Beijing has been continuing to increase its presence over the South China Sea via building reproduction isles, creating armed establishments as well as augmenting its efforts towards the prevention of entrée by other littoral states into the sea zone which creates a very complicated and high-tension problem between other coastal states located at this region and it.

In recent years and at the moment, China and other littoral countries as well as with the inclusion of U.S., one is able to observe the further escalation of conflict within the region among associated parties. Even though some states like Brunei, Vietnam have been successful on settling this issue with China, other countries namely Philippines, Indonesia, Taiwan are confronting with China and sometimes especially China and Taiwan are about to enter into confrontation on this issue.

To conclude, owing to the region's increasing prominence at the moment as well as its further probable augmentation of significance within the forthcoming terms, the military-based confrontation or other types of confrontation among the littoral stand / will stand high likely. And as the final analysis, due to the increasing importance of discovering and exploiting brand-new energy deposits in the contemporary world, it can easily be mentioned that the existing and prospective hydrocarbon deposits within SCS may perhaps trigger an all-inclusive conflict among the associated parties within this zone for forthcoming terms.

REFERENCES

Association of Southeast Asian Nations – ASEAN. (2012). "Declaration On The Conduct Of Parties In The South China Sea". https://asean.org/declaration-on-the-conduct-of-parties-in-the-south-china-sea-2/.

Beech, H. (2016). ''Just Where Exactly Did China Get the South China Sea Nine-Dash Line From?'', *Time*, https://time.com/4412191/nine-dash-line-9-south-china-sea/.

BRIA. (2018). ''The Dispute Over The SCS'', https://teachdemocracy.org /images/pdf/members/bria_33_2.pdf.

Buszynski, L. (2010). Rising Tensions in the South China Sea: Prospects for a Resolution of the Issue. *Security Challenges*, *6*(2), 85–104.

Carauna, A. (2023). ''Maritime Affairs Program (MAP) Handbill Spotlight'', ICAS, https://chinaus-icas.org/research/map-spotlight-nine-dash-line/.

Caşın, M. H. (2022). In Caşın, M. H., Kısacık, S., & Donduran, C. (Eds.), *"Yükselen Çin Deniz Gücünün Küresel Güç Dengelerine Yansıması", in 21. Yüzyılda Bütün Boyutlarıyla Çin Halk Cumhuriyeti 1. Cilt* (pp. 278–340). Nobel Akademik Yayıncılık.

Chang, T. K. (1991). China's Claim of Sovereignty over Spratly and Paracel Islands: A Historical and Legal Perspective. *Case Western Reserve Journal of International Law*, *23*(3), 399–420.

Chen, W. C., Ou, C. H., Yang, M. H., Shih, Y. C. (2024). "China's gray zone actions in the East China Sea, Taiwan Strait, and South China Sea: A comparative study and impact on fisheries", *Marine Policy* (167): 1-12, https://doi.org/.DOI: 10.1016/j.marpol.2024.106246

China Power. (n.d.), "How Much Trade Transits the South China Sea?", https://chinapower.csis.org/much-trade-transits-south-china-sea/.

Dar, K. B. (2023). "The South China Sea dispute and Sino-Vietnamese reconciliation", *Journal of International Studies* 19(1): 37-59. https://doi.org/.DOI: 10.32890/jis2023.19.1.2

Eco-Business. (2013), "South China Sea energy profile: critical world trade route and potential source of hydrocarbons", 12 February 2013, https://www.eco-business.com/news/south-china-sea-energy-profile-critical-world-trade-route-and-potential-source-of-hydrocarbons/.

EIA. (2024). ''Regional Analysis Brief: SCS'', https://www.eia.gov/international/analysis/regions-of-interest/South_China_Sea.

Emmers, R. (2010). "The changing power distribution in the South China Sea: Implications for conflict management and avoidance", *Political Science* 62 (2): 118-131, https://doi.org/.DOI: 10.1177/0032318710381519

Eurasia Review. (2024). "South China Sea Energy Profile: Critical World Trade Route – Analysis", 25 March 2024, https://www.eurasiareview.com/25032024-south-china-sea-energy-profile-critical-world-trade-route-analysis/.

Guoqiang, L. (2015). ''China Sea Oil and Gas Resources'', CIIS, https://www.ciis.org.cn/english/COMMENTARIES/202007/t20200715_2762.html.

Hsiung, J. C. (1995). "China's Omni-Directional Diplomacy: Realignment to Cope with Monopolar U.S. Power", *Asian Survey* 35 (6): 573-586. https://doi.org/10.2307/2645710.

Ian, C. J. (2023). "Still waters run deep: Taiwan's South China Sea strategy", *Clingendael Spectator*, 19 October 2023, https://spectator.clingendael.org/en/publication/still-waters-run-deep-taiwans-south-china-sea-strategy.

Idrus, P. G. (2024). "Nearly 80% of Indonesians see Beijing's South China Sea actions as threat", *Benar News*, 21 March 2024, https://www.benarnews.org/english/news/indonesian/80-percent-indonesians-see-china-threatens-sovereignty-03212024143829.html.

International Crisis Group. (2021). ''Vietnam Tacks Between Cooperation and Struggle in The SCS'', https://www.crisisgroup.org/asia/north-east-asia/china/318-vietnam-tacks-between-cooperation-and-struggle-south-china-sea.

Jian, S. (1997). "Multinational oil companies and the Spratly dispute", *Journal of Contemporary China* 6(16): 591-601, https://doi.org/.DOI: 10.1080/10670569708724298

Jianren, Z. (2019). Power Transition and Paradigm Shift in Diplomacy: Why China and the US March towards Strategic Competition? *The Chinese Journal of International Politics*, *12*(1), 1–34. DOI: 10.1093/cjip/poy019

Kasım, K., (2024). "Güney Çin Denizi Sorunlarının Bölgesel ve Uluslararası Güvenliğe Etkileri," *International Journal of Politics and Security (IJPS)* 6(1): 22-37. DOI: .DOI: 10.53451/ijps.1413751

Kim, J. (2015). Territorial Disputes in The SCS: Implications for Security in Asia and Beyond. *Strategic Studies Quarterly*, *9*(2), 107–141.

Kin, S. E., & Ryan, Z. (2023). "Malaysia: Securing sovereignty in the South China Sea through ASEAN centrality", *Yale Journal of International Affairs*, 15 May 2023, https://www.yalejournal.org/publications/malaysia-securing-sovereignty-in-the-south-china-sea-through-asean-centrality.

Kocadal, Ö. (2022). Asya-Pasifik'te ABD-Çin Rekabeti: Tukidides'in Tuzağı ve Liberal Uluslararası Düzen. In Al, A., & Kaya, H. (Eds.), *Uluslararası Politik Ekonomide Avrasya* (pp. 105–123). Nobel Akademik Yayıncılık.

Ku, J. (2014). "Can International Law Be an Obstacle to Peace? Some Thoughts on Taiwan's East China Sea Peace Initiative", *Opinio Juris*, 05 August 2014, https://opiniojuris.org/2014/08/05/just-long-can-shelve-sovereignty-disputes-thoughts-taiwans-east-china-sea-peace-initiative/.

Küçükdeğirmenci, O. (2024). Security Architecture in Indo-Pacific from the Past to Present: Bilateral Alliances and Multilateral Structures. In Güçyetmez, F., & Doğan, D. (Eds.), *Emerging Power in Indo-Pacific Geopolitics* (pp. 335–400). İdeal Kültür Yayıncılık.

Küçükdeğirmenci, O. & Zandamela, A. C. (2020). "From Balancing to Accommodation: Understanding the Philippines's Relations with the US and China in Post-Arbitration Period", *The International Journal of Humanities & Social Studies* 8 (12): 66-74, DOI No.: .DOI: 10.24940/theijhss/2020/v8/i12/HS2012-024

Kuisong, Y. (2009). "The theory and implementation of the People's Republic of China's revolutionary diplomacy", *Journal of Modern Chinese History* 3 (2): 276–309, DOI: .DOI: 10.1080/17535650903345346

Ma, X. (2016). The SCS dispute. *Atlantisch Perspectief, 40*(3), 39–41.

Macaraig, C. E., & Fenton, A. J. (2021). "Analyzing the Causes and Effects of the South China Sea Dispute", *The Journal of Territorial and Maritime Studies* 8(2): 42-58, https://www.jstor.org/stable/10.2307/48617340.

Malaysia Ministry of Foreign Affairs. (2023). "Malaysia's Position On The South China Sea", 08 April 2023, https://www.kln.gov.my/web/guest/-/malaysia-s-position-on-the-south-china-sea.

Ministry of Foreign Affairs Brunei Darussalam. (2013). "Joint Statement between Brunei Darussalam and the People's Republic of China", 11 October 2013, https://www.mfa.gov.bn/Lists/Press%20Releases/NDispForm.aspx?ID=106&ContentTypeId=0x0100DE0D91A42F563640A6718A29AE56AE67.

Nguyen, N. L. (2023). "Vietnam and China: Conflicting neighbors stuck in nationalism and memory", *Harvard International Review*, 03 May 2023, https://hir.harvard.edu/vietnam-and-china-conflicting-neighbors-stuck-in-nationalism-and-memory/.

Ogden, C., & Jones, C. (2023). "Chapter: 17 Chinese conceptions of the Indo-Pacific The impact of identity and history", in *Handbook of Indo-Pacific Studies*, edited by Barbara Kratiuk, Jeroen J. J. Van den Bosch, Aleksandra Jaskólska ve Yoichiro Sato, 343-365, New York: Routledge.

Osiewicz, P. (2023). "Chapter 14: International conflicts in the Indo-Pacific region", in *Handbook of Indo-Pacific Studies*, edited by Barbara Kratiuk, Jeroen J. J. Van den Bosch, Aleksandra Jaskólska ve Yoichiro Sato, 290-305, New York: Routledge.

Paraskova, T. (2024). "CNOOC Begins Oil Production at South China Sea Field", Oil Price, 27 June 2024, https://oilprice.com/Latest-Energy-News/World-News/CNOOC-Begins-Oil-Production-at-South-China-Sea-Field.html.

Peng, N. & Ngeow, C. B. (2022). "Managing the South China Sea Dispute: Multilateral and Bilateral Approaches, *Ocean Development & International Law* 1-23, https://doi.org/.DOI: 10.1080/00908320.2022.2034555

Putra, B. A. (2024). "Brunei's silent claims in the South China Sea: a case for the theory of trade expectations", *Cogent Social Sciences*, 10(1): 1-14, https://doi.org/.DOI: 10.1080/23311886.2024.2317533

Quyet, L. V., & Nguyet, N. T. A. (2023). Sovereignty Over The Paracel Islands in 1884-1945: An Approach From The Rivalry Between France, China and, Japan. *Journal of Liberty and International Affairs*, *9*(2), 275–296. DOI: 10.47305/JLIA2392347q

Ranade, J. (2014). "China's New Policy of Peripheral Diplomacy", *Centre For China Analysis & Strategy (CCAS)*, May 2014, Https://Ccasindia.Org/Article_Details.Php?Aid=14.

Singh, A. (2022). ''Securing Sea Lines of Communication in Asia'', ORF, https://www.orfonline.org/public/uploads/posts/pdf/20230717144443.pdf.

Storey, I. (2024). "Commentary: Malaysia and the South China Sea dispute - a sea change under PM Anwar Ibrahim?", *Channel News Asia*, 31 August 2024, https://www.channelnewsasia.com/commentary/south-china-sea-malaysia-anwar-dispute-policy-4575821.

Supriyanto, R. A. (2016). "Out of Its Comfort Zone: Indonesia and the South China Sea", *Asia Policy* (21): 21-28, https://www.jstor.org/stable/24905085.

Taiwan Today. (2013). “Caution needed in promoting East China Sea peace initiative”, 06 January 2013, https://taiwantoday.tw/news_amp.php?unit=2&post=2776 &unitname= Politics-Top-News&postname=Caution-needed-in-promoting-East-China-Sea-peace-initiative.

Thao, N. H. (2003). “The 2002 Declaration On The Conduct Of Parties In The South China Sea: A Note”, *Ocean Development & International Law* 34 (3-4): 279-285, Https://Doi.Org/10.1080/00908320390221849.

The Guardian. (2024). ‘‘Asean leaders cite 1982 UN treaty in SCS dispute’’, https://www.theguardian.com/world/2020/jun/27/asean-leaders-cite-1982-un-treaty-in-south-china-sea-dispute.

Tønnesson, S. (2002). “The Paracels: The “Other” South China Sea Dispute”, *Asian Perspective Special Issue on China-ASEAN Relations* 26(4):145-169, https://www.jstor.org/stable/42704389.

Tonnesson, S. (2021). The SCS: Historical Developments. In Zou, K. (Ed.), *Routledge Handbook of The SCS* (pp. 31–45). Routledge.

Turker, H. (2023). “Maritime Chessboard: The Geopolitical Dynamics of the South China Sea”, *Geopolitical Monitor*, 24 August 2023, https://www.geopoliticalmonitor.com/maritime-chessboard-the-geopolitical-dynamics-of-the-south-china-sea/.

Türkeş, H. (2018). “South China Sea ‘major’ trade route for crude oil”, *Anatolian Agency (AA) Energy Terminal*, 28 August 2018, https://www.aa.com.tr/en/energy/general/south-china-sea-major-trade-route-for-crude-oil-/21401

Tüter, M. (2022). “Vietnam’s Policy over South China Sea: Potential for Conflict Escalation?”, *International Journal of Political Studies* 8 (2): 63-74, Doi: , https://dergipark.org.tr/en/download/article-file/2544043.DOI: 10.25272/icps.1145238

Tzeng, W. F. (2023). “The Anatomy of Diplomatic Work among China’s Top Leaders”, *China Review Special Issue: External and Internal Factors Shaping the Outcomes of 2024 Elections in Taiwan* 23(4): 229-258, https://www.jstor.org/stable/10.2307/48750787.

Vu, K. (2024). “Why Vietnam Cannot Copy the Philippines’ China Policy”, *The Diplomat*, 14 February 2024, https://thediplomat.com/2024/02/why-vietnam-cannot-copy-the-philippines-china-policy/.

Wee, L. Z. (2022). ‘‘What is Nanyang art?’’, Think China, https://www.Thinkchina.sg /culture/what-Nanyang-art.

Wei, S. T. (2024). "YL Blog #60 – Caught in the Middle: The Measured Voice of Brunei's Foreign Policy Amidst the South China Sea Disputes", *Pacific Forum*, 29 February 2024, https://pacforum.org/publications/yl-blog-60-caught-in-the-middle-the-measured-voice-of-bruneis-foreign-policy-amidst-the-south-china-sea-disputes/.

Wong, A. C. (2024). "The 2012 Scarborough Shoal Standoff: Analyzing China in Crisis with the Philippines," Encounters and Escalations in the Indo-Pacific Perspectives on China's Military and Implications for Regional Security. In Mastro, O. S. (Ed.), *The National Bureau of Asian Research* (pp. 75–90).

Zhang, D. (2018). The Concept of 'Community of Common Destiny' in China's Diplomacy: Meaning, Motives and Implications. *Asia & the Pacific Policy Studies*, *5*(2), 196–207. https://onlinelibrary.wiley.com/doi/epdf/10.1002/app5.231. DOI: 10.1002/app5.231

Zhang, R. (2021). "Explainer | South China Sea: what are rival claimants building on islands and reefs?", *South China Morning Post*, 07 March 2021, https://www.scmp.com/news/china/diplomacy/article/3124309/south-china-sea-what-are-rival-claimants-building-islands-and.

Zhou, O. (2024). "CNOOC discovers Kaiping South oilfield in South China Sea with over 100 mil mt proven volume", *S&P Global*, 08 March 2024, https://www.spglobal.com/commodityinsights/en/market-insights/latest-news/oil/030824-cnooc-discovers-kaiping-south-oilfield-in-south-china-sea-with-over-100-mil-mt-proven-volume.

Zou, K. (2021). Introduction. In Zou, K. (Ed.), *Routledge Handbook of The SCS* (pp. 1–6). Routledge.

Zou, Y. (2023). "China and Indonesia's responses to maritime disputes in the South China Sea: forming a tacit understanding on security", *Marine Policy* (149): 1-8, https://doi.org/.DOI: 10.1016/j.marpol.2023.105502

Chapter 4
India's Power Struggle in South Asia

Emrah Yıldırımçakar
https://orcid.org/0000-0001-6501-5471
Avrasya University, Turkey

ABSTRACT

In recent years, India has made concerted efforts to expand its power and influence in South Asia. Asia. With the sharp increase in population, economy, and technology, India is expected to be more involved in both regional and global affairs in the future. India is unlikely to want China or any regional country or countries to assume the leadership of the region on its own. India aims to present a profile of cooperating with regional or global actors in terms of either ruling the region alone or jointly shaping the region. Any alternative policy of eliminating India from South Asia is likely to have a profound impact on the development and stability of the region. Although India is not yet a leading economy in South Asia, its economic and strategic position in the region is increasing significantly. As a growing power, India's new regional and global policy, especially its pioneering role in establishing new initiatives, demonstrates its intention to increase its power and influence both in South Asia and the world.

INTRODUCTION

There are significant political and economic transformations taking place in the international arena. Considering the balance of power shifts towards Asia, India is likely to be one of the major powers that will play critical roles in both regional and international political, economic, and military affairs. In recent years, India has surpassed China to become the world's most populous country. It has also become

DOI: 10.4018/979-8-3693-8109-0.ch004

one of the world's five largest economies, and its economic influence is likely to grow even faster in the future (World Population Review, 2024). However, India is not only a growing power in South Asia. At present, China, compared to India, has a more influential position in terms of politics, economy, technology, and military both in South Asian and world politics. Considering the current position of South Asia and the parameters of political, economic, military, and power competition in world politics, the competition in South Asia is most likely to progress between China and India. As rising powers, both China and India are competing for influence in the region through strategic cooperation, investments, infrastructure, economic corridors, military expansion, and diplomatic engagement. China has endeavoured to increase its influence across South Asia and the world within the scope of the BRI. Apart from its new economic initiative, India is striving to assert its leadership through regional cooperation initiatives and partnerships with global powers. in this context, both China and India struggling both for regional dominance and a larger role in international politics.

India aims to have more projects in the South Asia and other regions to compete with China and other regional powers. The economic projects such as the Asian Highway Network and India-Myanmar-Thailand with the support of the United Nations Economic and Social Commission for Asia and the Pacific (UNESCAP). The Trilateral Highway (IMTTH) is planned to reach Laos, Cambodia, and Vietnam and the Mekong-India Economic Corridor is designed to connect India to Myanmar (Gong, 2019). Parallel to these projects, India is trying to take a more active role against the rising political, economic, and military power of China. In the context of its 'Move East' policy, India is increasingly taking positions in Southeast Asian regional collaborations such as the South Asian Organisation for Regional Cooperation (SAARC) and the Bay of Bengal Initiative for Multi-Sectoral Technical and Economic Cooperation (BIMSTEC). These economic policies have the potential to change the Indo-Pacific landscape in favour of India (Pant, 2018). There are also two critical economic corridors, the India-Middle East-Europe Economic Corridor (IMEC) and the North-South Transport Corridor (INSTC), designed as alternatives to China's multi-level economic corridors that are still being built within the framework of the Belt and Road Initiative (BRI).

As a growing economic power, India is uneasy about China's growing influence in South Asia and is growing cooperative relations with Pakistan and other regional states. India is struggling to increase its influence in South Asia not only as leverage against China's growing presence but also to portray itself as a responsible power in the region. Moreover, India is an ally of Western powers, namely the United States. Therefore, India's growing power capabilities in the region are likely to be supported by the Western world. India does not have sufficient militaristic and economic resources to establish a more sustainable political, militaristic, and economic position or increase its influence and reduce China's influence in the region. Therefore, India may need to benefit from the influence of the United States to cope with political developments in the region. The dominant position of the United States is likely to assist India increase its credibility both regionally and globally (Tambi, 2023). However, this may pose a challenge not only to India's military presence but also to its political and economic interests. It may also carry the risks of closer cooperation between China and other regional states.

With the Modi Government, India has started to follow a more proactive foreign policy both regionally and internationally. India has joined some critical international organizations to be one of the most critical actors globally. India has also opened a new page in its relations with South and East Asian countries. Accordingly, India aimed to follow a new strategy under the motto of the "Look East" policy. India also changed its "Act East" policy to intensify its relations with East Asian countries to be more active in the South and East Asian regions (Hall and Ganguly, 2022). When we look at all these developments, India has realized, albeit belatedly, that one of the most important elements of being economically, politically, and militarily strong depends on its relations with its surroundings.

India's 'Look East' policy has developed in the context of its objectives of becoming a part of global power. This policy has progressed within the scope of India's changing policies moving away from its non-alignment policy and establishing closer relations with the United States (Ranjan, 2019). However, India needs to free itself from regional issues. Its efforts such as controlling its neighbors can damage its global image and interests. Instead of spending efforts on controlling its neighbors, India can benefit greatly from the presence of the United States in the South Asian region and develop more stable relations with its neighbors by increasing its influence in the region. (Basrur, 2010). Considering the current situation, India needs to further demonstrate its cooperative approach to its neighbors. By attracting them through a "win-win" concept similar to the approach China has adopted in its foreign relations. India can enhance its regional influence by promoting a strategy where benefits are shared. This kind of approach is more likely to yield positive results. This approach could encourage these neighboring states to recognize India's leadership and cooperate with India more willingly in terms of fostering stronger political, economic, and strategic ties between India and South Asia

This chapter focuses on India's power dynamics in South Asia. One of the key findings of this study is that India has made significant progress in expanding its power, enabling it to compete with China both regionally and internationally. Power competition is a central element of realist theory within the larger framework of International Relations. In this context, we seek to explore the questions and rationale behind India's growing influence in South Asia by addressing what are the key factors driving India's power struggle, and to what extent can India increase its influence in the region and the world, given its current political, economic, and military capabilities?

A REALISTIC ASSESSMENT OF INDIA'S POWER STRUGGLE

There are various approaches to seeking power, power balancing, and being more powerful in international relations. Power balancing or being powerful has become a critical topic of debate since ancient times. Theoretically, the paramount objective of states is to position themselves in a secure and stable international system. If a state struggles to increase its power and impact in the international arena, it can also cooperate with more powerful international actors to enhance its position (Waltz, 2014). In this sense, increasing power and capabilities are not solely limited to the capacity of a state, cooperation and collaboration are also critical in the process of competition and enhancing power.

As discussed in the international relations and political science scholarship, hard power and soft power are different from each other in the context of being more powerful or creating influence in global affairs. Hard power policies include military intervention, relatively more coercive diplomacy, and severe economic sanctions to reach desired outcomes based on national interests. Soft power usually focuses on common political values by aiming to create peaceful atmospheres for conflicts, providing economic cooperation, and creating an attractive atmosphere for resilient solutions. Joseph Nye emphasizes soft power by arguing that states can sometimes reach a desired outcome without using force or coercion. This kind of outcome can be considered the "second face of success" (Nye, 2004). As discussed in the realist ideology, being successful or getting a more advantageous outcome versus a rival is one of the main desired outcomes in international affairs.

> *"The dictionary tells us that power means an ability to do things and control others, to get others to do what they otherwise would not. Because the ability to control others is often associated with the possession of certain re- sources, politicians and diplomats commonly define power as the possession of popula- tion, territory, natural resources, economic size, military forces, and political stability. For ex- ample, in the agrarian economies of eighteenth-century Europe, population was a critical power resource since it provided a base for taxes and recruitment of infanty. Traditionally the test of a great power was its strength in war. Today, however, the definition of power is losing its emphasis on military force and conquest that marked earlier eras. The factors of technology, education, and economic growth are becoming more significant in international power, while geography, population, and raw materials are becoming somewhat less important." (Nye, 1990).*

Power, while a central concept in realist theory, is not merely an end goal for states to achieve and then abandon; power is also a primary source of insecurity that drives states to constantly compete for dominance. From a realist perspective, it is not enough to increase one's power. What is equally important is to limit the power of others and maintain one's superiority over rivals; this is crucial in power politics and balance of power theories. The acquisition and loss of power are crucial in international relations. As emphasized by Mearsheimer (2021), population size and a robust economy are essential components of military power. In this context, a country is expected to be more powerful in the future. However, a more powerful country is likely to be perceived as a threat by its own and other regional powers. Therefore, a country needs to focus on increasing its power and influence on the one hand, and on the other hand, manage the process of absorption from being perceived as a threat.

"Scholars of international politics are used to thinking about the problem of collective action in the context of a multipolar system, where buck-passing is the main obstacle to the formation of a counterbalancing coalition. Balancing is risky business. Strong states rarely welcome others standing in their way and can impose harsh penalties on those that do. In a multipolar system, major powers have a reasonable chance of defending themselves individually against even the strongest state in the system, and so each can try to make others pay the price for confronting the revisionist state. For this reason, states in a mulitpolar system are often slow to balance against powerful rivals, and the formation of a balancing coalition is generally an incremental process in which new members are added over time." (Pape, 2005).

Power-seeking and power-balancing strategies can be seen more commonly in a global and regional system supported by bilateral and multilateral cooperation, not only in terms of economy but also in terms of political, economic, and militaristic goals and technological advancement (Ikenberry, 2015). Waltz (2014) argues that states may need to cooperate with more powerful states and international actors to create an environment for stability and security in the international system to increase their power and influence. Slightly different from Waltz, Walt (1987) argues that offensive capabilities, proximity, and increased armament are the main reasons for posing a threat to other countries. To respond to these threats, rivals may pursue balancing strategies to limit the rise of rival states and form counter-alliances. However, states are generally not inclined to increase their power by forming alliances.

There is a great potential for power competition in South Asia namely between China and India. The military and economic development of China causes India to take measures for its military and economic interests. This competition is not limited to China and India, the competition between China-United States and India-Pakistan also creates challenges for the stability of the region. There are significant proofs demonstrating changes in India's foreign policy and its ambition for having a more important position in the international arena as well as a permanent seat in the United Nations Security Council. India's regional and global political strategies have transformed from hard to soft power strategies since the 1990s. As an emerging regional and global power, India can also be considered a dominant power in South Asia. However, India is not successful enough to be considered a power to influence the outcomes of bilateral or multilateral conflicts in the region and its neighbourhood (Wagner, 2005). In other words, India has the potential to become a leading political and economic power in the region. However, currently, India's political and economic capabilities and its advanced bilateral and multilateral cooperation are far away from being compared to that of China.

India aims to follow a soft power approach based on the concepts of non-reciprocity, asymmetric responsibility, and connectivity, which indicates its intention to attract neighboring countries with its economic development model (Hazarika and Mishra, 2016). It is also argued that soft power has become more important in the new era and countries are spending millions of dollars to increase their soft power. This era is mostly shaped by soft power strategies (Nye and Goldsmith, 2011). Unlike increasing hard power, soft power does not involve coercive solution methods and has the potential to be applied in many regions. It is used by both state and non-state actors worldwide (Hazarika and Mishra, 2016). In this sense, India's tendency to increase its power and influence in terms of soft power strategies both in South Asia and around the world will surely not only strengthen India's political and economic position but also enable India to play a more effective role in global governance.

Realist scholars such as Mearsheimer (2001) have argued that the rising power of one state is simultaneously the loss of another. India's South Asia strategy is a kind of power-balancing strategy in the region. To achieve its political and economic goals or implement its future policies, India needs to balance its power or increase its presence in the region against the power and presence of regional powers such as China. With the Modi Government, India has set many new principles in its foreign policy. One of the most notable policies of principles is the development of relations with neighbouring countries in terms of diplomacy and defence (Hall and Ganguly, 2022). In parallel with its efforts to develop trustworthy relations with its neighbours, India is likely to cooperate more closely with the United States, both to be more active in regional affairs and to increase its presence in the South Asian Sea, as well as to reduce China's growing dominance in the region. This strategy is quite likely to gain the support and satisfaction of the United States.

SOUTH ASIA IN THE INDIAN FOREIGN POLICY

During the Bandung Conference in 1955. China's then Prime Minister, Zhou Enlai proposed a significant political principle under the name of the "Five Principles of Peaceful Coexistence" in 1953. These principles were signed by the Chinese and Indian governments. They were majorly based on common respect for sovereignty, establishing an environment for peaceful coexistence, respecting territorial integrity and equality, providing a non-interference in domestic affairs as well as mutual benefiting from political and economic cooperation (Ministry of Foreign Affairs of the PRC, 2020). On one hand, China and India signed significant peaceful coexistence agreements, on the other hand, it can be observed that India and China have long-standing disagreements on the border between China and India. (Khilnani, et al. 2012). It seems that the rivalry between China and India will continue parallel to their political and economic cooperation in emerging organizations such as BRICS and the SCO.

In line with the multilateral political and economic developments in the international arena, India has aimed to reshape its foreign policy within the framework of the Non-Aligned 2.0 principles. This strategy includes a set of political principles that India has tried to follow to determine its next strategy for the national interests of India in its foreign relations. With these principles, India has aimed to manage its internal development and maximize its global and domestic options to prepare a better future for the benefit of the Indian People. (Khilnani, et al. 2012). Since India is one of the most populous countries in the world, it will not be easy to please the Indian People in a relatively short period. Moreover, the Indian Government has several disadvantages in achieving the desired results. India has the "big brother" problem that makes it difficult to please all its neighboring states. In other words, India is faced with a trust deficit problem mostly for Pakistan, Bangladesh, Sri Lanka, and Nepal (Hazarika and Mishra, 2016). Unless India can create a reliable environment among its neighbors, it will not be able to increase its presence in the region to the desired level and will not be accepted as a leading country in the region by its neighboring countries.

India and China are the two most popular soft power countries in South Asia to gain support and win the hearts of nations around the world. They aim to create a good global image and increase their influence. Unlike Western powers, the influence of the soft power of India and China has surpassed that of hard power in many regions. India and China are competing to increase their soft power globally. Both can pursue soft power strategies. However, if a country does not pay more attention to soft power or does not use it as a foreign policy objective, it will be of little importance to its national and international interests (Hazarika and Mishra, 2016). Compared to China's soft power, India's soft power expenditure is relatively limited. India's foreign direct investment is also limited both in South Asia and globally. Without soft power and increased foreign investment, India is unlikely to be recognized as a leading political and economic power.

In its political strategy in South Asia, India is not solely focused on competing with China, it also seeks opportunities for cooperation with China to establish a more advanced political and economic environment in the region. By engaging in multilateral cooperation with China and other regional actors, India can enhance the collective development and security of the region which may be more beneficial both for India and China in the long term. Collaborative efforts can play important roles in addressing shared issues based on infrastructure development, trade facilitation, and security concerns by creating a more stable and prosperous environment in South Asia. an approach based on both competition and cooperation may provide India with a broader objective of achieving sustainable growth and power influence in the region.

> *"In the multilateral fields also, such as on climate change and other issues involving the interests of the developing world, India and China are increasingly finding common ground and supporting each other. The frequency of dialogues between the two countries at all levels has increased manifold since the Look East Policy was heralded. Doubts remain, however, about China really wishing to have a strategic relationship with India due to its huge military relationship with Pakistan that extends into the strategic nuclear field and its manifest use of that country as a bulwark against India in the subcontinent." (Mehrotra, 2012).*

India has actively sought to enhance its soft power over the past five years. During this time, the Indian Council for Cultural Relations (ICCR) has established 22 cultural centers in 19 countries to improve India's global image. The Indian government has also promoted the learning of its language by organizing the annual World Hindi Conference, encouraging foreigners to engage with Indian culture and language (Blarel, 2012). In addition to its cultural efforts, India has aimed to establish both bilateral and multilateral relations with regional actors in South Asia, striving to assume a leadership role in political and economic matters. In contrast, China has focused more on forming bilateral relations with individual actors in the region (Wagner, 2016). Despite these different strategies, both India and China are ultimately striving to achieve similar strategic outcomes such as expanding their influence, securing regional leadership, and boosting their global power. This demonstrates that there are multiple paths to increasing power and influence, India and China are navigating different routes to achieve their multilateral goals.

China is more active in establishing cooperation in South Asia in the name of South-South cooperation not only to increase China's influence in the region but also to demonstrate that China is a responsible power. (Zhao, 2024). On one hand, some scholars think that China has lost its confidence due to the conflicts bombed out in Southern China. Consequently, the United States continues to be one of the most critical actors in the region. Due to the slight loss of its superiority and popularity, the United States is deeply concerned about the future of the region (Gong, 2019). India is aware of China's incessantly increasing influence in South Asia and its neighbourhoods. India's strategy is using pragmatic ways to overcome this competition. In this context, India has had some policies to enhance its cultural and economic relations with these neighbouring countries (Hazarika and Mishra, 2016). China and India have different objectives for soft power strategies. While China's soft power strategy is mainly based on harmony and peaceful development (Zhou & Estaban, 2018). India's soft power strategy is majorly based on promoting multiculturalism, a plural world order, and a democratic image (Hazarika and Mishra, 2016). Accordingly, the South Asian region is experiencing multilateral power-balancing strategies. Currently, the influence of China and the United States is relatively higher than India's influence. However, India has the potential to be a significant actor in the region in the future.

As many researchers have also admitted, India has not effectively used its soft power strategy in South Asia. There are three main reasons for these ineffective uses. First, India has not been able to use public diplomacy as effectively as China. Second, hard power and soft power should be expanded in parallel to a great extent. Some scholars argue that India has an undeniable tremendous potential for soft power based on its culture and rich civilizational heritage and it has no record of colonization or imperialism in its history. It has always been a victim of foreign occupation. Therefore, India has more advantages than China in pursuing soft power policies (Hazarika and Mishra, 2016). However, it should not be forgotten that China also has no historical record of colonization and imperialism in its long history. This criterion is likely to be accepted as one of the main concepts of being successful in pursuing the process of soft power in foreign relations, In this context, as a rival of India, China is also one of the most successful international actors in the world.

China is anticipated to create significant challenges for India in terms of foreign policy and security in the future. As one of the major global powers, China can directly influence India's geopolitical sphere. The expansion of China's economic and military capabilities is likely to widen the power differential between the two countries (Khilnani et al., 2012). Moreover, China has successfully pursued a policy of regionalism in South Asia, effectively engaging countries in the region through policy coordination on development and security issues (Freeman, 2018). India must deeply assess the strategies employed by its rivals both in the region and globally. A comprehensive evaluation of these geopolitical tactics likely enables India to formulate a more impactful and strategic foreign policy to strengthen its position both in its neighborhood and on the global stage.

INDIA'S REGIONAL AND INTERNATIONAL PROJECTS AS A STRATEGY TO INCREASE ITS POWER AND INFLUENCE

India is one of the most important and influential countries in South Asia. However, China holds a more dominant role in the economic affairs of South Asia, Central Asia, the Middle East, and the European Union (EU). Both the United States and the EU are concerned with China's dominant position in global and EU trade. Currently, China is a crucial trade partner of the EU, accounting for 16.2 percent of the EU's total product trade, while India's trade partnership with the EU accounts only 2 percent (European Commission, 2021). Recognizing its relatively limited economic influence in the EU and other regions, India has sought to enhance its economic standing to compete more effectively with China. In this context, India has pursued the development of additional economic routes and corridors versus China's political and regional strategies to deepen its cooperative relations with more regions and countries.

In recent years, India has been actively inclined to apply soft power in India's foreign relations. India has realized that it cannot be a major power without strong political and economic institutions (Blarel, 2012). As a result, India has sought to develop trade corridors and political and economic cooperation with many regions and countries to achieve its long-term political and economic goals. Although India is not a critical economic partner for the EU and is not a leading economy in South Asia, the Middle East, and Central Asia. However, its economic and strategic position is growing significantly in these regions and the world simultaneously. To compete with China, India needs to have more political strategies and economic projects in the Southeast Asia region. Along with the India-Middle East-Europe Economic Corridor (IMEC) and the North-South Transport Corridor (INSTC), India also needed to develop other cooperation projects such as the Asian Highway Network, with the support of the United Nations Economic and Social Commission for Asia and the Pacific (UNESCAP) and India-Myanmar-Thailand Trilateral Highway (IMTTH) which was planned to reach Laos, Cambodia and Vietnam (Gong, 2019). Consequently, India has developed a more active policy against China's rising political, economic, and military presence under the name of the "Act East" policy. In line with this policy, India has taken increasingly active positions in Southeast Asian regional cooperation such as the South Asian Organisation for Regional Cooperation (SAARC) and the Bay of Bengal Initiative for Multi-Sectoral Technical and Economic Cooperation (BIMSTEC). In this context, India has sought to change the future of the Indo-Pacific economic and strategic landscape in its favor (Pant, 2018). India's such an active policy will also create alternatives to the regional countries that are not willing to acknowledge the leadership of China in South Asia.

After much discussion among the Indian elite and the Indian leadership, the Government of India applied for membership in the SCO and AIIB. Although BRI was also an initiative established and led by China, like the SCO and AIIB, India refused to be a part of the BRI. Being a member of the SCO and AIIB was also controversial both internally and politically. Accordingly, being a member of the SCO and AIIB also created great unrest among the Indian people (Freeman, 2018). The reason why India did not support the BRI is that India does not want to be an economic power led by China. Instead of being part of Chinese initiatives, India is struggling to establish Indian-led economic initiatives. If India agrees to be an economic partner of BRI, India should stop establishing economic corridors and join Chinese-led economic initiatives. This is not a rational stance for a country that is trying to take the economic and political leadership of the region.

THE NORTH-SOUTH TRANSPORT CORRIDOR (INSTC)

Nearly a decade ago, India announced its intention to establish the International North-South Transport Corridor (INSTC), which is an economic route passing through Iranian territory to reach Central Asia, the Caspian Sea, and Russia. The corridor was planned to span approximately 7,200 kilometers and was anticipated to extend to the European Union (Khan, 2023). The decision to establish this corridor was made approximately two years after the announcement of the BRI. With the implementation of this corridor, India aimed to enhance connectivity with Central Asian and European countries by linking India to Iran's Chabahar port, thus providing access to the Caucasus and Central Asia. One of India's strategic goals in establishing the INSTC was to bypass Pakistan, which posed a significant geographical obstacle to India's access to Central Asian and Caucasian markets (Ali & Khan, 2024). This corridor allowed India to pursue two key objectives simultaneously: the first was eliminating Pakistan's land barrier, and the second was countering China's growing economic influence in Central Asia and the Caucasus.

China's growing political and economic presence in South Asia and other regions deeply worries India. Any step that allows China to go further is a step lost for India in regional and international relations. Currently, India's economic capabilities are not as sufficient as China's in terms of financing international trade projects and supporting the infrastructure of participating countries to solve their economic problems and achieve a satisfactory level of cooperation (Gupta (2020, p. 54). However, India has one of the significant advantages that has the potential to enable India to achieve the desired results in its presence in world affairs and its competition with China. This advantage is the support of the United States and the EU behind India.

According to Thaliyakkattil (2019), the United States has long been the most influential actor in South and Southeast Asia. While the rise of China in recent years has increasingly challenged the United States' dominance in the region, other scholars consider the hegemony of the United States to remain unparalleled in South Asia and many other regions (Shambaugh, 2018, Gong, 2019). Despite such different approaches to the future of South Asia, it is clear that China's close interaction with South Asian countries will ultimately pose challenges to India's political and economic position in the region. The competition in South Asia will not be limited to the competition between the United States and China. India's quest for power and influence will make India the third most influential power influencing competition in South Asia and has the potential to play a significant political and economic role in Central Asia, the Middle East, and Eurasia.

THE INDIA-MIDDLE EAST-EUROPE-ECONOMIC-CORRIDOR (IMEC)

India launched the India-Middle East-Europe Economic Corridor (IMEC) during the G20 Summit held in India in 2023. The IMEC is planned to begin in India, passing through the territories of the United Arab Emirates, Saudi Arabia, Jordan, and Israel, before continuing from Israel to the Greek port of Piraeus, and finally reaching the European Union (Korkmaz, 2023). The IMEC is designed as an alternative to China's BRI. It is designed to connect India, the Middle East, and the EU through a combination of highways and seaways. When fully operational, the IMEC is expected to influence over half of the global economy and connect approximately 40 percent of the global population (Rizvi, 2023). In this context, the IMEC is anticipated to be an alternative for India to increase its trade and investment in the Middle East and the EU versus China's dominant economic position.

As with the INSTC, India's financial resources are insufficient to fully fund the IMEC. Consequently, India cannot provide substantial financial assistance to its partner states to address infrastructure challenges and compete directly with China's Belt and Road Initiative (BRI). In this context, India may seek to leverage the support and influence of the United States to enhance its presence in the Middle East and attract cooperation from other international actors (Tambi, 2023). With the support of the U.S. and the EU, India aims to strengthen its economic and cooperative relations with Middle Eastern and European countries. To have a significant position in these regions, India must set up more bilateral and multilateral relations with regional states. Moreover, the IMEC is not solely an initiative designed to serve India's political and economic interests. Rather, it appears to be a multilaterally planned project that aligns with the strategic interests of the United States, the EU, and Israel. Therefore, with the peaceful environment in the Middle East and the EU, the IMEC has the potential to play a critical role in the world economy.

With the announcement of the BRI's economic corridors and its infrastructure investments along with the deepening bilateral cooperation through Chinese corridors such as the China-Pakistan, China-Myanmar, and China-Bangladesh partnerships, India felt increasingly concerned about falling significantly behind China (Darshana, 2020). India places great importance on its relations with South Asian states, as the Asian market is one of the key markets for its economic interests. In this context, India has sought to establish free trade agreements and expand its economic engagements with other Asian economies (Khilnani et al., 2012). As a result, India realized the need to strengthen its bilateral and multilateral relations with neighboring and strategic countries in various regions to counter China's growing power and influence in South Asia and globally. It is stated that the strategy behind IMEC was developed on the same concept. In this concept, India aimed to strengthen its influence in the region by increasing its economic connections and serving its objectives against China's BRI supported by the US and the EU (Kaygusuz, 2023). Therefore, it would not be wrong to claim that IMEC is planned to serve as a long-term common policy developed by India, the United States, and the EU.

The Asian Infrastructure Investment Bank (AIIB) and the Silk Road Fund are critical financial supporters of the BRI. China established them to support the infrastructure expenses of the BRI. It is thought that the AIIB provides $100 billion in financial support to the BRI, while the Silk Road Fund provides $40 billion. The China Development Bank, the BRICS New Development Bank, and Eximbank are other important supporters of the BRI (Roland, 2017; Zou et al., 2021). In fact, since the announcement of the BRI in 2013, India has declared its opposition to the BRI and its other alternative paths such as the China-Pakistan Economic Corridor (CPEC), which is one of the sub-critical components of the BRI (Siddiqa 2023). As the IMEC does not have sufficient financial opportunities compared to the BRI, it will not have more alternative corridors like the BRI to support its financial and infrastructure issues. However, it should be noted that the countries located on the IMEC line are relatively accessible and do not need as much financial or infrastructure support as those along the BRI line.

With the establishment of the IMEC, India aims to increase its economic influence in the Middle East and establish advanced trade links with the EU by reducing the increasing presence of China on a global scale (Das, 2024). This seems to be one of the most preferable strategic policies for India to compete with China. IMEC also puts countries that support China's BRI with choosing to support the BRI or IMEC. In this context, recently, Italy decided to leave the BRI to become a member of IMEC (Rossi, 2023). However, the route that the IMEC plans to establish is becoming unsafe and risky day by day. One of the critical factors that make the corridor unsafe is the conflict between Israel-Palestine and Israel-Arab countries. Accordingly, due to the long-term Israeli attacks on the Gaza Strip and finally Israel's attacks on Lebanon and Yemen, despite the warnings and pressures of international organizations, Israel does not want to stop attacking these countries with the support of the United States, the completion of the corridor faces critical difficulties (Sładkowski, A. et al. (2024). If the conflict between Israel and Palestine spreads to Iran and other neighbouring countries, the future of the region and IMEC will be in danger. The recently rising tense relations between Israel and Iran are posing serious problems for the security of the region.

Another reason for India's non-participation in BRI Forums is that Indian officials claim that BRI lacks transparency processes in both governance and implementation. Moreover, it carries the risk of unmanageable debt burden. While BRI provides great benefits for economic flows, it also has the potential to strengthen China's military power (Freeman, 2018). India's negative attitude towards cooperation with China may also have negative political and economic consequences for India in the long run. However, instead of these negative attitudes, India should change its political approach towards BRI positively in order to derive multilateral economic and political benefits from cooperation and contribute to the development and prosperity of the region (Juutinen 2018). The reluctance of Indian elites and politicians to support the BRI may stem from the concern that supporting BRI means supporting a more advanced China, both economically and militarily.

THE TRILATERAL SECURITY PARTNERSHIP BETWEEN AUSTRALIA, THE UNITED KINGDOM, AND THE UNITED STATES (AUKUS)

The AUKUS is an abbreviation of the names of the three member countries, Australia, the United Kingdom, and the United States, established in 2021. AUKUS is another form of cooperation established to counter China's emerging presence in South Asia and the entire world. In this sense, a trilateral cooperation strategy has been put in place by the United States with the support of the United Kingdom and Australia to increase India's political and economic presence in South Asia. (US Secretary of Defense, 2023). This cooperation will not only increase India's existing political and economic influence in the region but will also serve the political and economic interests of Australia, the United States, and the United Kingdom in the region.

It is claimed that no region is more critical than South Asia for India. Without enhanced multilateral and bilateral cooperation with South Asian countries, India will probably feel more concerned and disappointed about its future economic political, and militaristic objectives (Khilnani, et al. 2012). For India being successful starts with its neighbourhoods. In other words, with a well-managed neighbouring policy, India may have a more influential role in world politics. If India is carefree for the future of South Asia, it will be more comprehensively involved in increasing its presence in other regions and the international arena.

Being dominant in the vast Asian oceans also creates a potential for maritime competition. However, while it creates great concern for the region, it also creates comparative advantages for India. (Khilnani, et al. 2012). Therefore, the AUKUS is a cooperation based on such a policy. India's leadership in the region may increase the potential for conflict among the regional powers, however, not only India and Australia but also the United States will benefit from India's dominant position under the AUKUS cooperation in the region versus the increasing dominance of China.

THE COOPERATION OF INDIA-ISRAEL AND THE UNITED STATES-THE UNITED ARAB EMIRATES (I2U2)

I2U2 is a strategic cooperation between India, Israel, the United Arab Emirates, and the US, established in 2022. 2I stands for India and Israel and 2U stands for the US and the United Arab Emirates. The motivation behind this cooperation was expected to shift the balance of power in favor of the West. However, I2U2 is also argued to play a role like the role played by the QUAD (an informal strategic forum comprising four nations, namely the United States, India, Australia, and Japan) in the context of rising tensions between China and the United States in South Asia, the Indo-Pacific, and the Middle East (Tamer, 2022; Shorbagy, 2024).

The I2U2 cooperation is a political strategy developed by the United States to establish more advanced cooperation among its alliances. This cooperation is strongly supported by the Indian Government to increase its presence in the Middle East and deepen its strategic relations with oil and energy-rich countries in the region (Kugelman, 2022). The I2U2 cooperation is an opportunity for India to enhance its relations with the Middle East and then be able to establish economic corridors like China to reach the European Market.

THE SOUTH ASIAN ASSOCIATION FOR REGIONAL COOPERATION (SAARC) AND THE BAY OF BENGAL INITIATIVE FOR MULTI-SECTORAL TECHNICAL AND ECONOMIC COOPERATION (BIMSTEC)

India aimed to give priority to the establishment of new initiatives in the context of its willingness to develop or increase its soft power. India's policy continues in the context of a series of new initiatives to attract neighbor and regional countries instead of imposing hard power. Following this policy, regardless of whether in the establishment or after the establishment process, India guided initiatives such as the SAARC, the South Asia Co-operative Environment Programme, the South Asian Economic Union, and BIMSTEC. With these initiatives, India aimed to both create economic cooperation and enhance its trustworthiness for the countries relatively less trusted in India. (Blarel, 2012) The idea of SAARC was first brought to the agenda by Bangladesh in 1983. Shortly, the SAARC was established in 1985, with the first summit at Dhaka Bangladesh. The first summit was carried out with the attendance of heads of the government. (Partha, 2013). A short period later, the SAARC cooperation organization expanded with the participation of many other regional countries.

The South Asian Regional Cooperation Organization (SAARC) was established to play a strategic cooperation role in the region. However, compared to other regional cooperation organizations such as ASEAN (Association of South East Asian Nations) and NAFTA (North American Free Trade Association), SAARC has not made any significant progress in deepening cooperation (Partha, 2013). South Asia is one of the least integrated regions in the world. It is also one of the regions where the poorest people live in the world (Khilnani, et al. 2012). Security and economic inefficiency are critical factors for the fragmentation of the South Asian region. However, a well-planned regional integration seems to be one of the most preferable options for the economic and infrastructural development of the region. it will also enable the region to get rid of poverty and set an integration atmosphere to solve regional education, infrastructure, development, and economic issues.

Other factors such as Pakistan will gain multilateral economic benefits and strengthen its regional influence through its close relations with China. An increase in Pakistan's power could lead to a relative decline in India's influence and credibility in the region. In parallel with these kinds of risky developments, India should focus more on maximizing the opportunities provided by SAARC and BIMSTEC benefit from the advantages of cooperation (Juutinen, 2018). By pursuing interconnected and multilateral cooperation through platforms like SAARC and BIMSTEC, India should solidify its position as an emerging and leading power in the region.

THE CHALLENGES AHEAD FOR INDIA IN SOUTH ASIA

China is one of the critical actors that has the potential to limit India's power projection by establishing close political and economic cooperation with Southeast and South Asian countries. Pakistan and China's cooperation is another proof of this policy of restraint. China's close relations with the region and its strategic relations with countries like Pakistan and Bangladesh may create long-term challenges for India and other countries' cooperation relations (Blarel, 2012). South Asia region and its neighbouring countries have needed cooperation to benefit from investment, infrastructure projects, and economic corridors. China has created a relatively good project to support the needs of the countries in the region in terms of win-win co-operation. However, India has not been successful in providing such an opportunity to the region in terms of win-win cooperation. If India was able to undertake such policies, the SAARC could be a step for such an initiative. If India is willing to undertake such projects at present or in the future, Indian projects could make the opportunities provided by BRI less attractive (Pant, 2016; Juutinen, 2018). India has this potential since India has also different alternatives such as IMEC and INSTC that can be implemented to increase India's soft power and cooperation opportunities.

Some challenges for India stem from the politics of the United States in the Middle East. India's IMEC and INSTC economic corridor develops with the co-operation of Middle Eastern countries. In the establishment process of the IMEC, the Iran-United States and Iran-Israel tense relations have the potential to create challenges for India-Iran relations. To eliminate this risk, India received assurance from the United States in 2019 to get Iran's Chabahar port out of the sanction list of the United States against Iran (Kashif and Koch, 2024). However, the policies of the United States for backing Israel may result in radical changes for the region in the long run. Another challenge for India to enhance its power and influence is the India-Pakistan conflict. India-Pakistan has had relatively unstable relations for a long time. Pakistan-China intimate cooperation and Pakistan's enabling China to implement Pakistan's Gwadar port provides critical advantages to accomplish one of the important branches of the BRI with the name of China-Pakistan Economic-Corridor (CPEC). the Gwadar port is close to the Baluchistan region, and it is not appropriate for India to take advantage of it. After Pakistan obtained nuclear weapons capabilities, India followed a policy based on perceiving Pakistan with antagonistic feelings (Basrur, 2010). The CPEC is planned to allow China to reach the Indian Ocean without traveling through the Malacca Strait. The CPEC is expected to enhance China's cooperation with other countries by diminishing transportation expenses and reducing the time of delivery. This may lead the other countries to cooperate with China instead of India which was always considered to be near to them.

The instability of the Middle East and the conflict between Israel and Palestine have the potential to jeopardize the process of building IMEC or create difficulties for other countries willing to cooperate with India (Khan et al., 2024; Shinde, 2023). Only peaceful Israeli-Arab relations could enhance the stability of the Middle East. Since the conflict erupted once again in October 2023, the Israeli Army's continued asymmetric attacks despite the calls for a ceasefire from the UN and other countries have negatively affected the stability of the Middle East. This also seems to be a clear example of the insincere approach of the United States to resolving the conflicts in the Middle East. While the United States on one hand, appears to be making efforts to normalize Arab-Israeli relations, on the other hand, it supports Israel's continued fighting in the region (Baabood, 2023). A policy like this, pursued by the United States and Israel, is likely to impact not only ongoing and developing projects in the region but also India's cooperation with Middle Eastern countries in the context of establishing the IMEC. Such a policy can also have an impact on facilitating alignment and cooperation to enhance the success of IMEC. It will also be indicative of how regional actors respond to broader geopolitical dynamics. The success of the IMEC corridor will largely depend on how effectively India manages these evolving political issues.

The rise of China as an emerging power has intensified competition between India and China, particularly in South Asia and the Middle East. This rivalry has largely been driven by China's increasing influence in these regions, especially through infrastructure and economic projects (Zhao, 2024). In this context, China has focused heavily on the Belt and Road Initiative (BRI), offering economic, financial, and commercial alternatives to regional countries. China's strategy targets provide underdeveloped nations with financial support framed as "win-win" cooperation (Huang, 2016). Some scholars argue that existing political and economic conflicts may pose challenges for certain countries when it comes to cooperating with India and the India-Middle East-Europe Economic Corridor (IMEC). However, many nations are likely to seek cooperation with India, particularly with the backing of Western powers (Elmali, 2023; Siddiqa, 2023). Unlike IMEC, the BRI emphasizes connecting people and cultures through a "people-to-people bond" to foster collaboration and enhance relations between participating actors. From 2013 to 2023, China implemented public health, education, agriculture, and 1,600 anti-poverty foreign aid projects to build credibility and promote a more peaceful and friendly approach within the region and globally. This poses a positive effect on regional countries in terms of deepening their relations with China.

India has a significant advantage in attracting cooperation from other democratic countries. These shared democratic values may also foster a sense of ideological alignment with countries that prioritize democratic values, the rule of law, and transparent governance to cooperate with India. However, India also has negative records such as poor health care, child mortality, illiteracy, and social strife (Blarel, 2012). In addition, the oppression of the Muslim population in India may also create difficulties for India in cooperating with Muslim-majority countries. In this context, India needs to focus more on resolving its internal problems that create injustice towards Muslims or other population groups.

India also has a critical role in global governance. In particular, it has the potential to take the initiative in the context of strengthening multilateralism in the world and balancing power between the United States and China. Some scholars argue that China is increasing its presence in the South China Sea and the Indian Ocean in parallel with the BRI cooperation. Thus, China's presence is likely to threaten India and the region. With the establishment of the BRI, China will likely have the potential to increase its military capabilities in the region. Moreover, China can squeeze India in the context of increasing its strategic relations with countries that do not have good relations with India (Juutinen 2018). India should leverage its large population and rising power status to address and overcome both the alleged and anticipated challenges it faces. As a rapidly growing economy with a significant demographic advantage, India has the potential to utilize its human capital, economic growth, and strategic positioning to have greater influence in regional and global affairs.

China holds significant power in terms of military hardware and strategic investments in South Asia. In response, India has been working to strengthen its military relations with neighboring countries. Nearly a decade ago, India's National Security Advisor, Shiv Shankar Menon, emphasized the need for India to enhance its security posture in South Asia and the Indian Ocean to counter China's expanding presence and influence in the region. Indian Prime Minister Narendra Modi also pointed this concern out during his official visits to SAARC countries and Indian Ocean island states in 2015 (Wagner, 2016). Despite Modi's efforts, Indian foreign policy has not seen significant shifts under his leadership. While Modi may appear to pursue new strategies aimed at bolstering India's political and economic position regionally and globally, scholars argue that he has not implemented a fundamentally new or more comprehensive strategy than his predecessors (Ranjan, 2019). However, Modi has launched several economic corridors to increase India's cooperation power with many regions and other international actors.

CONCLUSION

India is one of the key rising powers in South Asia. With its growing population and expanding economy, India seeks to extend its influence beyond South Asia to compete with other global powers, particularly China. To enhance its political, economic, and military capabilities, India must play a pivotal role in its neighborhood and forge cooperative partnerships with regional and international actors to strengthen its influence multilaterally. In this context, India has sought to establish economic corridors, similar to China's initiatives, to expand its reach into more countries and regions, with the goal of boosting its political and economic stature. Both China and India, as developing countries, aim to increase their participation in the global economy by enhancing trade connectivity and fostering more advanced economic relations with other nations and regions. They also aim to enhance their regional and global trade and investment capabilities to solidify their roles as emerging powers in the global economy.

Not only India but also several Western powers, such as the United States and the European Union, are reluctant to collaborate with China within the framework of the BRI. These countries are concerned about China's growing regional and global influence and are thus eager to support India in its competition with China, particularly in regions such as South Asia, Southeast Asia, Central Asia, the Middle East, and Europe. To this end, the U.S. and the EU are interested in limiting China's influence in these regions and on the global stage. They are actively supporting India's economic initiatives, such as the IMEC and other regional projects, to help bolster India's economic capabilities and enhance its geopolitical influence.

To increase its power and influence in South Asia and the globe, India has endevoured to establish multilateral cooperation organizations, encouraging regional and global actors to collaborate with India. By promoting these partnerships, India aims to strengthen its political, economic, and strategic presence both in the region and beyond. Some of these initiatives are similar to China's BRI, which was launched a decade ago to create new highways, railways, and maritime routes connecting China to the rest of the world. While India lacks the financial and infrastructural resources to provide the same level of support to member countries as China does, its initiatives aim to boost India's multilateral capabilities in terms of power balancing, as well as increasing its political, economic, and military influence. Despite facing several political and economic challenges, India is determined to strengthen its regional and global presence by positioning itself as a counterweight to other rising powers, particularly to China.

REFERENCES

Baabood, A. (2024) "The Geopolitics of Economic Development in the Middle East", February 15, Carnegie Middle East Center, https://carnegie-mec.org/2024/02/15/geopolitics-of-economic-development-in-middle-east-pub-91650

Basrur, R. M. (2010). Global Quest and Regional Reversal: Rising India and South Asia. *International Studies, 47*(2-4), 267–284. DOI: 10.1177/002088171104700412

Blarel, N. (2012) India: the next superpower?: India's soft power: from potential to reality? IDEAS reports - special reports, Kitchen, Nicholas (ed.) SR010. LSE IDEAS, London School of Economics and Political Science, London, UK.

Das, D. (2024). Revisiting the contours of the evolving Middle Eastern order through the India-Middle East-EU Corridor: Mapping India's scopes and limitations. *Asian Journal of Political Science, 32*(1), 1–22. DOI: 10.1080/02185377.2024.2322498

Elmali, B. (2023) "Unrest in the Middle East Is Bad for Both CPEC and IMEC", Retrieved from The Diplomat: https://thediplomat.com/2023/11/unrest-in-the - middle-east-is-bad-for-both-cpec-and-imec/

European Commision. (2021) "EU trade relations – India", Retrieved from European Commission, https://policy.trade.ec.europa.eu/eu-trade-relationships-country-and -region/countries-and-regions/india_en

Freeman, C. P. (2018). China's 'regionalism foreign policy' and China-India relations in South Asia. *Contemporary Politics, 24*(1), 81–97. DOI: 10.1080/13569775.2017.1408168

Gong, X. (2019). The Belt & Road Initiative and China's influence in Southeast Asia. *The Pacific Review, 32*(4), 635–665. DOI: 10.1080/09512748.2018.1513950

Gupta, A. (2020). Global Strike vs. Globalization: The US-China Rivalry and the BRI. In Leandro, F. J. B. S., & Duarte, P. A. B. (Eds.), *The Belt and Road Initiative: An Old Archetype of a New Development Model*. Palgrave Macmillan. DOI: 10.1007/978-981-15-2564-3_3

Hall, I., & Ganguly, Š. (2022). Introduction: Narendra Modi and India's foreign policy. *International Politics, 59*(1), 1–8. DOI: 10.1057/s41311-021-00363-8

Hazarika, O. B., & Mishra, V. (2016). South Asia As A Battleground: Soft Power Contestation between India and China. *World Affairs: The Journal of International Issues, 20*(3), 112–129. https://www.jstor.org/stable/48505297

Huang, Y. (2016). Understanding China's Belt & Road Initiative: Motivation, framework and assessment. *China Economic Review*, *40*, 314–321. DOI: 10.1016/j.chieco.2016.07.007

Ikenberry, G. J. (2015). Between the Eagle and the Dragon: America, China, and Middle State Strategies in East Asia. *Political Science Quarterly*, *XX*(XX), 1–35.

Juutinen, M. (2018). Kautilyan foreign policy analysis: Sino-Indian dynamics in South Asia and the Indian Ocean region. *Journal of the Indian Ocean Region*, *14*(2), 206–226. DOI: 10.1080/19480881.2018.1472859

Kashif, H. K., & Koch, H. (2024) "'INSTC and Chabahar Port': An Introduction, Edited Kashif Hasan Khan, India's Economic Corridor Initiatives", March, Routledg, New York, pp. 3-19. DOI: DOI: 10.4324/9781003454540-2

Kaygusuz, B. (2023) "Hindistan'ı Avrupa'ya bağlayacak koridor hakkında bilinenler", Independent Turkish, Sebtember *12,*https://www.indyturk.com/node/660456/dünya/hindistanı-avrupaya-bağlayacak-koridor-hakkında-bilinenler

Khan, K. H., Bastanifar, I., & Omidi, A.. (2024). Integrating gravity models and network analysis in logistical strategic planning: A case of the India Middle-East Europe Economic Corridor (IMEC). *Maritime Economics & Logistics*, *26*(2). Advance online publication. DOI: 10.1057/s41278-024-00289-x

Khilnani, S., Kumar, R., Mehta, P. B., Menon, P., Nilekani, N., Raghavan, S., Saran, S., & Varadarajan, S. (2014). *NonAlignment 2.0: A foreign and strategic policy for India in the 21st century*. Penguin Publications.

Korkmaz, H. (2024) İsrail'deki Savaş IMEC Projesini Rafa Kaldırabilir, Tasam, September 14, https://tasam.org/tr-TR/Icerik/72436/israildeki_savas_imec_projesini_rafa_kaldirabilir

Kugelman, M. (2022) Another Quad Rises, Foreign Policy, July 14. https://foreignpolicy.com/2022/07/14/i2u2-quad-india-israel-uae-us-south-asia/#fn:2

Mearsheimer, J. J. (2021). The inevitable rivalry: America, China, and the tragedy of great-power politics, *Foreign Affairs,* 100(48). Pdf available: https://www.foreignaffairs.com/articles/china/2021-10-19/inevitable-rivalry-cold-war

Mehrotra, L. (2012). India's Look East Policy: Its Origin and Development. *Indian Foreign Affairs Journal*, *7*(1), 75–85.

Ministry of Foreign Affair of the People's Republic of China. (2020). China's initiation of the five principles of peaceful. *Co-Existence (Glasgow, Scotland)*, *29*(June). http://ir.china-embassy.gov.cn/eng/dtxw/201407/t20140702_1894012.htm

Nye, J. S. (1990). *Soft Power,* Foreign Policy, *No. 80*. JSTOR., Retrieved October 14, 2024, from, DOI: 10.2307/1148580

Nye, J. S. (2004) Soft Power, New York, Public Affairs.

Nye, J. S., & Goldsmith, J. L. (2011). The Future of Power. *Bulletin - American Academy of Arts and Sciences. American Academy of Arts and Sciences*, *64*(3), 45–52. https://www.jstor.org/stable/41149419.#

Pant, H. V. (2018) "The future of India's ties with ASEAN", The Diplomat, January, 26, Retrieved from, https://thediplomat.com/2018/01/the-future-of-indias-ties-with-asean/

Pape, R. A. (2005). Soft Balancing against the United States. *International Security*, *30*(1), 7–45. https://www.jstor.org/stable/4137457. DOI: 10.1162/0162288054894607

Partha, S. G. (2013). An Enigma that is South Asia: India versus the Region. *Asia-Pacific Review*, *20*(1), 100–120. DOI: 10.1080/13439006.2013.788336

Ranjan, A. (2019). India's South Asia Policy: Changes, Continuity or Continuity with Changes. *The Round Table*, *108*(3), 259–274. DOI: 10.1080/00358533.2019.1618611

Rizvi, O. (2023) "From India to Europe: What Opportunities and Challenges will the New Corridor Bring?", December 12, https://www.euronews.com/business/2023/12/15/from-india-to-europe-economic-corridor-to-offer-new-trade-opportunities

Rolland, N. (2017). China's "Belt and Road Initiative": Underwhelming or Game-Changer? *The Washington Quarterly*, *40*(1), 127–142. DOI: 10.1080/0163660X.2017.1302743

Rossi, E. (2023) "How IMEC (and Italy) can reshape trade and ties. A conversation with Soliman", Decode 39, September 12, https://decode39.com/7712/imec-italy-reshape-trade-ties-soliman/

Shambaugh, D. (2014). The Illusion of Chinese Power. *National Interest*, *132*, 39–48. https://www.jstor.org/stable/44151213

Shinde, V. (2023) "History Repeats: A new (old) Economic Corridor Emerges", Lowy Institute, November 1, https://www.lowyinstitute.org/the-interpreter/history-repeats-new-old-economic-corridor-emerges

Shorbagy, M. (2024). Triangular Dymamics: US Response to China's Assertivenes in the Middle East. *Arab Studies Quarterly*, *46*(2), 137–161. DOI: 10.13169/arabstudquar.46.2.0137

Siddiqa, A. (2023). Corridor Politics IMEC vs. BRI: Another Geopolitical Face-off in U.S.-China Rivalry. *Journal of Pakistan-China Studies*, *4*(1), 1–22. DOI: 10.55733/jpcs.v4i1.69

Sładkowski, A., Bošnjak, R., Kezić, D. and Krile, S. (2024) BRI Project: Are There Alternatives? Transactions on Maritime Science. Split, Croatia, 13(1). .DOI: 10.7225/toms.v13.n01.018

Tambi, R. (2023) "India pushes back against China's economic influence" September 9, https://eastasiaforum.org/2023/09/09/india-pushes-back-against-chinas-economic-influence/

Tamer, C. (2022) "The 'I2U2' Alliance in West Asia: A New 'QUAD'", July 25, ANKASAM, https://www.ankasam.org/the-i2u2-alliance-in-west-asia-a-new-quad/?lang=en

Thaliyakkattil, S. (2019). *China's Achilles' Heel: The Belt and Road Initiative and Its Indian Discontents*. Palgrave Macmillan. DOI: 10.1007/978-981-13-8425-7

U.S. Defence Secretary. (2023) AUKUS: The Trilateral Security Partnership Between Australia, U.K. and U.S., September 12, https://www.defense.gov/Spotlights/AUKUS/

Wagner, C. (2005) From Hard Power to Soft Power? Ideas, Interaction, Institutions, and Images in India's South Asia Policy, Heidelber Papers in South Asian and Comparative Politics. Working Paper No. 26.

Wagner, C. (2016). The Role of India and China in South Asia. *Strategic Analysis*, *40*(4), 307–320. DOI: 10.1080/09700161.2016.1184790

Waltz, K. N. (2014). Anarchic orders and balance of power. In Elman, C., & Jensen, M. A. (Eds.), *Realism Reader* (pp. 104–123). Routledge.

World Population Review. (2024) world population by country 2024, https://worldpopulationreview.com/countries/by-gdp

Zhao, M. (2024). The belt & road initiative and U.S.-China competition over the global South. *China Economic Journal*, *17*(2), 166–181. DOI: 10.1080/17538963.2024.2344270

Zhou, W., & Esteban, M. (2018). Beyond Balancing: China's approach towards the Belt and Road Initiative. *Journal of Contemporary China*, *27*(112), 487–501. DOI: 10.1080/10670564.2018.1433476

Zou, L., Shen, J. H., Zhang, J., & Lee, C. C. (2021). What is the rationale behind China's infrastructure investment under the Belt and Road Initiative. *Journal of Economic Surveys*, *36*(3), 605–633. DOI: 10.1111/joes.12427

Chapter 5
India's Policies in the South China Sea

Şeyma Kızılay
Bursa Uludag University, Turkey

ABSTRACT

This study analyzes India's position in South China Sea policies. The policies followed by New Delhi are examined within the framework of the question of which actors defend which theses in the conflicts in the region. As a rising actor that creates significant impact in its own geography, India also plays a policy-determining role in the South China Sea issues with the relations it has developed with various countries. On this basis, India's steps are especially important for the strategic interests of China, with which it is in competition. The South China Sea (SCS) dispute has become an issue in which other actors in the region have been involved in recent years. Territorial conflicts and disputes over maritime jurisdictions are increasing tensions among Vietnam, the Philippines, Taiwan, Malaysia and Brunei, and China. The aforementioned countries claim that China is trying to increase its sovereign territory and Exclusive Economic Zones (EEZ) through various activities.

INTRODUCTION

The South China Sea (SCS) dispute has become an issue in which other actors in the region have been involved in recent years. Territorial conflicts and disputes over maritime jurisdictions are increasing tensions among Vietnam, the Philippines, Taiwan, Malaysia and Brunei, and China. The aforementioned countries claim that China is trying to increase its sovereign territory and Exclusive Economic Zones

DOI: 10.4018/979-8-3693-8109-0.ch005

(EEZ) through various activities. Issues that cause problems between coastal countries are shaped within the framework of territorial waters, territorial affiliation and EEZ.

The development that caused the issue to escalate was China's nine-line map move in 2009. Beijing had claimed dominance in the area within the nine lines of the United Nations (UN). This map borders the riparian countries. Moreover, the area affects not only the riparian countries, but also the countries in the region that use this area for commercial activities and need its geopolitical influence. However, China's claims of dominance over the region are not new. One of the issues of regional competition during World War I was actually the SCS region. China, which has a deep-rooted history, bases its claims of dominance over the region on the period of the Chinese empire. The SCS dispute arose when the Philippines, Vietnam and Malaysia claimed rights in the region in the 1970s. Since this date, the issue has remained a conflict between regional actors until today. However, in recent years there have been developments that will cause the problem to escalate.

Riparian countries, disturbed by China's ongoing activities and recent steps, and regional countries negatively affected by these activities are also developing moves against Beijing's activities. Although the problem has a historical background, it has become more prominent in recent years due to China's increasing activities in this field and the involvement of different countries in the issue. A more complex equation has recently emerged with the policies followed by other states in the region. The shift of attention to Asia in global politics also brought the disputes in the SCS to the fore. In this equation, India's position as a rising actor in the region and international politics is also quite critical. Based on this, this study examines India's position on the SCS disputes and its policies towards the issue.

WHO IS ON WHICH SIDE IN THE SCS DISPUTES?

While the territorial disputes in the SCS were an issue between the countries of the region, they have gradually taken on an expanding perspective. The escalation of tension over the sovereignty of the Spratly and Paracel Islands deeply affects the balances in the region. One of the factors affecting the escalation of the conflict, from which no country has backed down, is that the SCS is a strategic shipping route. Its contribution to world trade is the primary point that attracts the attention of states. One third of the transportation in global trade is provided from here (Magramo, 2023). However, areas with rich natural resources and fishing grounds, such as the Spratly Islands, also attract the attention of countries (Center for Preventive Action, 2024). According to US Energy Information Agency estimates, there are approximately 190 trillion cubic feet (TCF) of natural gas and 11 billion barrels of proven and probable oil reserves in the SCS (Sunariyanto and Hanan).

China, Vietnam and the Philippines stand out as the parties to the problem in the region. Especially in recent years, there have been serious conflicts among these three countries (China-Philippines and China-Vietnam). There have been various naval conflicts between the parties over the Spratly and Paracel Islands from past to present. They also followed methods aimed at undermining each other's influence in the region through mutual moves. For example, in 2023, the Philippines allegedly used lasers to negatively affect the vision of Chinese ship crews. There are also claims that China is trying to block the way of Filipinos with various maneuvers (BBC, 2023). In response to the Philippines' claim, the Spokesperson of the Chinese Ministry of Foreign Affairs stated in his statement that the Philippine ship entered Chinese waters without permission and that the Chinese Coast Guard responded "in a professional and measured manner". It is noteworthy that there is no mention of laser in the statement. Another development regarding the incident is that the Philippine Department of Foreign Affairs sent a diplomatic protest to the Chinese embassy in Manila (Guzman, 2023). This incident, which is the latest example of increasing tension in the region, is not the first. Various incidents have occurred between the parties in the region before. For example, the claim that two Vietnamese reconnaissance operations were sabotaged by China in 2012 is one of them (BBC, 2023). This incident, which caused anti-China protests, is also important in terms of revealing what issues related to the SCS may lead to. Therefore, it is understood that each development in the region deepens the disagreements and may cause serious consequences.

The escalation of tensions between China and Vietnam and especially the Philippines has the potential to have a global impact. As a matter of fact, 2023 was a period in which tensions increased the most and diplomatic conflicts occurred in the region. The involvement of regional and global actors who will support or oppose the parties in a possible escalation may also ignite a large-scale conflict.

Countries are divided into three regarding the SCS issue. In particular, the 2016 arbitration decision led the countries to choose sides between China and the Philippines. The first category includes actors who support the Philippines' position and oppose China. Japan comes first. The second category consists of countries that support China. Here there are Pakistan, Cambodia and some African countries. In the third group, there are actors who are in favor of solving the problem through peace negotiations. In addition to this positioning, the main factor affecting the attitude of countries is the dilemma created by China's economic power and support and the military power and support of the United States (US) (Wen and Xiaochen, 2016).

INDIA'S PERSPECTIVE ON THE SCS ISSUE

As a rising power in Asia, India acts with the aim of playing a decisive role in the overall order. It also seeks strategic autonomy in international politics. Countries that aim to be rule-makers rather than rule-abiders in the international system are pursuing strategic autonomy. India is one of these countries, especially in search of autonomy against US hegemony (Kaya 2024). However, it basically pursues a policy of balance in world politics. On the one hand, it is careful to maintain its relations with the US and European countries, and on the other hand, it is trying to increase its influence in the Asian geography. In line with this purpose, it strives to improve its dialogue with the countries in the region. BRICS and QUAD memberships also show that it is trying to achieve balance by taking part in various platforms. In addition to corporate commitments, it also takes steps towards its goal of becoming a rising power in the region.

Regarding the SCS, it followed an economically focused strategy, especially within the framework of the Act East Policy. Act East Policy is a diplomatic initiative that aims to promote economic, strategic and cultural relations at different levels in the Asia-Pacific geography in general. In this context, the method of strengthening ties with Southeast Asian countries is followed. It is also used as a counterbalance to China's regional influence and strategic control. It has deepened its relationship with the region in order to strengthen regional economic integration (Pant and Basu, 2023). In this context, India has followed a development strategy with the economic reforms it has adopted, has turned to multi-dimensional foreign relations, and the Act East Policy has become a tool used in the fight against regional challenges. Within the scope of this policy, India has developed a method around three basic headings. These are elaborate institutional mechanisms; economic interests including infrastructure development and connectivity; and common strategic interests (Debates, 2020). The strategy of being active in the SCS region and strengthening its ties with other actors is based on these three pillars.

India is not one of the main actors in the region and does not have a coastline on the SCS. However, it benefits from the strategic route feature of the region. On this basis, it pays attention to the protection of rule-based order and freedom of navigation in maritime communication routes (Saha, 2021). The importance of the region for India can be explained as follows: The SCS waterways are the second most used waterways in the world. This region is used for trade worth approximately 200 billion dollars every year. 55% of India's trade with the Indo-Pacific region takes place via the SCS waterway (via the Strait of Malacca) (Keck, 2014). Therefore, the region is of great importance for New Delhi. It also has a strategic role in strengthening India's ties with Southeast Asia and increasing its regional growth (Saha, 2021).

Another important point is the Andaman and Nicobar Islands, located at the entrance to the Strait of Malacca. There are possibilities that these two areas will become a power struggle area between India and China within the scope of the SCS. These islands have the potential to become a new point of conflict in the maritime competition between the two countries. China is taking various steps to prevent India's activities towards the Andaman and Nicobar Islands. One of these is its efforts to prevent India from using the islands strategically by expanding its submarine fleet (Joshi 2019). China's activities in this area also disturb India. Because this area, especially the Andaman, provides India with military and strategic power. It also provides a passage from the Eastern Indian Ocean to the Pacific Ocean. Therefore, gaining dominance and influence around the Andaman means also exerting influence over Malacca. This triggers the struggle between New Delhi and Beijing (Joshi 2019).

India is also taking initiatives to increase its influence in the Andaman and surrounding areas. Its policy towards the region is developing to balance China's activities. In addition, New Delhi wants to strengthen its control over the islands and deepen its position in the Asia-Pacific region. India has a special Andaman and Nicobar Command unit that increases its military capacity on the islands. New Delhi has also announced a project for the islands. The project aims to transform the Andaman and Nicobar Islands into a shipping and tourism center (Sharma 2024). All of these demonstrate the importance India attaches to these islands and indicate that this area will be one of the main areas of competition for maritime dominance in Asia in the coming years.

India's policy and attitude towards the SCS disputes are generally based on a strategy of maintaining balance. New Delhi's policy was clearly stated in the The Association of Southeast Asian Nations (ASEAN)-India joint Vision Statement that emerged in 2012. According to the declaration, India promotes maritime cooperation to overcome disputes and challenges in maritime matters (Jawli, 2016: 89). In addition, New Delhi has always stated that it is in favor of ensuring freedom of navigation and flight in the region. Today, it emphasizes that the SCS is a global common area. It also states that all disputes should be handled and resolved within the framework of international law, in a way that does not harm the legitimate interests of any of the parties (Saha, 2021). With this attitude, it seems that she is pursuing a more active policy today than before. This change in New Delhi's attitude is a reflection of its economic goals, energy needs and military strategies that have grown over the years. Like other countries, India also has strategic interests in the region. At the same time, ensuring freedom of navigation is deemed necessary within the scope of commercial activities and energy needs. Therefore, every development in the field in question has started to play a decisive role in terms of India's basic needs and interests over time.

KEY FACTORS IN NEW DELHI'S SCS POLICIES

New Delhi aims to maintain balance in all equations within the framework of its relations with China, partnerships with the US and the aim of preserving its strategic autonomy. Its stance on the SCS issue is also generally neutral. In addition, its policy towards the issue is shaped in line with the three basic strategies and balance policy goals mentioned. However, in recent years, claims have emerged that New Delhi's neutral attitude has begun to change. Issues such as border tensions with China, close cooperation policy with the Philippines, global competition dynamics and India's strategy to stand out and play a decisive role in the region are effective in this regard. Therefore, there are multiple dynamics in its policy towards the SCS. Based on this, the main factors shaping India's SCS policies can be listed as follows:

Relations and disputes with China: Sino-Indian relations have different dynamics but are based on competition at the regional level. In particular, the issue of border disputes comes to the fore between the two countries at various times and increases tension. The foreign policy steps of the parties are also affected by these tensions. There are even hot conflicts. Activities at the border have increased in 2020 and beyond. Both countries intimidate each other and show power, sometimes through military exercises and sometimes through military cooperation (Kızılay, 2023).

Indian and Chinese troops faced each other in the Galwan Valley in the summer of 2020 and a conflict broke out between them. In December 2022, China launched an attack on the Aranuchal Pradesh region (Chellaney, 2023). Aranuchal Pradesh is the border state of India and has strategic importance. Such initiatives also affect New Delhi's other strategies and policies. As tensions escalated, New Delhi turned to a more active and vocal strategy. The statement made by External Affairs Minister Subrahmanyam Jaishankar of India at the 15th East Asia Summit in 2020 is an indication that the attitude towards China and SCS policies will work differently. Jaishankar said; "China's actions and events in the SCS have shaken confidence in ongoing negotiations on proposed rules of conduct in the region" (Saha, 2021). This shows that the policies followed will not be pro-China. The tensions with China are also reflected in its SCS policy and relations with the countries in the region (Saha, 2021). Especially his stance against the 2016 arbitration decision strengthens thoughts in this direction.

On the other hand, conflicts such as Galwan Valley clashes and Arunachal Pradesh attacks on the China-India border cause New Delhi to turn to methods that will further pressure Beijing. In this context, India can be expected to follow a two-dimensional strategy. The first of these is to increase defense elements and military capacity. India's military modernization moves have accelerated especially after 2014. Improving military qualities not only provides regional deterrence for India, but also serves its global rise. Strengthening military capacity does not only aim to pressure China on border issues. It can also be used as a tool to restrict China's influence in relations with various countries. This constitutes the second dimension of the strategy to improve military qualifications. Accordingly, India can use the development it will gain as a result of military modernization to improve its relations with countries with which China has problems within the scope of SCS. This means, in the long run, that the bloc against China in the region, especially in the SCS issues, will strengthen militarily and act more boldly in taking various steps. India's border conflicts with China and its moves to develop its military capacity may have an impact that will shape the regional security equation in the long term, in order to make China lose influence.

There is distrust between India and China regarding respect for territorial integrity and sovereignty. After the recent clashes in the Galwan Valley, India sent a warship to the SCS (India Times, 2020). This is important as it shows that China can exert influence in the area of control. Its further involvement in the SCS can also be seen as a trump card against China. Thus, India both gives a message to China and instrumentalizes it as a counterbalance to influence and limit China's Indian Ocean activities. Its recent increased interest in the SCS problems also shows that it will continue to use this card. Therefore, it seems that the India-China competition will not be limited to border problems. It can be predicted that maritime competition will come to the fore in the future. Because creating more influence and gaining influence in South Asia is of strategic importance for India in terms of reaching world markets through global maritime routes.

Strong relations with the Philippines: The Philippines is a development and security partner for India in South Asia. The rapprochement in India-Philippine relations has increased since 2014 against China's increasing regional demands. In this context, New Delhi displays an attitude that supports the Philippines' position in the SCS. The increasing rapprochement in recent years is an indication that a common attitude and policy will be followed in the region. High-level visits between the two countries strengthen cooperation and partnerships. Minister of National Defense Delfin Negrillo Lorenzana visited India with a delegation of five people between 8-11 March 2018. This is vital to bilateral relations as it is the first bilateral defense minister-level visit from the Philippines to India (Saha, 2021). In 2023, Philippine Secretary of Foreign Affairs Enrique A. Manalo paid an official visit to India. Various agreements were made to deepen India-Philippines relations. The areas of cooperation include many areas such as maritime, trade-investment, law enforcement, development cooperation (Ministry of External Affairs Government of India, 2023). In addition, in the joint statement made between New Delhi and Manila in 2023, China was called to comply with the rules-based maritime order and accept the decision of the International Court of Justice in favor of Manila in 2016 (Pant and Basu, 2024).

In March 2024, Indian External Affairs Minister Jaishankar, in his statement during his visit to Manila, expressed India's full support to the Philippines in protecting its national sovereignty (Haidar, 2023). Also in April 2024, India delivered the strategic BrahMos cruise missile and declared its full support for the protection of the national sovereignty of the Philippines. In addition to their partnership in various fields, the two countries also display a common stance within the scope of SCS policies. It is understood that relations will continue to grow stronger in the coming years.

Cooperation with regional actors: India is taking steps to improve its relations and cooperation not only with the Philippines but also with other countries in the region. For example, New Delhi provided a 100 billion loan to Vietnam to supply high-speed patrol boats. There is also a sale of strategic parts of the Indian navy between the parties. Vietnam has made efforts to purchase India's warship INS Kirpan in 2023 (Singh, 2023). Military cooperation with Vietnam dates back to the past. In 2016, India and Vietnam upgraded their relations to the level of "comprehensive strategic partnership". Seven agreements were signed during the virtual meeting between Prime Minister Modi and his Vietnamese counterpart Nguyen Xuan Phuc in December 2020. One of these included regulations on the implementation of regulations on defense industry cooperation, and the other included nuclear cooperation between the Indian Atomic Energy Regulatory Board and the Vietnam Radiation and Nuclear Safety Agency (Saha, 2021).

Trade and energy-based relations between the two countries also have an increasing momentum. Historical and cultural ties from the past and geographical proximity also have a great impact on the development of relations. In the past, India supported Vietnam's independence from France and also opposed US intervention. In addition, deep ties are established in the fields of green economy, circular economy, digital transformation, software and energy. It is expected that dialogue in these areas will be increased in the future. Indian investments in Vietnam are quite remarkable. For example, Adani, one of India's leading companies, stated that it wants to invest in thermal power plants in Vietnam and take part in both renewable energy and thermal energy projects in the country (Hanoi Times, 2023).

Partnerships in the field of defense are also on the rise. In 2015, a five-year cooperation commitment was made in the fields of defense trade and education (Pant, 2018). Various steps are being taken on the basis of this common vision statement. For example, in 2017, Vietnam announced that it purchased BrahMos anti-ship missiles from India (Bisht, 2023). There is also naval cooperation between the two. The two countries are cooperating in security to "increase coast security and prevent illegal activities." Joint naval exercises are also one of the key parameters of Vietnam-India defense cooperation (Sang, 2022).

India is also developing its relations with the countries involved in the problem within the scope of ASEAN. The SCS is a major and essential maritime corridor for trade and shipping. India also wants to be more active in the region and tries to establish closer ties with ASEAN countries (Villaruel, 2015).

ASEAN is central to India in implementing its Indo-Pacific strategies and vision. ASEAN countries are also trying to increase cooperation with India in order to balance China. On the other hand, ASEAN countries do not have a common stance on the SCS dispute. A common policy is not followed against China and its practices. While some member countries greet Chinese policies with silence, some countries do not directly participate in the conflict and act cautiously in line with their economic interests. India is also developing its relations in this context. For example, in 2011, it signed an agreement with Vietnam to expand and encourage oil exploration in the SCS. Offshore energy projects between the two countries date back to the 1980s (Sang, 2022: 137). Over time, the importance of Vietnam in Indian foreign policy has also increased. Vietnam is a valuable partner for India in security partnership. The two countries have common interests in a safe and stable South Asia. Vietnam also pays attention to its relations with India in accordance with its policy of establishing safe and multidimensional ties.

Vietnam has also served as a bridge in India's relations with other regional countries and ASEAN. New Delhi also sees Hanoi as one of the key actors in implementing regional policies, providing security cooperation and increasing its influence (Sang, 2022: 133). Moreover, Vietnam is one of the countries that have a territorial dispute with China. SCS developments are also among the security dynamics between New Delhi and Hanoi. A comprehensive strategic partnership was signed between the two in 2016. The main driving factor of this partnership is defense and security (Sundaram, 2024). Vietnam also focuses on the security of the SCS and resolving issues in accordance with international law. India supports this policy of Vietnam. Hanoi is also pleased with New Delhi's presence in the SCS (Krishnan and Boudreau, 2014).

In this context, the two countries are strengthening ties in security-defense, diplomatic support and energy cooperation. In April 2024, two Indian Navy ships made a port visit to Vietnam (Singh, 2024). The India-Vietnam Maritime Dialogue meetings held regularly by the two countries also create a suitable atmosphere for discussing regional policies and establishing new partnerships.

On the other hand, Malaysia and Brunei, which are official plaintiffs against China, also have strategic value for New Delhi. These countries may play a greater role in India's eastern policy in the future. It is likely that new alliances and partnerships will come to the fore to make deep strategic moves in the region. For example, in its relations with Kuala Lumpur, India maintains a stable and cooperative dynamic in terms of political, economic, military and defense unity. Deepening the connection with Malaysia is among the critical strategies followed by New Delhi in consolidating its Indo-Pacific policies and influence in the region. Developing relations have risen to the level of strategic partnership over time. By 2023, this partnership has deepened to include the fields of politics, diplomacy and strategic defense (Bonesh, 2024).

In addition, these countries' relations with China and their regional problems shape India's regional policies. In particular, their strategies regarding the SCS issues have an effect on increasing their ties with India. For example, Malaysia, which has had close relations with India for many years, has been following a policy in line with New Delhi regarding the SCS in recent years. In addition, Malaysia's energy policy enables it to stand against China and alongside India in its SCS strategies. This attitude has become clearer in recent years. In 2023, Malaysia sided with India by rejecting China's map claiming maritime areas near the island of Borneo (South China Morning Post, 2023). Borneo is a strategic region for Malaysia. Oil and natural gas extracted from industrial drilling wells constitute one of the most important items of the country's economy. In addition, Malaysia, which wants to operate further in search of resources, is confronted by Chinese forces (Tan, 2024). Therefore, Malaysia is positioned opposite Beijing on the SCS issue. This is also a factor that brings rapprochement in India-Malaysia relations. Additionally, Malaysia does not recognize China's SCS claims.

Aim to play a decisive role in regional and global politics: India, as a rising power in Asia, wants to be a decisive actor in global politics. For this purpose, it follows a strategy of increasing its influence by developing its relations. Therefore, it has turned its passive and cautious stance on regional issues in the past into a more active dimension. For example, at the ASEAN Regional Forum Summit held in Phnom Penh in 2012, New Delhi emphasized strong support for freedom of navigation and access to resources such as fisheries and gas, in accordance with the principles of international law. In 2014, it issued a joint statement with Vietnam, calling on all relevant parties in the SCS to act with restraint, avoid threats or use of force, and resolve disputes by peaceful means (Villaruel, 2015).

However, in addition to India's aim to play a decisive role, its energy policy also directs its SCS strategies. India is the fourth largest energy consumer in the world. Therefore, it is seriously dependent on energy imports. The great need for energy also pushes India to develop cooperation with countries such as Vietnam. This cooperation is also reflected in SCS policies and India's aim to gain regional influence. For example, India accepted Vietnam's invitation to explore for oil and gas in disputed waters in the SCS in 2011. Thus, India's energy policy and its SCS moves intersect. This makes India an effective actor in regional conflict (Villaruel, 2015).

Seeking strategic autonomy in global politics, India takes a more active and independent stance in regional and global issues. In addition, preventing the tension in the region from being reflected in the Indian Ocean is among India's main goals. The Indian Ocean is New Delhi's core area of interest and influence. The reflection of tensions and conflicts in this area poses a threat to India's regional sphere of influence. Therefore, being indirectly involved in solving the problems is crucial for New Delhi to maintain its regional dominance. The intensity and complexity of international issues also provide a favorable environment for India to pursue various policies. India has been increasing its military, political and diplomatic effectiveness with the strategic ties it has established in recent years and its developing economic preferences.

The multidimensional relationships it has established, its international corporate activities and its active role in various platforms also serve New Delhi's goals of increasing its global and regional influence and protecting its interests. Every change in the geopolitics of South Asia has strategic value for India, which sees this region as its core sphere of influence. Its interest in the region is based on its strategic interests, the desire to protect freedom of navigation, and the need for energy (Peng, 2023). Within the scope of these three basic goals, India is involved in the SCS issues and tries to keep the spread of tensions at a controllable level. In addition, it displays a will to be in a position to direct events in the struggle for regional dominance or to shape events through various partnerships.

CONCLUSION: THE FUTURE OF INDIA'S SCS POLICIES

India has generally followed a cautious policy towards SCS issues. The main reason for this attitude is that it does not want to be a party to regional disputes. In addition, New Delhi avoids getting involved in issues that do not directly affect its interests or concern itself. However, in recent years, the intense interest in Asia and the escalation of the SCS issue have reached a level that affects New Delhi's interests and dominance in the Indian Ocean region. This has led India to pursue a more active policy. However, it also maintains a balanced attitude towards China. Because India's interest and intervention in the developments in this field may pave the way for China to engage in activities against India's interests in the Indian Ocean. The SCS strategy may also be shaped, especially regarding the protection of strategic targets in the Andaman Sea (Singh, 2023). Because, for India, protecting its core interests is a more priority issue. However, as has been seen obviously recently, India is trying to balance China while also putting pressure on Beijing. Related to this, it has a greater presence in the SCS disputes. In this context, India is instrumentalizing the SCS issues in order to break the power of China, with which it has border problems. It can be predicted that he will continue to use this strategy in the future.

In addition, its relations with the countries that are parties to the problem are improving and it is making moves to pressure China. In this context, it is likely that China will take steps to increase this pressure on China in the future. Increasing the closeness established especially with ASEAN countries may be one of the prominent policies in this sense. Increasing dialogue, especially in the economic and military-defense fields, can provide regional actors with a basis to be in a stronger position against China. Towards this goal, steps can be taken to deepen strategic cooperation with countries that are coastal to India or have interests in the region. In terms of regional security balances, such partnerships may also create tension-escalating effects. However, this will mean further internationalization of SCS issues (Peng, 2023).

The emerging Asian struggle has led India to a strategy of strengthening its multi-dimensional and multi-actor relations regionally and globally. However, Beijing is a compelling factor for New Delhi and its regional goals. It can be said that India will strengthen its regional connections and participate more in SCS problems in line with the aim of limiting China and protecting strategic interests. The deepening of its partnership with the countries party to the problem, especially the Philippines and Vietnam, confirms this. Protecting its interests in the region also depends on the sustainability of this strategy. The partnerships it has established, especially with actors in direct conflict with China, such as Vietnam and the Philippines, are of great importance in terms of creating a force against China gaining ground.

REFERENCES

BBC. (July 7, 2023). What is the South China Sea dispute? https://www.bbc.com/news/world-asia-pacific-13748349

Bisht, I. S. (2023). Vietnam Negotiating BrahMos Missile Purchase With India: Report, The Defense Post, https://www.thedefensepost.com/2023/06/14/vietnam-brahmos-missile-india/#google_vignette

Bonesh, F. R. (2024). India-Malaysia Economic Partnership: Challenges, Prospects, and Strategic Collaborations, *India Briefing*, https://www.india-briefing.com/news/india-malaysia-economic-partnership-challenges-prospects-and-strategic-collaborations-30687.html/

Center for Preventive Action. (May, 2024). Territorial Disputes in South China Sea, *CFR*, https://www.cfr.org/global-conflict-tracker/conflict/territorial-disputes-south-china-sea

Chellaney, B. (2023). The Sino-Indian Rivalry is Reshaping Asia, *Project Syndicate*, https://www.project-syndicate.org/commentary/china-cannot-win-india-himalayan-border-dispute-by-brahma-chellaney-2023-04

Debates, R. (2020). India's 'Act East' Policy and Regional Cooperation, *Observer Research Foundation (ORF)*, https://www.orfonline.org/expert-speak/indias-act-east-policy-and-regional-cooperation-61375

Donnellon-May, G. (2023). India and China's rivalry is reshaping South Asia, *ASPI The Strategist*, https://www.aspistrategist.org.au/india-and-chinas-rivalry-is-reshaping-south-asia/

Guzman, C. (2023). Philippines Coast Guard Accuses China of Blinding Crew With 'Military-Grade' Laser, *Time*, https://time.com/6255012/philippines-laser-south-china-sea-tensions-escalate/

Haidar, S. (2023). India supports Philippines' sovereignty, says Jaishankar, sparking response from China, *The Hindu*, https://www.thehindu.com/news/national/india-supports-philippines-in-upholding-its-national-sovereignty-eam-jaishankar/article67993485.ece

India Times. (August 30, 2020). Post-Galwan clash, Indian Navy quietly deployed warship in South China Sea. *Indian Times*, https://timesofindia.indiatimes.com/articleshow/77834259.cms?utm_source=contentofinterest&utm_medium=text&utm_campaign=cppst

Jawli, N. (2016). South China Sea and India's Geopolitical Interests. *Indian Journal of Asian Affairs*, *29*(1/2), 85–100.

Joshi, Y. (2019). China and India's maritime rivalry has a new flashpoint: the Andaman Sea, *South China Morning Post*, https://www.scmp.com/week-asia/opinion/article/3042032/china-and-indias-maritime-rivalry-has-new-flashpoint-andaman-sea

Kaya, E. (2024). ABD Hegemonyasına Karşı Orta Ölçekli Güçlerin Stratejik Özerklik Arayışı, *Gumushane University. The Social Science Journal*, *15*(1), 220–236.

Keck, Z. (2014). India Wades Into South China Sea Dispute, *The Diplomat,*https://thediplomat.com/2014/03/india-wades-into-south-china-sea-dispute/

Kızılay, Ş. (2023). A Possible Scenario for 2023 India: Opportunities and Challenges, *ANKASAM,*https://www.ankasam.org/a-possible-scenario-for-2023-india-opportunities-and-challenges/?lang=en

Krishnan, U., & Boudreau, J. (2014). Vietnam Seeks India Role in China Sea as Dung Meets Modi, *BBC,*https://www.bloomberg.com/news/articles/2014-10-28/vietnam-seeks-india-role-in-china-sea-spat-as-dung-meets-modi

Magramo, K. (2023) Tensions are flaring once more in the South China Sea. Here's why it matters for the world, *CNN,*https://edition.cnn.com/2023/09/29/asia/south-china-sea-tensions-philippines-china-us-explainer-intl-hnk/index.html

Ministry of External Affairs Government of India. Joint Statement on the 5th India-Philippines Joint Commission on Bilateral Cooperation, Ministry of External Affairs Government of India, https://www.mea.gov.in/bilateral-documents.htm?dtl/36743/Joint+Statement+on+the+5th+IndiaPhilippines+Joint+Commission+on+Bilateral+Cooperation

Pant, H. V. (2018). India and Vietnam: A "Strategic Partnership" in the Making, *RSIS*, https://www.rsis.edu.sg/wp-content/uploads/2018/04/PB180409_-India-and-Vietnam.pdf

Pant, H. V., & Basu, P. (2024). India's nuanced approach in the South China Sea, *The Hindu*, https://www.thehindu.com/opinion/op-ed/indias-nuanced-approach-in-the-south-china-sea/article68080577.ece

Peng, N. (2023). India's Growing Involvement in the South China Sea Disputes, *The Diplomat,*https://thediplomat.com/2023/11/indias-growing-involvement-in-the-south-china-sea-disputes/

Saha, P. (2021). India Calibrates its South China Sea Approach, *Observer Research Foundation (ORF)*, https://www.orfonline.org/research/india-calibrates-its-south-china-sea-approach

Sang, H. T. (2022). The Growing Importance of Vietnam to India's South China Sea Policy, *Journal of Indo-Pacific Affairs*, 133-150.

Sharma, R. (2024). India's Plan To Develop "China Chokepoint" At Strategic Andaman & Nicobar Islands, In The Eye Of Storm, *Eurasian Times*, https://www.eurasiantimes.com/indias-plan-to-develop-china-chokepoint-at-strategic-andaman-nicobar-islands-in-the-eye-of-storm/

Singh, A. (2023). Despite the excitement, India's South China Sea policy remains unchanged, https://www.lowyinstitute.org/the-interpreter/despite-excitement-india-s-south-china-sea-policy-remains-unchanged

Singh, M. (2024). India, Vietnam deepen defense partnership to confront regional challenges, *Indo-Pasific Defence Forum*, https://ipdefenseforum.com/2024/04/india-vietnam-deepen-defense-partnership-to-confront-regional-challenges/

South China Morning Post (SCMP). (August, 2023). South China Sea: Malaysia joins India in rejecting new Chinese map over land claim ahead of G20 summit, *SCMP*,https://www.scmp.com/news/asia/southeast-asia/article/3232887/south-china-sea-malaysia-joins-india-rejecting-new-chinese-map-over-land-claim-ahead-g20-summit

Sunariyanto, B. P., & Hanan, A. (2022). The Importance of the South China Sea Energy Perspective. *Purnomo Yusgiantoro Center (PYC)*,https://www.purnomoyusgiantorocenter.org/the-importance-of-the-south-china-sea-energy-perspective/

Sundaram, R. (2024). China Factor in India-Vietnam Strategic Relations, *India Defence Review*, https://www.indiandefencereview.com/news/china-factor-in-india-vietnam-strategic-relations/

Tan, R. (2024). Malaysia's appetite for oil and gas puts it on collision course with China, *The Washington Post*,https://www.washingtonpost.com/world/2024/05/11/china-malaysia-south-china-sea/

Villaruel, J. J. C. (2015). India's Interests in the South China Sea, *Center for International RElations & Strategic Studies (CIRSS), Vol 2 No. 8*, https://fsi.gov.ph/indias-interests-in-the-south-china-sea-by-jemimah-joanne-c-villaruel-vol-ii-no-8-march-2015/

Wen, W., & Xiaochen, C. (2016). Who Supports China in the South China Sea and Why, *The Diplomat,*https://thediplomat.com/2016/07/who-supports-china-in-the-south-china-sea-and-why/

Chapter 6
Malaysia's South China Sea Policy: The Role of Small States in Peacebuilding?

Halil Deligöz
https://orcid.org/0000-0003-0878-9299
Independent Researcher, Turkey

ABSTRACT

This chapter analyzes Malaysia's orientations within the context of strategic competition, mainly between the US and China. Since the Cold War, Malaysia has been mindful of the negative repercussions of power competition in Southeast Asia and has consistently insisted on maintaining strategic independence from this rivalry. Therefore, Malaysia often seeks to de-escalate tensions in the South China Sea and prioritizes peaceful solutions. Instead of playing a role in drawing larger alliance partners into conflict, Malaysia exemplifies the opposite: the role of an asymmetrically smaller state in alleviating regional tensions, particularly by maintaining a strategic distance from the main rival states, even though its room for maneuver is limited.

INTRODUCTION

The South China Sea (SCS) has held strategic importance for both littoral and non-littoral states throughout history, serving as a key route for major sea lanes of communication (SLOCs). Today, it remains significant due to its hydrocarbon resources, fisheries, and deposits of minerals and rare earth elements. It is also situated in a geography that has become a hotspot due to strategic competition between

DOI: 10.4018/979-8-3693-8109-0.ch006

the US and China, garnering the interest of forces for navigational, defense, and balancing reasons in this rivalry (Wu, 2013, p. 7).

This chapter aims to summarize the Malaysian policy, role and conflict resolution approach within the SCS dispute context. Ministry of Foreign Affairs of Malaysia reiterated in April 2023 that "Malaysia is unequivocally and firmly committed to protecting Malaysia's sovereignty, sovereign rights and interests in its maritime areas in the South China Sea, as depicted by our 1979 Map" (MOFAM, 2023). The Ministry also clarified the country's conflict resolution approach to the matter: "Malaysia firmly holds the view that matters relating to the South China Sea must be resolved peacefully and constructively, in accordance with the universally recognised principles of international law, including the 1982 United Nations Convention on the Law of the Sea (1982 UNCLOS)" (MOFAM, 2023).

The SCS has become an important domain in the strategic competition between the US and China. In this contingency, how the regional countries and Malaysia maintain their strategic autonomies without compromising their national interests becomes a daunting strategic task. Malaysia's Defence White Paper underlines that "non-alignment and shared security are the basis of Malaysia's credible partnerships" (Malaysian Ministry of Defence, 2020, p. 4). As C.C. Kuik argues, Malaysia's non-alignment is a contextual choice that emerged from the late 1960s. Malaysia had formed an alliance with the UK after its independence in 1957 especially to confront the communist threat. However, the UK's declaration in 1968 that it wouldn't honour its commitments "east of Suez", the 1969 "Nixon Doctrine" (also known as Guam Doctrine) signalling that the US would withdraw its soldiers from the Asia, and eventually the Nixon-Mao rapprochement led to the regional countries to change their hitherto alignment with the West. The policy adjustments that scholars call "hedging" emerged within this context (Kuik, 2024, p. 44). Malaysia is a $415.57 billion economy with a 33 million population among the upper-developing countries (IMF, n.d.), and wants to maintain its peaceful development (Malaysian Ministry of Defence, 2020, p. 14). To this end, as this chapter argues, Malaysia's actions are motivated by, on one hand, hedging for insurance against potential risks in the context of the global strategic competition (See Lui & Kuik, 2021), and on the other hand, by reducing the overall risk in the region in order to refrain from potential costs and spillovers. Signalling its unwillingness to jump on one of the two rival trains is meaningful, as such a stance potentially messages disapproval of belligerency and slows down the process of war preparations in a variety of ways, such as slowing alignment formation and reducing the likelihood of flash points. In other words, Malaysia follows a strategy beyond hedging or "hedging plus" to protect its strategic autonomy and maintain peace in the region (He & Feng, 2023, p. 46).

In history, peoples of the region interacted in times of peace and disputes. In the bright 14th and 15th centuries, the Malay Peninsula was a destination of people, including "merchants of Cairo, Mecca, Aden, Abyssinia, Kalwa, Malindi, Hormuz, Persia, Rum, Turks, Christians of Armenia, Dable, Goa, Malabar Coast, Keeling, Oresia, Ceylon, Bengal, Arakan, Peugeot, Siam, Industrious, Malaya, Pahang, Pattani, Kampaya, Cochin, China, Bruno" (Al-Aboudi, 2021, p. 506). The traders used to find shelter in the Malacca Sultanate during the monsoon periods before heading towards their destinations. The fact that about 84 languages were spoken then in Malacca is a good indication of a sophisticated commercial center (Abdullah, 2013). Meanwhile, a common trade and socio-cultural environment existed in the region as exemplified in Malacca sultan Sultan Mansur Shah's marriage with a Chinese princess Hang Liu (Hang Li Po) and the development of a Chinese-Malaysian community called *Peranakan Chinese*[1] (Abdullah, 2013, p. 143 & 146). Before colonial times, China was occasionally called upon to assume the role of hegemon to maintain regional order. Between the years roughly 1405 and 1435, Malacca Sultanate[2] sent about 20 messengers to the Chinese emperor (Ming Dynasty) for protection (Abdullah, 2013, p. 145). For example, in the year 1407, the King of Malacca and Sumatra, who was a Muslim, submitted a complaint about the King of Siam because of the latter's actions violating the equality among the small kingdoms under the Chinese tributary system[3] (Al-Aboudi, 2021, p. 498). Likewise, Ming Dynasty dispached Admiral Zeng "as a special envoy to the Asian countries", demonstrating China's recognition of its role. Thus, Malacca's position as an important commercial hub was recogized by Admiral Zeng, providing the city with a leverage against Siam's hostilities (Abdullah, 2013, p. 145).

With the decline of the science and technology in the dynastic Chinese and the rise of the West in the global scene after the geographical explorations and the First Industrial Revolution, the region was colonized by the Western powers, and thus, China's order-imposing influence vanished. In particular, the defeat of the First Opium War (1840) signified the beginning of China's "century of humiliation." Fast forward, after the victory of the Communist Revolution in 1949, China mainly focused on protecting its regime in the Cold War context, especially until the Nixon-Mao consensus in 1972. However, the nature of influence was dominated by the bloc politics and the region was very much intruded during the Cold War rivalry, as a Chinese scholar states:

> *Although the US and the Soviet Union, the two superpowers, did not occupy any features in the Nansha Islands [i.e., the Spratlys], they were involved in the disputes to different extents. The balance of power in the SCS area may directly influence the balance of power in the Asia-Pacific region and the overall international political order (Wu, 2013, p. 9).*

The article intends to contribute to the literature by tracing how Malaysia strives to reduce the overall risk in the region during the great power rivalry, rather than merely resorting to hedging focused on self-insurance based on a narrow definition of national interest. The role of small states to draw their major allies into war is a phenomenon often mentioned. However, small states' role as peacebuilders is not recognized regarding that they lack enough carrots and sticks to shape major powers' behaviors (Holsti, 1970). The Malaysian* case demonstrates that small states not only merely hedge but also feel the need to act as a peacemaker to decrease the overall tension. Malaysia's role as a small peacekeeper is inferred from the speeches, announcements, and behaviors of Malaysian politicians and institutions.

The article proceeds with the following sections: first, the strategic importance of the SCS region; second, the great power rivalry in the region and ASEAN's stance to cope with this context; third, overlapping claims in the SCS; fourth, China's approach to the SCS; fifth, Malaysia's non-confrontational approach; sixth, competing trade regimes; seventh, academic search for a regional order; and eighth, conclusion.

STRATEGIC IMPORTANCE OF THE STRAIT OF MALACCA AND SCS MARITIME AREA

The Strait of Malacca connects the Andaman Sea in the Indian Ocean and the SCS in the Pacific Ocean. Three ASEAN member countries, Malaysia, Singapore, Indonesia, and with a small area, Thailand, harbour the Strait (Britannica, 2024), which is known as "the world's busiest shipping route and therefore of great strategic importance" (Yu, 2024, p. 44). Today's Malaysian state of Malacca was historically a strategic territory for world powers. Its people, wealth and customs were lavishly described by the European travellers, who accompanied Ferdinand Magellan in his voyage to East Indies from 1519 to 1522 (see Pigafetta & Stanley, 2010, p. 111-113). Among them, Duarte Barbosa highlighted in his diaries that "He who is lord of Malacca has his hand on the throat of Venice" (Abdullah, 2013, p. 144), meaning that "who rules Malacca can control the world trade" (Al-Aboudi, 2021, p. 507). This strategic importance incentivized colonialists to control the city, the first being the Portuguese in 1511 (Malaysian Ministry of Defence, 2020, p. 17).

This is also true of today's great powers: For the US, the strait and the larger SCS region is crucial to contain China. And, for China, SCS maritime area constitutes a strategic power resource from both geopolitical and geoeconomic fronts. According to Alfred Thayer Mahan's sea power theory, who rules the ocean waters can rule the whole world. Patrolling nuclear submarines is key for China to deter the US. Moreover, the area can serve as a "buffer zone" in a military confrontation. The SCS is also particularly crucial for China regarding that it has not competitive advantage to dominate Central Asia or South Asia comparing to Russia and India, respectively, in its proximity (Nguy n et al., 2024, p. 8, 11; Khaliq, 2021). Myers contends that in hot war conditions, China's military base in Djibouti would be too remote to be useful, while a secret base reportedly under construction in Cambodia would not be adequate to defend Chinese interests beyond the SCS (Myers, 2023). From a geoeconomic perspective, China is an economy that can produce all goods and materials in the UN Industrial Classification of Economic Activities, demonstrating a high degree of self-sufficiency. Moreover, it is catching up rapidly technologically. However, its main dependence remains on access to raw materials and energy resources, and the SCS is rich in hydrocarbons (Munir & Sajjad, 2022) and is considered the "second Middle East" with "at least 11 billion barrels of oil and 190 trillion cubic feet of natural gas" according to the US Energy Information Administration estimations (Lui&Kuik, 2021, p. 285). Moreover, as Wu (2013, p. 6) notes, China depends on maritime routes for 90% of its foreign trade and "more than half of its foreign transactions by value occur via the SCS". Thus, the Malacca Strait is a gateway in China's 21st Century Maritime Silk Road, which is the maritime leg of Xi Jingping's signature project, i.e., the Belt and Road Initiative. As President Hu Jintao said in 2003, China has been concerned about the potential control of the Malacca Strait by "certain major powers". The term "Malacca Dilemma" refers to the risk of a Malacca Strait blockage by the US or other powers, cutting China's route to outside (Myers, 2023). Mutually, Western sources predict that a potential disruption of SCS trade due to, for example, potential economic coercion by China would lead to a crisis at global scale (Cordesman et al. 2019). Almost the halt of the container trade in the Red Sea during the Israel-Palestine war after October 7, 2023, reminds this. Comparing the Suez Canal, which accounts for 12% of global shipping, with the Strait of Malacca, which accounts for 60% of the global sea trade, a crisis involving the latter would have truly global impact (*Asia Financial*, 2023; Ryan, 2023).

The SCS is also of strategic importance for Malaysia. Malaysia is the third largest LNG exporter, and hydrocarbon production contributes a third of the country's GDP. Likewise, SCS's fish stock and tourism potential can be tapped only within a cooperative environment (Lui&Kuik, 2021). However, resource richness is not only regarded as a "cure" for economic development but also as a "curse", an idea, which largely emphazises the domestic dynamics to explain causes of resource-rich countries' underdevelopment (See Stevens, 2004). Beyond domestic dynamics, history also shows how resource richness invites "curse" in the form of colonization, occupation and inter-state conflicts. So, comparing the SCS area to the "Middle East" has both positive and negative connotations: aside development potential the region has been subject to external powers' influences, both today and in the history. In response, Malaysia chooses a balanced approach toward the external forces: it strives to maintain good neighbourly relations with China without bandwagoning firmly (Kuik, 2008; Lai& Kuik, 2021), and highlights the resolution of issues under international law, i.e., balancing through lawfare and capitalizing on its diverse relations in the region and globally. If SCS riparian states, and China in particular, can shape a cooperative environment and ensure uninterrupted production and trade, external powers will have less clout to intervene in disputes in the future. In this context, the perceptions and SCS policies of Malaysia and other riparian states will be largely shaped by the messages and actions of China and the USA in the future.

GREAT POWER RIVALRY AND THE ASEAN

Malaysia became a founding member of ASEAN in 1967, along with the Philippines, Thailand, Indonesia and Singapore, in the context of the Cold War. Then, the Association's foundation ethos was articulated by Shee Poon-Kim: "it was hoped that ASEAN could, through regional cooperation, minimize manipulation and domination by the great powers" (Poon-Kim, 1977, p. 754). To emphasize this intent, the five ASEAN member states signed the Zone of Peace, Freedom and Neutrality (ZOPFAN) in 1971, declaring their aim to keep Southeast Asia away from the great power rivalry. The declaration stated that the signing countries were:

> *determined to exert initially necessary efforts to secure the recognition of, and respect for, South East Asia as a Zone of Peace, Freedom and Neutrality, free from any form or manner of interference by outside Powers (Signature states of ASEAN, 1971).*

Malaysian leaders were particularly conscious of the risks that the region's resources, including then newly discovered hydrocarbons, could attract great power rivalries. Therefore, the only viable option for "the survival of the small nations in Southeast Asia" was political neutralization (Poon-Kim, 1977, p. 755). During the Cold War, the Communist threat and underground activities within the regional countries prompted the ASEAN states to confront communist expansion in the context of the Vietnam War (1955-1975) (Poon-Kim, 1977, p. 754) and to seek economic and security support from the Western allies, as then the Malaysian Prime Minister Al-Haj expressed this need in the Commonwealth Prime Ministers' Conference in 1969 (Al-Haj, 1969). Diversification of relations was also emphasized on the occasion of the Soviet Trade and Industrial Exhibition in Kuala Lumpur on September 23, 1969, by then Acting Prime Minister and Director of Operations, Tun Abdul Razak bin Hussein: "We believe that in the final analysis, a country's sovereignty and territorial integrity can best be safeguarded by a policy of friendly relations with as many countries as possible" (bin Hussein, 1969).

Coming to the present context, Chinese "redness" has been navigating within capitalism relatively smoothly, as the country has been a crucial pillar of the global supply chain and welfare, even though the Communist propaganda is still unwanted as verified in the case of the movie, *the Battle at Lake Changjin* (2020), which was produced by the Chinese Communist Party's Central Propaganda Department and not approved by Malaysia for screening (Chen & Bandurski, 2021). Like toward China, Malaysia also maintains a level of suspicion on the US's conflictual actions in the SCS, especially after the beginning of wars in Ukraine in 2022 and Palestine in 2023. Former PM Mahathir Mohamad said in June 2024:

> *Even though the US is not in the South China Sea, it seems to like provoking confrontation between nations to the point of causing them to go to war against each other, as happened between Ukraine and Russia. The US is a big arms dealer. They can only sell their arms when there is tension and war (Global Times, 2024c).*

In 2023, Mr. Mohamad envisaged that the the rise of the West-East tension might be culminating in a war (Global Times, 2023).

Regarding the new war fronts, namely Ukraine and in Palestine, and the major powers' involvement -even if undeclared and indirect- in these conflicts such as through arms support, ASEAN countries' suspicion toward the US actions can increase, as Malaysian PM's mentioned thoughts above. A survey by ISEAS-Yusof Ishak Institute among the ASEAN respondents showed that when asked which county they would choose if they had to choose between the US and China, respondents' alignment choice tilted toward China from 2023 to 2024. In 2023, 61.1% chose the US and 38.9% China, while in 2024, 50.5% chose China compared to 49.5% choosing the US (ISEAS-Yusof Ishak Institute, 2024, p. 5). This change is congruent with the survey results on "the region's top geopolitical concerns". The first of these is the Israeli-Palestinian conflict with 46.5%; second, aggressions in SCS with 39.9%; and the third is the Russia-Ukraine War with 39.4%. Among Malaysians, the Israeli-Palestinian conflict was the top concern with 83.1%, while aggressions in the SCS was ranked second with a 47.6%, compared to 90.2% among Philippinos and 72.5% among the Vietnamese. According to the survey, Israel's war on Gaza "diminished trust in international law and rules-based order" (ISEAS-Yusof Ishak Institute, 2024, p. 4, 16). Moreover, China is viewed as the "most influential economic power" (59.5%), and "most influential political and strategic power" (43.9%) (ISEAS-Yusof Ishak Institute, 2024, p. 4). On the other hand, 50.1% expressed distrust over China and 45.5% are in the opinion that "China could use its economic and military power to threaten their country's interest and sovereignty" (ISEAS-Yusof Ishak Institute, 2024, p. 4). In other words, the US involvement in the proxy fronts in the Middle East and Eastern Europe affected the ASEAN people's trust perceptions between the two major powers. This could enhance China-ASEAN rapprochement to prevent the opening of a third front in the SCS in the context of great power competition.

Aside US's conflictual actions, which requires maintaining a strategic distance, China as a regional hegemon also lacks credible commitment not to do the same. Credible commitment is best made through institutions, however in the SCS context, there is not a particular institution to coordinate the issues, other than UN mechanisms, to which China shows selective respect, alike the US. In this context, China and the ASEAN relations constitute an important aspect of the SCS-related issues' coordination for conflict resolution, even if so far only at the level of written "declaration" and "guideline", short of institutionalized binding. In this respect, China and ASEAN members produced two reference documents: the Declaration on the Conduct of Parties in the South China Sea (DOC) in 2002, and the Guidelines for Implementing the DOC in 2011 (ASEAN, 2012; ASEAN, 2011; Wu 2013, 109).

On the occasion of the 50th anniversary of diplomatic relations between Malaysia and China, the two countries released a joint statement, in which, "China welcomes Malaysia taking on the role of country coordinator for ASEAN-China Dialogue Relations in 2024, and firmly supports Malaysia in assuming the chairmanship of ASEAN in 2025" (MOFAM, 2024b). Overall, the ASEAN has a confirmed history of "neutrality", which creates a dependable path today to alleviate great power tensions through the efforts of middle powers. One hurdle is that Southeast Asians view ASEAN as increasingly inadequate to address evolving challenges, with 77% of Malaysian respondents saying so in 2024. This risks the "irrelevance" of the organization. What's more, the people of the region also fears -with a high margin of 76.4%- that ASEAN might become a competition arena in the great power rivalry, with its members potentially becoming proxies of major powers (ISEAS-Yusof Ishak Institute, 2024, p. 14). ASEAN is expected to become the forth largest economy by 2030, which will provide important clout to the organization if the members can maintain their strategic autonomy in the great power rivalry (Hahn, 2024). Malaysia's history under colonial powers after its fall to the Portuguese in 1511, to the Dutch in 1641, and to the British in 1824 until the country's independence in 1957 can be regarded as a factor for the country's preference for the strategic distance (Government of Malaysia, n.d.). Moreover, foreign powers' interference left a bitter memory as in Vietnam in 1970s. Malaysia also needed to fight againt communist anarchy and expansion plans led by Malayan Communist Party (MCP), and in this context, the country embraced democracy, which located it within the liberal world (Shuib et al., 2009). After his 1974 election victory, Tun Razak government became a member of the "Five Power Defense Arrangement, (FPDA), involving Malaysia, Singapore, United Kingdom, New Zealand and Australia" (Shuib et al., 2009, 97). So, ASEAN and Malaysia has a history of ideological and security alignment with the West since the Cold War era, while they see China a new partner particularly in economic realm.

OVERLAPPING CLAIMS

The regional countries, Philippines, Malaysia, Brunei, China, Taiwan and Vietnam have overlapping claims over the Spratly Islands. China claims approximately 90% of the 3.5 million square kilometers of the SCS maritime area through its nine-dash-line designation (Khaliq, 2021; Mahadzir, 2014, p. 209). Philippine, Malaysia, and Brunei's claims over the Spratlys are based on their Exclusive Economic Zone regulated under the UNCLOS, while China bases its claim on its "effective control" of the area: firstly in the period from the ancient times until the French occupation in 1933, and secondly from the end of the Second World War (Philippine, Malaysia, and Brunei) (Khalid, 2019). As Hayton (2018, p. 4) states, "in response to France's annexation of six of the Spratly Islands" in July 1933, Chinese journals published several articles to confront the French in this area. China's designation was first pronounced by the Republic of China (i.e., today's Taiwan) in 1947 with an 11-dash-line (US Energy Information Administration, 2024). After Peoples' Republic of China's foundation in 1949, Mao Zedong followed the same policy. However, the tension soared in 2009, when China renewed its claims for the majority of the SCS with the release of a new nine-dash-line map, while until then the issue was swept under the carpet. Recently in 2023, Chinese Ministry of Natural Resources declared a 10-dash-line map, which encompasses Taiwan as well (Clayman, 2023).

The Chinese Foreign Ministry issued a document "Historical Evidence To Support China's Sovereignty over Nansha Islands" on November 17, 2000, claiming that "Chinese seafarers were the first to name and 'develop' the various disputed islands and areas" in the South China Sea (Song et al., 2020; Evers, 2014, p. 6). On the other hand, when the Philippines filed an arbitration case under UNCLOS on China's nine-dash line claim in 2013[4], China objected to the arbitration. So, in this case, China vaguely referred to the "historic title" phrase of Articles 15 and 298 of UNCLOS (Ma, 2017) while it was not ready to hear other littoral states' counter-claims. The US Department of State rejects China's claims, underlying that "No provision of the Convention contains the term 'historic rights,' nor is there a uniform understanding of what, specifically, the term means as a matter of international law" (US Department of State, 2022, p.9). Thus, US rejects the legitimacy of the Chinese claims, and signals its willingness to play a balancing role.

Malaysia claims 12 features in the form of rocks, shoals, reefs, islands, atolls within the framework of its 1979 map. Out of these, 10 features are situated near the Malaysian state of Sabah in the Spratly Islands, while the Luconia Shoals (*Bet-*

ing Patinggi Ali in Malaysian) is close to Sarawak. The Luconia Shoals is rich in oil resources (Ryan, 2023). Malaysia maintains presence in five of these features, namely: "Pulau Layang-Layang (Swallow Reef), Terumbu Mantanani (Mariveles Reef), Terumbu Ubi (Ardasier Reef), Terumbu Siput (Erica Reef), and Terumbu Peninjau (Investigator Reef)." Philippines occupies one of them (Terumbu Laksamana/ Commodore Reef), and Vietnam occupies another feature (Pulau Amboyna Kecil/Amboyna Cay) (Mahadzir, 2014, 208-209). According to the US Energy Information Administration, Malaysia's claims cover around "five billion barrels of oil reserves and 80 trillion cubic feet of gas reserves" (Ryan, 2023, referred to the US Energy Information Administration, 2024). After China's 10-dash-line, Malaysia's Ministry of Foreign Affairs immediately rejected the "unilateral maritime claims" and said that the country would continue its oil and gas explorations off the Borneo island (Aljazeera, 2023). India, Vietnam, Philippines and Taiwan also condemned the new claims (Clayman, 2023).

Khalid (2019) argues that SCS "is fast becoming a hotbed of tensions among littoral states". It could be more likely to reach an equitable conclusion among the states with roughly equal powers in the absence of a major power party to the dispute. From this perspective, China's direct stakes in the SCS constitute an important impediment to reaching an equitable conclusion, while other external forces' stakes also add complexity to the picture.

A former Malaysian Member of Parliament, Dr. Ong Kian Ming, argued after the 2016 Permanent Court of Arbitration (PCA) in The Hague ruling that the ruling would "strengthen Malaysia's claim on features such as James Shoal or Beting Serupai, which lies a mere 80 km northwest of Bintulu, Sarawak and is well within the continental shelf of Malaysia and the 200 nautical mile EEZ". He continued, "Malaysia's claim to the North Luconia Shoals (or Gugusan Beting Raja Jarun) and the South Luconia Shoals (Gugusan Beting Patinggi Ali), which are located approximately 100 km from Sarawak, would also be strengthened" (Ming, 2016). Mr. Ming also recommended international arbitration way for Malaysia if better options are exhausted (Ming, 2016).

Several hydrocarbon fields within Malaysia's EEZ are also located within China's nine-dash-line, leading to overlapping claims by Malaysia and China. The Kasawari gas field is a case in point. Regarding the Malaysian state oil company Petronas' activity in the gas field, China conveyed concern to the Malaysian PM Anwar Ibrahim in Beijing in April 2023. The Kasawari gas field is located within Malaysia's Exclusive Economic Zone (EEZ), approximately 200 kilometers from the Sarawak coast line (Strangio, 2023).

When it comes to fishing, Vietnamese fishing boats top the numbers in the Malaysian waters: "748 vessels and 7,203 Vietnamese crew members were detained between 2006 until 2019", while "89 times Chinese Coast Guard vessels were detected to have encroached into the country's waters from 2016 to 2019" (Nordin, 2020). In 2016, an ASEAN declaration was adopted on regional cooperation against "Illegal, Unreported and Unregulated (IUU) fishing", followed by further measures in 2019 (Nordin, 2020). Malaysia-Philippines relations depict good neighbourly moments. When typhoons and earthquakes hit the Philippines, Malaysia willingly offered its hand to its neighbour, for example, during the 2013 Bohol earthquake, Typhoon Durian in 2006 and Typhoon Haiyan in 2013 (Department of Foreign Affairs of the Philippines, 2013). Malaysia reiterates its suggestion that SCS-related disputes are best solved through multilateral mechanisms among the ASEAN states (Galvez, 2023).

Wu (2013, p. 4) argues that Malaysia (and the Philippines) joined the debate only after the 1970s. Malaysia started oil drilling operations with two vessels in 1970 after the country declared an area of 80,000 square kilometres as its mining zone in the Spratly Islands (Wu, 2013, p. 8). This argument seems to be caused from the denial of historical rights to these countries. However, it should not give way to an argument that previously inactive littoral states' rights can be compromised by historically more active ones. States, which prefer pacific relations don't mean that they forgo their rights. In other words, China's historically active fishing and navigational activities shouldn't mean it has the right to create a *fait accompli* against the neighbouring states.

As Hans-Dieter Evers (2014) argued, China, as a party to UNCLOS, claims to utilize Article 15, which mentions "reason of historic title or other special circumstances" as a base for its claims in the South China Sea. In response, Evers suggests that Malaysia and other littoral states can also bring their claims regarding historical rights in the SCS:

> *As Malay seafarers have dominated trade and shipping in Southeast and East Asia in line with their Austronesian ancestry, historical claims to the South China Sea could be posted by most ASEAN states as well, but no documents could be found to that effect (Evers, 2014, p. 7).*

However, on July 12, 2016, the PCA ruled that "there was no legal basis for China to claim historic rights to resources within the sea areas falling within the 'nine-dash line'" (Ming, 2016). So, the debate on "historical rights" has ended so far with this ruling. Moreover, the US, as the primary defender of the existing world order, defends this position (US Energy Information Administration, 2024). China rejected the PCA ruling, arguing that its island in the SCS entitle it EEZ as its "dotted line" showed. Chinese ambassador to the US, Cui Tiankai, also argued that the ruling would diminish motivations for negotiation and "intensify conflict and even confrontation" (Brunnstrom & Blanchard, 2016).

So far, only Malaysia and Brunei solved their "overlapping claims" through bilateral agreements (Khalid, 2019, p. 3).

MALAYSIA'S ROLE AND AMICABLE STYLE

In 2004, then PM Abdullah Badawi described Malaysia-China relations as "a triumph of good diplomacy and good sense", and suggested others to follow a similar track (Kuik, 2008, p. 175). Malaysia insists on its friendly approach towards China even though the latter's actions have been criticized by the US, ASEAN and the regional states. Malaysian Defence Minister Hishammuddin Hussein said in 2014 "Just because you have enemies, doesn't mean your enemies are my enemies" (Thayer, 2014).

Malaysia pays attention to negotiation and diplomacy to solve issues and sustain the development environment in the region. Malaysian Ministry of Defence's *Defence White Paper* (2020) has a subtitle "A secure, sovereign and prosperous Malaysia", for which, then PM Mahathir Mohamad recognizes "the consequential role of economic sustainability" (p. 1). However, in April 2023 Malaysia's Ministry of Foreign Affairs needed to clarify Prime Minister Anwar Ibrahim's use of the word "negotiation" on the issue of the South China Sea after the opposition leader Muhyiddin Yassin claimed that the PM acknowledged China's claims on the Malaysian territories (Strangio, 2023). In order not to be interpreted Malaysia's diplomatic style mistakenly, the Ministry re-confirmed the country's policy by stating that:

Malaysia's position on the South China Sea is consistent and remains unchanged. The Government of Malaysia is unequivocally and firmly committed to protecting Malaysia's sovereignty, sovereign rights and interests in its maritime areas in the South China Sea, as depicted by our 1979 Map. Malaysia firmly holds the view that matters relating to the South China Sea must be resolved peacefully and constructively, in accordance with the universally recognised principles of international law, including the 1982 United Nations Convention on the Law of the Sea (1982 UNCLOS) (MOFAM, 2023).

The Malaysian approach of insisting on negotiation and dialogue was reiterated in PM Anwar Inrahim's comments on 15 June 2024, as well. Upon a question on China's maneouvres in the SCS, he said:

Why this obsession, the tendency to exaggerate the problem, border issues with China, when we, in Malaysia, or the Thais, or Brunei or Indonesia all have problems with their neighbours? We haven't actually cemented agreement in all areas with the borders. But does it mean that it is tension and that it is tense, or causing difficulty in relations? No. The relationship with Singapore is super-excellent, with Tailand, with Indonesia... But all these countries, we have problems with the borders. So, why then, pick and choose and exaggerate the issues with China? Do we have a problem? Yes. Have we encountered any serious clashes or problems? No. Do we think this is going to be easily resolved? No. But what is the mechanism? Discussions, dialogue. Will we concede, then? No. (South China Morning Post, 2024).

In this lenghty quotation, the Prime Minister's "role conception" implies that Malaysia acts as a tranquilizer. Malaysia tries to persuade the international public opinion to shape a peaceful perception in the region and prevent a chain of hostile reactions.

Comparing to China's choice of "bilateralism" vis-a-vis "multilateralism", Malaysia prefers the latter (Munir & Sajjad, 2022; Ibrahim, 2023). In response to two Parliamentary questions in May 2010, Deputy Foreign Minister Kohilan Pillay clarified Malaysia's approach of conflict resolution on the SCS dispute as follows: "Malaysia believes that the overlapping claims should be resolved at the negotiating table, with reference to third parties such as the International Court of Justice (ICJ) or the Arbitration Tribunal being the last option to obtain a solution" (Mahadzir, 2014, p. 210. In the same context, the minister stated: "Malaysia views that the issue of overlapping claims in the South China Sea should be resolved on a bilateral or multilateral basis and involve only countries who have overlapping claims" (Mahadzir, 2014, p. 211). As Mahadzir argues, Malaysia chose not to publicize the Chinese ships' incursions into the Malaysian waters, while demonstrating firm commitment to protect its waters through patrolling and shadowing the Chinese ships until they left the scene. Such shadowings were exercized against the Chinese incursions near Layang-Layang (Swallow Reef) in the Spratlys on verious times (Mahadzir, 2014, p. 220-221).

Istishara meaning consultation and discussion is practiced as part of Malaysian and Islamic culture in family and business issues (Ahmed et al., 2022, p. 39; Kavas et al., 2020, p. 693). Cultural patterns also feed into the diplomatic style. So, Malaysian culture, a crucial part of the national identity, also helps to adopt a role conception as peacemaker in the political field. However, considering China's claims for the larger area of the SCS with its nine-dash-line, it appears that if the region is left to bilateral negotiations dominated by China, the latter will be asserting its claims easily. Therefore, on 6 May 2009, Malaysia and Vietnam jointly submitted an application to the Commission on the Limits of the Continental Shelf (CLCS) to identify the continental shelf beyond the 200-miles (UN, 2024). This action drew protest from China. China's UN mission's letter to the then UN General Secretary Ban Ki-Moon stated that Malaysia and Vietnam's action "seriously infringed China's sovereignty, sovereign rights and jurisdiction in the South China Sea" (Permanent Mission of PRC to UN, 2009). Wu defined Vietnam's policy as "regionalising or internationalising the disputes" by aligning its interests with those of the ASEAN members (Wu, 2013, p. 116). About the Philippines' submission on China's nine-dash-line in 2013 under UNCLOS, the PCA, which was established under Annex VII of UNCLOS, ruled on 12 July 2016, rejected China's claims based on historical rights (Permanent Court of Arbitration, 2013 & 2016). The littoral states were supportive of the tribunal's decison. As Marvel (2024, p. 485) states, "as of 2020, Vietnam and Malaysia tacitly supported the Award by rejecting China's 'historic rights,' while Indonesia 'endorsed' the Award, with Taiwan stating that 'any claim inconsistent with international law should not be accepted'". China's assertiveness and the inconclusive bilateral negotiations were the main reasons for the littoral states to resort to lawfare. Also, in 2019, Malaysia singly submitted an application to the CLCS for the identification of its continental shelf which also drew protest from both Vietnam and China (Lui & Kuik, 2021).

In 2024, in a common declaration after the meeting between Prime Minister Anwar Ibrahim and Prime Minister of Australia, Anthony Albanese, the two leaders,

> *expressed serious concern about developments in the South China Sea and highlighted the importance of freedom of navigation and overflight by international law. The Leaders emphasised the need for all States to comply with international law, including the 1982 United Nations Convention on the Law of the Sea (UNCLOS) (MOFAM, 2024a).*

So, although Malaysia prefers non-confrontational diplomacy in the region, it feels a need to reiterate its messages to check the regional superpower, China, through international law and institutions. The regional countries are well aware of the perils of the Western dominance in different forms. Therefore, Malaysia has a deep motivation to solve issues equitably among the regional countries. However, China's expansionist SCS policy narrows the littoral states' options and pushes them to seek balancing through lawfare and limited alignment with the US and like-minded balancers, such as Australia and Japan.

RECENT MALAYSIA-CHINA RELATIONS

China has been "Malaysia's largest trading partner for 15 consecutive years since 2009, representing 17.1% share of Malaysia's total trade" (Embassy of Malaysia, Beijing, 2024). The economy is considered to constitute a path facilitating a neofunctionalist momentum to solve higher political issues. However, recent years saw narrowing the cooperation and accommodation space from the Malaysian perspective. For example, Malaysia summoned China's ambassador in June 2021 for breaching Malaysia's air space due to the flight of 16 military aircraft near Sarawak Malaysia, and again in October 2021, due to the Chinese ships' "presence and activities" within its exclusive economic zones near Sabah and Sarawak states in the Borneo island (BBC, 2021; Aljazeera, 2021).

Despite the Chinese assertiveness, the two countries maintained neighbourly relations and signalled positive messages for the bilateral relations. During his meeting with his Malaysian counterpart Utama Haji Mohamad bin Haji Hasan on 25 April 2024, China's Foreign Minister Wang Yi said that his country was ready to "stand up for justice on the international stage, oppose unilateralism and bullying, and defend the common interests of the Global South" (Global Times, 2024b). However, China doesn't present consistent self-restraint as implied in its defining SCS as its "core interest" and claiming a large part of it by means of its "nine-dash line" designation.

In his congratulatory message on January 31, 2024 on the occasion of Sultan Ibrahim Sultan Iskandar's throning as Malaysia's new king, Xi Jinping pointed out the neighbourly relations since 1974 and the beginning of the establishment of diplomatic relations based on "mutual respect, equality, mutual benefit and win-win cooperation". The message mentioned that Xi and Prime Minister Anwar Ibrahim had "reached important common understandings on jointly building a China-Malaysia community with a shared future, drawing a new blueprint for the development of bilateral relations in the new era" (Ministry of Foreign Affairs of PRC, 2024).

China expects that Malaysia's coordinatorship of the China-ASEAN relations would also contribute to the two countries' positive relations (Ministry of Foreign Affairs of PRC, 2024). A *Global Times* editorial column commented in February 2024 on how ASEAN-US and ASEAN-China economic relations evolved since 2000:

> *In 2000, US trade with ASEAN was more than three times that of China-ASEAN trade. By 2020, China's trade was almost double that of the US. Today, China has become the largest trading partner of almost all ASEAN countries. Larger economies of ASEAN, including Indonesia, Malaysia, Thailand and Vietnam, are not willing to take sides. All of them hope to leverage the contradictions between China and the US to maximize their own interests (Global Times, 2024a).*

The article also mentioned the US's investment commitment of merely $150 million in all the ASEAN during the US-ASEAN Special Summit in Washington in 2022. It ridiculed the amount, saying "What a chicken feed" (Global Times, 2024a). According to the journal, China's investment was a factor in Malaysia's "tilt toward China", as Malaysian PM Anwar interpreted: "Because they're investing more" (Global Times, 2024a). Thus, China's economic statecraft toward the region was perceived positively by Malaysia. This economic picture attests to the fact that the region has increasingly become China's economic sphere of influence, even though the US maintains important leverage in the region, especially securitywise. Paraphrasing the arguments of Chen Xiangmiao, director of the World Navy Research Center at the National Institute for South China Sea Studies, the *Global Times* editorial said:

Malaysia is one of the most "neutral" countries in ASEAN. It has a bitter memory of colonial aggression and the harm caused by the power games during the Cold War, it is thus very averse to great power competition and unwilling to take sides (Global Times, 2024a).

Chen Xiangmiao argued that taking sides would even lead to a disintegration of ASEAN, considering that its members have different relationships with the US and China. The commentator argued that such a one-sided dependence would make ASEAN "become a vassal state" (Global Times, 2024a). According to the article, Malaysian PM Anwar's "pragmatic" approach in maintaining relations with both the US and China and "protecting the interests of his country and ASEAN" was "represent(ative)" of ASEAN's "mainstream" policy (Global Times, 2024a). This line of view argues that external factors have the potential to disturb the ASEAN-China development environment, also because the ASEAN states are not homogenous (Yu, 2024, 54). Hong Yu (2024, 43) states, the term "Southeast Asea" has been used only since the Second World War, when the British referred to the region as a conflict zone. The mentioned *Global Times* editorial argued, the US was trying to influence the ASEAN countries that their relations with China was against their countries' interests. However, the article argued that "Only the feet know if the shoes fit", meaning that ASEAN states were following their national interests, despite the US efforts (Global Times, 2024a).

Overall, a positive economic statecraft agenda has been at the heart of China's ASEAN strategy: trading more, and investing for the development of these neighbouring countries in an amount that compares to the US investment level. So far, the top three beneficiaries of China's investments in ASEAN were "Singapore, Indonesia and Malaysia… with US$ 32.57 billion, US$ 29.97 billion and US$ 18.67 billion, respectively" (Yu, 2024, p. 57). In 2024, a survey found that 66.7% of Malaysian respondents viewed China as "the most influential economic power in Southeast Asia", while only 9.3% of them viewed the US as such (ISEAS-Yusof Ishak Institute, 2024, 35). However, the other side of the coin is that for the year 2022 for example, the US was the top investor in the ASEAN with US$37 billion, while Japan came second with US$27 billion and China only third with US$15 billion (ASEAN & UNCTAD, 2023, p. 12). Similarly, in Malaysia, the US was the top investor in 2022 with US$ 8.6 billion, which constituted almost half of the total FDI inflows in that year, followed by Singapore with US$ 2.6 billion, and Japan with US$ 2.2 billion. Hong Kong came fourth with US$1.4 billion (ASEAN & UNCTAD, 2023, p. 18). So, in fact, China does not have quantitative advantage in terms of mobilizing positive economic statecraft vis-a-vis its rivals in Malaysia. Moreover, instead of grand projects, Malaysia emphasizes "small but beautiful projects" to green and digitalize the economy and raise human capital for development where the US companies might have competitive advantage. For the training of Malaysian workforce, several Chinese-Malaysian projects stand out in these "smart" areas as well: "Malaysia-China Kuantan Industrial Park (MCKIP); Digital Free Trade Zone; D&Y Textile; Alliànce Steel; Jinko's solar investments in Penang; China Railway Rolling Stock Corp.'s Rolling Stock Center (CRCC) in Batu Gajah, Perak; and Geely's automotive investments in Proton, the national auto company" (Busbarat, 2023). Regarding the utility of economic statecraft, countries' economic models also affect their influence potential. As Norris (2010, p. 308-309) argued, success factors of the Chinese economic statecraft included firmer control of commercial activities by the state. It can be argued that US investors could be investing more in a less visible market mechanism, while China's investments might be more visible and state-guided subject to bilateral political negotiations.

On security matters, Malaysia signals a balanced relationship with both the US and China. It conducts military exercises with both, by which it gives the message that Malaysia maintains a balanced approach and sees the events through a friendship lens (Marston, 2023, 27). Diplomatically, Malaysia offers Chinese citizens visa-free entry for 30 days on each visit between 1 December 2023 and 31 December 2024. Visa liberalisation decisions are taken only between highly trusting states (Embassy of Malaysia, Beijing, 2023). China also has a visa-free regime for ordinary tourists from 12 countries: Germany, France, Italy, the Netherlands, Spain, Malaysia, Switzerland, Ireland, Hungary, Austria, Belgium and Luxembourg (Yuying & Jingyi, 2024).

A fellow at the Wilson Center's Asia Program argues,

China's failure emerges largely as a result of unreliable relationships, unstable host countries, and limited near-term naval power in the Indian Ocean. U.S. policy should therefore aim to exacerbate these issues to ensure China continues wrestling with the Malacca Dilemma (Myers, 2023).

From this point of view, if the US statecraft focuses on destabilizing the China-ASEAN counries' relations, regional countries might be challenged in maintaining stable relations with China. The Cold War experience shows that regime or leadership changes are also supported by great powers in times of strategic rivalry.

COMPETING ECONOMIC STATECRAFT STRATEGIES AND MALAYSIA

The Obama Administration's Sceretary of State Hillary R. Clinton's article dated October 11, 2011 and titled "America's Pacific Century" sketched the US's "Pivot to Asia" strategy (Stewart & Reininger, 2016, p. 4-5). A year later, in 2012, the Regional Comprehensive Economic Partnership (RCEP) negotiations were initiated by 10 ASEAN member states and the Association's six FTA partners (Australia, PRC, India, Japan, Republic of Korea, and New Zealand) during the ASEAN

Summit in Phnom Penh, Cambodia. However, India opted out of the negotiations in 2019. According to the ASEAN website, "RCEP is committed to providing fair regional economic policies that mutually benefit both ASEAN and its FTA partners" (ASEAN, n.d.). Regarding that the trade arrangements led by the West has been criticized for not being egalitarian (see Wade, 2003 & 2020), RCEP's emphasis on mutual benefit is noteworthy. RCEP has an ambitious trade liberalization agenda among the participating countries: 90% of tariffs will be eliminated within 20 years among the trading parties, and common rules on intellectual property, e-commerce and trade (Zhou, 2020). On the occasion of the 50'th anniversary of China-Malaysia relations, Chinese premier Li Qiang met with the Malysia's Sultan Ibrahim and PM Anwar Ibrahim in June 2024. In a joint statement, the two countries committed to a "high-quality implementation" of the RCEP, expressed their willingness to speed up the negotiations on the ASEAN-China Free Trade Area 3.0 Upgrade. They also committed active participation to "the 2024 ASEAN-China Year of People-to-people Exchanges" to enhance "the ASEAN-China Comprehensive Strategic Partnership" and "build a closer ASEAN-China community with a shared future" (MOFAM, 2024b).

In 2013, Malaysia-China Comprehensive Strategic Partnership was established, and in 2014, Malaysia-US relations were defined as "comprehensive partnership" (Kuik, 2024, p. 57). On 29 November 2022, Malaysia became a party to the Comprehensive and Progressive Agreement for Trans-Pacific Partnership (CPTPP), which is the successor of the originally Obama-initiated Trans-Pacific Partnership (TPP). CPTPP aims to eliminate 99% of tariffs among its partners (Zhou, 2020). US president Donald Trump had withdrawn from TPP on 23 January 2017, i.e., on the third day of his incumbancy, as he had conceived protective trade policies. Moreover, Malaysia is a founding member of the Indo-Pacific Economic Framework for Prosperity (IPEF), initiated in 2022 during the Biden Administration. However, the people of ASEAN and Malaysia is "unsure" about the future of this framework. Many believe that the IPEF does not ensure better access to the US market, while requesting various adjustments from others. Also, Malaysia fears potential Chinese reprisals as it has strong trade links with China (ISEAS-Yusof Ishak Institute, 2024, p. 28, 31). On July 28, 2024, Malaysian PM Ibrahim announced that he sent an application letter to the present chair of BRICS, Russia, to join the intergovernmental organization dominated by China and Russia. BRICS is regarded the main platform to contemplate de-dollarization through the use of local currencies (Bernama, 2024). PM Ibrahim thinks that an Asian Monetary Fund is a necessity as well as de-dollarization and a fair trade between the developing and developed countries (Nambiar, 2024).

So, Malaysia, as other ASEAN countries, participates in trade arrangements dominated by both China and the West rather than discriminating one for the other. Malaysia also underlines Japan's role in manufacturing projects especially in the early period of Malaysia's industrialization (Malaysian Investment Development Authority, 2024). Malaysia's participation in competing trade frameworks transcends bloc politics, and is congruent with a hedging strategy. Malaysia signals that the country does not fit bloc politics dictated by the great power rivalry, rather, it wants to maintain good relations with both sides, even though the maneouvring space diminishes.

In the liberal international relations theory, trade is viewed as an insurance against war (Russett, 2016, p. 77-78). Malaysia thinks that this is also valid for China. In his interview with the *Global Times* published on June 23, 2024, former Malaysian PM Mahathir Mohamad said,

> *I don't think the Chinese can accept what is happening in Ukraine and the South China Sea. China wants to grow economically. And when you have tensions, you cannot trade, you cannot grow, and you are going to waste your money fighting and killing people. I don't think that is China's objective (Global Times, 2024c).*

As Mr. Mohamad articulated, war needs to be prevented to achieve economic development, be it in Ukraine, Palestine or the South China Sea (*Global Times*, 2024c). That's why, Malaysia's main policy is to persuade the actors to proactively prevent a war in the region beyond hedging. Malaysia's narrative and actions imply this.

IN SEARCH OF REGIONAL ORDER

Alike most other ASEAN countries, Malaysia's strategy has been defined as "hedging" (Kuik, 2008; Rahmanillah et al., 2023), which generally refers to "insurance-seeking behaviour" of actors "under high-stakes and high-uncertainty conditions" (Lui & Kuik, 2020, p. 280). Three attributes of it, as summarized by Lui & Kuk, are: "an insistence on not taking sides; (b) attempt(ing) to pursue opposing measures, i.e. concurrent adoptions of selective defiance and selective deference vis-à-vis competing powers; and (c) diversification to cultivate a fall-back position" (Lui & Kuik, 2021, p. 280). As this chapter argues, Malaysia's rhetoric and moves are purposed to reduce the overall tension and benefit from the generally peaceful development environment. This is logical because in the case of increased tension, hedging might not be adequate to insure middle powers' security and survival. Nowadays authors increasibly debate on the limits of hedging (Rahmanillah et al., 2023; He & Feng, 2023, p. 2) and argue that "after hedging" context has been arriving (He & Feng, 2023, p. 49). Even though small states' role in drawing major powers to war is well studied, their role to de-escalate the conditions of security dilemma has not been emphasized. Malaysia employs and promotes de-escalatory methods and "quiet diplomacy" (Nordin, 2020), mainly, negotiations among the ASEAN and China and unpublicizing the naval infringes so that they are not used to escalate the situation further and invite external powers' interests. This is also to keep "ASEAN centrality…despite the Big Powers and its allies' competition in South China Sea" (Nordin, 2020).

So far, the US has been a crucial partner of the regional countries' hedging or balancing strategies to check China's hegemony in the SCS through signalling friendship, on the one hand, while also taking some measures to increase their capabilities, on the other. As Rahmanillah et al. (2023) argue for Indonesia, middle powers' hedging has its limits, as in the scenario of an increased rivalry between the US and China, the middle powers' manoeuvring space might be seriously diminished and they might be forced to take a side.

Amitav Acharya (2014, p. 159) envisages a peaceful regional order, based on a "Consociational Security Order" (CSO). Acharya refutes the applicability of extant international relations theories, primarily offensive realism and liberal institutionalism, for the Asia-Pacific context. Rather, he draws on both domestic political theories and IR theories to suggest a peaceful order. As he argues, the existing IR theoretical approaches tend to balance between "anarchy" and "society". In his CSO, he identifies "four enabling conditions: interdependence, equilibrium, institutions under shared leadership, and elite restraint" (Acharya 2014, 159). Briefly summarized, firstly, interdependence does not require integration, instead, it recognizes "national independence and sovereignty" (Acharya, 2014, p. 161). Secondly, "equilibrium" refutes hegemony and requires "multiple balances of power" due to the fear of releasing a security dilemma (Acharya, 2014, p. 161). Thirdly, institutions in the region tend to be "intergovernmental, rather than supranational" and "cooperative" rather than "collective" (Acharya 2014, 161). Finally, "elite restraint" refers to the elite's self-restraint as they "understand the perils of political fragmentation" (Lijphart, 1962, p. 216, quoted in Acharya, 2014, p. 161).

Potentially wider set of world affairs can also change countries' dialogue partners and negotiation environment. For example, Malaysia welcomed UN Resolution 2728 on March 25, 2024, on the immediate ceasefire in Gaza. China mainly supported Russia in pushing the Western UNSC members for a ceasefire resolution, which will surely affect Malaysia's positive attitude toward China, indirectly. So, regarding that great power rivalry might be fought in different geographies and forms, seemingly isolated events to the SCS context can factor into the policy evaluations of the regional countries in the future.

CONCLUSION

This article analyzes Malaysia's political position in the context of the SCS maritime area disputes characterized by overlapping claims. With its nine-dash-line policy claiming much of the SCS maritime area based on the "historical rights" argument, China posed an important challenge in conflict resolution, rather than credibly committing to self-containment. This reality leaves for the littoral states little room but to find solutions by other means, including lawfare. Lawfare strategy refers to the littoral states' utilization of legal bodies of the UN to have their rights legally confirmed and thus to gain political recognition under the rule-based international order. Upon the Philippiness application, PCA clarified on July 12, 2016 that "there was no legal basis for China to claim historic rights to resources within the sea areas falling within the 'nine-dash line'" (Ming, 2016). So, the debate specifically over China's "historical rights" has been legally concluded. Other littoral states, including Malaysia, also benefits from this ruling with regard to balance of claims.

Economic statecraft has gained a renewed currency as an influence mechanism within the great power rivalry context. China promotes its Belt and Road projects in the ASEAN countries and specifically Malaysia in recent years. China has been the biggest trading partner of Malaysia consecutively for 15 years since 2009. This partnership supports liberal expectations to allow peaceful relations and potentially mobilizes neo-functional dynamics to facilitate cooperation in higher political areas. Mutually, this also offers important leverage for Malaysia to push for multilateral solutions to the SCS dispute on a win-win basis among all the neighbours, as it is the only way for the region's sustainable peace and development.

Malaysia declares itself as a "non-aligned" country and promotes multilaterally-produced or equitably negotiated settlements. A bitter Cold War experience reminds that power rivalries between the great powers often prove destabilizing for smaller states. Therefore, ASEAN countries have crucial incentives principally not to bandwagon with or balance against a great power. Malaysia's policy has been defined by scholars as hedging, i.e., a strategy to keep an equidistance between the rival superpowers. However, middle powers' hedging strategies have their limits, because in the case that the rivalry intensifies, their strategic autonomy to maneouver diminishes. Cognizant of this, Malaysian policy goes beyond hedging and intends to alleviate the total risk perception and the vicious cycle of security dilemma. Relational positions toward the US and China also can be fine-tuned according to the changing perceptions. New fronts in Ukraine and Palestine make Malaysia concerned that the SCS could become a third front. This creates new incentives for Malaysia (and the ASEAN in general) to find accommodation with China to keep the region peaceful. In this regard, Malaysia's application in July 2024 to become a BRICS member can be interpreted within this context.

In this framework, Malaysia's principled stance to act together with ASEAN in finding solutions to the SCS dispute is a strategy to prevent the escalation of the crisis without feeding into the emerging strategic rivalry. Presently, the context is fragile as there is not a binding mechanism to deliberate the SCS issue in a credible way with all the interested states. China and other littoral states' overlapping claims in the SCS require effective utilization of ASEAN-China cooperation to find a resolution. To this aim, a major international conference to discuss the matter can be convened. Malaysia's historically friendly relations and its position as a hub of trade could help deliver peace dividends and calm the waters. Moreover, Malaysia can increase its participation in the UN mechanisms, diversify its economic relations with major players and enhance its defence capabilities.

Finally, Malaysia's strategy can be characterized as mitigating the overall risk at source, beyond insuring against risks in the short to medium term. Put differently, Malaysia performs a role to reduce the overall tension in the region as a peacemaker. This role is more for the long term, because states need to ensure their long-term survival beyond risk management. With this implicit strategy, Malaysia considers its national interest within the regional peace and stability. Contrary to the examples that small allies are often responsible for drawing bigger allies to the conflict, Malaysia's advocacy for de-risking seems to function to prevent potential conflagrations. Therefore, asymmetrically smaller states' roles in peacebuilding in the context of great power rivalries are worth further study.

REFERENCES

Abdullah, S. (2013). Effect of Malay-China Trade Relations During the Malacca Sultanate on the Emergence of Chinese Peranakan Community. *World Journal of Islamic History and Civilization*, *3*(4), 143–149. DOI: 10.5829/idosi.wjihc.2013.3.4.3401

Ahmed, G. G. J. W., Nasrin, M. I., & Abdullah, M. M. A. (2022). Study on Significance of Shura in Islam and its Practice in Contemporary Muslim Family Affairs. *Al-Bukhari Journal of Arabic and Islamic Studies*, *2*(1), 38–49.

Al-Aboudi, N.K.M. (2021). The Islamic Sultanate of Malacca: a study of its inception and the factors of its development into a global trade center in the first half of the 15th century. *PalArch's Journal of Archaeology of Egypt/Egyptology* 18(5), 491-510.

Al-Haj, T. A. P. (1969, January 8). Statement by the Prime Minister, Tunku Abdul Rahman Putra Al-haj, at the Commonwealth Prime Ministers' Meeting in London. *Foreign Affairs Malaysia*, 2 (1), 2-4. https://www.kln.gov.my/documents/8390448/8418517/VOLUME+2.pdf/148bc9c1-a73e-429f-be86-9477db7a3c35?version=1.0&download=true

Aljazeera (2021, October 5). Malaysia summons China envoy over South China Sea 'encroachment'. https://www.aljazeera.com/news/2021/10/5/malaysia-summons-china-ambassador-over-south-china-sea-incursion

Aljazeera (2023, August 31). Malaysia rejects new China map claiming entire South China Sea. https://www.aljazeera.com/news/2023/8/31/malaysia-rejects-new-china-map-claiming-entire-south-china-sea

ASEAN. (2011). Guidelines for the Implementation of the DOC. https://www.asean.org/wp-content/uploads/images/archive/documents/20185-DOC.pdf

ASEAN. (2012, May 14). Declaration on the Conduct of Parties in the South China Sea. https://asean.org/declaration-on-the-conduct-of-parties-in-the-south-china-sea-2/

ASEAN. (2012, May 14). Declaratıon on the conduct of parties in the South China Sea. https://asean.org/declaration-on-the-conduct-of-parties-in-the-south-china-sea-2/

ASEAN. (n.d.). The Regional Comprehensive Economic Partnership (RCEP). https://asean.org/our-communities/economic-community/integration-with-global-economy/the-regional-comprehensive-economic-partnership-rcep/

ASEAN & UNCTAD. (2023). A Special ASEAN Investment Report 2023 International investment trends: Key issues and policy options. https://asean.org/wp-content/uploads/2023/12/AIR-Special-2023.pdf

Asia Financial (2023, December 19). Red Sea Attacks Disrupt Key Asia-Europe Sea Trade Route. https://www.asiafinancial.com/red-sea-attacks-disrupt-key-asia-europe-sea-trade-route

BBC (2021, June 2). South China Sea dispute: Malaysia accuses China of breaching airspace. https://www.bbc.com/news/world-asia-57328868

Bernama (2024, July 28). Malaysia has applied to join BRICS-Ibrahim. https://www.bernama.com/en/news.php?id=2322706#:~:text=BRICS%2C%20which%20initially%20included%20Brazil,and%20the%20United%20Arab%20Emirates

Bin Hussein, T. A. R. (1969, September 23). Text of speech by the Acting Prime Minister and Director of Operations, Tun Abdul Razak bin Hussein, at the opening of the Soviet Trade and Industrial Exhibition at Dewan Bahasa dan Pustaka, Kuala Lumpur, at 4.00 p.m. September 23, 1969. *Foreign Affairs Malaysia*, 2 (1), 22-25. https://www.kln.gov.my/documents/8390448/8418517/VOLUME+2.pdf/148bc9c1-a73e-429f-be86-9477db7a3c35?version=1.0&download=true

Britannica (n.d.(a)). Peranakan. https://www.britannica.com/topic/Peranakan

Britannica (n.d.(b)). Sultanate of Malacca. https://www.britannica.com/place/sultanate-of-Malacca

Britannica (The Editors of Encyclopedia Britannica) (2024, June 4). Strait of Malacca. https://www.britannica.com/place/Strait-of-Malacca

Brunnstrom, D., & Blanchard, B. (2016, July 13). South China Sea ruling will 'intensify conflict', says Chinese envoy. *Malaysiakini*.https://www.malaysiakini.com/news/348366

Busbarat, P., Camba, A., Pratiwi, F. I., Po, S., Đ , H., Sengkhamkhoutlavong, B., Yean, T. S., & Thuzar, M. (2023, December 5). How Has China's Belt and Road Initiative Impacted Southeast Asian Countries? https://carnegieendowment.org/posts/2023/12/how-has-chinas-belt-and-road-initiative-impacted-southeast-asian-countries?lang=en

Clayman, T. (2023, December 22). China's New Map: The 10-Dash Line. *The Boston Political Review*.https://www.bostonpoliticalreview.org/post/china-s-new-map-the-10-dash-line

Cordesman, A. H., Burke, A. A., & Molot, M. (2019). The Critical Role of Chinese Trade in the South China Sea. Report by Center for Strategic and International Studies (CSIS). http://www.jstor.com/stable/resrep22586.30

Department of Foreign Affairs of the Philippines. (2013, November 14). PHL embassy expresses gratitude for assistance from the Malaysian government and, general public for Yolanda victims. https://dfa.gov.ph/authentication-functions/148-typhoon-yolanda/1281-phl-embassy-expresses-gratitude-for-assistance-from-malaysian-government-general-public-for-yolanda-victims

Embassy of Malaysia. Beijing (2023). Important announcement on visa exemptions for Chinese passport holders. https://www.kln.gov.my/web/chn_beijing/news-from-mission/-/blogs/visa-exemptions-for-chinese-passport-holders?_33_redirect=%2Fweb%2Fchn_beijing%2Farchives

Embassy of Malaysia. Beijing (2024, January 30). Ambassador of Malaysia Presents Letter of Credence to President Xi Jinping. https://www.kln.gov.my/web/chn_beijing/home/-/asset_publisher/uilwCm9JrwYv/blog/ambassador-of-malaysia-presents-letter-of-credence-to-president-xi-jinping?inheritRedirect=false&redirect=https%3A%2F%2Fwww.kln.gov.my%2Fweb%2Fchn_beijing%2Fhome%3Fp_p_id%3D101_INSTANCE_uilwCm9JrwYv%26p_p_lifecycle%3D0%26p_p_state%3Dnormal%26p_p_mode%3Dview%26p_p_col_id%3D_118_INSTANCE_NF5xaQSGH7fe__column-2%26p_p_col_count%3D2

Evers, H. D. (2014). Nusantara: Malaysia and the Governance of the South China Sea. The 9th International Malaysian Studies Conference (MSC9) Malaysia's Development: 2020 and Beyond. 18 –20 August 2014. Universiti Malaysia Terengganu. https://www.researchgate.net/publication/265057806

Galvez, D. (2023, March 1). Malaysia vows continuing support for Mindanao peace, aid to Bangsamoro. https://globalnation.inquirer.net/211584/malaysia-vows-continued-support-for-mindanao-peace-process-continued-aid-to-bangsamoro-people

Global Times. (2023, May 9). Exclusive: GT's interview with former Prime Minister of Malaysia Mahathir bin Mohamad. https://www.globaltimes.cn/page/202305/1290398.shtml

Global Times (2024a, February 26). Malaysian PM's remarks reveal US' self-entertaining hegemonic diplomacy. https://www.globaltimes.cn/page/202402/1307708.shtml

Global Times (2024b, April 26). China willing to cooperate with Malaysia in standing up for justice on intl stage, opposing unilateralism: official. https://www.globaltimes.cn/page/202404/1311325.shtml

Global Times (2024c, June 23). US profits from confrontations it provokes in Ukraine, South China Sea: Mahathir. https://www.globaltimes.cn/page/202406/1314662.shtml

Government of Malaysia. (n.d.). Summary Of Malaysia's History. https://www.malaysia.gov.my/portal/content/30120

Hahn, L. C. (2024, April 18). Revitalising US relations with Southeast Asia through public diplomacy. https://eastasiaforum.org/2024/04/18/revitalising-us-relations-with-southeast-asia-through-public-diplomacy/

He, K., & Feng, H. (2023). *After Hedging: Hard Choices for the Indo-Pacific States Between the United States and China*. Cambridge University Press. DOI: 10.1017/9781009420570

Holsti, K. J. (1970). National role conceptions in the study of foreign policy. *International Studies Quarterly*, *14*(3), 233–309. DOI: 10.2307/3013584

Ibrahim, A. (2023, September 22). National Statement by the Honourable Mr. Anwar Ibrahim Prime Minister of Malaysia at the General Debate of the 78th Session of the United Nations General Assembly New York, 22 September 2023. https://gadebate.un.org/sites/default/files/gastatements/78/my_en.pdf

IMF. (n.d.). Malaysia. https://www.imf.org/en/Countries/MYS

Kavas, M., Jarzabkowski, P., & Nigam, A. (2020). Islamic Family Business: The Constitutive Role of Religion in Business. *Journal of Business Ethics*, *163*(4), 689–700. DOI: 10.1007/s10551-019-04384-5

Khalid, M. (2019). Littoral States Conflicts in the South China Sea: a Constant Danger to Regional Peace. *South China Sea: Emerging Scenario*, 193. https://www.researchgate.net/publication/340174502_Littoral_States_Conflicts_in_the_South_China_Sea_A_constant_danger_to_regional_peace

Khaliq, R. U. (2021, February 25). '3 reasons' China tries to control South China Sea. *AA*.https://www.aa.com.tr/en/asia-pacific/3-reasons-china-tries-to-control-south-china-sea/2157110

Kuik, C. C. (2008). The Essence of Hedging Malaysia and Singapore's Response to a Rising China. *Contemporary Southeast Asia*, *30*(2), 159–185. DOI: 10.1355/CS30-2A

Kuik, C. C. (2024). Explaining Hedging. *Contemporary Southeast Asia*, *46*(1), 43–76. DOI: 10.1355/CS46-1c

Lai, Y. M., & Kuik, C. C. (2021). Structural sources of Malaysia's South China Sea policy: Power uncertainties and small-state hedging. *Australian Journal of International Affairs*, *75*(3), 277–304. DOI: 10.1080/10357718.2020.1856329

Mahadzir, D. (2014). Malaysia's maritime claims in the South China Sea: security and military dimensions. In Chachavalpongpun, P. (Ed.), *Entering unchartered waters: ASEAN and the South China Sea* (pp. 208–222). Institute of Southeast Asian Studies.

Malaysian Investment Development Authority. (2024, August 1). PM Anwar: Strong Malaysia-Japan ties key to sustainable economic growth. https://www.mida.gov.my/mida-news/pm-anwar-strong-malaysia-japan-ties-key-to-sustainable-economic-growth/

Malaysian Ministry of Defence. (2020). Defence White Paper: A secure, sovereign and prosperous Malaysia. https://www.mod.gov.my/images/mindef/article/kertas_putih/KPP2.pdf

Marston, H. (2023). The Struggle for Autonomy amidst Great Power Rivalry in Southeast Asia. In The National Institute for Defense Studies, Japan. *NIDS ASEAN Workshop 2023 The Era of Great Power Competition in the Indo-Pacific Region*, pp. 22-34.

Marvel, M. J. C. (2024). The South China Sea Arbitration: Navigating Compliance Strategies through the Lens of Raya and the Last Dragon. In Voigt, C., & Foster, C. (Eds.), *International Courts versus Non-Compliance Mechanisms: Comparative Advantages in Strengthening Treaty Implementation* (pp. 471–488). Cambridge University Press. DOI: 10.1017/9781009373913.029

Ming, O. K. (2016, July 14). What the decision on South China Sea means to Malaysia. *Malaysiakini*. https://m.malaysiakini.com/news/348469

Ministry of Foreign Affairs of PRC. (2024, January 31). Xi Jinping Sends Message of Congratulation to Malaysia's New King Sultan Ibrahim Sultan Iskandar. https://www.fmprc.gov.cn/eng/zxxx_662805/202402/t20240201_11237752.html

MOFAM (Ministry of Foreign Affairs of Malaysia). (2023, April 8). Malaysia's Position on The South China Sea. https://www.kln.gov.my/web/guest/-/malaysia-s-position-on-the-south-china-sea

MOFAM (Ministry of Foreign Affairs of Malaysia). (2024a, March 4). Joint Statement for the 2nd Australia-Malaysia Annual Leaders' Meeting Monday 4 March 2024. https://www.kln.gov.my/web/guest/speeches-statements/-/asset_publisher/statement/content/joint-statement-for-the-2nd-australia-malaysia-annual-leaders-meeting-monday-4-march-2024?inheritRedirect=false&redirect=https%3A%2F%2Fwww.kln.gov.my%2Fweb%2Fguest%2Fspeeches-statements%3Fp_p_id%3D101_INSTANCE_statement%26p_p_lifecycle%3D0%26p_p_state%3Dnormal%26p_p_mode%3Dview%26p_p_col_id%3Dcolumn-2%26p_p_col_count%3D1

MOFAM (Ministry of Foreign Affairs of Malaysia). (2024b, June 20). Joint Statement between the People's Republic of China and Malaysia on Deepening the Comprehensive Strategic Partnership towards China-Malaysia Community with a Shared Future. https://www.kln.gov.my/web/guest/speeches-statements/-/asset_publisher/statement/content/joint-statement-between-the-people-s-republic-of-china-and-malaysia-on-deepening-the-comprehensive-strategic-partnership-towards-china-malaysia-commun?inheritRedirect=false&redirect=https%3A%2F%2Fwww.kln.gov.my%2Fweb%2Fguest%2Fspeeches-statements%3Fp_p_id%3D101_INSTANCE_statement%26p_p_lifecycle%3D0%26p_p_state%3Dnormal%26p_p_mode%3Dview%26p_p_col_id%3Dcolumn-2%26p_p_col_count%3D1

Munir, T., & Sajjad, N. (2022). Strategic rebalancing: SinoUSs interplay in the South China Sea. *International Journal of Applied Research in Social Sciences*, *4*(7), 221–236. DOI: 10.51594/ijarss.v4i7.371

Myers, L. (2023, March 22). China's Economic Security Challenge: Difficulties Overcoming the Malacca Dilemma. Georgetown *Journal of International Affairs*. https://gjia.georgetown.edu/2023/03/22/chinas-economic-security-challenge-difficulties-overcoming-the-malacca-dilemma/

Nambiar, S. (2024, August 2). Will Malaysia build ASEAN with BRICS? (The Lowy Institute). https://www.lowyinstitute.org/the-interpreter/will-malaysia-build-asean-brics

Nguy n, A. C., Ph m, M. T., Nguy n, V. H., & Tr n, B. H. (2024). Kennedy, P. S. J. (2022). Explaining the Increase of China's Power in The South China Sea Through International Relation Theories. *Cogent Arts & Humanities*, *11*(1), 1–16. DOI: 10.1080/23311983.2024.2383107

Nordin, N. A. B. M. (2020, October 20). Maritime Security-Malaysia and South China Sea. https://midas.mod.gov.my/gallery/publication/midas-commentaries/219-maritime-security-malaysia-and-south-china-sea-by-nor-aini-binti-mohd-nordin

Permanent Court of Arbitration. (2013, August 27). PCA Press Release: Arbitration between the Republic of the Philippines and the People's Republic of China: Arbitral Tribunal Establishes Rules of Procedure and Initial Timetable. https://www.pcacases.com/web/sendAttach/227

Permanent Court of Arbitration. (2016, July 12). Award: PCA Case No 2013-19, in the matter of the South China Sea arbitration before an arbitral tribunal constituted under annex vii to the 1982 united nations convention on the Law Of The Sea between the Republic of the Philippines and the People's Republic of China. https://pcacases.com/web/sendAttach/2086

Permanent Mission of PRC to UN. (2009, May 7). Submission No. CML/17/2009. https://www.un.org/Depts/los/clcs_new/submissions_files/mysvnm33_09/chn_2009re_mys_vnm_e.pdf

Pigafetta, A., & Stanley, H. E. J. (Eds.). (2010). *The First Voyage Round the World by Magellan: Translated from the Accounts of Pigafetta and Other Contemporary Writers*. Cambridge University Press. DOI: 10.1017/CBO9780511708046

Rahmanillah, A. R., Bastian, T. P., & Ihsan, R. (2023). Indonesia's South China Sea Policy: The Limits of Hedging. *Edunity*, *2*(11), 1279–1291. DOI: 10.57096/edunity.v2i11.177

Russett, B. (2016). Liberalism. In Dunne, T., Kurki, M., & Smith, S. (Eds.), *International Relations Theories: Discipline and Diversity*. Oxford University Press. DOI: 10.1093/hepl/9780198707561.003.0005

Ryan, S. E. K. Z. (2023). Malaysia: Securing sovereignty in the South China Sea through ASEAN centrality. *Yale Journal of International Affairs*. (March 15). https://www.yalejournal.org/publications/malaysia-securing-sovereignty-in-the-south-china-sea-through-asean-centrality

Shuib, M. S., Keling, M. F., & Ajis, M. N. (2009). The Implications of Cold War on Malaysia State Building Process. *Asian Culture and History*, *1*(2), 89–98. DOI: 10.5539/ach.v1n2p89

Signature states of ASEAN (Indonesia, Malaysia, Philippines, Singapore, Thailand) (1971, November 27). Zone of Peace, Freedom and Neutrality Declaration. https://www.pmo.gov.my/wp-content/uploads/2019/07/ZOPFAN.pdf

Song, V. S., Don, N. T., & Khoi, N. L. H. (2020, June 16). Examining the "historical evidence" for China's sovereignty over the South China Sea islands (Part 1). https://usvietnam.uoregon.edu/en/examining-chinese-historical-evidences-of-sovereignty-over-the-south-china-sea-islands-part-1-china-was-the-first-to-discover-and-name-the-nansha-islands/

South China Morning Post (2024, June 15). Anwar Ibrahim on navigating Malaysia through China-US tensions- Talking Post with Yonden Lhatoo. *Youtube*. https://www.youtube.com/watch?v=xtM-wPrgl6k&list=LL

Stevens, P. (2004). Resource curse and investment in energy industries. In C. Cleveland (Ed.) *Encyclopedia of Energy 5*, pp. 451-9. DOI: 10.1016/B0-12-176480-X/00548-9

Stewart, S., & Reininger, B. (2016). Executive Summary. In Fung, E. & Loong, A. (Eds.). *Assessing the Obama Administration's Pivot to Asia*. Jackson School of International Studies, University of Washington. https://digital.lib.washington.edu/researchworks/bitstreams/e3fe0493-a6c6-4787-b5ea-2a62465ccc33/download

Strangio, S. (2023, April 11). Malaysia Clarifies South China Sea Policy Following PM's Comments. *The Diplomat*. https://thediplomat.com/2023/04/malaysia-clarifies-south-china-sea-policy-following-pms-comments/

Thayer, C. (2014). 'Speak Softly and Carry a Big Stick': What is Malaysia Playing At? *The Diplomat*. https://thediplomat.com/2014/03/speak-softly-and-carry-a-big-stick-what-is-malaysia-playing-at/

UN. (2024, April 11). Commission on the Limits of the Continental Shelf (CLCS) Outer limits of the continental shelf beyond 200 nautical miles from the baselines: Submissions to the Commission: Joint submission by Malaysia and the Socialist Republic of Viet Nam. https://www.un.org/Depts/los/clcs_new/submissions_files/submission_mysvnm_33_2009.htm

US Department of State. (2022). Limits in the Seas No. 150: People's Republic of China: Maritime Claims in the South China Sea. United States Department of State Bureau of Oceans and International Environmental and Scientific Affairs. https://www.state.gov/wp-content/uploads/2022/01/LIS150-SCS.pdf

US Energy Information Administration. (2024, last updated on March 21). South China Sea: Overview. https://www.eia.gov/international/content/analysis/regions_of_interest/South_China_Sea/south_china_sea.pdf

Wade, R. H. (2003). What strategies are viable for developing countries today? The World Trade Organization and the shrinking of 'development space'. *Review of International Political Economy*, *10*(4), 621–644. DOI: 10.1080/09692290310001601902

Wade, R. H. (2020). Rethinking the world economy as a two bloc hierarchy. *Real-World Economics Review*, Issue no. 92. https://www.paecon.net/PAEReview/issue92/Wade92.pdf

Wu, S. (2013). *Solving disputes for regional cooperation and development in the South China Sea: A Chinese perspective*. Chandos Publishing. DOI: 10.1533/9781780633558

Yi, W. (2024, April 26) Written Interview with Al Jazeera Media Network by Foreign Minister Wang Yi. https://www.fmprc.gov.cn/eng/wjb_663304/wjbz_663308/2461_663310/202404/t20240426_11289693.html

Yuying, Z., & Jingyi, C. (2024, May 7). China extends visa exemption for 12 countries to 2025 year-end. *Global Times*. https://www.globaltimes.cn/page/202405/1311838.shtml

Zhang, Y., & Buzan, B. (2012). The tributary system as international society in theory and practice. *The Chinese Journal of International Politics*, *5*(1), 3–36. DOI: 10.1093/cjip/pos001

Zhou, L. (2020, November 12). What is RCEP and what does an Indo-Pacific free-trade deal offer China? *South China Morning Post*. https://www.scmp.com/news/china/diplomacy/article/3109436/what-rcep-and-what-does-indo-pacific-free-trade-deal-offer

ENDNOTES

* Malaysia is not a "small state" per se, however, this article refers to the country's asymmetrical power gap with both the USA and China in the strategic competition context (see Wey, 2017).

1 The word "peranakan" refers to the people with foreign anchestral ties in Malaysia, Singapore and Indonesia (Britannica, n.d.(a)). "Peranakan Chinese", also nicknamed as "Chinese guard", denotes their Chinese descent and "protected" status in the history. They were mainly Chinese traders, who married with local women, while today, this naming doesn't pricesly confirm their Chinese descent due to demografic movements and changes, such as during the colonial times (Abdullah, 2013, p. 146).

2 Malacca Sultanate was founded by the Sumatran prince Paramesvara (later renamed Sultan Iskandar Shah) and existed from roughly 1403 until Portuguese colonial rule in 1511 (Britannica, n.d.(b)).

3 The Chinese tributary system can be described as as a value-based, hierarchical and concentric institutional construct of a *Pax Sinica* international society (Yongjin & Buzan, 2012, p. 12-16).

4 PCA Case No. 2013-19 award text: https://pcacases.com/web/sendAttach/2086

Chapter 7
Narrative Power: Taiwan's South China Sea Claim as a Strategy in Securing Its International Visibility

Eva Ermylina
https://orcid.org/0009-0008-3595-9672
National Chung Hsing University, Taiwan

Ali Demir
https://orcid.org/0000-0002-7659-0356
National Chengchi University, Taiwan

ABSTRACT

This paper delves into Taiwan's strategic use of its territorial claims in the South China Sea as a means of constructing a narrative that asserts its sovereignty and enhances its international visibility. Amidst the complex geopolitical landscape of the region, Taiwan's involvement serves not only to maintain its territorial interests but also to affirm its identity as a sovereign state independent of the PRC, which claims Taiwan as its province. Taiwan's involvement in the South China Disputes is not to confront the other claimants but to craft a narrative that portrays it as a responsible and peaceful actor committed to regional stability. The chapter explores the intricacies of this narrative construction by applying Strategic Narrative theory (Formation and Projection Stages). This narrative is essential for Taiwan's efforts to counteract its diplomatic isolation and secure a place in international discourse, demonstrating that it is not merely a claimant in the territorial dispute but also a proactive participant in the global geopolitical landscape.

DOI: 10.4018/979-8-3693-8109-0.ch007

INTRODUCTION

The South China Sea dispute has raised concerns about security issues in the geopolitical landscape (Yi, 2024). Taking a spot in the Indo-Pacific region, this territorial dispute involves multiple claimants and layers of complexity. Located in the West Pacific Ocean (Huang, Wang, Li, & Li, 1994), this long-standing conflict happened due to China's claim of the "Nine-Dash Line" based on the historical narrative, that this U-shaped line encompasses most of the sea area, extending deep into other countries' maritime zones namely Vietnam, Philippines, Malaysia, and Brunei. China's growing influence has caused the dispute to intensify, where over recent decades, China's economic and military capabilities have significantly increased, leading to more assertive actions in disputed areas. This included the construction of artificial islands and military installations, which have escalated tensions with other claimant states (Kusuma, Kurnia, & Agustian, 2021).

In August 2023, China released a new "Ten-Dash line" map, shifting from the previous nine-dash line covering Taiwan's east maritime zone, incorporating Taiwan into its central territory, and strengthening China's claims in Southeast Asia. This new map has boiled the issue into a new phase of conflict. China's previous Nine-Dash Line and related claims are already contentious. Under international law, countries are permitted to claim and utilize territory within 200 nautical miles of their coastlines, known as their Exclusive Economic Zones (EEZs). This limit is established by the United Nations Convention on the Law of the Sea (UNCLOS) and represents the maximum area of water that countries can claim, along with various other restrictions and regulations. As a signatory to these agreements, China technically cannot claim these territories, having already agreed to the established standards for national waters (Clayman, 2023). Several countries including Indonesia, Malaysia, Vietnam, the Philippines, India, and Taiwan have rejected this baseless claim (Lema, Blanchard, Lee, & Vu, 2023). China's assertive behaviour clashes with the international treaty, which has alarmed the countries around the region and endangered the liberal world order.

While the world focuses on China as the main claimant of the South China Sea versus other involved countries, Taiwan is unseen and seemingly unforgotten in this dispute. The South China Sea dispute initially began on the claim from the Republic of China (ROC) which now positions in Taiwan (Republic of China). After World War II, under the nationalist Kuomintang party's rule, the Republic of China marked its territorial claims in the South China Sea with an eleven-dash line on a map. This claim encompasses most of the region, including the Pratas Islands, the Macclesfield Bank, and the Paracel and Spratly Islands, which China reclaimed from Japan (Council on Foreign Relations, 2024). When the communists declared their sovereignty over the whole China area under the name of the People's Republic of China (PRC)[1] in

1949, the PRC inherited the South China Sea claim. Unlike the ROC's claim of an eleven-dash line, China simplified it into a nine-dash line, removing the two dashes between northern Vietnam and China (Wang, 2015). Despite the complex situation after the Chinese Civil War when the nationalists relocated to Taiwan, the ROC stand on the South China Sea remains the same. Consequently, both China and Taiwan assert the same territorial and maritime claims in the South China Sea, though they each contend these claims belong to a different China. Although both sides agree that the territory and waters within the Dash Line belong to China, they each refer to their own version of China (Herscovitch, 2017).

The existence of two versions of China—the Republic of China in Taiwan and the People's Republic of China on the mainland—stems from the unresolved civil war between the Communists and Nationalists. This division has, for decades, contributed to unstable cross-strait relations in the region. In the early stage of the status quo, the Nationalist leader, Chiang Kai-shek persisted in regaining control of the whole of China from the Communists at the same time, the ROC was still the representative of China in the United Nations. After China replaced the Republic of China (ROC) in the UN in 1971, Taiwan gradually lost diplomatic relations and became increasingly isolated internationally (Shattuck, 2021). Differing interpretations of the "One China" policy have further impacted Taiwan's status. As China's influence has grown, it has reinforced its "One China Policy," asserting that Taiwan has no political rights in the international arena and claiming full sovereignty over Taiwan. As of August 2024, Taiwan has only 12 diplomatic allies, facing significant challenges in engaging with the international community. China's isolation tactic has successfully blurred Taiwan's status and dimmed Taiwan's international visibility (Dewi & Dewi, 2019). Therefore, Taiwan's overshadowed claim in the South China Sea dispute is unsurprising, given that Taiwan itself is claimed as an inseparable part of China (Kuok, 2015).

Taiwan has made small yet significant efforts to clarify that its claims on the South China Sea are based on land and comply with UNCLOS and international law. For example, President Ma Ying-jeou stated in a speech in September 2014 that "the principle that 'sovereignty over land determines ownership of the surrounding waters,' which is established in the United Nations Convention on the Law of the Sea, applies to disputes concerning sovereignty over both land and sea." Additionally, Taiwan has taken a more conciliatory stance by advocating for the application of its East China Sea Peace Initiative, which encourages parties to shelve disputes and promote joint exploration and development in the East China Sea (where China, Taiwan, and Japan have competing claims), to the South China Sea as well (Kuok, 2015). In May 2015, Taiwan officially released the South China Sea Peace Initiative, it firstly asserted Taiwan's sovereignty on the South China Sea based on the perspectives of history, geography, and international law, that the Nansha (Spratly)

Islands, Shisha (Paracel) Islands, Chungsha Islands (Macclesfield Bank), and Tungsha (Pratas) Islands, along with their surrounding waters, are an inherent part of ROC territory and waters. Then, the initiative called for the countries surrounding the disputed area to safeguard peace and stability, promoting the "Sea of Peace and Cooperation" (MOFA Taiwan, 2015).

Moreover, under Tsai Ing-wen's presidency in 2016, Taiwan reiterated that will continue to uphold the ROC's territorial sovereignty guided by the values of peace, humanitarianism, ecological conservation, and sustainable development. The ROC is willing to engage in negotiations based on equality with all concerned states to promote peace and stability and protect and develop resources in the South China Sea, which has formulated four principles and five actions: UNCLOS, multilateral mechanisms, freedom of navigation and overflight, and promoting joint development (MOFA Taiwan, 2016). Unlike the prior President Ma who had visited Itu Aba (Taiping) Island (Tiezzi, 2016), Tsai's approach has been characterized by a degree of restraint, avoiding high-profile actions that could provoke China or complicate relations with the US. This includes not making a significant visit to Taiping Island, which some viewed as a missed opportunity to assert sovereignty. In contrast, following the July 12, 2016, arbitration ruling that dismissed China's "nine-dash line" claim and classified Taiping Island as a rock, Tsai's government strongly rejected the ruling's legal impact on Taiwan. They stated that since Taiwan was not a party to the arbitration, it does not recognize the ruling's authority and emphasized that referring to Taiwan as the "Taiwan Authority of China" was inappropriate. In response, Tsai dispatched naval ships to the SCS to demonstrate Taiwan's commitment to its claims. Avoiding the escalation of conflict, Tsai's government has sought to balance Taiwan's interests between the US and Japan while distancing itself from China's influence. This strategy includes supporting US initiatives for freedom of navigation in the SCS while maintaining Taiwan's historical claims. The administration has emphasized non-traditional security issues, such as environmental protection and humanitarian assistance, to position Taiwan as a cooperative regional player rather than a confrontational one (Lee, 2017).

Furthermore, in response to China's latest ten-dash line claim, Taiwan has positioned itself as a claimant against China, slightly shifting from its role as the main claimant contesting other countries. China's latest map concurs all parts of Taiwan's island as its territory. Taiwan's Ministry of Foreign Affairs has firmly rejected China's new map, which includes the 10-dash line. They emphasized that Taiwan is not part of the People's Republic of China and that Beijing has never ruled the island. Jeff Liu, a spokesperson for Taiwan's Foreign Ministry, stated, "No matter how the Chinese government twists its position on Taiwan's sovereignty, it cannot change the objective fact of our country's existence" (Flemming, 2023). From that statement, Taiwan's primary struggle is not the territorial dispute in the South China

Sea, but rather its fight for international status against China's extensive claims that Taiwan is an inseparable province. This layered complexity positions Taiwan as a unique actor in the South China Sea dispute.

It is believed that Taiwan's primary interest in the South China Sea dispute is not to disrupt regional peace, as this would contradict Taiwan's capabilities and Taiwan's will to be a peace safeguard in the region. Firstly, by positioning itself as a claimant opposing China, Taiwan aims to distinguish itself as a separate entity from China. Taiwan's national interest lies in enhancing its soft power to garner sympathy from the international community and secure its international visibility. This issue is considered an ideational one, as Taiwan seeks to portray itself as a legitimate actor with issues similar to those of other claimants against China. This paper examines the issue through the narrative framework, analyzing how Taiwan strategically utilizes discourse and storytelling. It is a game of discourse narrative to boost Taiwan's international image. Accordingly, this chapter aims to provide an overview of Taiwan's interest in the South China Sea dispute in this changing geopolitics as more than material power but ideational through narrative power. To arrive at this point, firstly it will delve into Taiwan's claims and position in the South China Sea dispute. It will also highlight the construction of Taiwan's image in the South China Sea dispute by employing the strategic narrative framework to understand the narrative level (issue, identity, and international system) and the stages of strategic narrative (formation and projection). It then discusses Taiwan's interest by emphasizing the importance of power narrative over material power for Taiwan's international visibility.

TAIWAN IN SOUTH CHINA SEA DISPUTE: HISTORICAL BACKGROUND AND THE POSITION

The South China Sea is a region fraught with territorial disputes involving several countries, including China, Vietnam, the Philippines, Malaysia, Brunei, and the ROC[2] (Taiwan). The historical backdrop of Taiwan's involvement in the South China Sea disputes is rooted in the complex geopolitical changes in East Asia throughout the 20th century. Taiwan's territorial claims in the South China Sea date back to the era of the ROC before the Chinese Civil War. In 1947, the ROC government published the "U-shaped line" (also known as the "nine-dash line"), which delineated its claims over the South China Sea, including the Spratly Islands, Paracel Islands, and other features. The history of territorial claims in the South China Sea began in the 18th century with European colonizers, who were primarily focused on exploiting minerals and crops for export from the Pacific to other regions of the world. During the 18th and 19th centuries, islands and coastal areas gained strategic importance for European powers seeking to maintain trade supremacy. Under British colonialism, the mapping and demarcation of land borders became significant, leading the British Empire to claim the Spratly and Paracel Islands until 1933. Despite facing numerous challenges, such as the Opium War and the Chinese Revolution in the first half of the 20th century, the Qing Dynasty's authorities contested France's sovereignty over the Paracel Islands. Additionally, after the invasion of Manchuria in 1932, the Japanese Empire did not oppose the claims of France and the United States over the region. However, Japan invaded the Spratly Islands following the Sino-Japanese War, and the Governor-General of Taiwan, under Japanese colonial rule, asserted sovereignty over these islands in March 1939. In 1947, the ROC, which at that time did not have authority over Taiwan, declared the reintegration of the Spratly and Paracel Islands into its sovereignty and jurisdiction. Prior to this, in 1936, Bai Meichu had introduced the U-shaped line in "the Chinese National Humiliation Map[3]," which formed the controversial historical basis for the ROC's claims over the South China Sea. After World War II, the ROC reaffirmed its claims over several islands in the South China Sea by stationing troops on key features, such as Itu Aba (Taiping Island), the largest of the Spratly Islands, which remains under the ROC's control to this day. The ROC's consistent administration of these islands has been a key element of its ongoing claim to sovereignty over parts of the South China Sea (Kipgen, 2020).

During World War II, Taiwan Island was under the control of the Japanese Empire, and its sovereignty over the South China Sea was not directly related to Chinese historical claims. Nevertheless, Taiwan's strategic location played a crucial role in the ROC's claims over the South China Sea, creating a critical naval base in the Pacific region following the Kuomintang (KMT)'s retreat to Taiwan Island (Chen, 2016). Following the Treaty of San Francisco in 1951 and the Sino-Japanese Peace Treaty in 1952, Japan returned Taiwan, the Penghu Islands, and the Spratly Islands to the ROC. However, neighbouring countries did not accept this power shift in the South China Sea and maintained their own territorial claims against the ROC's assertions. The Permanent Court of Arbitration (PCA) in The Hague also did not recognize the ROC's claims, making the issue a controversial political and historical phenomenon that continues to involve the PRC today. The ROC's claims in the South China Sea were not based on the UNCLOS but stem from historical claims dating back to mainland China and its asserted sovereignty over the South China Sea from a nationalistic perspective. Despite this, the ROC's approach was less aggressive compared to the PRC's stance at the time. The loss of recognition in the United Nations in 1971 significantly weakened the ROC's position within the international system, negatively impacting its claims in the South China Sea. As a result, the ROC's political priorities shifted after the 1970s, focusing more on sustaining economic development and ensuring political survival in the face of the growing influence of the PRC. During this period, under the leadership of Chiang Ching-kuo, the ROC deprioritized its claims in the South China Sea, largely due to the geopolitical dynamics of the Cold War and the increasingly close relationship between the PRC and the United States. The ROC's strategic focus during this time was more on internal consolidation and external survival rather than territorial disputes (Hwang & Frettingham, 2021).

The ROC's historical claims evolved after the 1990s with the rise of Taiwanese nationalism in domestic politics and at the presidential level. Taiwan entered a new era of democratization under President Lee Teng-hui, which influenced its approach to the South China Sea claims. However, Lee initially adhered to the policies of his predecessors, as his political position was not yet strong enough to implement fundamental changes. Despite this, the arms conflict between China and Vietnam over the Spratly Islands prompted a more assertive political response from Taiwan due to the dual and overlapping claims between the PRC and the ROC. In response to the escalating tensions, Taiwan announced the South China Sea Policy Guideline in 1993, which was grounded in historical claims rather than international law. This policy move intensified the clash of interests between Taiwan and the PRC over the South China Sea, marking a significant moment in the region's geopolitical landscape. Taiwan's priorities were shifted towards economic development and securing its international presence during the mid-1990s. Thus, Taiwan's stance on its South China Sea claims evolved from a historical perspective to a more nuanced approach that respected the UNCLOS and the positions of neighbouring countries. This shift was marked by the enactment of the 'Law on the Territorial Sea and the Contiguous Zone of the Republic of China' in 1998, which effectively undermined the previous U-shaped line policy. The political developments involving South Korea, Japan, and the PRC over the Exclusive Economic Zone (EEZ) brought new challenges to Taiwan's territorial disputes in the South China Sea. A central issue in these disputes is Taiwan's position relative to the PRC, raising ongoing debates about whether Taiwan is part of China or a separate political entity. As China's political and economic power grew in the international system, Taiwan began to adopt a more defensive posture to assert its sovereignty over the Spratly and Paracel Islands at the turn of the 21st century. For instance, the responsibility for defending these islands transitioned from military defence to the coast guard administration. This shift led to a weakening of Taiwan's military presence against Chinese naval forces, thereby undermining Taiwan's claims in the South China Sea (Hwang & Frettingham, 2021).

The early 2000s marked the rise of Taiwanese nationalism and the implementation of de-Sinification policies, which significantly influenced Taiwan's approach to its South China Sea claims. During the first term of President Chen Shui-bian, Taiwan's stance on these claims became more passive compared to the assertiveness of the Lee Teng-hui era. This shift was primarily due to the Chen administration's reluctance to establish historical ties with China based on the "historic waters" concept that had previously underpinned Taiwan's claims. Within the Democratic Progressive Party (DPP) during Chen's presidency, two distinct perspectives shaped Taiwan's South China Sea policy. The first advocated for a passive role, arguing that Taiwan's lack of historical claims and differing political agenda from mainland China necessitated a more restrained approach. However, this passivity led to a diplomatic setback for Taiwan, particularly in its relations with ASEAN countries, as it found itself increasingly isolated in the face of China's aggressive and expansionist policies in the South China Sea (Hwang & Frettingham, 2021). The signing of the 'Declaration of Conduct of Parties in the South China Sea' between China and ASEAN countries in 2002 signalled the need for a more active Taiwanese stance. This second perspective within the DPP emphasized the importance of diplomatic engagement to protect Taiwan's international standing and territorial claims, aligning with the UN Charter and UNCLOS principles. This shift towards a more proactive policy was demonstrated by President Chen's visits to the Spratly (Taiping) and Pratas Islands—the first such visit by a Taiwanese president—which underscored Taiwan's commitment to asserting its presence in the disputed region. Following these visits, the Chen administration launched the "South China Sea Initiative," marking a significant departure from previous policies. The initiative was further supported by the publication of a White Paper that advocated for environmental diplomacy and a cooperative, non-sovereignty-based approach with other South China Sea claimants. Through these actions, Taiwan sought to distance itself from the U-shaped line traditionally associated with Chinese claims, thereby crafting a distinct Taiwanese foreign policy and reinforcing its separate political identity from China (Shih, 2020).

Following the Chen administration's distinct Taiwanese approach to the South China Sea claims, Ma Ying-jeou's presidency marked a return to the traditional KMT stance, aligning with the "One China" principle established after the ROC lost its UN representation in 1971. Ma's approach to the South China Sea was tested by Malaysia and the Philippines' sovereignty claims over parts of the Spratly Islands in 2008 and 2009, respectively. In response, Ma's administration began deploying both military and civilian personnel to the disputed islands, signalling Taiwan's serious commitment to its claims. Despite this, Taiwan continued to emphasize "environmental issues" concerning the reefs and islands, aiming to garner international attention while cooperating closely with China on the South China Sea disputes. Taiwan's diplomatic isolation from the UN, a consequence of its lack of official recognition, hindered its ability to participate actively in negotiations and military exercises in the region. However, the Ma administration remained steadfast in defending Taiwan's claims against US and Vietnamese operations around

Taiping Island in 2012. Ma's visit to Taiping Island underscored Taiwan's resolve not to relinquish its claims, despite the growing power of China's naval forces and economic influence in the South China Sea (Chiang, 2015).

Under Tsai Ing-wen's leadership, Taiwan's approach to the South China Sea disputes shifted from focusing on arbitration to using the claims to assert Taiwan's status as a sovereign and independent state within the international system. Tsai's administration adopted an ambiguous policy, avoiding the strong rhetoric of her predecessors while striving to balance internal and external priorities. Domestically, Tsai aimed to demonstrate that Taiwan's foreign policy was distinct from China's, highlighting Taiwan's unique stance. Internationally, she advocated for multilateral cooperation in resolving the South China Sea disputes, seeking to elevate the issue to an international level where China's claims could be challenged by the global community. This strategy not only aimed to undermine China's territorial assertions but also sought to bolster Taiwan's identity and international image—crucial elements in its ongoing struggle for sovereignty (Chung, 2016). By promoting multilateralism and diplomatic engagement, Tsai's administration worked to position Taiwan as a responsible actor on the global stage, while simultaneously reinforcing its independent identity separate from that of China. In addition to defining the fundamental differences between Taiwan's and China's claims—rooted in identity and historical relations—Taiwan under the Tsai administration focused on safeguarding its security and economic ties with the United States and ASEAN countries. This was done within the framework of multilateral dialogue concerning the South China Sea disputes. Consequently, Tsai's administration aligned more closely with the U.S. both politically and militarily, aiming to bolster Taiwan's sovereignty and independent stance against China. However, unlike the Ma administration, Tsai's government did not maintain a strong physical presence around Taiping Island to assert its claims in the South China Sea (Chang I.-w. J., 2020).

The establishment of the PRC in 1949 and the subsequent retreat of the ROC to Taiwan set the stage for dual claims over the South China Sea by both the PRC and the ROC. Despite the PRC's rise as a major regional power, Taiwan has maintained its claims, though its geopolitical standing and international recognition have shifted significantly over the decades. Taiwan's position in the South China Sea dispute is multifaceted, balancing its historical claims, geopolitical interests, and strategic narrative construction. Taiwan's claims in the South China Sea serve as an assertion of its sovereignty and territorial integrity. By maintaining control over Taiping Island and other features, Taiwan reinforces its status as a sovereign entity distinct from the PRC. This is a critical aspect of Taiwan's identity and ontological security, as it seeks to affirm its existence as an independent state. Taiwan strategically employs narratives that emphasize its role as a responsible and peaceful actor in the region. By framing its involvement in the South China Sea as a commitment to regional stability and international law, Taiwan seeks to enhance its international visibility and counteract diplomatic isolation. This narrative positions Taiwan as a proactive participant in global geopolitics rather than merely a claimant in the territorial disputes. Despite its lack of formal diplomatic recognition by most countries, Taiwan engages with the international community through non-traditional means. Participation in international forums, scientific research, and humanitarian initiatives in the South China Sea are part of Taiwan's strategy to project itself as a constructive and cooperative entity in the international arena. Taiwan's position in the South China Sea also involves defence and security considerations. The control of strategic locations like Taiping Island provides Taiwan with a strategic foothold in the region. Taiwan has invested in upgrading its facilities on Taiping Island to strengthen its defence capabilities and sustain its claims. Taiwan's involvement in the South China Sea is also a delicate balancing act vis-à-vis the PRC. While both the PRC and Taiwan lay claim to the same historical boundaries, Taiwan seeks to differentiate its stance by emphasizing peaceful resolution and adherence to international norms, contrasting with the PRC's more assertive approach (Lin, 1997).

Taiwan's decision to base its territorial claims on the UNCLOS rather than on historical rights represents a significant shift in its legal strategy, distinguishing its stance from China's nine-dash line claims. By invoking Article 121(3) of UNCLOS, particularly concerning Itu Aba (Taiping Island), Taiwan underscores its commitment to international legal frameworks, positioning itself as a more responsible and law-abiding actor in the South China Sea dispute. This legal rationale may enhance Taiwan's international legitimacy and potentially attract greater global support for its position. Taiwan's increased military presence on Itu Aba, including the extension of the runway and regular military exercises, highlights the island's strategic significance. These actions reflect Taiwan's determination to assert its sovereignty and deter other claimants, while also carefully avoiding direct confrontation with China. The military activities conducted by Taiwan in the region have broader implications for regional security, as they could potentially escalate tensions with neighbouring claimants, particularly Vietnam and the Philippines (Woods, 2016). However, Taiwan's approach seeks to balance deterrence with a commitment to maintaining regional stability, illustrating the delicate equilibrium it must navigate between asserting its claims and avoiding provocation. Taiwan's diplomatic strategy of carefully asserting its claims without directly confronting China reflects the complex dynamics of its relationship with Beijing, while simultaneously ensuring that Taiwan remains an active player in the regional dispute. This nuanced approach could potentially open avenues for cooperation with other Southeast Asian nations that also seek to counter China's expansive territorial claims in the South China Sea. To strengthen its position, Taiwan could engage more proactively with ASEAN countries, building alliances that support a rules-based order in the region. This might include confidence-building measures and collaboration in areas such as environmental protection and search and rescue operations, where Taiwan's expertise and commitment to international norms could be particularly valuable. Additionally, Taiwan's efforts to participate in multilateral dialogues about the South China Sea, even as an observer, would enhance its international visibility and legitimacy. By adopting a strategy of strategic restraint, focusing on non-military aspects of its claims, such as environmental conservation and humanitarian assistance, Taiwan could reinforce its image as a responsible and constructive actor. This approach not only reduces the risk of military escalation but also aligns Taiwan more closely with international norms, potentially garnering broader support for its position (Tønnesson, 2020).

TAIWAN-CHINA'S CLAIM ON ENERGY RESOURCES IN SOUTH CHINA SEA DISPUTE

The South China Sea is believed to hold substantial reserves of oil and natural gas. According to estimates by the U.S. Energy Information Administration (EIA), the region may contain around 11 billion barrels of oil and 190 trillion cubic feet of natural gas. These resources make the SCS a valuable area for energy security and economic development for both China and Taiwan (US Energy Information Administration, 2024). As the world's largest energy consumer, China is heavily reliant on imported energy to sustain its industrial and economic growth. The SCS is a critical area for China not only as a source of potential energy reserves but also as a crucial shipping lane through which approximately 80% of its energy imports pass (Turcsány, 2017). Taiwan, being resource-poor, is similarly dependent on energy imports. Access to the SCS's resources is essential for Taiwan to enhance its energy security, reduce dependency on external suppliers, and maintain economic stability (Schofield, 2014). The strategic importance of the South China Sea lies not just in its vast energy reserves but also in the opportunities it presents for bolstering energy security and economic independence. These energy-related interests drive both China and Taiwan to adopt strong sovereignty claims in the region, creating a direct link between resource potential and national policy priorities.

Energy resources amplify the importance of territorial claims over disputed areas in the SCS, such as the Spratly Islands, the Paracel Islands, and the Pratas Islands, all of which are claimed by multiple countries, including China and Taiwan. China asserts its historical claims over nearly the entire SCS through the "nine-dash line," a demarcation line that conflicts with international norms under the United Nations Convention on the Law of the Sea (UNCLOS). The presence of energy resources strengthens China's resolve to enforce these claims. By securing these resources,

China aims to reduce its dependence on energy imports from external sources and enhance its energy independence. To back its claims, China has engaged in militarization and infrastructure-building activities, such as constructing artificial islands with airstrips and ports that can support exploration activities (Raditio, 2018). Taiwan has similar sovereignty claims over the SCS, with its claims mirroring China's nine-dash line. Taiwan controls the largest naturally occurring feature in the Spratly Islands, Taiping Island (Itu Aba), which it uses as a basis for its territorial and resource claims. Taiwan emphasizes adherence to international law, including UNCLOS, and calls for cooperative development of resources while maintaining its claims. This aligns with Taiwan's broader strategy to project itself as a responsible and constructive actor in international politics. Access to energy resources strengthens Taiwan's argument for self-sufficiency and reduces its vulnerability to energy blockades by China (Song & Zou, Major Law and Policy Issues in the South China Sea: European and American Perspectives, 2016). While sovereignty claims over the SCS have long been contested, the potential for energy resource extraction has elevated the stakes for both China and Taiwan.

The potential to exploit energy resources drives both sides to assert control over key areas. China has heavily invested in energy exploration and drilling activities in disputed areas. State-owned enterprises, such as the China National Offshore Oil Corporation (CNOOC), have been deployed to explore and extract resources, often in areas that overlap with Taiwan's claims. China's activities are frequently accompanied by the deployment of naval and coast guard forces, leading to heightened tensions and confrontations with other claimants, including Taiwan (He, 2018). Taiwan has been relatively constrained in its ability to explore or exploit resources in the SCS due to its diplomatic isolation and the military threat from China. Nonetheless, Taiwan has conducted limited exploration activities around Taiping Island, seeking to assert its rights over surrounding waters and maintain a physical presence in the region (Song, 2013). The contrasting approaches of China and Taiwan to energy exploration not only highlight their different levels of capacity and strategy but also reflect their broader objectives in the region. Beyond material gains, these efforts are deeply tied to questions of identity and sovereignty, which can be better understood through the lens of ontological security.

From an ontological security perspective, the energy resources in the SCS are not just about material gain but also about symbolic affirmation of identity and sovereignty. For China, asserting control over the SCS, including its energy resources, is part of its broader narrative of restoring historical greatness and countering foreign encroachment. The SCS is central to China's national identity as a rising global power, and securing energy resources there is seen as a validation of its sovereignty and territorial integrity (Tien & Cheng, 2016). For Taiwan, maintaining control over its claimed territories in the SCS and accessing resources is tied to its assertion of independent governance and sovereignty. Taiwan's approach to resource management in the SCS reflects its desire to strengthen its international image as a responsible and cooperative actor, distinct from China (Liu F.-k., 2021). The role of ontological security adds a symbolic dimension to the dispute over energy resources, making it a matter of identity and legitimacy for both sides. Taiwan supports the use of international law, particularly UNCLOS, to resolve disputes and promote joint development of resources under the United Nations framework. In contrast, China has rejected international arbitration rulings, such as the 2016 Permanent Court of Arbitration decision, which invalidated its claims under the nine-dash line. The United States has a vested interest in ensuring freedom of navigation in the SCS and reducing the possibility of Chinese hegemony over the region's resources. The U.S. regularly conducts Freedom of Navigation Operations (FONOPs) and supports Taiwan as part of its broader strategy to counterbalance China's influence in the region. The involvement of international law and third-party actors, such as the United States, further complicates the energy dispute between China and Taiwan. These factors add layers of complexity to the already contentious competition, making cooperation over energy resources increasingly challenging (Kucharski, 2022).

Despite the mutual interest in energy resources, cooperation between China and Taiwan on resource exploitation is unlikely due to political tensions and strategic concerns. For instance, the unresolved sovereignty dispute and China's refusal to recognize Taiwan's government create significant barriers to collaboration. Both sides view control over resources as critical to their broader strategic goals, making compromise difficult. Furthermore, Taiwan's support for UNCLOS and multilateral solutions contrasts with China's preference for bilateral negotiations, further complicating joint efforts. Given these challenges, the dispute over energy resources in the South China Sea appears to be an intractable issue, deeply rooted in both material and symbolic interests and these dynamics underscore the broader implications of the energy-driven conflict (McGillis, 2021).

The existence of energy resources in the South China Sea exacerbates the sovereignty dispute between China and Taiwan. These resources are not only valuable for economic and energy security but also serve as symbolic markers of sovereignty and identity. While China adopts an assertive approach to secure these resources, Taiwan positions itself as a proponent of international law and cooperative development. The competition over energy resources thus deepens the geopolitical and ontological tensions between the two sides, contributing to the complexity of the broader regional dispute.

STRATEGIC NARRATIVE: THE CONSTRUCTION OF TAIWAN'S IMAGE AS A LEGITIMATE INTERNATIONAL ACTOR

In the context of new media, narrative has become a critical tool in constructing a nation's image. The advent of advanced technologies particularly the internet and digital media has facilitated rapid and widespread dissemination of information, allowing global populations to interact and access political content with unprecedented speed. This dynamic has necessitated adjustments in diplomacy strategies, prompting nations to craft narratives that effectively enhance their soft power (Anna, 2017). On social media and news platforms, communities both influence and are influenced by the information they receive. The rapid spread of issues and the presence of multiple perspectives on any given story necessitate the construction of effective narratives to maintain visibility (Özdemir & Yıldız, 2024). Miskimmon et al. (2014) formulated a strategic narrative framework, highlighting the significance of using narratives strategically for political actors. This framework is also theoretically valuable for understanding international relations through the lens of strategic narrative.

The strategic narrative framework will be employed to explain Taiwan's interest in engaging with the South China Sea dispute in the contemporary geopolitical climate. Strategic Narrative explains how narrative, storytelling, and communication are strategically employed to shape the international order, promoting interests, values, and aspirations by managing expectations and influencing the discursive environment (Miskimmon, O'Loughlin, & Roselle, 2017). The evolution of media ecology has amplified the importance of narrative, transforming media into an agent of order that enhances connectivity and redistributes power. As people increasingly engage with diverse media channels and online platforms, narratives become vital not just in communicating messages but in shaping perceptions and influencing power dynamics within this interconnected environment. Thus, narratives play a crucial role in communication. Firstly, a compelling narrative can serve as a power resource, such as a historical explanation of events or policies. Secondly, narrative communication as a process is a key means through which power resources operate, with soft power, for example, aligning with pre-existing narratives. Finally, narrative as a tool for influencing specific audiences reveals the competitive nature of international relations within a complex media environment (Roselle, Miskimmon, & O'Loughlin, 2014). Hence, this chapter assumes that Taiwan strategically utilizes narratives to achieve its goals, such as securing international visibility and affirming its status as a sovereign and legitimate actor in global affairs in the involvement of the South China Sea dispute despite its own complex status on the international stage. By emphasizing its adherence to the UNCLOS and the liberal world order regime, Taiwan reinforces its identity as a contributor to regional stability and the international order, this narratives allow Taiwan to differentiate itself from China which is portrayed as an assertive actor.

The process of the strategic narrative emplotment involves creating a compelling storyline that spans the past, present, and future. This storyline is then applied at various levels such as issue, identity/national, and international system narrative to form a narrative that is coherent, persuasive, and strategically effective. The storyline across different levels of a strategic narrative must be consistent and aligned. If there are contradictions between the issue, identity, and international system narratives, it undermines the coherence of the overall narrative. Such inconsistencies can damage the narrative's credibility, making it less persuasive and failing to convey a reliable and compelling image of the entity being portrayed (Miskimmon, O'loughlin, & Roselle, 2014). In Taiwan's case, the narrative surrounding its involvement in the South China Sea dispute as a legitimate actor as well as a contributor to the region's stability is consistently portrayed across all levels- issue, identity/national, and international system narratives.

At the level of issue or policy narrative, Taiwan actively engages in promoting development in the South China Sea dispute. The issue/policy narrative is about how specific policies, agendas, or issues are framed and communicated to influence public perception and persuade a particular policy objective. This narrative is strategic because it influences how a topic is discussed and understood. By framing the issue in a specific way, these narratives guide policy discussions and shape decisions to align with the interests of the actor creating the narrative. Essentially, they set the stage for how policies are debated and decided (Miskimmon, O'loughlin, & Roselle, 2014). The issue narrative is closely related to the South China Sea dispute, where Taiwan emphasizes its way "Sea of Peace and Cooperation" of solving the dispute without jeopardizing each claimant's sovereignty. Taiwan as one of the claimants in the dispute focuses on promoting the development possibilities in the area. President Ma Ying Jeou, for instance, has released the plan "South China Sea Peace Initiative" drawing attention to the narrative of "settling territorial disputes to jointly developing resources. Although sovereignty cannot be divided, resources can still be shared" (Ma, 2015). Taiwan also advocates for its participation in regional dialogues and cooperation activities showcasing Taiwan's will to shift the territorial dispute in the South China Sea into a collaborative effort for mutual benefits (Kuok, 2015). Further, President Tsai Ing-wen underlined "advance peace and stability, as well as protect and develop resources" by publishing several actions in the South China Sea such as scientific collaboration, humanitarian assistance, and rescue, and multilateral collaboration under the principles of the disputes should be resolved by setting aside differences and promoting joint development (MOFA Taiwan, 2016). In a 2019 interview with The Sunday Telegraph, President Tsai responded to the question related to the South China Sea mentioning any actions that will be helpful towards maintaining peace and freedom of passage would be welcomed (Smith, 2019). This issue narrative not only advances Taiwan's approach but also reinforces its identity as a leading actor committed to peace and cooperation.

The issue narrative cannot be separated from the identity/national narrative, as Taiwan constructs its identity on the international stage, defining its role and core characteristics. In this context, Taiwan's identity is not just a representation but a crafted portrayal of its character as an actor in international relations. The identity narratives detail who Taiwan is, what its key attributes are, and what intentions it holds within the international community. Through this process, Taiwan aims to solidify its standing and clarify its purpose and goals on the world stage. Firstly, the fundamental national interest of Taiwan must be understood in order to interpret Taiwan's intention on the international stage. Over a decade, Taiwan's main interest has been to maintain its sovereignty and secure Taiwan from China's threat. Taiwan actively engages with the world, continuously striving for international participation and making significant contributions to the global community. Through the exertion of its soft power and international cooperation, including humanitarian aid, Taiwan enhances its international profile and positions itself as a force for good. This approach aims to strengthen its foreign relations and bolster its international status. As stated in Article 141 of the ROC Constitution:

> *"The foreign policy of the Republic of China shall, in a spirit of independence and initiative and based on the principles of equality and reciprocity, cultivate harmonious relations with other nations, and respect treaties and the Charter of the United Nations, in order to protect the rights and interests of overseas compatriots, promote international cooperation, advance international justice, and ensure world peace." (MOFA Taiwan, 2022)*

Accordingly, Taiwan identifies itself as a contributor to regional development and the peace-guard in regional stability. On May 26, 2015, the ROC government proposed the South China Sea Peace Initiative, emphasizing the principle that "while sovereignty cannot be compromised, resources may be shared." This initiative led to the Agreement Concerning the Facilitation of Cooperation on Law Enforcement in Fisheries Matters between the ROC and the Philippines in November of the same year (Kim, 2016). President Ma then visited Taiping Island in a mission to reiterate Taiwan's sovereignty over land in the South China Sea and promote the island as a base for humanitarian assistance and scientific research. In his speech, he publicized some concrete actions in making the island of peace and rescue operations,

> *"Through these concrete actions, we aim to demonstrate to the international community that the Republic of China is committed to fulfilling its international obligations and actively serving as a peacemaker and provider of humanitarian aid, so as to truly transform the South China Sea into a sea of peace and cooperation." (Office of the President Republic of China (Taiwan), 2016)*

This approach was further continued under President Tsai Ing-wen. During her first National Security Council meeting in July 2016, President Tsai issued a directive to cultivate greater interest in Taiping Island as a base for cross-border scientific studies by foreign researchers. This initiative was highlighted during the ministry-organized International Science Forum on the South China Sea, held on September 4-5, 2016, in Taipei City. On September 6, 2017, Taiping Island was visited for the first time by an international group of academics and researchers, organized by the Republic of China (Taiwan) Ministry of Science and Technology (MOST). Building on the South China Sea Peace initiative, the South China Sea International Science Project Office was launched by MOST in November 2016. The office is tasked with promoting collaboration between Taiwan and other countries and territories in the region, as well as inviting experts to conduct research on Dongsha and Taiping Islands (Taiwan Today, 2017). This development underscores Taiwan's focus on constructing its image as a contributor and peacekeeper in the region.

Taiwan constructs itself as a contributor and peacekeeper in regional stability. This narrative is driven by Taiwan's interest in enhancing its soft power and avoiding conflict with other actors. Taiwan's challenging position on the international stage, primarily due to the One China policy, makes it difficult for the country to be recognized politically as a sovereign entity. Consequently, Taiwan seeks to bolster its soft power to increase its attractiveness, with the hope that the international community will take notice of its presence. By emphasizing its role as a contributor and peacekeeper, Taiwan frames itself as a protagonist in the region, while simultaneously portraying China as the antagonist. This narrative positions China as the main villain, consistently creating instability in the South China Sea through assertive actions, such as unilateral military operations. This is related to the international system narrative, where Taiwan gives prominence to the liberal world order.

Additionally, Taiwan's international system narrative delves into the nature and structure of global affairs. This narrative reflects Taiwan's understanding of how the international order is organized, the composition of the world's structure, the key players involved, and the mechanisms through which the system functions. The current dominant narrative of world order is rooted in constitutionalism and liberalism, characterized by central tenets such as liberal democracy, industrial capitalism, secular nationalism, and open trade. This narrative shapes the international system by upholding principles like state sovereignty and non-interference, which are foundational to International Relations. It also underscores the importance of cooperation and negotiation within established international organizations, advocating for a peaceful global order (Chang Y.-Y., 2021). The international system, grounded in the principles of liberal internationalism, is crucial for promoting universal human rights, freedom, and democratic values. Liberal internationalism envisions a world where nations collaborate based on shared values and collective progress, emphasizing diplomacy, multilateralism, and the rule of law (Ikenberry, 2014).

However, this system faces significant challenges from the rise of authoritarian states, particularly China, which offers an alternative governance model. China's emergence on the global stage has introduced a competing narrative focused on sovereignty, national development, and a distinct interpretation of human rights and freedoms (Weiss & Wallace, 2021). Taiwan's stand on liberal world order aligns closely with its ally, the United States, in upholding and promoting the principles of the liberal international order. Taiwan's strategic narrative emphasizes the perceived threat to this order, portraying China as the antagonist (Yuan & Fu, 2020). Under this narrative, China’s assertive behaviour in the South China Sea is a major threat to world stability. In the broader context of a global struggle between autocracy and democracy, Taiwan positions itself as a responsible actor, contributing to regional stability and acting as a protector of peace. This has created a complex dynamic in which the established liberal order must contend with the principles and practices of a rising power that does not fully align with its norms (Liu & Yang, 2023).

In the liberal world order, which underscores the importance of multilateralism and adherence to international regimes, Taiwan has strategically aligned itself with these principles in its approach to the South China Sea claims. Taiwan's stance highlights its commitment to international norms and cooperative frameworks as key to addressing regional disputes. Taiwan has consistently supported the UNCLOS as a foundation for resolving maritime disputes, including those in the South China Sea. The UNCLOS provides a comprehensive legal framework for maritime boundaries and rights, aligning with the liberal international order's emphasis on a rules-based system. Taiwan's adherence to the UNCLOS is evident in its public endorsement of the arbitral tribunal's ruling under UNCLOS concerning the Philippines' claims against China, despite not being a party to the case. This endorsement underscores Taiwan's support for international legal mechanisms.

Furthermore, Taiwan advocates for multilateral dialogue and cooperation as essential components in addressing the South China Sea dispute. This approach is consistent with the principles of liberal internationalism, which prioritize collective action and diplomatic engagement. In addition to supporting international legal frameworks, Taiwan promotes peaceful dispute resolution methods and expresses a willingness to negotiate with other claimant states through diplomatic channels. This approach reflects Taiwan's alignment with the liberal order's emphasis on peaceful conflict resolution and international cooperation. For instance, Taiwan has proposed joint development agreements and collaborative resource management initiatives in contested areas to foster cooperation and mitigate tensions.

Taiwan also actively supports the principles of international law and the rule of law as foundational to resolving disputes. By emphasizing adherence to these norms and standards, Taiwan seeks to position itself as a responsible actor in the international community, dedicated to upholding the liberal world order's principles. This commitment is demonstrated through Taiwan's participation in international discussions and efforts to build international support for its position on the South China Sea. Moreover, Taiwan has engaged in diplomatic initiatives to garner support from other countries and international organizations. This includes lobbying for recognition of its stance and building alliances with nations that advocate for a rules-based international order. Such efforts underscore Taiwan's proactive role in seeking international backing and reinforcing its position within the liberal world order. By championing UNCLOS and advocating for multilateral cooperation, Taiwan aims to advance a resolution to the South China Sea dispute that adheres to international norms and emphasizes collaborative engagement. This approach not only aligns with the principles of the liberal world order but also reinforces Taiwan's role as a proactive and constructive participant in regional and global affairs.

The three levels of narrative -issue, identity, and international system narrative- in the South China Sea dispute are intertwined to construct Taiwan's image as a legitimate actor within the international order. This strategic narrative assists in addressing its primary challenge of gaining global recognition. Global recognition, though not necessarily diplomatic or formal ties, is a significant interest for Taiwan, particularly because Taiwan is claimed by China as a rebel province. China's metanarrative of "Taiwan's question" together with isolation tactics in all sectors such as international organizations and civil sectors has severely diminished Taiwan's international visibility. As a result, Taiwan carefully engages in the South China Sea claims, aiming to avoid conflicts with other regional claimants that could undermine its efforts to enhance its appeal to the international community. This strategic approach allows Taiwan to boost its global visibility. Simultaneously, Taiwan seeks to distinguish itself from China by portraying China as the antagonist in the dispute, highlighting how China's actions could threaten the established liberal world order. The entire storyline aims to foster a perception within the international community that Taiwan is a separate entity from China and a legitimate country, therefore it is beneficial for Taiwan in securing its international presence. Further detail will be provided in the examination of the communication process of strategic narrative: formation and projection stage.

The formation stage plays a crucial role in the communication process of strategic narratives. It is the initial phase where the actor crafts the narrative, determining the long-term and short-term goals to be achieved through it and the types of communication. The goal might include agenda-setting, legitimation, diverting attention, enhancing popularity, and mobilization. Actors may employ various communication methods, such as persuasion, argument, and representational force. These different forms of communication serve as the foundation for crafting and driving the intention behind a strategic narrative (Miskimmon, O'loughlin, & Roselle, 2014). The formation stage of Taiwan's strategic narrative concerning its South China Sea claims is crucial for defining its international role. During this phase, Taiwan carefully develops its narrative, outlining both long-term and short-term goals to shape regional and global perceptions. These goals include legitimizing its sovereignty, diverting attention from China's dominance narrative, and enhancing its visibility as a significant regional actor.

Taiwan's main long-term objective is to secure its presence in the region by aligning with international norms while reinforcing its identity as a sovereign state distinct from the People's Republic of China. Taiwan seeks to bolster its global standing by highlighting its contributions to regional stability and promoting its democratic values, aiming to build international solidarity in facing China, a common concern for all other claimants. Taiwan's actions in the South China Sea are also focused on asserting its sovereignty, countering China's narrative that portrays Taiwan as merely a renegade province. By asserting its own claims in the South China Sea, Taiwan underscores its ability to make independent decisions on matters of national interest and security, thereby challenging the PRC's narrative of "One China". By presenting itself as a peaceful, law-abiding actor, Taiwan contrasts its approach with China's, positioning itself as a more favourable partner in the region. This strategy is closely linked to Taiwan's broader goal of ensuring its voice is heard in regional security discussions. Taiwan seeks to establish itself as a key player in these discussions, advocating for peaceful resolutions and adherence to international law. In doing so, Taiwan not only protects its own interests but also gains recognition as a legitimate participant in regional security, helping it to build international support against China's attempts to diplomatically isolate it. Taiwan's narrative emphasizes its role as a responsible and cooperative stakeholder in the South China Sea, aiming to resonate with the global community, especially democratic nations that share Taiwan's values and strategic interests.

In the formation stage of its strategic narrative, Taiwan employs various types of communication to effectively convey its message and achieve its objectives in the South China Sea. These communication strategies are carefully selected to influence both domestic and international audiences, and they play a crucial role in shaping perceptions, garnering support, and legitimizing Taiwan's claims. The key types of communication Taiwan utilizes include persuasion, argumentation, and representational force. Persuasion is a central communication method Taiwan uses to influence the attitudes and beliefs of other states, international organizations, and the broader global community. Taiwan seeks to present itself as a peaceful, democratic, and rule-abiding actor in the South China Sea, contrasting its behaviour with that of the People's Republic of China (PRC). For example, Taiwan emphasizes its adherence to international law and its commitment to regional stability, which helps to build trust and support among other nations. Taiwan also uses public diplomacy to persuade global audiences of its responsible and constructive role in the South China Sea. By fostering a positive image internationally, Taiwan aims to gain support and recognition from other countries. Moreover, Taiwan positions itself as a defender of democratic values and international norms, contrasting this with China's authoritarian approach. By framing its claims in moral and ethical terms, Taiwan appeals to the values of democratic nations and seeks to build alliances based on shared principles. Taiwan also engages in humanitarian and environmental efforts on Itu Aba, such as providing medical services to fishermen and conducting environmental conservation projects. These initiatives are intended to showcase Taiwan's responsible stewardship of the island and its surrounding waters, further reinforcing its narrative as a legitimate and constructive player in the South China Sea.

In the next stage after the formation of narrative is reception, which emphasizes how the narrative is communicated, disseminated, and challenged within the new media environment. The goal is to strategically present, promote, and convey the narrative in order to shape perceptions, influence opinions, and gain support or understanding from the intended audience. The type of communication selected plays a crucial role in customizing the message, particularly by adapting the narrative to suit the communication medium within the new media landscape. Consequently, understanding the media technology employed by the actor, the timing of communication, and the dissemination networks is essential in the projection process (Miskimmon, O'loughlin, & Roselle, 2014). The projection stage of Taiwan's claim in the South China Sea dispute is a critical component of its broader strategy to secure international visibility and reinforce its status as a sovereign entity. Taiwan strategically communicates and disseminates its narrative to shape global perceptions, influence international opinions, and garner support from key stakeholders.

Taiwan has employed various strategies in the projection stage to effectively communicate its narrative on the South China Sea dispute to a global audience. One key approach has been through social media diplomacy, where Taiwan has actively utilized platforms like Twitter, Facebook, and YouTube to articulate its stance. Government officials, particularly from the Ministry of Foreign Affairs (MOFA), regularly post multilingual updates, statements, and videos that emphasize Taiwan's legal claims, peaceful intentions, and its role as a responsible stakeholder in regional security. The MOFA Twitter account, for instance, has become a central platform for engaging with global audiences and disseminating Taiwan's positions. Through these digital platforms, Taiwan not only presents its narrative but also counters opposing claims, thereby enhancing its visibility on the international stage. Taiwan further bolsters its international presence through official statements and press releases, which are distributed via global media outlets and published on government websites. These documents are meticulously aligned with international legal frameworks, such as the United Nations Convention on the Law of the Sea (UNCLOS), and are strategically timed to coincide with significant regional events or global discussions about the South China Sea. By doing so, Taiwan ensures that its legal and diplomatic positions are included in the global conversation. Engagement with international media such as Taiwan Today has also been a strategic component of Taiwan's projection efforts. This media engagement allows Taiwan to reach a broad audience, ensuring that its perspective on the South China Sea dispute is understood.

NARRATIVE POWER OVER MATERIAL POWER FOR TAIWAN'S INTEREST IN THE CURRENT SOUTH CHINA SEA DISPUTE

This section delves into the theoretical content which explores the essence, role, and power narrative, comparing the material power. By unpacking the concept of narrative power, it becomes evident how it serves as a critical tool for states, particularly those with limited material resources, to shape perceptions, influence international norms, and advance their strategic interests. In juxtaposition, material power is often associated with tangible assets such as military might, economic strength, and territorial control. However, narrative power offers a more nuanced and flexible means of exerting influence, particularly in the realm of international diplomacy and conflict resolution. Following this, the analysis transitions to a discussion that bridges the theoretical concepts with empirical evidence, specifically examining Taiwan's interests in the South China Sea dispute.

The importance of narrative in shaping international politics is supported by the effort to develop the concept of "Narrative Power," which, according to the authors, is closely related to soft power. Narrative power centers on the influence of storytelling and the construction of narratives to shape international politics. It highlights how narratives create meaning, shape beliefs, and influence perceptions, becoming a tool to communicate and enhance attractiveness, thereby impacting the dynamics of international relations. This concept examines how narratives wield power within global politics, including their ability to provoke antagonism in a region. It also explores how these issues can be addressed or mitigated through the dissemination of "counter-narratives" or "small" stories that challenge and counteract dominant narratives. Conversely, Strategic Narrative refers to the intentional creation and spread of specific stories or narratives aimed at achieving particular strategic objectives, particularly in the realms of politics and international relations. This approach involves the deliberate use of narratives to shape perceptions, influence behavior, and fulfill strategic goals, often by state and non-state actors (Hagström & Gustafsson, 2019).

Taiwan's approach to the South China Sea dispute exemplifies the strategic use of narrative power to advance its national interests, particularly given its relatively limited material resources. Unlike other claimants in the region who may emphasize territorial control and resource extraction, Taiwan has focused on shaping a narrative that aligns with international norms and promotes cooperation. By advocating for principles such as freedom of navigation and peaceful dispute resolution, Taiwan positions itself as a responsible global actor committed to regional stability. This narrative not only distinguishes Taiwan from China's more assertive and unilateral actions but also enhances its diplomatic influence, garnering support from the international community.

For Taiwan, the South China Sea is less about asserting territorial dominance and more about securing international recognition and support. Taiwan is acutely aware of the constraints imposed by its geopolitical situation, particularly the ongoing conflict with China, which claims Taiwan as part of its territory. As a result, Taiwan's strategy in the South China Sea does not prioritize territorial ambitions but instead seeks to gain narrative power that can bolster its standing in international affairs. By emphasizing cooperation and shared benefits in the South China Sea, Taiwan aims to attract international allies who value these principles, thereby strengthening its position on the global stage.

The South China Sea also serves as a crucial platform for Taiwan to demonstrate its commitment to international peace and stability. Taiwan's narrative stresses the importance of collective exploration and resource management, opposing any unilateral actions that could lead to conflict or exploitation by a single country. This narrative approach allows Taiwan to project an image of a peace-oriented nation that contributes positively to regional dynamics, further differentiating itself from China's more confrontational stance. Through this strategic use of narrative power, Taiwan not only advances its interests in the South China Sea but also reinforces its broader diplomatic goals in an increasingly complex international environment.

CONCLUSION

This chapter has analysed Taiwan's strategic narrative construction in the South China Sea dispute. It has highlighted how Taiwan employs narrative power as a tool to assert its sovereignty, promote regional stability, and gain international visibility. Taiwan's emphasis on adherence to international law, such as the UNCLOS, and its peaceful initiative and, namely the South China Sea Peace Initiative and the Scientific Collaboration Initiative, underscore its identity as a responsible actor in the region which distinct itself from China. Through strategic narratives, Taiwan seeks to shape perceptions, gain global recognition, and reinforce its independent identity. Henceforth, the key contribution of this paper lies in its application of the strategic narrative framework to demonstrate how Taiwan leverages soft power in the face of limited material resources. By aligning itself with the liberal international order and emphasizing regional cooperation, Taiwan distinguishes itself from China's assertive actions, projecting itself as a peace-oriented and law abiding entity. This approach emphasizing the narrative power to bolster Taiwan's international legitimacy instead of *de jure* way to assert its sovereignty which is difficult for Taiwan particularly facing diplomatic isolation.

However, this research has limitations. First, while it primarily focuses on Taiwan's strategic narrative, it does not examine the effectiveness of these narratives in altering international perceptions or policy outcomes. Second, the research is constrained by its scope, emphasizing Taiwan's perspective while offering a limited exploration of the responses from other regional actors. Further research on the last stage of strategic narrative, the reception stage is needed to understand how the narrative is perceived. In addition, comparative studies analyzing the narrative strategies of other claimants in the South China Sea dispute could provide a broader understanding of the role of narratives in regional geopolitics.

REFERENCES

Anna, K. (2017). Strategic Narratives of Public Diplomacy and the Enactment of Soft Power: An Exploratory Study. *Dissertation*. Retrieved from https://hdl.handle.net/11244/51905

Chang, I.-J. (2020, July 15). *Taiwan's Delicate Balancing Act in the South China Sea.* Retrieved from Global Taiwan Institute: https://globaltaiwan.org/2020/07/taiwans-delicate-balancing-act-in-the-south-china-sea/

Chang, Y.-Y. (2021). The post-pandemic world: Between constitutionalized and authoritarian orders–China's narrative-power play in the pandemic era. *Journal of Chinese Political Science*, *26*(1), 27–65. DOI: 10.1007/s11366-020-09695-3 PMID: 33071536

Chen, H.-Y. (2016, August). Republic of China's Decision-Making Process in Regards to Drawing a U-shaped Line on the Map of the South China Seaand Its Implications. *Pacific Focus*, *31*(2), 283–306. DOI: 10.1111/pafo.12074

Chiang, H.-c. (2015, April 2). *Itu Aba claim a distracting waste.* Retrieved from Taipei Times: https://www.taipeitimes.com/News/editorials/archives/2015/04/02/2003614945

Chung, L. (2016, July 13). *Tsai Ing-wen tells warship crew to defend Taiwan's interests as they set off for island in South China Sea.* Retrieved from South China Morning Post: https://www.scmp.com/news/china/diplomacy-defence/article/1989282/tsai-ing-wen-tells-warship-crew-defend-taiwans

Clayman, T. (2023, December 22). *China's New Map: The 10-Dash Line.* Retrieved from Boston Political Review: https://www.bostonpoliticalreview.org/post/china-s-new-map-the-10-dash-line

Council on Foreign Relations. (2024). *Timeline: China's Maritime Disputes.* Retrieved from https://www.cfr.org/timeline/chinas-maritime-disputes

Dewi, I. F., & Dewi, K. U. (2019, October). Strategi Pemerintahan Xi Jinping terhadap Taiwan dalam Mengamankan Kedaulatan Tiongkok. *Jurnal Hubungan International*, *7*(2), 161–168.

Flemming, T. (2023, September 1). *The South China Sea has been contested for decades, so what does China's new map mean?* Retrieved from ABC News: https://www.abc.net.au/news/2023-09-01/why-chinas-latest-map-is-causing-new-south-china-sea-conflict/102803902

Hagström, L., & Gustafsson, K. (2019). Narrative power: How storytelling shapes East Asian international politics. *Cambridge Review of International Affairs*, *32*(4), 387–406. DOI: 10.1080/09557571.2019.1623498

He, B. (2018). Security Regionalism: A New Form of Strategic Competition or Cooperation between the United States and China in the South China Sea? In Feng, H., & He, K. (Eds.), *US-China Competition and the South China Sea Disputes* (pp. 151–169). Routledge. DOI: 10.4324/9781351214308-10

Herscovitch, B. (2017). *A Balanced Threat Assessment of China's South China Sea Policy*. Cato Institute. Retrieved from http://www.jstor.com/stable/resrep04873

Huang, Q.-z., Wang, W.-z., Li, Y. S., & Li, C. W. (1994). Current Characteristics Of The South China Sea. In *Oceanology of China Seas* (pp. 39-47).

Hwang, Y. J., & Frettingham, E. (2021). *Maritime and Territorial Disputes in the South China Sea: Faces of Power and Law in the Age of China's Rise*. Routledge. DOI: 10.4324/9781003035855

Ikenberry, G. J. (2014, August 18). *Book Review: Liberal Internationalism: Theory, History, Practice By Beate Jahn*. Retrieved from Foreign Affairs: https://www.foreignaffairs.com/reviews/capsule-review/2014-08-18/liberal-internationalism-theory-history-practice

Kim, J. (2016, May 7). *Where Does Taiwan Stand on the South China Sea?* Retrieved from The National Interest: https://nationalinterest.org/blog/the-buzz/where-does-taiwan-stand-the-south-china-sea-16099

Kipgen, N. (2020). *The Politics of South China Sea Disputes*. Routledge. DOI: 10.4324/9781003026334

Kucharski, J. (2022, September 13). *Taiwan's Greatest Vulnerability Is Its Energy Supply*. Retrieved from The Diplomat: https://thediplomat.com/2022/09/taiwans-greatest-vulnerability-is-its-energy-supply/

Kuok, L. (2015, May 22). *Taiwan's Evolving Position in the South China Sea—And Why Other Actors Should Take Notice*. Retrieved from Asia Maritime Transparency Initiative: https://amti.csis.org/taiwans-evolving-position-in-the-south-china-sea-and-why-other-actors-should-take-notice/

Kuok, L. (2015, May 7). *Tides of change: Taiwan's evolving position in the South China Sea*. Retrieved from Brookings: https://www.brookings.edu/articles/tides-of-change-taiwans-evolving-position-in-the-south-china-sea/

Kusuma, W., Kurnia, A., & Agustian, R. A. (2021). *South China Sea: Conflict, Challenge, and Solution*. Lampung Journal of International Law., DOI: 10.25041/lajil.v3i1.2266

Lee, W. (2017). Taiwan, the South China Sea Dispute, and the 2016 Arbitration Decision. *Journal of Chinese Political Science, 22*(2), 229–250. DOI: 10.1007/s11366-017-9470-2

Lema, K., Blanchard, B., Lee, L., & Vu, K. (2023, August 31). *Philippines, Taiwan, Malaysia reject China's latest South China Sea map*. (M. Petty, & F. Kerry, Editors) Retrieved August 2024, from Reuters: https://www.reuters.com/world/asia-pacific/philippines-taiwan-malaysia-reject-chinas-latest-south-china-sea-map-2023-08-31/

Lin, C.-y. (1997, April). Taiwan's South China Sea Policy. *Asian Survey, 37*(4), 323–339. DOI: 10.2307/2645651

Liu, F.-k. (2021). Mainland China-Taiwan interplay in the South China Sea. In *K.-Y. Zou, Routledge Handbook of the South China Sea* (pp. 376–391). Routledge. DOI: 10.4324/9780367822217-26

Liu, R., & Yang, S. (2023). China and the liberal international order: A pragmatic and dynamic approach. *International Affairs, 99*(4), 1383–1400. DOI: 10.1093/ia/iiad169

Ma, Y.-j. (2015, June 11). *A Plan for Peace in the South China Sea*. Retrieved from Wall Street Journal: https://www.wsj.com/articles/a-plan-for-peace-in-the-south-china-sea-1434040267

McGillis, J. (2021, December 15). *Taiwan's Energy Security and the Threat of a PRC Blockade*. Retrieved from Global Taiwan Institute: https://globaltaiwan.org/2021/12/taiwans-energy-security-and-the-threat-of-a-prc-blockade/

Miskimmon, A., O'loughlin, B., & Roselle, L. (2014). *Strategic narratives: Communication power and the new world order*. Routledge. DOI: 10.4324/9781315871264

Miskimmon, A., O'Loughlin, B., & Roselle, L. (2015). Strategic Narratives: A response. *Critical Studies on Security, 3*(3), 341–344. DOI: 10.1080/21624887.2015.1103023

Miskimmon, A., O'Loughlin, B., & Roselle, L. (2017). *Forging The World: Strategic Narratives and International Relations*. University of Michigan Press. DOI: 10.3998/mpub.6504652

Miskimmon, A., O'Loughlin, B., & Roselle, L. (2018). Strategic Narrative: 21st Century Diplomatic Statecraft. *Revista Mexicana de Política Exterior, 113*. Retrieved from https://pure.qub.ac.uk/en/publications/strategic-narrative-21st-century-diplomatic-statecraft-narrativa-

Office of the President Republic of China (Taiwan). (2016, January 28). *Remarks by President Ma on Taiping Island*. Retrieved from https://english.president.gov.tw/NEWS/4832/Remarks%20by%20President%20Ma%20on%20Taiping%20Island

Özdemir, G. S., & Yıldız, A. K. (2024). Bringing Diplomacy to the Digital Age: The Implementation and Impact of Digital Diplomacy in the USA. In Akıllı, E., Güneş, B., & Güner, O. (Eds.), *Digital Diplomacy in the OSCE Region* (pp. 113–123). Spronger., DOI: 10.1007/978-3-031-50966-7_11

Raditio, K. H. (2018). *Understanding China's Behaviour in the South China Sea: A Defensive Realist Perspective*. Springer.

Roselle, L., Miskimmon, A., & O'Loughlin, B. (2014). Strategic narrative: A new means to understand soft power. *Media, War & Conflict*, *7*(1), 70–84. DOI: 10.1177/1750635213516696

Schofield, C. (2014). Adrift on complex waters: geographical, geopolitical and legal dimensions to the South China Sea disputes. In Roberts, C. B., & Buszynski, L. (Eds.), *The South China Sea Maritime Dispute: Political, Legal and Regional Perspectives* (pp. 24–45). Routledge. DOI: 10.4324/9781315858029-2

Shattuck, T. J. (2021, October 25). *A New Type of Diplomacy: Taiwan 50 Years after UN Expulsion*. Retrieved from Foreign Policy Research Institute: https://www.fpri.org/article/2021/10/a-new-type-of-diplomacy-taiwan-50-years-after-un-expulsion/

Shih, Y.-C. (2020, January). Taiwan's progress towards becoming an ocean country. *Marine Policy*, *111*, 1–7. DOI: 10.1016/j.marpol.2019.103725

Smith, N. (2019, January 5). *Taiwan president signals support for UK base in South China Sea*. Retrieved from The Telegraph: https://www.telegraph.co.uk/news/2019/01/05/taiwan-president-calls-international-support-defend-democracy/

Song, Y.-h. (2013). The South China Sea Workshop Process and Taiwan's Participation. In *N.-T. A. Hu, & T. L. McDorman, Maritime Issues in the South China Sea: Troubled Waters or A Sea of Opportunity* (pp. 70–86). Routledge.

Song, Y.-h., & Zou, K. (2016). *Major Law and Policy Issues in the South China Sea: European and American Perspectives*. Routledge. DOI: 10.4324/9781315593210

Taiwan, M. O. F. A. (2015, May 26). *South China Sea Peace Initiative*. Retrieved from https://www.mofa.gov.tw/News_Content.aspx?n=604CBAA3DB3DDA11&sms=69594088D2AB9C50&s=4589151C339E71C5

Taiwan, M. O. F. A. (2016, July 19). *Sustainable Governance and Enduring Peace in the South China Sea*. Retrieved from https://en.mofa.gov.tw/theme.aspx?n=1462&s=40&sms=294

Taiwan, M. O. F. A. (2022, July 7). *Foreign Policy Guidelines*. Retrieved March 25, 2024, from https://en.mofa.gov.tw/cp.aspx?n=1302

Taiwan Today. (2017, September 08). *Taiping Island visited for 1st time by international science group*. Retrieved from https://nspp.mofa.gov.tw/nsppe/news.php?post=121166&unit=390

Tien, H.-M., & Cheng, T.-j. (2016). *The Security Environment in the Asia-Pacific*. Routledge. DOI: 10.4324/9781315292090

Tiezzi, S. (2016, January 28). *Taiwan's President Ma to Visit Disputed South China Sea Island*. Retrieved from https://thediplomat.com/2016/01/taiwans-president-ma-to-visit-disputed-south-china-sea-island/

Tønnesson, S. (2020). Four aspects of the crisis in the South China Sea. In Buszynski, L., & Hai, D. T. (Eds.), *The South China Sea: From a Regional Maritime Dispute to Geo-Strategic Competition* (pp. 9–23). Routledge.

Turcsány, R. Q. (2017). *Chinese Assertiveness in the South China Sea: Power Sources, Domestic Politics, and Reactive Foreign Policy*. Springer.

US Energy Information Administration. (2024, March 21). *South China Sea*. Retrieved from US Energy Information Administration: https://www.eia.gov/international/analysis/regions-of-interest/South_China_Sea

Wang, Z. (2015). Chinese Discourse on the "Nine-Dashed Line": Rights, Interests, and Nationalism. *Asian Survey*, *55*(3), 502–524. DOI: 10.1525/as.2015.55.3.502

Weiss, J. C., & Wallace, J. L. (2021). omestic politics, China's rise, and the future of the liberal international order. *International Organization*, *75*(2), 635–664. DOI: 10.1017/S002081832000048X

Woods, S. (2016, July). The Sino-Philippine South China Sea Dispute. *American Journal of Chinese Studies*, *23*(1), 159–171.

Yi, S. W. (2024, January 04). *Navigating South China Sea Security in2024*. Retrieved from The Diplomat: https://thediplomat.com/2024/01/navigating-south-china-sea-security-in-2024/

Yuan, Z., & Fu, Q. (2020). Narrative Framing and the United States' Threat Construction of Rivals. *The Chinese Journal of International Politics, 13*(13), 419–453. DOI: 10.1093/cjip/poaa008

ENDNOTES

1 Furthermore, in this paper, the PRC will be named China and the ROC will be named Taiwan or the ROC.

2 For clarity, the term "Taiwan" will be used to refer to the ROC in this discussion, reflecting the change in political discourse over time.

3 It should be noted that since its establishment, the People's Republic of China (PRC) has used the same map to support its claims over these territories.

Chapter 8
Navigating the Geopolitics of the South China Sea:
Re-Emerging Maritime Dynamics in the Systemic World Order

Bilal Ersin Elikoğlu
https://orcid.org/0000-0002-1424-7691
Istanbul Technical University, Turkey

ABSTRACT

This Study will not solely focus on the tensions between China/USA or the frictions regarding the South China Sea. To put it more precisely, the focus will not be on the regional sub-security systems of the international system. No specific geographical area or time period on the globe will be specifically examined, and the perspective will not be narrowed. The system will be considered as a whole. The cyclicality of the historical process and the entirety of the System will be evaluated by considering differential time and space, and Geopolitical Dualism will be highlighted. The purpose of this study is to provide you with an unconventional, different perspective on the competition between powers that have been able to dominate the peaks of the System from the past to the present. From this point of view, the classic, actor-based geopolitical picture has been avoided. Study aimed to contribute to the literature a geopolitical perspective dominated by "blue tones" in the context of the competition between Continental Power and Sea Power.

DOI: 10.4018/979-8-3693-8109-0.ch008

INTRODUCTION

The South China Sea has been highly "securitized" during the last couple of decades. The international public opinion constructed the judgment that there is a crisis environment in this maritime area and that the crisis is caused by some maritime activities originating from China. Moreover, the transformation of the China-Taiwan dispute from an issue to be resolved between these two actors into an international issue has been particularly noticeable. Furthermore, various problems debated within the context of the South China Sea, under the framework of International Maritime Law and strongly advocated by the United States, continuously escalate tensions and increase geopolitical pressure in the region. The securitization of the South China Sea provides the foundation for the controlled escalation of tensions between the United States and China. Throughout history, crisis zones, which are sustainable, controllable and artificial in nature, constructed by the hegemon, are often observed in various regions of the international system. One of the most prominent reflexes that the hegemon displays during the phase of changing power in the international system is to manoeuvre to create crisis and geopolitical pressure zones.

In this study, the focus will not solely be on the tensions between China and the USA or the frictions regarding the South China Sea. To be precise, the focus will not be on the regional sub-security systems of the international system. In addition, there will be no specific focus on a particular geographical area and/or a particular period of time on the globe; nor will there be any limitation of the perspective. The system is going to be considered as a whole. The cyclicality of the historical process and the holistic nature of the international system will be assessed, taking into account time and space differentiation, and geopolitical dualism will be emphasised. The purpose of this study is to offer you an unconventional, different perspective on the competition between the powers that have dominated the summits of the international system from the past to the present. From this point of view, the traditional actor-based geopolitical picture has been avoided. In addition, it aims to contribute to the literature a geopolitical perspective influenced by "blue tones" in the context of the competition between Continental Power and Sea Power.

Historical processes have witnessed the competition between Continental Powers (Tellurocracy) and Sea Powers (Thalassocracy). It may be seen as an oversimplification to reduce the entire historical process to this dualism. However, the nature of the competition and the parties involved were determined by the seas and oceans. This dualism extends beyond geopolitical competition. For instance, the dualism of Maritimity and Continentality also strikingly emerges within the topics such as the ways states govern and in political/social life (Khikmatov, 2022). Any other issue outside of the Geopolitical Dualism are beyond the scope of this study and will not be discussed for now. To return to the topic, blocking the Continental Powers' goals of access to the seas has always been the primary strategic reflex of the Sea Powers.

The fundamental cause of the geopolitical dualism between Sea Power and Continental Power is simply the endeavour to access resources and achieve the "accumulation" and "volume" required by the capitalist system, or to maintain the existing volume. Sea Power aims to maintain access to Sea Choke Points and Sea Lines of Communication, as well as the control of the sea, while Continental Power aims to gain access to these. Sea Powers build their strategies on the coastlines of continental islands and also the islands close to the continent, without aiming to penetrate into the interior regions of the continent. In this way, the Continental Power's access to the sea shall be minimized (Dugin, 1997).

For a Continental Power to aim for access to the seas, a maritime strategy is a must. By successfully implementing this strategy, the path for the evolution of Continental Power to a Sea Power is opened. Consequently, the necessity for the Sea Power holding hegemony to share its accumulation and volume arises. This is the reason behind the competitive nature of the geopolitical dualism. In fact, whoever wants to be a leading actor in the international system must first obtain access to the seas and then, as a further step, build long-distance maritime trade networks. (Arrighi, 2010).

The manoeuvres of Maritimisation and access to the seas, historically seen in many examples and implemented by China in the 21st century, pose a direct threat to the current hegemon, the United States. Ultimately, the focus is shifting from the narrative of China's "rise" to China's potential to compete with the hegemon and possibly aspire to hegemony in one of the future power transition phases. As a continental power, China is one of the most serious actors seeking access to the seas and making steady progress towards this goal. As a result, the South China Sea, the focus of scholars in disciplines such as International Relations and Political Science, is regarded as a critical issue for the geopolitical equations of the international system in the upcoming decades.

As can be deduced from the geopolitical perspective that I have briefly outlined above, when I speak of "navigation" in the South China Sea, I do not mean a physical navigation. Without isolating it from other maritime areas, it is a matter of considering the geopolitical realities of this sea and, moreover, its geopolitical dynamics. In other words, it is a search for geopolitical routes across the seas. Geopolitics, like the sea, presents a sense of wholeness. The 'Geography of Water' cannot be isolated from each other. Oceans surrounding continental islands within this wholeness facilitate communication and interaction between continental areas that host human life, thus providing the basis for geopolitical unity.

Evaluating the International System by looking at the South China Sea would be simplistic and meaningless, given the complex structure of the system. Today, the crises, events, phenomena and geopolitical pressures emerging in the South China Sea should be evaluated within a framework of causality. The focus on the South China Sea is a consequence. It is essential to carefully examine the "causes" that led to this "consequence". At this point, the differentiation of time and space and the wholeness of geography will help us understand the modus operandi of the dualism between Continental and Sea Power.

SPACE AND WHOLENESS

The perspective becomes much deeper when events in the South China Sea are framed in the context of differential space, the geographical wholeness of the historical process, and geopolitical dualism. Moreover, from this point of view, the geography that needs to be taken into account is also broadened. Although such an expansion can be daunting, it is a vital price to pay in order to understand and absorb the dynamics of the system. At the same time, focusing on the system itself rather than on the state-centred approach of actors within the functioning of the international system will help to concentrate more on the role of geopolitics and geoeconomics within the system. This will help to establish a much more rational systemic equation.

As Immanuel Wallerstein has pointed out, understanding what he called the world-economy (Wallerstein, 1991) and the different stages of capitalism is essential for understanding maritime geo-economics and geopolitics. It is therefore crucial to first understand the international system. The rise of China or the future of the hegemonic power of the United States cannot be explained without a deep understanding of the system. It is crucial to recognise that capitalism, often perceived as an ideology, is a complex system that exhibits cyclicality and encompasses the entirety of the world's commercial and economic existence. It is more appropriate to consider capitalism as a systemic phenomenon that has evolved and transformed throughout history, manifesting itself in different forms and intensities and undergoing a metamorphosis from a natural economy to a market economy (Kocka, 2016). While emphasising that a market economy existed before the emergence of capitalism, it is important to acknowledge that capitalism has redefined all exchange relations, including those within the market economy.

By examining capitalism in the context of the historical wholeness and differential space of the international system, we are also touching on one of the most plausible explanations for an approach that foregrounds the system and does not rely on the state within the system. Throughout the ages, when states in the modern sense did not exist, there were different types and structures of geo-economic and geopolitical operational mechanisms. In terms of these mechanisms, states were political entities that could be classified as actors pursuing capitalist strategies and actors pursuing territorial strategies, rather than states that did not exist in their present form. Among these, those pursuing capitalist strategies were the Sea Powers. The territorial strategy, on the other hand, was the roadmap of the Continental Powers (Arrighi, 2010). In other words, capitalism and maritimization were concepts that occurred in an almost intertwined and parallel journey; and economic exchange relations also correlated with social structure (Gilpin, 1987).

Capitalism is a phenomenon transported by sea. This explains its frequent and exclusive association with Pax Britannica (Campling & Colas, 2021). However, it seems inaccurate to date capitalism, which was already present before the 'ism' era, spatially and historically, if not by name, to that period. True geographical expansion occurred with the Great Geographical Discoveries, and the substantial emergence of capitalist volume followed this geographical expansion with the Industrial Revolution. Therefore, although Britain's situation may seem exceptional, the Pax Britannica, which is a continuation of a legacy transferred from the Northern Italian City-States to the United Provinces and later to Britain, cannot be considered as the first or the greatest step (Modelski, 1978). Moreover, even the Pax Americana that followed the Pax Britannica should be questioned. On the other hand, the understanding of the dynamics of the international system in a general framework, the connection between capitalism and maritime expansion on a sub-layer, and specifically the "rise of China", is only possible through an understanding of the Long Cycles of the system, i.e. its "cyclicality". The prominence of a single actor in a particular period will not go beyond being a reflection of the conjuncture of that period.

The global spread of capitalism via maritime trade routes across all latitudes and longitudes has had significant consequences for the historical process. First of all, it is remarkable for the absolute interconnectedness of vast geographical areas. This is due to the inherent need of capitalism to achieve a large volume of trade. Secondly, one of the most striking outcomes of the need for long-distance maritime trade is the emergence of the naval-trade complex. As the need for fast and secure transportation across all the world's seas and oceans through maritime commercial networks arose, navies took on additional doctrinal and strategic duties alongside their previous roles (Pearsall, 1986).

As technology advanced and transportation costs were reduced, the foundations of a global financial system were laid (Bailey, 2017). Thus, in the cyclical adventure of the historical process, the transition from market economies to capitalism was observed. The growth of trade, along with increasing transportation and security needs, made it imperative for navies to consistently ensure security of supply and control of the seas. This is because one of the most important sources of wealth for nations is maritime trade (Smith, 2005), and the domain of this trade is now the controllable part of the global islands' ocean. The strategy of capitalism has been to extend this control through long-distance trading networks and naval bases. This is the most striking aspect of the geopolitical dualism between Thalassocratic and Tellurocratic powers. Thalassocracies are those that have used and developed the capitalist strategy of expanding naval trade complexes on an enormous scale. Tellurocratic powers, on the other hand, were more concerned with taxation, land acquisition, the costs of state-building and the defence of the land.

A careful examination of the historical process reveals the impressive route taken by maritime geopolitics to the depths of the continental islands. The fact that the high seas, as international waters, are a global commons accessible to all humankind means that the sovereignty claims of states are excluded from these high seas. Consequently, the limited/uncertain legal authorities and responsibilities in these waters necessitate a focal point for maritime geopolitics and careful management of security concerns emanating from the sea (Larsen, 2024). Unlike terrestrial/continental areas, the seas are locations that cannot be fortified, delineated with borders, or defended in the same way as land (Brodie, 1965).

Today, much like other grey zone issues, the vast majority of studies on the South China Sea are negatively affected by Sea Myopia. Not only scientific studies, but also the work of international and transnational/supranational institutions suffer from this Myopia (Larsson, 2024). One reason for this is that non-maritime societies and institutions have no choice but to operate with a terrestrial mindset. In the literature, this situation is referred to as Sea Blindness (Bueger & Edmunds, 2017). I am inclined to refer to this adverse condition as Sea Myopia rather than Sea Blindness. After all, people, societies, states and international/supranational institutions do see the seas, albeit metaphorically. However, I consider myopia to be a more appropriate term because of their inability to develop cognitive skills despite seeing them, resulting in a limited range of vision. In fact, those suffering from this myopia exacerbate the situation by shying away from even the term "geopolitics", perceiving it as something evil. Another related reason is that the dynamics of the international system have not been thoroughly analysed in terms of how much they have been influenced by maritime geopolitics throughout history. Otherwise, in the specific context of the South China Sea issue, the threat posed by China's land-based missiles to the US Navy, the tensions between the Philippines and China, the focus on the Taiwan Strait, or even the US Navy's Freedom of Navigation Operations (FONOPs) would be less prioritised issues.

On the other hand, the changing nature of maritime geopolitics, the unpredictability of the nature of the sea, and humanity's current distance from possessing the technical and technological capabilities to conquer nature, combined with the inherent ambiguity in the multifaceted definitions of "security" within the discipline of International Relations, easily lead us to believe that the concept of maritime security has a high potential for continuous transformation in the present and coming decades, thus making the concept more flexible. Under these conditions, it is challenging to predict in advance the potential incidents or phenomena that could threaten the security of the South China Sea or any other part of the ocean, and to test the effectiveness of conventional solutions. According to Bueger, maritime security is a multi-layered concept built on pillars such as geo-economics, geopolitics, the marine environment and national security (Bueger, 2015). Therefore, it is necessary to remain within the reality of maritime geopolitics, to distance oneself from ideological thinking, and to remain connected to rationality.

What, then, is this rationality? Simply put, in order to achieve stability in maritime geographies that are referred to as grey zones, such as the South China Sea, there needs to be international harmony on topics such as capacity building, ocean governance, economic development, maritime awareness, situational awareness at sea, and the legal status of open sea areas (Feldt, Roell, & Thiele, 2013). This state of harmony cannot be provided by the cooperation of a single state, group of states, or supranational organisation, but rather by the harmonisation or unipolarity that the great powers themselves can establish. Ensuring maritime security does not appear to be a matter that can be addressed solely on the initiative of a single, ordinary actor. In addition, when considered in the context of international relations, with Great Power competition and the evolution of the international system towards multipolarity, and with hegemony shifting away from the United States, especially as the aftermath of the Vietnam War, which was a signal crisis, and Iraq, which was a systemic crisis, become increasingly evident, it would be overly optimistic to expect governance and cooperation in any particular body of water in the global islands ocean. Particularly after the 2003 Iraq operation, the USA strongly felt the hegemonic descent phase of the power transition period (Arrighi, 2009).

It is therefore not difficult to predict the occurrence of artificial crises and wars. Historically, hegemony has changed hands in two ways: one through economic stagnation followed by an economic crisis, and the other through war. The irrationality lies in approaches that are detached from the geopolitical reality and do not take into account the cyclicality of the system. The international system is in turmoil. While geopolitical pressures have increased sufficiently in various regions of the world and the power transition phase is working against hegemony, the effectiveness of the aforementioned concepts of cooperation and collaboration should be questioned.

Therefore, time and space present a wholeness, and what deepens and reveals its isotopy is derived from its differentiation. This is how Fernand Braudel describes it: Historical Capitalism, for approximately five centuries, has determined the dynamics of the international system by following the phases of its systemic cyclicalities. Within these dynamics, the most striking variable in the equation of transitional phases is maritime geopolitics and maritime security. What lies behind the high impact of the sea in this equation is its role as a variable that paves the way for, and in a sense prepares the ground for, financial expansion. This variable also serves as a triggering mechanism for the cyclical reorganisation necessary for the world capitalist system (Arrighi & Silver, 2001).

Currently, the sustained crises between China's neighbours in the South China Sea that have existed since independence after the Second World War to the present day continue. The crucial point is that China prefers manoeuvres aimed at gaining access to the ocean rather than deepening its focus on the continental expanse of Eurasia, a significant landmass. With this orientation, China is confidently pursuing maritime expansion, steadily developing its civilian maritime sector, its navy and, perhaps most importantly, its industrial capacity as part of its capitalist strategy. While it is possible to describe this development using various statistical data, it is widely accepted in the Social Sciences that numbers do not always reflect reality. It seems more reasonable to explain China's maritime expansion and evolution into a sea power in terms of its vision, mission, projection and diplomatic initiatives. For example, it is a fact that China's development of maritime capabilities and growth of its navy has greatly unsettled the United States as it moves towards becoming a dominant force in the East and Indian Pacific (Cordesman, 2022). Moreover, it is not just a matter of quantitative naval growth; China is expanding its sea power by increasing the volume of ports and maritime infrastructure, investing in ports and infrastructure in various geographical locations. Also, the United States is known to be concerned about China's ability to build naval platforms. Economic, industrial, political and influence projects such as the Belt and Road Initiative and the Maritime Silk Road underline China's ambitions as a contender for hegemony and as a Great Power.

Just like the other Sea Powers that, in the historical process, conquered the dominant heights of the international system, attained hegemony and power within the dynamics of the system... Over a period of about 500 years, the maritime trading complex of the northern Italian city-states, especially those of Venice and Genoa, brought the riches of the Mediterranean to the Italian coasts, allowing them to trade with the more powerful empires on equal and sometimes better terms. Subsequently, the United Provinces became the warehouse of Europe, with its extensive maritime trade networks, its stock exchange and the institutionalised companies created by its maritime commercial complex. Later, Great Britain became the empire on which the sun never sets, a formidable empire backed by an unrivalled navy and capitalist strategy. Finally, the age we live in, defined as the rules-based world order, is the American age. The most tangible manifestation of American power is its navy, which since the end of the Second World War has always been fleet in being and flagged in the world's oceans.

Was the Cold War a merely fictional phenomenon in terms of power projection? Could the end of the Cold War have been the "end of history"? Did the American dream come true? Is it now China's turn? These are the questions that need to be asked. However, direct answers to these questions are difficult to provide using conventional methods and are considered akin to fortune telling. Therefore, rather than answering these questions directly, I prefer to focus on the cyclical nature of the international system, centring on capitalist strategy and maritime geopolitics, to understand the phase of hegemonic transition. When will this transition take place? Who will succeed? What process will unfold? Historical processes would provide the answers.

THE RISING SUPERPOWER OF ASIA: CHINA ON THE PATH TO THALASSOCRACY

Let's approach the dispute and the geopolitical tensions in the South China Sea from a perspective outside the classical one, in other words, not from the window of international law, but from a geopolitical perspective. Spykman's Rimland was one of the geopolitical theories that conceptualised the rise of the United States to hegemony. Although Spykman did not present a conceptualisation that went as far as distinguishing between Sea Power and Continental Power, if we add a bit of a blue tone to his theoretical approach, we arrive at the same parallel. The idea is that the Sea Power (the United States) could increase its chances of isolating the continent in two separate ways. The first is to gain allies on the coast of the continental island of Eurasia. The second is to gain allies in island states close to the continent (Spykman, 1944). By doing so, it could isolate the Continental Power (Russia) from the world's oceans, thereby preventing the emergence of a potential Sea Power with access to the seas. This meant maintaining the strategic superiority and naval presence advantage of the existing Sea Power in the oceans (Gerace, 1991). During the Cold War, this idea was brought to life in much the same way as George F. Kennan's Containment Policy. It is, of course, impossible that Kennan was unaware of the theorists who preceded him.

On the other hand, like Spykman, Mackinder developed theories about the continental island of Eurasia in the global ocean of islands. This continental island was rich in resources. It was necessary for a capitalist strategy to have it under the control of the hegemon. Mackinder, who developed the idea of a continental island to be controlled for domination, also had the idea that the ever-developing land transport should be taken into account by those involved in the maritime commercial complex and trade, and that the volume of maritime trade could be increased in parallel. No matter how large the land area of the continental island, intermodal transport reaching the coast by rail had the potential to have a multiplier effect on the financial expansion of historical capitalism (Mackinder, 1904). Therefore, the control of the Eurasian lands was of serious importance. At the logical base of the *Heartland* lay a blue tone and a Thalassocratic mindset. As mentioned above, maritime geopolitics does not end with the contact of the sea with the coast and the waterfront, but also penetrates the inland areas of the continental islands.

Ultimately, Russia could not reach the seas. Instead of the warm seas it had desired for centuries, the Russians remained stuck in the vast expanse of Soviet lands. Consequently, first they lost their empire and then the Soviet Union. Even today, accessing the seas remains a dream for the Russians. However, the biggest obstacle to their access to the seas was themselves. They were prisoners of territorial strategy and, like many empires, were deprived of the financial accumulation of Historical Capitalism.

This situation has a certain connection with socio-genetic codes. Just as not every island or coastal state can become a Sea Power, not every continental state can become a Continental Power. However, some have managed to become more than a Continental Power and have also become a Sea Power. There are also those who have had this chance many times but failed for various reasons. The French are among the leaders in this respect. The fact that they meticulously implemented a capitalist strategy, at least in their own country, but failed to become a Sea Power is a topic that deserves further study (Attali, 2018). However, a power like Russia never even dreamed of pursuing this path. Thus, at the end of an era, in the cyclical nature of the international system, hegemony was sustained on the other side of the ocean without passing through this region. Of course, geography is also changing; the Arctic, for example, is no longer an impenetrable natural frontier on which the Russians could rely. The political conjuncture and the dynamics of the international system are also busy redefining their own boundaries.

As a result of the Cold War, or more accurately, the sudden absence of a rival, the USA managed to keep its adversary landlocked and pushed it onto the continent. This was a thoroughly Thalassocratic reflex. The Russians, with their tradition of Continental Empire, were too terrestrial to make use of the capitalist strategy. They were essentially a "fortress navy" (Mahan, 1987). China, however, seems to have made the prelude to a very different story. In terms of national industry, productive capacity, population and foreign policy manoeuvres, China does not resemble pre-World War I Germany, Nazi Germany during World War II or Imperial Japan. Ultimately, China's actions could even create its own Systemic Cycle of Accumulation, and through this accumulation drive its material and financial growth as a candidate for hegemony. Another way in which China differs from other actors in Asia is that it is not an American vassal like Japan. Nor is it a city-state like Hong Kong, Singapore, etc. Moreover, if one carefully examines the financial accumulation of historical capitalism, which has its origins in the pre-capitalist period, especially in the Italian city-states, and emerged during the Commercial Revolution between the 11th and 14th centuries, it is correct to conclude that it reached its peak in Europe. However, it should not be overlooked that national markets, nation-states and inter-state sub-systems are not Western inventions. As Adam Smith pointed out, even in the eighteenth century the region with the largest market volume and national markets was not Europe but Asia (Smith, 2005). In this region, the most prominent actor in terms of the volume of historical capitalism is China.

China, which partly by coincidence and partly by historical necessity has embarked on the road to a hegemony capable of dominating the international system, reflects a potential similar to that of other Thalassocracies in the cyclicality of the historical process. The critical point here is that the United Kingdom's cycle of accumulation was the first to merge capitalism and imperialism in one pot, with both capitalist and territorial strategies working in harmony. This method worked so well that it was adopted and developed by the American accumulation cycle. Both maximised national power through global long-distance maritime trade and control of Sea Lines of Communication. They owed their systemic power transition environment, created by *Military Keynesianism*, to capitalist-imperialist harmony. Both, like their predecessors, turned the transition of power to their advantage through crisis and war. As mentioned above, historical experience shows that power transition requires a phase of war or economic crisis once a certain geopolitical pressure is reached in the system (Arrighi, 2007). What increases this pressure is China's "maritime expansion" and its maritimization process, which fuels geopolitical dualism.

As Stopford emphasises in his work "Maritime Economics", when considering the significant impact of maritime and waterway transportation on development over more than five thousand years, the cyclicality that emerges is quite remarkable in terms of the dynamics of the international system. The maritime economy and the geographical phases in which maritime trade is positioned, beginning with the maritime trade centres of the Mediterranean and Indian Oceans, then shift towards the North Atlantic, the Pacific and the China Sea (Stopford, 2008). In these maritime trade centres, where transitions from East to West are observed, the newly emerging centres, resulting from the failure of Eastern societies to maintain their dominance and to lose their central status, are mainly Western-controlled, especially European, port cities. These port cities are not only rising in maritime trade, but also represent Sea Powers that understand and successfully exploit the symbiotic relationship between maritime and economic development to their advantage.

In the 21st century, the transition from East to West is once again turning eastwards, manifesting itself economically and industrially in China. This time, China seems to have adopted a systematic approach to the maritime economy and maritimisation, placing capitalist strategy at the centre of its political roadmap. Centuries ago, during periods when China's international trade networks with India and the Arab world were developing, particularly around the 8th century, port cities that could be considered financial centres were on the rise. One of the most important of these was the port of Guangzhou.

It was a lively, substantial and developed port, as well as a trading city. Foreign merchants who visited the city praised it for its high standard of living. During the Song Dynasty, Chinese merchants sought to develop and expand their trading networks through the safe navigation and trading opportunities provided by the administration and navy it established. Southeast Asia, India, the Arabian Peninsula and even Egypt felt the impact of China's overseas maritime trade. However, within this economic development and maritime system, a situation that clogged up the system and hindered sustainability became increasingly apparent. This was the control of economic activities by the state, a blockage in which the territorial strategy even dominated the market. As a result, all the accumulation and volume left the Chinese ports (Kocka, 2016). Whether it is explained by the lessons learned from historical processes or by the experience gained, it is not clear, but the situation is not the same for China today. So much so that China, as a state, is playing by the rules to become the centre and focus of financial growth in the capitalist system.

China aims to build comprehensive interests by establishing extensive long-distance maritime trade networks and acquiring overseas military bases. The targeted interests here are to increase economic capacity and maximise industrial production capabilities to generate economic wealth. Due to the increased need for capitalist accumulation, access to broader geographical areas such as Africa, Europe, etc. becomes a necessity to pursue capitalist strategies (Shelton, 2001). This broader access refers not only to physical reach, but also to engagement with influence and market opportunities, and the use of these engagements as usable tools in line with national interests (Alden, 2012). In the geopolitical dualism of the international system, China cannot achieve this through the use of hard power solely. In fact, doing so through hard power alone would only awaken a sleeping dragon and amount to a generous waste of existing energy (Narramore, 2008). Therefore, China's investments in Europe and, more importantly, the African continent - the most important of the developing regions - are critical manoeuvres. Another outcome of this investment and influence-focused policy is establishing overseas relations to gain access to strategic ports and infrastructure facilities in the region (Alden, 2008).

The step to ensure the sustainability of prosperity is the establishment of a naval trade complex that will maintain and expand this state of prosperity within a cyclical system. Thus, it is clear that the demonstration of a naval presence in the open seas fulfils the need to access the widest possible geographical area in the ocean of continental islands (Feldman, Eiran, & Rubin, 2021). On the other hand, considering the whole historical process, during the phases of hegemonic transitions and power shifts, the naval-trade complex in question is an indispensable variable for the transfer of power from one actor to another. The most recent and concrete example of how powerful this variable can be was seen during the Second World War, in the immense impact of the unified American navy and merchant marine during the war.

To achieve success in this regard, China is taking steps to harness the sea and gain prosperity from it, and to maintain that prosperity through maritime power. It is taking firm and strong steps to become a maritimized state. The Differential Space is reflected in different geographies through strategic policies such as the Maritime Silk Road Initiative and the String of Pearls. The underlying logic of differential space involves examining how space is conceived and designed (Lefebvre, 1991) and recognising that it can be restructured. This involves deconstructing and rethinking the perception of space in order to reconstruct it. It is natural for a powerful actor like China to see the Maritime Silk Road as a window of opportunity both regionally and globally.

Due to this initiative, many investments are being directed towards ports and facilities with high development potential, particularly in developing countries, as well as into critical infrastructure projects. These investments are ones that will create positive externalities. It is undeniable that they have an impact on expanding China's sphere of influence as well as being economically beneficial. Therefore, China might be aspiring not just to be a Regional Power, or a Continental Power that desires access to the seas but cannot achieve it, but rather to become a Maritime Power capable of penetrating the global ocean and its hinterland, and power projecting as globally as a potential Superpower. If this is the case, it seems highly likely that China is targeting more than just the South China Sea. Thus, we should stop focusing solely on the South China Sea. In other words, we should stop shaping our perspectives in relation to the geopolitics and the international system by looking at a specific maritime area or any particular geography.

China has succeeded in gaining access to the seas, and despite attempts by Sea Power to push it back to the continent, it has reached the world's oceans and seas. As a power that has been able to use and benefit from the sea, it has taken its place in the international system. After global projects such as the Belt and Road Initiative, another notable step in China's maritimization efforts is the initiative known as the Maritime Silk Road. One of its initiatives is the "String of Pearls", which involves a series of military bases, trade ports and marine infrastructure investments along the Sea Lines of Communication (SLOCs). China is continuing these moves, which are reminiscent of historical periods when dominant powers made the right strategic moves during power transitions. In other words, it seems to be building a Thalassocracy by focusing its capitalist strategy on the use of seas and oceans. From Fujian Province, through Guangdong, Guangxi, Hainan, to Kuala Lumpur, Kolkata and Colombo via the Straits of Malacca, to Nairobi via the Indian Ocean, then north through the Gulf of Oman and the Yemen Sea, and finally to Athens via the Suez Canal to Venice (with special emphasis on the Piraeus Port, one of the busiest in the Mediterranean), this "String of Pearls" strategy is truly a Thalassocratic Grand Strategy. It's worth noting that this expansive continental and maritime geographical area also includes the South Pacific.

The string of pearls, extending from Asia to Europe and Africa, also appears to be designed with the aim of gaining strategic bases on Maritime Sea Lines of Communication and Choke Points from the Middle East to China. In line with this objective, China is seeking to develop local connections in various regions. This step taken by a global player to expand its sphere of influence and influence will be followed by the establishment of commercial relations and direct investment. The series of maritime links and investments, referred to as the String of Pearls, includes the remarkable naval base built at the Pakistani port of Gwadar. The radar facilities at Gwadar have given China the ability to monitor shipping in the Gulf of Oman and the Strait of Hormuz. It is important to note that through these and similar initiatives, China is not only expanding its sphere of influence and trade volume, but also building its capabilities in terms of maritime control (Conrad, 2017).

Investing in maritime infrastructure from the South China Sea to the Indian Ocean, the eastern Mediterranean, northern Europe and even the Baltic ports, China is certainly not considering Gwadar and nearby Chabahar separately, especially in the Indian Ocean. Given the multi-billion dollar trade agreements recently signed with Iran, China seems to be realising an impressive vision and projection of maritime use with a carefully woven network and chain of bases in the oceans. These manoeuvres by China, typical of Sea Power manoeuvres, transform the potential force it is building at sea into an apparatus that positively affects its national power by supporting it from diplomatic, commercial and military perspectives. It is laying the foundations of an area of influence that extends from maritime areas to the most inland areas of continental geography, including the Middle East (Gresh, 2017). In this respect, China reflects the rise and development of Thalassocracies created by the international system in the field throughout history. Whether this reflection evolves into "Chinese hegemony" will be shaped by its success in implementing geopolitical decisions and global maritime projections.

CONCLUSION: HEGEMONY RISES FROM THE SEA

With the collapse of the Soviet Union, the world entered a new geopolitical era known as multipolarity. Since the early 1990s, the sidelining of the Western Bloc's main adversary, the Soviet Union, has been characterised in international relations as America's "unipolar moment". This period marked the end of the communist threat and was seen as the beginning of a system to be sustained by actors from the 'liberal' world. However, the Russian Federation and the former Eastern Bloc countries in need of integration into the New World Order, instability in the Balkans, chronic problems in the Middle East and the rise of Asia were prominent issues in the general framework of this era. Today, the body of ideas that forms the backbone of studies in International Relations, Security and Global Politics largely revolves around these themes. This situation contradicts one of the main goals of this study: that historical processes should be considered as a whole without being divided into specific periods, that geography should be considered in a holistic way, and that geopolitics should analyse the security systems of the entire globe without isolating them from each other. The purpose of highlighting this contradiction is to construct a different perspective.

On the other hand, the International System, within its own mechanics and the equations formed by these mechanics, does not operate in a way that allows any actor to make manoeuvres that are incompatible with the modus operandi of the system. In other words, capitalist strategy and maritimisation, which have been shaped over centuries, have certain dynamics that determine the trajectories of the actors. One of the most important dynamics in question are the elements of national power. The elements of National Power are the fundamental reference values that determine what kind of variable an actor can be within this equation. The positioning of other variables is determined by geopolitics, geo-economics and geo-culture. This is what we mean by the international system, the world economy and the world system.

The studies of International Relations and related fields, as described above or approached through a critical argumentation, risk leading us into academic/ intellectual myopia if we continue to focus on conventional methods, ignoring the historical, temporal and spatial, geopolitical and systemic wholeness. For example, the notion that almost all current habits - the functioning of world politics - should now be designed or revised according to the new order is most evident in areas such as security, geopolitics, economics and social life. This notion was propagated during the period of absolute US dominance, which has been called the "unipolar moment", despite the fact that the US had already experienced a crisis of signals and hegemony and had entered a phase of stagnation. It is no longer appropriate to claim that actors such as the Russian Federation and China were moving in line with Western norms, systems and institutions, or had the inclination and orientation to do so during this period.

Moreover, the ambiguity of the reasons for the need for such a belief is even more remarkable. It is observed that the orientations of Russia and China, rather than being Western or hegemonically persuaded, are more focused on becoming regional powers. By establishing regional spheres of influence and creating subsystems, they are contributing to the construction of a multipolar world order, thereby building a position against hegemony and waiting for the moment of systemic transition. We can only grasp this assumption by thinking in terms of historical processes, geography and geopolitical dualism as a whole. This wholeness leads us to focus on the cyclical nature of history and the competition between Sea Power and Continental Power. The international system has been shaped by this dualistic operation.

The main reason why the US and its "allies"- such as Japan, South Korea, the Philippines, Indonesia and Australia - perceive China as a threat is because of its high capability to access seas such as the Korea Sea, the Yellow Sea and the East and South China Seas, as well as the oceans beyond. Due to its proximity to key geopolitical waterways and its infrastructure investments in distant ones, China is now more than a rising power. It is an old Continental power that has adopted a capitalist strategy and vision of maritimisation, maximising its maritime power and emerging from the continent to the sea as a potential hegemonic maritime power. Its global capacity is evident in its ports, shipbuilding and shipyard facilities. Moreover, China is at the centre of the world's economic production and commercial distribution systems. In short, it has built its naval/commercial complex to a level that influences the dynamics of the international system, supported by its industrial infrastructure. While it is possible to focus on an important and attractive area such as the South China Sea, this focus also means missing the big picture and leaving the systemic analysis incomplete and superficial. Chinese decision-makers are quite happy with this incomplete and superficial analysis. By taking advantage of global public opinion and the hegemon's focus on specific maritime areas, they can channel their efforts into larger Grand Strategic Projections.

For China, which aims to connect marine and continental geographies through the establishment and integration of railway, maritime, land road and intermodal transport systems, the primary objective of this goal is to create a volume that will maximise capitalist accumulation and fluid capital. In this direction, China is seeking to establish an intermodal production and distribution system that also links gas and oil pipelines.

The main point to focus on is that China may engage in disputes in the South China Sea and many other maritime areas. It may expend energy on Law of the Sea disputes, face certain crisis regions, or construct crises as useful apparatuses. However, under the current conditions, with its workforce, industrial capacity, economic size, production capabilities, and perhaps related large-scale maritime manoeuvres, China has gone beyond merely disrupting the hegemon in terms of maritime capacity building. China's positioning as a new potential Thalassocratic Power within the cyclical nature of the international system will be the natural outcome of the systemic world economy structure in the coming decades. Issues such as rights, claims and disputes in the South China Sea are contextual. A new Maritime Law Conference could well be convened with the shift in hegemony. It should be noted that even the concepts and forms of Territorial Waters and the Continental Shelf, which have given rise to the territorialisation of the sea within the framework of Maritime Law, are subject to change. Just as Selden's *Mare Clausum* and Grotius' *Mare Liberum* have been conceptually developed and transformed, International Maritime Law and its related texts are not sacred. They will naturally be configured according to the needs of the times, the dynamics of the international system and the interests of the hegemon. The historical process has shown that the evolution of these configurations always takes shape on a geopolitical basis, with the Law of the Sea and the International Law also serving as a useful apparatus in this geopolitical process.

REFERENCES

Alden, C. (2008). China and africa: A new development partnership. *Strategic Analysis, 32*(2), 297–304. DOI: 10.1080/09700160801994902

Alden, C. (2012, September). China and Africa: The Relationship Matures. Strategic Analysis. Retrieved from DOI: 10.1080/09700161.2012.712365

Arrighi, G. (2007). *Adam Smith in Beijing : lineages of the twenty-first century*. Verso.

Arrighi, G. (2009). *Adam Smith in Beijing: Lineages of the 21st Century*. Verso Books.

Arrighi, G. (2010). *The long twentieth century : money, power, and the origins of our times*. Verso.

Arrighi, G., & Silver, B. J. (2001). Capitalism and world (dis)order. Source[[]. Retrieved from]. *Review of International Studies, 27*(5), 257–279. https://about.jstor.org/terms. DOI: 10.1017/S0260210501008117

Attali, J. (2018). *Denizin Tarihi*. Kırmızı Kedi Yayınevi.

Bailey, M. (2017). Supporting the wartime economy: Imperial maritime trade and the globalised maritime trade system, 1914–1916. *Journal for Maritime Research, 19*(1), 23–45. DOI: 10.1080/21533369.2017.1331617

Brodie, B. (1965). *A Guide To Naval Strategy*. Praeger.

Bueger, C. (2015). What is maritime security? *Marine Policy, 53*, 159–164. DOI: 10.1016/j.marpol.2014.12.005

Bueger, C., & Edmunds, T. (2017). Beyond seablindness: A new agenda for maritime security studies. *International Affairs, 93*(6), 1293–1311. DOI: 10.1093/ia/iix174

Campling, L., & Colas, A. (2021). *Capitalism and the Sea: The Maritime Factor in the Making of the Modern World*. Verso.

Conrad, M. P. B. (2017). China's Access to Gwadar Port: Strategic Implications and Options for India. *Maritime Affairs, 13*(1), 55–62. DOI: 10.1080/09733159.2017.1317123

Cordesman, A. H. (2022). The Other Side of Chinese Sea Power: 'White Area Warfare'.

Dugin, A. G. (1997). *Foundations of Geopolitics*. Arktogeja.

Feldman, N., Eiran, E., & Rubin, A. (2021). Naval Power and Effects of Third-Party Trade on Conflict. *The Journal of Conflict Resolution, 65*(2–3), 342–371. DOI: 10.1177/0022002720958180

Feldt, L., Roell, P., & Thiele, R. D. (2013). ISPSW Strategy Series: Focus on Defense and International Security Maritime Security-Perspectives for a Comprehensive Approach Maritime Security-Perspectives for a Comprehensive Approach. Retrieved from http://www.ispsw.de

Gerace, M. P. (1991). Between Mackinder and Spykman: Geopolitics, containment, and after. *Comparative Strategy*, *10*(4), 347–364. DOI: 10.1080/01495939108402855

Gilpin, R. (1987). The Political Economy of International Relations.

Gresh, F., G. (. (2017). A Vital Maritime Pinch Point: China, the Bab al-Mandeb, and the Middle East. *Asian Journal of Middle Eastern and Islamic Studies*, *11*(1), 37–46. DOI: 10.1080/25765949.2017.12023324

Khikmatov, F. K. (2022). Geopolıtıcal Power In The 21st Century Clash Of Tellurocracy And Thalassocracy. *British Journal of Global Ecology and Sustainable Development*, *10*, 53–64.

Kocka, J. (2016). *Capitalism: A Short History*. Princeton University Press. DOI: 10.2307/j.ctvc77kv8

Larsen, J. (2024). Maritime security: How geopolitics hardens threat patterns at sea and challenges known solutions.

Larsson, O. L. (2024). Sea blindness in grey zone preparations. *Defence Studies*, *24*(3), 399–420. Advance online publication. DOI: 10.1080/14702436.2024.2359913

Lefebvre, H. (1991). *The Production of Space*. Blackwell Publishing.

Mackinder, H. J. (1904). The Geographical Pivot of History. Source. *The Geographical Journal*, *23*(4), 421. DOI: 10.2307/1775498

Mahan, A. T. (1987). *The Influence of Sea Power Upon History, 1660-1783*. Dover Publications.

Modelski, G. (1978). The Long Cycle of Global Politics and the Nation-State (Vol. 20). Retrieved from https://about.jstor.org/terms

Narramore, T. (2008). China and Europe: Engagement, multipolarity and strategy. *The Pacific Review*, *21*(1), 87–108. DOI: 10.1080/09512740701868930

Pearsall, A. W. H. (1986). The royal navy and trade protection 1688–1714. *Renaissance and Modern Studies*, *30*(1), 109–123. DOI: 10.1080/14735788609366499

Shelton, G. (2001). China and Africa: Building an economic partnership. *The South African Journal of International Affairs*, *8*(2), 111–119. DOI: 10.1080/10220460109545365

Smith, A. (2005). An Inquıry Into The Nature and Causes of The Wealth of Natıons.

Spykman, N. J. (1944). THE Geography of the Peace. New York: HARCOURT, BRACE AND COMPANY. Retrieved from www.questia.com

Stopford,M.(2008).*MARITIMEECONOMICS*(3rded.).DOI:10.4324/9780203891742

Wallerstein, I. (1991). *Geopolitics and Geoculture: Essays on the Changing World-System*. Cambridge University Press.

Chapter 9
The South China Sea Disputes:
International Law

Zeynep Fırat Erkan
https://orcid.org/0000-0003-3114-8764
Recep Tayyip Erdoğan University, Turkey

ABSTRACT

The South China Sea (SCS) dispute involves overlapping territorial claims among China, Taiwan, the Philippines, Vietnam, Malaysia, and Brunei over the Paracel and Spratly islands, which are rich in resources and strategically located. The conflict also tests the limits of international law, particularly the United Nations Convention on the Law of the Sea (UNCLOS). This document examines the legal framework of the dispute, its historical evolution, and the claims of the involved countries in light of international law. It highlights the complexities arising from differing interpretations of UNCLOS, the role of international arbitration, and the challenges in enforcing legal outcomes due to geopolitical tensions. This study calls for a reevaluation of UNCLOS to address the ongoing territorial disputes in the SCS effectively.

INTRODUCTION

The South China Sea (SCS) dispute is a complex and multifaceted geopolitical challenge that has captivated the attention of scholars, policymakers, and the international community for decades. China's significant land reclamation and construction initiatives in the South China Sea, particularly commencing in September 2013, have further intensified international interest and scrutiny regarding developments

DOI: 10.4018/979-8-3693-8109-0.ch009

in the region. At its core, the dispute revolves around overlapping territorial and maritime claims among several sovereign states, including China, Taiwan, the Philippines, Vietnam, Malaysia, and Brunei. These claims encompass, in particular, Paracel and Spratly islands and the surrounding water areas including reefs, atolls, cays, which are believed to harbor significant natural resources and are strategically located along some of the world's most important shipping lanes. For these reasons, the problem has taken on an international dimension, with major and non-regional powers such as the United States, Russia and also Australia and India commenting and intervening in addition to the countries in the region.

The SCS dispute is not merely a contest over physical territory; it is also a battle of legal interpretations and principles. The competing claims have led to a series of diplomatic standoffs, military posturing, and legal arguments that have tested the limits of international law, particularly the United Nations Convention on the Law of the Sea (UNCLOS). Adopted in 1982, entered into force in 1994, and accepted by all countries in the region except Taiwan, UNCLOS is frequently invoked by the parties to the dispute. As the largest claimant in the South China Sea, and despite its acceptance of UNCLOS, China uses a map of historical origin, the so-called "nine-dash line", which covers almost 80 percent of the sea, to legitimize itself.

This chapter aims to examine the complex interplay between the SCS dispute and international law. It examines how UNCLOS and other legal instruments have been interpreted and applied by the claimant states and the international community in an attempt to resolve the dispute. The chapter also explores the role of international arbitration, as exemplified by the 2016 ruling of the Permanent Court of Arbitration (PCA) in The Hague, which was a landmark decision that addressed the legality of certain maritime claims and activities in the SCS. Furthermore, the chapter discusses the challenges and limitations of international law in addressing the SCS dispute, such as the UNCLOS' failure to elaborate on some of its terms and the resulting variability of interpretation. It also addresses the political, economic and strategic factors that complicate legal solutions and the ongoing debate on the effectiveness of international law in managing territorial disputes in an era of shifting global power dynamics. In this context, the study will be structured into three main parts. The initial part will delve into the legal framework that will serve as the foundational toolkit for our analysis. In this part the rights recognized by UNCLOS and their limitations will be addressed. The second part will trace the issue's historical origins of the dispute and how the current situation was reached. . The final section will critically examine the claims of the regional countries in the context of international law. The research will draw upon a comprehensive array of sources, including legal documents, policy papers, press conference transcripts, national research reports, and various online articles and books.

LEGAL FRAMEWORK OF THE SOUTH CHINA SEA DISPUTE

The South China Sea dispute is complex because of the overlapping territorial and maritime claims among littoral states. The complexity arises from the fact that the claims are not only overlapping but also often based on different interpretations of international law, particularly the United Nations Convention on the Law of the Sea (UNCLOS). UNCLOS provides a comprehensive framework for the governance of the world's oceans, including rules on territorial seas, exclusive economic zones (EEZs), and continental shelves. However, the application of these rules to the specific features in the South China Sea has been contentious. For instance, the dispute over the legal status of various maritime features is critical, as it determines the extent of a state's maritime rights under UNCLOS. The disagreement over whether certain features are capable of generating an EEZ or continental shelf further complicates the situation. Additionally, the concept of "historic rights," as claimed by China through its Nine-Dash Line, is a point of contention, with other states and legal experts debating its validity under international law. Nevertheless, in this section we will provide the legal framework that will facilitate the analysis of the legal situation in the South China Sea.

It is a fundamental principle of international law that sovereignty over land territory serves as the foundation for the determination of maritime rights. As the International Court of Justice (ICJ) has affirmed many times, maritime rights are derived from the coastal state's sovereignty over the land, a principle that can be encapsulated as "the land dominates the sea"[1] (Maritime Delimitation and Territorial Questions (Qatar v. Bahrain), 2001; Territorial and Maritime Dispute (Nicaragua v. Colombia), 2012). This principle leads to two distinctions according to whether sovereignty is claimed over them or not. They are land territory and submerged features. Islands, rocks, and other land features above water at high tide are considered land territory in a legal sense. These features can generate maritime zones, including the territorial sea, contiguous zone, EEZ, and continental shelf. Despite land territory, submerged features, such as reefs, banks, and other formations that are naturally below sea level at high tide, do not generate their own maritime zones. Their legal status depends on the maritime zone in which they are located (Beckman, 2013). For instance, if a submerged feature is located within the EEZ or continental shelf of a coastal state, it may be subject to that state's sovereign rights for the purpose of exploring and exploiting natural resources. This distinction is crucial in the context of the South China Sea dispute, where various features, including islands, reefs, and low-tide elevations, are claimed by multiple states. The legal status of these features, whether they are considered land territory or submerged features, directly impacts the maritime claims and rights of the coastal states involved in the dispute.

UNCLOS provides a framework for understanding and claiming maritime zones based on various offshore geographic features. They differ from each other with their nature and significance.

Islands: An island is a naturally formed area of land, surrounded by water, which is above water at high tide and generate a territorial sea, contiguous zone, exclusive economic zone (EEZ), and continental shelf (Article 121/1, 2).
Rocks: Rocks which cannot sustain human habitation or economic life of their own shall have no exclusive economic zone or continental shelf (Article 121/3).
Low-Tide Elevations: A low-tide elevation is a naturally formed area of land which is surrounded by and above water at low tide but submerged at high tide. If a low-tide elevation is within the territorial sea, it may be used as the baseline for measuring the breadth of territorial sea. And if it is situated out of the territorial sea, it has no territorial sea of its own (Article 13).
Artificial Islands, Installations, and Structures: The coastal State shall have exclusive jurisdiction over them. Before construction of them, due notice must be given. The coastal State may, where necessary, establish reasonable safety zones up to 500 meters in length around such artificial islands, installations and structures in which it may take appropriate measures to ensure the safety both of navigation and of the artificial islands, installations and structures. Artificial islands, installations and structures do not possess the status of islands. They have no territorial sea of their own, and their presence does not affect the delimitation of the territorial sea, the exclusive economic zone or the continental shelf (Article 60/2, 3, 4, 5, 8).
Submerged Features: Submerged features, such as reefs, banks, and other formations that are naturally below sea level at high tide. When determining the territorial sea for islands on atolls or with fringing reefs, the measurement starts from the seaward low-water line of the reef, as indicated by the appropriate symbol on officially recognized charts (Article 6).

When we look at the definition of rocks and islands, it is seen that rocks cannot generate EEZ and continental shelf as they cannot sustain human habitation or economic life. They are entitled only to a territorial sea and contiguous zone. However, UNCLOS does not provide a specific, standardized method or criteria for determining whether a particular land feature can sustain human habitation or economic life. This determination is left to the interpretation and judgment of states and international bodies and still controversial. Furthermore, the lack of a clear definition of low-tide elevations in the treaty whether it has a territory or not is also mentioned by the International Court of Justice (ICJ) in its 2001 judgment in Maritime Delimitation and Territorial Questions Between Qatar and Bahrain (Maritime Delimitation and Territorial Questions (Qatar v. Bahrain) (Merits), 2001).

The term "artificial island" is not explicitly defined in UNCLOS. Nonetheless, it commonly refers to a feature that remains above water at high tide due to land reclamation or other human activity (Beckman, 2013). Based on the terms of the convention, the difference between artificial island and natural island is related to be man-made or not. While this distinction gives the sovereign state to generate maritime zones for its natural island, it gives only the exclusive right to construct and to authorize and regulate the construction, operation, and use of them to them in their EEZ and on the continental shelf.

The application of the United Nations Convention on the Law of the Sea (UNCLOS) to the offshore geographic features in the South China Sea raises several important issues. It is estimated that less than forty of the features in the Spratly Islands meet UNCLOS's definition of an island, with the total land area of the thirteen largest islands being only about 1.7 km^2 (Beckman, 2013). None of the claimant states have clarified which features they consider to be islands, rocks, low-tide elevations, artificial islands, and so on. Moreover while certain states claim some features as islands, they have been deemed rocks by others, or by international legal analyses. This uncertainty is compounded by the fact that most features are not above water at high tide. Additionally, there are cases where claimant states have built installations on low-tide elevations or submerged features within 200 nautical miles (nm) of another claimant, without clarifying their entitlements. Many of the country claims examined cannot be directly associated with UNCLOS or other international legal instruments. This section will not go into the UNCLOS definitions of the object of these claims, as these specific cases will be discussed in detail later. However, it is clear that ambiguities in the definitions of UNCLOS contribute to keeping the SCS dispute unresolved and encourage differences of interpretation between States.

SOUTH CHINA SEA PROBLEM FROM PAST TO PRESENT

The South China Sea has been and continues to be the scene of many disputes. In short, from a legal perspective the crisis in the South China Sea is characterized by two opposing viewpoints: China's insistence on its historical rights and maritime claims based on its interpretation of international law, and the stance of the Southeast Asian claimants and the Arbitral Tribunal, which favors a strict application of the United Nations Convention on the Law of the Sea (UNCLOS). Before going into the legality of states' claims over the South China Sea, seeing how these disputes have developed may help us to understand the sovereignty claims of the claimant states.

Colonial Period and Early Claims

Although the importance of the sea is well known, the 19th century was relatively quiet in terms of claims. At the end of the 19th century, Vietnam had exercised sovereignty over the Paracel and Spratly Islands for roughly two centuries, supported by the legislation of that time. No international disputes challenged Vietnam's sovereignty over these islands during this period[2] (Quyet & Nguyet, 2023). Until the end of the 19th century, the authorities in the southernmost region of China were unaware of the Paracel Islands, despite their proximity to China, and had even less knowledge of the Spratly Islands (Quyet & Nguyet, 2023). After the signing of the Patenôtre Treaty in 1884, France solidified its control over Vietnam and subsequently expanded its influence throughout Indochina. This treaty marked the formal establishment of French colonial rule in Vietnam, laying the groundwork for the expansion of French influence across the broader Indochinese region. In 1933, the French colonial government in Indochina annexed the Spratly Islands (Truong Sa archipelago) into Ba Ria Province, and in 1938, it included the Paracel Islands (Hoang Sa archipelago) in Thua Thien Province for administrative purposes (Ha, 2020). France's actions in South China Sea, including the establishment of administrative units, the stationing of troops, and the construction of lighthouses and meteorological stations, were driven by a combination of strategic, economic, and security interests. These interests included the protection of maritime navigation routes, the combating of piracy, and the exploitation of natural resources (Quyet & Nguyet, 2023).

China had opposition France's actions in the Paracel Islands. Prior to this, China had claimed sovereignty over the Pratas and Paracel Islands in response to 1909 Pratas Island crisis, which was started on Pratas Island by a Japanese merchant in 1907 and was interpreted as a Japanese invasion (Hayton, 2019). To assert China's sovereignty in the South China Sea, in January 1930, the Chinese government initiated a consultation process involving several ministries and the Committee of Mongolia and Tibet, leading to the revision and expansion of existing regulations in September 1931. This resulted in the creation of "The Revised Inspection Regulations of Land and Water Maps." Subsequently, a Land and Water Maps Inspection Committee was formed on June 7, 1933, comprising representatives from various relevant institutions and departments (Hong N., 2020). In 1935, China published a map of the islands which was an assertion of its claim to sovereignty over the entire South China Sea (Keyvan, 2017). The Chinese government, after conducting additional investigations and studies, distributed an atlas within its administration in 1947. This atlas featured an eleven-dash line or U-shape dashes that delineated the territorial extent of China's jurisdiction over the South China Sea (nearly %80 of the sea), extending as far as the Zengmu Ansha, also known as the James Shoal

(Gao & Jia, 2013). During these dates, South Vietnam took over French installations in the southern Paracels, and the Philippines claimed much of the Spratlys as a Philippine Freedomland (Kalayaan) (Tønnesson, 2020). After the triumph of the Chinese Communist Party in the civil war of 1949, the People's Republic of China embraced the cartographic claim represented by the eleven-dash line. However, it modified this claim by removing two dashes from the Gulf of Tonkin and giving the majority of the Tonkin Gulf to Vietnam in 1953, resulting in the "nine-dash line." This gesture was made to appease their communist allies in Vietnam, although no formal treaty was established between the two nations to formalize this territorial adjustment (Malik, 2013; Zhao, 2020).

Mid-20th Century Developments

In the 1970s, the territorial dispute in the South China Sea began to receive heightened interest and scrutiny. The discovery of oil and the UN Convention on the Law of the Sea (UNCLOS III) prompted a global race to declare maritime zones. China took the Crescent group in the Paracels by force from South Vietnam in 1974, leading to a scramble for islands in the Spratlys by other claimants. In 1977, Vietnam asserted that the Paracel and Spratly Islands were part of its territorial waters and declared an exclusive economic zone that extended two hundred miles (Hyer, 1995). This set the stage for the conflict. The PRC established itself on reefs in the Spratly area and engaged in a firefight with Vietnamese forces in 1988. (Tønnesson, 2020). While China was responding Vietnam in this way, in the late 1970s and 1980s, China's approach to the dispute with Malaysia was similar to its approach with the Philippines. After Malaysia claimed several islands in the Spratlys in 1979, Beijing responded quietly through diplomatic channels. Public mention of the Sino-Malaysian dispute did not occur until 1983, and even then, it was indirect, included within a general statement of China's claim to the entire Spratly Islands (Hyer, 1995).

Despite the fact that most of the competing claimants are The Association of Southeast Asian Nations (ASEAN) member states, China has historically preferred to address the territorial dispute on a bilateral basis with each of the claimants. This approach is aimed at preventing the issue from becoming a complication within the China-ASEAN relationship, which is primarily focused on economic matters. This has increased the perception of "China threat" among the claimant states and this threat together with the search for global actors has paved the way for the globalization of the problem (Hong Z., 2013).

China enacted its "Law on the Territorial Sea and the Contiguous Zone" on February 25, 1992. This law, in Article 2, incorporates into China's land territory the four island groups in the South China Sea, as well as other islands, to which

China applies a twelve-mile territorial sea. Article 3 of the law permits the use of straight baselines for measuring the breadth of the territorial sea (National People's Congress of PRC, 1992). This law reaffirmed China's claims to have "undisputed sovereignty" over the disputed areas such as Paracel, Spratly and Pratas Islands and Scarborough Reef. This law also authorized China to use military force if necessary to prevent other countries from occupying the islands (National People's Congress of PRC, 1992). Subsequently, the "Manila Declaration" was announced at the ASEAN meeting held in the Philippines in July 1992. The declaration underscored the importance of avoiding the use of force in the South China Sea dispute and highlighted the need for any potential crises to be resolved through peaceful means (1992 ASEAN Decleration on the South China Sea, 2017).

In 1995, following the adoption of the Law of the Sea Convention, China took control of Mischief Reef, which is part of the Spratly Islands, not far from the Philippine Island of Palawan and claimed by the Philippines. This was the first time China had a military confrontation with an ASEAN member other than Vietnam. The incident put a strain on Sino-Philippine relations and prompted the Philippines to renew its military ties with the United States (1895 – 2024 China's Maritime Disputes, 2024) (Burgess, 2003). Since then, the Scarborough reef has become an area of conflict between China and the Philippines[3]. The Philippines took the issue to ASEAN, and ASEAN issued its second declaration on the South China Sea dispute in March 1995, calling for "avoiding actions that could harm freedom of navigation and aviation and promoting confidence-building measures" (Thayer, 2020). On June 26, 1998, China introduced its Law on the Exclusive Economic Zone (EEZ) and the Continental Shelf. This law includes an article that states China's historical rights are not affected by the law's provisions (Gao & Jia, 2013). In 1999, ASEAN ministers decided to create a set of rules with China to avoid conflicts and refrain further takeovers in the South China Sea. After three years of talks, they signed the Declaration on the Conduct of Parties in the South China Sea at the ASEAN summit in Phnom Penh in 2002. Although the declaration is not binding, China and all ASEAN countries except Taiwan sign the declaration. In this declaration, the parties promised to follow the rules set by "the Charter of the United Nations and 1982 UN Convention on the Law of the Sea, the Treaty of Amity and Cooperation in Southeast Asia, the Five Principles of Peaceful Coexistence, and other universally recognized principles of international law." They also agreed to settle their disputes through negotiations without resorting to the threat or use of force (Declaration on The Conduct of Parties in The South China Sea, 2012). Together with this declaration and agreements were signed by Vietnam and China about delimitation of the Maritime Boundaries, EEZ and Continental Shelf and subsequently regulating fisheries in the Gulf of Tonkin in 2000, South China Sea was relatively quieten till 2009.

In 2009, the crisis that continues to present began with the UN deadline for submitting information on the outer limits of continental shelves. Vietnam and Malaysia made joint submissions for the southern part of the South China Sea, and Vietnam made a separate submission for the northern part. And both of them extend the continental shelf to 200 miles. As a response to this submission, China and Philippines who did not submit their own claims for the South China Sea protested. And China responded with a note of what it saw as a violation of its sovereignty and for the first time submitted a map with a U-shaped line to the UN. This map showed approximately 80% to 90% of China's South China Sea as "maritime territory" (Tønnesson, 2020). However, China still did not state whether the line demarcated a claim to land features or to both islands and waters. Vietnam, Malaysia, Indonesia and lastly the Philippines have separately responded to China's claims, saying the disputed islands belong to them (Gao & Jia, 2013).

Modern Disputes and Legal Standpoints

The crisis in the South China Sea since 2009 has been marked by frequent confrontations at sea, damaged equipment, and strained diplomatic relations. China has been particularly assertive, reclaiming land and building city[4] and military installations on several reefs and islands in the Spratly archipelago without significant international opposition, leading only to protests. To counterbalance China, some of the claimant states have granted privileges to and have expectations from third parties such as India and the United States of America. This has led to increased interest from third countries. These states including Japan increased their activities along the disputed islands such as joint naval exercises. Despite its aggressive actions, China has shown restraint by avoiding direct armed conflict. It has used non-lethal tactics, such as water cannons, to assert its dominance without provoking military intervention from the United States. On the other hand, China has significantly enhanced its military capabilities in the region over the past two decades, outpacing the combined efforts of the ASEAN nations. It has built a formidable navy and air force, strengthened by advanced missiles and surveillance systems (Tønnesson, 2020).

The Philippines, in response to China's persistent disruptive activities in the South China Sea, sought to raise the issue within ASEAN in 2010 but was blocked by Cambodia (Tønnesson, 2020, p. 13). Unable to find support within ASEAN, the Philippines turned to the United States and Japan for help (Hong Z., 2013). With the support of these two major powers, the Philippines independently filed a case with the Permanent Court of International Arbitration in January 2013. In the opening argument of its 15-point legal submission to the Arbitral Tribunal, the Philippines challenged the validity of China's maritime claims as delineated by the nine-dash line, which encompasses approximately 80% of the South China Sea and 90% of the exclusive economic zones within it. The Philippines insisted on the application of international law to scrutinize these claims (Tanrıverdi, 2021). This action was taken against the backdrop of a territorial distribution where the PRC held control over the entirety of the Paracel Islands and eight of the Spratly Islands. In contrast, Vietnam exercised control over 29 of the Spratly Islands, the Philippines over eight, Malaysia over five, Brunei over two, and Taiwan over one. This intricate mosaic of territorial claims underscores the multifaceted nature of the South China Sea disputes (Mermer, 2022).

While China continues to change the geography of the region and build military facilities on the islands, building mini airports on Fiery Cross Reef and Mischief Reef, the tribunal announced its award. The Arbitral Tribunal resolved 14 of the 15 issues, with the exception of one that dealt with military matters and announced that China's claims are contrary to the Convention. Briefly, in the Tribunal's view, any application of straight baselines to the Spratly Islands and historic rights of China encompassed by "nine-dash line" are contrary to the UNCLOS and Tribunal concluded that "none of the high-tide features in the Spratly Islands is capable of sustaining human habitation or an economic life of their own, the effect of Article 121(3) is that such features shall have no exclusive economic zone or continental shelf. Furthermore, The Tribunal has also held that Itu Aba, held by Taiwan, generate no exclusive economic zone or continental shelf. The Tribunal also made a judgment that China's construction of installations and artificial islands at Mischief Reef without the authorization of the Philippines, is contrary to the Convention and undermines Articles 60 and the Philippines' sovereign rights in its exclusive economic zone and continental shelf (The South China Sea Arbitration, 2016).

Following the announcement of the ruling, the Chinese government released a white paper stating its stance of "four noes": it would not participate in the arbitration, not recognize the arbitration panel's authority, not accept the ruling, and not enforce the decision. Furthermore, Chinese Foreign Minister Wang Yi characterized the tribunal's decision as having "three illegals": the arbitration was illegally initiated, the arbitration court was illegally formed, and the ruling was itself illegal. He argued that the tribunal had no jurisdiction, was prejudiced, and lacked a legal foundation for its decisions (Zhao, 2020). Because the new government of the Philippines prioritized Chinese economic aid and avoids military conflict, The Duterte administration did not use the 2016 legal victory. The rest of the ASEAN was the same and avoided the Tribunal's award directly, as economic sanctions were deemed ineffective against the world's second-largest economy and could have provoked retaliation. Military action was also not considered an option; even the US was hesitant to intervene militarily due to concerns about escalating tensions (Tønnesson, 2020; Zhao, 2020). Taiwan has sided with China against ASEAN, considering the potential long-term implications of the Permanent Court of International Arbitration's ruling on its control over Itu Aba (Taiping Island) (Mermer, 2022). The Belt and Road Initiative (BRI), unveiled by China in the fall of 2017 in the name of One Belt One Road, also promised economic development for ASEAN countries, contributing to an increase in China's soft power in the region and pushing South China Sea issues into the background. While the Belt and Road Initiative strengthened China's position in South Asia, the Quadrilateral Security Dialogue (QUAD)[5] was doing the opposite by supporting ASEAN countries that opposed China over the South China Sea.

By aligning with both current and potential victims of the China's claims, QUAD has sought to create a platform to address their shared security concerns. In this context, Japan has provided economic and military support to Vietnam and the Philippines, countries that are vulnerable to the PRC's actions in the South China Sea, and has enhanced cooperation with them. This has resulted in Southeast Asia becoming a focal point where QUAD countries aim to curb the PRC's expansion, transforming the region into an arena of competition between the PRC and QUAD (Mermer, 2022).

Since 2015, tensions have escalated in the South China Sea due to China's assertive actions, including the deployment of ships near Philippine and Vietnam-occupied islands, construction of military facilities, extensive reclamation and construction on several reefs[6] in the Spratly Island chain and aggressive maritime maneuvers. With this large-scale reclamation China increased the size of some land features by several times and created completely new land features that had previously been submerged reefs (Dolven, Elsea, Lawrence, O'Rourke, & Rinehart, 2015). These activities were responded other claimant states in various way. Philippine President Rodrigo Duterte threatened military action in response to Chinese incursions in April 2019, while Vietnam was protesting China's presence in its EEZ and the sinking of a Vietnamese fishing boat to the UN in April 2020. Despite the challenges posed by the pandemic, China has continued to assert its territorial claims, leading to increased tensions with the Philippines and Vietnam. In a positive development, Indonesia and Vietnam resolved their EEZ border disputes after twelve years of negotiations in 2022, but The Philippines' decision to welcome an expanded U.S. military presence and China's expanded territorial map in by adding a new dash, which includes Taiwan and the Spratly Islands, has indeed contributed to heightened regional tensions. At the time of writing this chapter, the China-Philippines dispute over the Second Thomas Shoal is escalating because of the collisions (1895 – 2024 China's Maritime Disputes, 2024). These developments show that the region's problems are far from being resolved.

EXAMINATION OF THE TERRITORIAL AND MARITIME CLAIMS OF COUNTRIES INVOLVED IN LIGHT OF INTERNATIONAL LAW

Having examined the historical context of the South China Sea dispute and its current state, it is crucial to understand the specific territorial and maritime claims of the involved parties and evaluation of the legal basis and implications of these claims under international law. This section aims to offer a concise overview of the claims by China, Taiwan, the Philippines, Vietnam and Malaysia, and the legal analysis of their claims in terms of international law which have been briefly mentioned earlier. A clear grasp of these claims is essential for a comprehensive understanding of the subsequent legal analysis.

China

As mentioned above, after enacted the "Law on the Territorial Sea and the Contiguous Zone" in 1992, China signed the UN Convention on the Law of the Sea on May 15, 1996. China's decision to ratify the United Nations Convention on the Law of the Sea (UNCLOS) in 1996 was driven by the belief that the convention, as a whole, was in harmony with its maritime positions and beneficial for safeguarding its long-term interests at sea (Seo, 2024). Then, in 1998, the "Exclusive Economic Zone and Continental Shelf Law" was enacted, and in 2009, the limits of the continental shelf were defined. By these legislative steps, China aimed to legitimize its claims in the region. Despite these legal measures, China continues to base its claims more on historical assessments than on international law. China's claims in the South China Sea are multifaceted and can be categorized into four main types:

Nine-Dash Line and "Historic Waters": Created in 1935, distributed in 1947, submitted to international platforms in 2009, and continued to repeat in many platforms, nine-dash line is a map that China often cites for its claims in the South China Sea. According to this map, as repeated in many times earlier, %80 of the South China Sea is belonged to China. China claims to be the first to have discovered, named, and utilized the resources of these islands, and to have continuously exercised sovereign powers over these groups of islands (Chinese Society of International Law, 2018). China claims the "sovereignty, rights and interests in the South China Sea were established in the long course of history, and are solidly grounded in history and the law, which are in compliance with the UN Charter and international law, including the United Nations Convention on the Law of the Sea" (Foreign Ministry Spokesperson Mao Ning's Regular Press Conference on March 5, 2024, 2024). As it is seen, China bases its sovereignty over these disputed islands on historical rights and asserts that its claim is in accordance with international law. Accordingly, The Philippines' taken control of several maritime features within these islands since

1970s and grouping them under the name “Kalayaan Island Group” are illegal. Additionally, the claim over the Scarborough Shoal and exploiting its resources are not based on legal authority (Foreign Ministry Spokesperson Mao Ning’s Regular Press Conference on March 5, 2024, 2024).

When these claims are evaluated in terms of international law, it will be seen that nine-dash line and historical waters are not recognized under international law. Furthermore, China signed UNCLOS in 1996. From this moment on, its national law contradicted the 1982 convention. Article 2 of the 1992 Law defines four group of islands (Spratly Islands, Paracel Islands, Pratas Islands and Macclesfield Bank) as 'territorial waters', referring to historical rights. According to Convention, state’s territorial waters could be 12 nm from their baseline. Furthermore, one of the areas that China claims is actually part of the Philippines' EEZ (The South China Sea Arbitration, 2016; Kuok, 2019). While China has the right to make declarations regarding the application of the 1982 Convention, its national law is in conflict with international law, as it cannot go against the legal principles of the Convention to support its historical claims (Buszynski, 2013). China's assertion of ancient records for sovereignty is therefore inconsistent with principles of international law. As stated above, this inconsistency was also repeated in the South China Sea Arbitration in 2016 (The South China Sea Arbitration, 2016).

Before this point, we have assumed that the map and historical rights are “legal” and said that they have become invalid with China's acceptance of the rules of international law. However, the status of the map and the historical right as legal evidence in international law is controversial. The China International Law Association, an international academic exchange center, published a study in 2016 criticizing the Arbitration Tribunal's decision, arguing that nine-dash line has a foundation in international law. According to them, the nine-dash line has consistently been supported by the principle of the customary laws related to discovery, occupation, and historic title, as well as the United Nations Convention on the Law of the Sea. They argue that its historic rights, which involve zonal implications, are generally “seen as a relevant factor in maritime delimitation” and should be taken into account. (Chinese Society of International Law, 2018).

Three counter-arguments can be advanced. First, because the nine-dash line claim is not well-defined and there is no specific geographical coordination that points the exact location of each line in the South Asian Sea, makes it difficult to treat it as a legal document. Moreover, without a clear basis, these claims undermine the stability and predictability of maritime borders, potentially leading to increased tensions and disputes. Second, the International Court of Justice (ICJ) in the 1986 Burkina Faso/ Republic of Mali Frontier Dispute Case has ruled that maps alone do not constitute a territorial title under international law, as they are merely informational and vary in accuracy. For maps to have legal force, they must be expressions of the will of the State. Last, even if the People's Republic of China (PRC) and the Republic of China (ROC) have long claimed the dotted line in the South China Sea without protest from other states, a unilateral claim must not blatantly violate international law. If the claim is so obviously illegal, it cannot become a legal right. Additionally, in the 1951 Anglo-Norwegian Fisheries Case, the ICJ found that coastal states cannot freely delimit their coastal sea areas without considering international law. If the ROC or PRC claims to have exercised authority over the South China Sea for an extended period, they must prove it. This is challenging for ancient claims unless there is written evidence. The rigorous requirement of effective authority, as outlined in the 1928 Island of Palmas Arbitration, would be difficult to demonstrate for those sea areas (Miyoshi, 2012).

The same contradiction applies to historical rights. The United Nations Convention on the Law of the Sea (UNCLOS) does not explicitly define "historic rights," and there is no uniform interpretation of this term in international law (US Department of State Bureau of Oceans and International Environmental and Scientific Affairs, 2022). The Convention mentions "historic bays" or "historic title" in two specific contexts: Article 10, which addresses bays, and Article 15, which pertains to the delimitation of the territorial sea between states with opposite or adjacent coasts. These provisions are geographically and substantively limited, applying only to bays and similar coastal configurations. They are drafted as safeguards, indicating that the provisions of Article 10 and Article 15 "do not apply" in situations involving historic bays and title, respectively. Notably, there is no provision in the Convention that safeguards "historic rights." Therefore, any claim to such rights must conform to the Convention's provisions, including those related to the Exclusive Economic Zone (EEZ), continental shelf, and high seas. The Gulf of Maine Chamber of the International Court of Justice (ICJ) emphasized in its 1984 judgment that the exclusive jurisdiction of a coastal state over fisheries within 200 nm of its coast supersedes the prior usage and rights of other states in that area (US Department of State Bureau of Oceans and International Environmental and Scientific Affairs, 2022, pp. 9-10). As stated in Article 309, UNCLOS's maritime zones and their geographic limits establish a framework that governs all parts of the sea, with no allowance for reservations.

Sovereignty Claims over Maritime Features: Issues arise regarding maritime features claimed by coastal states, including those subject to territorial claims or within such claims, and their ability to generate maritime zones. These features vary in size from proper islands to atolls, cays, islets, rocks, banks, shoals, and reefs. The status of these features, their eligibility for territorial claims, and their capacity to create maritime zones can be disputed. This is particularly true for features in the South China Sea, which are central to land disputes (Rothwell, 2013).

China asserts ownership over four distinct island groups within the South China Sea. They are Spratly Islands, Paracel Islands, Pratas Islands and Macclesfield Bank, and, along with their surrounding waters (National People's Congress of PRC, 1992; The South China Sea Arbitration, 2016). Spratly Islands comprise over 100 islands, reefs, and cays and are the most hotly contested area in the South China Sea, with overlapping claims from several countries. Paracel Islands are located to the north-east of the Spratly Islands and also claimed by Vietnam, but China has maintained effective control over most of these islands since the 1970s. Pratas Islands are the northernmost islands claimed by China, consisting of a single atoll and several rocks. They are also claimed by the Republic of China (Taiwan) and Macclesfield Bank is largely submerged and only exposed at low tide. However, China considers the Macclesfield Bank as one of its island groups. It includes Scarborough Shoal, which is also claimed by the Philippines.

The states asserting sovereignty over these island groups, including China, have not provided clear definitions of the status of these maritime features. However, as it stated, international law imposes restrictions on the types of territorial formations that can be claimed. According to widely accepted legal principles such as Article 121(3) of the Convention, sovereignty can be claimed over natural formations, regardless of their material (such as mud, coral, sand, or rock), as long as they are above water at high tide and are sufficiently large to support human habitation. In contrast, a substantial portion of the Spratly Islands and other islands are either completely submerged or only partially visible at high tide (Huysal, 2015). In this case, ownership and sovereignty cannot be claimed submerged features outside territorial waters. And these features cannot generate maritime zone.

In order to claim sovereignty over these features thus assert maritime zones, China has engaged in some land reclamation activities. She has been turning submerged features such as reef into islands, making some islands bigger by building on them and establishing military installations since December 2013. Such activities between 2017- 2019 increased significantly (Kuok, 2019). Satellite imagery has revealed that the physical size of the islands has been expanded, with the construction of ports, military installations, and airstrips, particularly on the Paracel and Spratly Islands (Biber & Ateş, 2021). With this land reclamation, China builds artificial islands with a belief that generate maritime zones and airspace zone. By doing so, China is violating international law. According to UNCLOS, artificial structures can only be built for security purposes. The construction of artificial structures is permissible solely for the purpose of preventing the erosion of formations that are naturally located above the water level. This does not infringe upon the legal rights of the sovereign state. However, the artificial elevation of a submerged formation, as has been undertaken by China, is deemed a violation of international law (Symmons, 1979). For instance, Tribunal also ruled that China's constructions on Mischief Reef are illegal because it is a low-tide elevation and therefore forms part of the Philippines' continental shelf (The South China Sea Arbitration, 2016). It should be noted that China is not alone in building artificial structures. Each of the areas undergoing reclamation - including Cuarteron Reef, Fiery Cross Reef, Gaven Reef, Hughes Reef, Johnson South Reef, Mischief Reef, and Subi Reef - is disputed between China and at least one other claimant, including the Philippines, Vietnam, Malaysia, and Taiwan (Dolven, Elsea, Lawrence, O'Rourke, & Rinehart, 2015). However, China's reclamation activities and militarization efforts far exceed those of other claimants in scale (Dolven, Campbell, & Ronald O'Rourke, 2023).

***Archipelagic State Claims*:** China is not recognized as an archipelagic state under international law, yet it has attempted to claim the rights associated with such status by drawing straight baselines around the Paracel Islands, effectively claiming the waters between the islands as internal waters (Mastro, 2021). China is asserting this on the basis of Article 46(a) of the UNCLOS, which allows for the establishment of straight baselines for archipelagic states. With this legality, China argues that the four archipelagos under its administration should be considered a single unit and granted the status of an archipelagic regime. These are the Southern Archipelago (Spratlys), the Western Archipelago (Paracels), the Eastern Archipelago (Pratas), and the Middle Archipelago (Macclesfield Bank and Scarborough Shoal) (Tønnesson, 2020). In particular, she claims that the Spratlys is an archipelago that is "widely recognized and acknowledged" in the international community (Chinese Society of International Law, 2018).

There are several reasons why it should be treated as a single unit. Firstly, these archipelagos fulfill the criteria of being a cohesive political, security, and economic unit. Secondly, historical precedent allows for the identification of a legal archipelago, and these islands have been consistently administered as a single entity by China. Additionally, there is a growing customary international law principle that permits the use of straight baselines for outlying archipelagos of continental states. Lastly, the archipelagic regime is designed to balance the sovereign interests of the archipelago with the rights of other states, such as navigation and fishing rights, and applying this regime to the Spratlys would ensure this balance (Nong, 2018). Despite this, according to Chinese Society, in the Award of 12 July, the Tribunal did not adequately consider China's view that the archipelago should be treated as a single entity for purposes of sovereignty, maritime entitlements, and delimitation. Instead, it incorrectly addressed the status of individual features within China's Southern and Middle Archipelago separately, effectively dismantling the two archipelagos and fragmenting the territorial and maritime delimitation dispute between China and the Philippines in the South China Sea (Chinese Society of International Law, 2018).

With this archipelago claim based on historical rights, China is trying to make South China Sea her closed sea. However, as could be understood this is a controversial move, as it goes against the UNCLOS and China's continental status. There are only limited archipelagos in the world according to UNCLOS. At the end of the UNCLOS III, various delegations announced their intention to claim the status of archipelagic states, as defined by UNCLOS. These included the Bahamas, Cape Verde, Fiji, the Netherlands Antilles, Papua New Guinea, the Philippines, and the Solomon Islands (Nong, 2018). As it is seen, China is not one of them. By ratifying this convention, China cannot claim to be an archipelago state.

Maritime Zones Claims: Through her national laws and public declarations, China lays claim to a territorial sea, a contiguous zone, an EEZ, and a continental shelf in the South China Sea. This includes a 12-nm territorial sea where China exercises full sovereignty, a 24 nm contiguous zone for enforcing customs, immigration, and sanitary regulations, a 200-nm EEZ for exploiting marine resources, and a continental shelf that extends to the outer edge of the continental margin or up to 200-nm, whichever is greater, with the possibility of further extension if justified by geological evidence. Despite this, China claims a 12-nm territorial sea from the Paracel baseline and also claims territorial waters around features in the Spratly Islands that do not qualify for such status under international law. China's interpretation of the territorial sea gives it exclusive rights to enforce its laws, which is a broader interpretation than that provided by UNCLOS, which allows for innocent passage of all ships, including military vessels (Mastro, 2021). China maintains a selective application of UNCLOS, adopting a "closed sea" (mare clausum) perspective when interpreting core provisions. This cautious approach extends across a range of maritime topics, such as innocent passage, navigational freedoms, delineation of maritime boundaries, the international seabed's legal framework, and scientific research in the marine environment (Seo, 2024).

China claims a 200 nm EEZ from the end of the territorial sea, where it asserts the right to regulate military activity. China asserts that the EEZ is distinct from the high seas under UNCLOS, implying that the freedoms of navigation and overflight within and above an EEZ do not equate to those on the high seas. According to this reasoning, China contends that foreign military operations and maritime surveillance are not automatically granted the same freedoms within an EEZ and must comply with the coastal state's laws and regulations, as per articles 58(1) and (3) of UNCLOS (Seo, 2024). This position is particularly emphasized by China in its legal arguments which mentioned above. This is in contrast to the views of the US and Australia, which argue that freedom of navigation for military vessels is a universally accepted practice under international law (Mastro, 2021). Several other countries, including some claimants in the South China Sea, support China's position on limiting military activities in EEZs. China, Vietnam, and a few other nations maintain the minority position that the UNCLOS permits them to control both economic activities and the navigation and overflight of foreign military vessels within their EEZs (Dolven, Campbell, & Ronald O'Rourke, 2023).

China's these expansive maritime claims in the South China Sea have significant geopolitical implications. They affect the rights and interests of other claimant states, such as Vietnam, the Philippines, Malaysia, and Brunei, as well as the broader international community that relies on the South China Sea for maritime trade and navigation. Despite a tribunal ruling, China has persisted in encroaching upon the EEZs of other coastal states. For instance, China has obstructed Vietnam's efforts to drill for oil and gas in its EEZ and has taken similar actions against the Philippines. However, as Kuok note with the carrot- stick analogy, China also employs incentives; in November 2018, China and the Philippines signed a Memorandum of Understanding on Cooperation for Oil and Gas Development, aiming for a framework for joint development by November this year, though this now seems improbable (2019). Despite this, by increasing its naval presence, China continues to infringe upon the sovereignty rights of the coastal states. China's violations are not only directed against regional states, but also against the United States, India, Australia and other nations conducting freedom of navigation operations and exercises in the South China Sea.

Until now, we have evaluated China's allegations and these allegations within the framework of international law. As it has been said many times, China's claims cover approximately 80 percent of the South China Sea. This situation has inevitably caused the claims of other littoral states to overlap with China's, and in this context, has shaped their reactions against China. These developments have been mostly mentioned under the China heading. For this reason, the following coastal state headings have been prepared only for a compact analysis. This will make our study more comprehensible. Before moving on to other headings, one more note should be stated. Taiwan will not be dealt with under a separate heading as it continues to claim to be the continuation of the Republic of China, adopts the map published by the Republic of China in 1947 (Liu, 2013) and asserts the same rights claims as China. Nevertheless, it must be said that Taiwan has remained in the background in the South China Sea issue due to the representation crisis. Despite this, it also builds artificial islands on the reefs.

Vietnam

Vietnam, alongside China, has been a key player in the South China Sea dispute and is the nation with the most frequent conflicts with China[7] in the South China Sea. It is the sole country in the region that also faces issues with China along its land borders and asserting sovereignty over the entire Spratly Islands, which it considers part of its Khanh Hoa Province (Hong Z., 2013). It also lays claim to the Paracel Islands, currently under Chinese control since 1976. Vietnam argues that its continental shelf, as defined by UNCLOS, grants Vietnam the right to occupy the Spratly Islands and proposes that each coastal state should have a 200 nm EEZ from its main coastline, with any high seas beyond that distance governed by the International Sea-Bed Authority. However, in 1982, Vietnam used straight baselines from its coasts that were inconsistent with UNCLOS. Under international pressure, Vietnam has reassessed its baseline claim (Rowan, 2005). Then In 2009, Vietnam expanded its continental shelves beyond the typical 200 nm from its shores, reigniting tensions over maritime sovereignty in the South China Sea. In June 2012, Vietnam enacted a maritime law that claimed authority over the contested Spratly and Paracel Islands, mandating that foreign naval vessels must notify Vietnam when traversing the area. China, of course, responded with sanctions and violations. Following a dozen years of negotiations, Indonesia and Vietnam concluded an agreement in 2022, establishing the definitive boundaries of their respective EEZs (1895 – 2024 China's Maritime Disputes, 2024).Vietnam has maintained a substantial military presence in these areas, including fortifications on the islands with soldiers, anti-aircraft batteries, and coastal artillery. The country has also engaged in activities to build artificial platforms and airstrips on the reefs in contravention of international law (Dolven, Elsea, Lawrence, O'Rourke, & Rinehart, 2015). In July 2024, Vietnam has submitted a claim to the United Nations for an extended continental shelf in the South China Sea, following a similar move by the Philippines. The claim aims to extend the continental shelf beyond the standard 200 nm from its territorial waters' baselines. Vietnam also reasserted its sovereignty over the Paracel and Spratly archipelagos, emphasizing that its submission complies with international law. China has expressed strong opposition to Vietnam's claim and has made formal protests to Vietnam.

Vietnam is the regional country most exposed to China's violations of international law. In response to Chinese encroachments, Vietnam has taken both diplomatic and strategic steps. It has cancelled oil drilling projects with Spain's Repsol after warnings from China (Hayton, 2017) and has instead partnered with Russia's Rosneft for oil block licensing, despite Beijing's opposition. This strategic move highlights Vietnam's shrewdness in navigating the complex geopolitical landscape (Yee, 2019). However, the Blue Whale gas-to-power project with U.S. company ExxonMobil has faced challenges, with rumors suggesting ExxonMobil may divest due to pressure from China (Clark, 2019). Vietnam has also sent its coast guard to register objections to Chinese survey activities in its EEZ and has issued strong diplomatic statements through its Ministry of Foreign Affairs (Vu, 2019) (Kuok, 2019).

Vietnam's foreign policy is guided by the "Three No's" principle, which precludes military alliances, cooperation against a third country, and the establishment of foreign military bases on its territory. This principle shapes Vietnam's approach to the South China Sea dispute, emphasizing the assertion of its rights under international law, such as its EEZ and continental shelf, in cooperation with other regional countries. Vietnam's strategic engagement with the US and other international partners aims to balance the influence of the People's Republic of China (PRC) while maintaining its sovereignty and territorial integrity (Mermer, 2022).

Philippines

Historically, the Republic of the Philippines was viewed as an archipelago by its former colonial rulers, encompassing a large area that included both waters and land features. Over the years, the Philippines adjusted its claims to align with the 1982 UN Law of the Sea Convention, establishing 80 archipelagic baselines that comply with UNCLOS through various enactments from 1961 to 2009 (Rosen, 2014). The Philippines has laid claim to Scarborough Shoal and a group of 50 Spratly Island features, known as the Kalayaan island group (KIG). These claims are independent of its archipelagic status and are based on historical and legal grounds. Scarborough Shoal, being a feature visible at high tide, can be claimed under international law.

The Republic of the Philippines has two primary external South China Sea claims: one to the features known as Scarborough Shoal, and another to the additional features within the geometric area that the Philippines asserts are part of the Kalayaan Island Group (KIG) (Rosen, 2014). These claims are independent of its archipelagic status and are based on historical and legal grounds. For instance, Scarborough Shoal, being a feature visible at high tide, can be claimed under international law. In 2009, the Philippines enacted a law establishing maritime baselines that comply with UNCLOS, specifically categorizing Scarborough Shoal and the Kalayaan Island Group under the island regime outlined in Article 121. The country also notified the CLCS of its plan to submit its continental shelf boundaries in the South China Sea. This indicates that the Philippines will assert an EEZ from its main archipelago and an extended continental shelf beyond the EEZ's outer limit (Beckman, 2013). However, The Philippines struggled to align its maritime claims with UNCLOS, as its constitution previously claimed "Freedomland" (Kalayaan) with a square-shaped line encompassing most of the Spratly area, similar to China's U-shaped line (Tønnesson, 2020). As mentioned in detail in the part of China, map is not likely to be legally sufficient to establish sovereignty over ocean territories on its own.

The Philippines is entitled to a 200-nm EEZ and continental shelf, which includes sovereignty over features classified as low-tide elevations, such as Reed Bank and Mischief Reef. These features cannot be claimed under international law. Any interference by China with the Philippines' use and management of its continental shelf resources is illegal. Other features within the KIG that are illegally occupied by China and Taiwan include Subi Reef, Zhongzhou Jiao Reef, Gaven Reef, McKennan Reef, and Cornwallis South Reef (Beckman, 2013). Arbitration Tribunal in 2016 had the same conclusion about these disputed areas between Philippines and China. Although the tribunal's decision in 2016 was a landmark victory for the Philippines, as it invalidated China's extensive maritime claims based on the "nine-dash line" and affirmed the Philippines' rights to the disputed areas under international law. However, the enforcement of this ruling has been hampered. The Philippines, one of the United States' two treaty allies in Southeast Asia (Kuok, 2019), has taken a more conciliatory stance toward China under President Rodrigo Duterte's leadership as mentioned before. The Philippines has set aside the South China Sea Tribunal ruling and instead concentrated on finalizing an agreement to collaborate on oil and gas development with China. After many years since this award issued, in June 2024, the Philippines submitted a claim to the UN for recognition of an extended continental shelf in the South China Sea, encompassing the disputed Spratly Islands off the western island of Palawan. The Philippines asserted its entitlement to establish the outer limits of its continental shelf up to 350 nm, the maximum permitted under the UN Convention on the Law of the Sea (UNCLOS). In response, China issued a diplomatic note urging the UN not to review the Philippines' submission, arguing that it gravely infringes upon China's "sovereignty, sovereign rights, and jurisdiction in the South China Sea." (Shin, 2024) At the time of writing these paragraphs, the UN has not reached a conclusion and it is expected to take some time.

Malaysia

Malaysia asserts sovereignty over 12 islets located in the region south of the Spratly Islands, which are situated on the continental shelf. Malaysia maintains a physical presence on five of the features in the South China Sea: Swallow Reef, Mariveles Reef, Dallas Reef, Ardasier Reef, Erica Reef, and Investigator Reef and two submerged feature as James Shoal and North Luconia Shoals and South Luconia Shoals. Three other features within Malaysia's claims are occupied by the Philippines and Vietnam. The Philippines occupies Commodore Reef, and Vietnam occupies Amboyna Cay and Barque Canada Reef. Almost all of them are claimed by China and Taiwan. Especially The Luconia Shoal is a subject of dispute between the littoral states due to the vast resources of oil and natural gas beneath the seabed and its richness in fish. Malaysia has also built oil platforms on this shoal (Roach,

2014). (Mahadzir, 2015). Most the nature of these features are not stated. Malaysia's claims to these maritime features in the South China Sea are grounded in its claim to a continental shelf, as outlined in a 1979 map, which depicts its claims to various maritime features and waters in the South China Sea, and other areas, a 1966 law, and a joint submission with Vietnam to the Commission on the Limits of the Continental Shelf in 2009 (Country Profile from the Maritime Awareness Project Malaysia, 2020). Malaysia is a rather moderate claimant who has generally sought to pursue policies in line with regional countries in the South China dispute. Malaysia strongly believes that issues concerning the South China Sea should be resolved peacefully and constructively, in line with the universally accepted principles of international law, including the UNCLOS (Ministry of Foreign Affairs, 2023).

When Malaysia submitted a proposal to the UN Commission on December 12, 2019, to extend its continental shelf, it encountered reactions from China the Philippines, and Vietnam. Subsequently, Malaysia has adopted a more critical stance towards China and has voiced its opposition to the China's activities that violate its airspace and EEZ. Having changed its policy towards China in 2019, Malaysia has increased its military cooperation with the US and also intensified its unilateral energy exploration activities in areas of the South China Sea where its claims overlap with those of China and Vietnam. In 2021, Malaysia participated in the Southeast Asia Cooperation and Training (SEACAT) exercise led by the United States. This exercise involved 21 countries, including key US allies like Australia and Germany. The drills aimed to improve the operational environment, build capacity for humanitarian missions, and uphold international laws and norms (Heydarian, 2021).

CONCLUSION

The South China Sea is a crucial semi-enclosed sea due to its strategic location connecting the Indian and Pacific Oceans, making it a vital maritime route. The sea is rich in marine life, offering economic opportunities and potential for scientific research. It also contains significant oil and gas reserves. The Paracel and Spratly Islands, located within this sea, are key strategic points for controlling access to these resources and sea lanes, leading to territorial disputes among the surrounding countries. Currently, from the surrouding states, China, Vietnam, Malaysia, Brunei, the Philippines, and Taiwan have claims over parts or all of the Spratly Islands, with Vietnam and China disputing the sovereignty of the Paracel Islands. These claims result in overlapping maritime jurisdictions not only within the Spratly and Paracel

Islands but also between these areas and the maritime zones of the mainland territories of the South China Sea's littoral states.

In addition to the disputes among regional countries, the involvement of numerous extra-regional actors, each pursuing their own interests, further complicates the issue. The problem also has a significant international law dimension. International maritime law, characterized by Gerry Simpson (2004) as "legalized hegemony," has been shaped by powerful states seeking to preserve the mare liberum system. The United Nations Convention on the Law of the Sea (UNCLOS), crafted with their dominant interpretations, is not universally accepted at this juncture. States interpret UNCLOS in accordance with their historical experiences and national identities. These interpretations are both inevitable and neutral, not favoring any one state over another. Currently, UNCLOS serves as the primary reference in maritime territorial disputes.

No multilateral agreement is permanent, and UNCLOS will eventually become obsoleteAlthough UNCLOS has made substantial contributions to maritime affairs, it remains silent on certain critical issues such as delimitation, tidal criteria, and feature delineation, which pose significant challenges in the South China Sea. In this context, the modification of UNCLOS is a consideration that should be explored to address these problems. Additional protocols to UNCLOS or special provisions for conflict zones such as the South China Sea may be more effective in resolving disputes in the region.

REFERENCES

1895 – 2024 China's Maritime Disputes. (2024). Council on Foreign Relations: https://www.cfr.org/timeline/chinas-maritime-disputes adresinden alındı

1992 - ASEAN Decleration on the South China Sea. (2017, July). Retrieved from Center for International Law: https://cil.nus.edu.sg/wp-content/uploads/2017/07/1992-ASEAN-Declaration-on-the-South-China-Sea.pdf

Beckman, R. (2013, January). The UN Convention on the Law of the Sea and the Maritime Disputes in the South China Sea. *The American Journal of International Law*, *107*(1), 142–163. https://www.jstor.org/stable/10.5305/amerjintelaw.107.1.0142. DOI: 10.5305/amerjintelaw.107.1.0142

Biber, A. B., & Ateş, H. Y. (2021, March 3). *Güney Çin Denizi'nde ABD ve Çin'in güç mücadelesi*. Retrieved from TRT Haber: https://www.trthaber.com/haber/dunya/guney-cin-denizinde-abd-ve-cinin-guc-mucadelesi-566452.html

Burgess, J. P. (2003, March). The Politics of the South China Sea: Territoriality and International Law. *Security Dialogue*, *34*(1), 7–10. DOI: 10.1177/09670106030341002

Buszynski, L. (2013, September 5). The development of the South China Sea maritime dispute. (L. Buszynski, & L. Buszynski-, Eds.) *National Security College Occasional Paper*, pp. 3-7.

Chinese Society of International Law. (2018). The South China Sea Arbitration Awards: A Critical Study. [Retrieved from Chinese Society of International Law.]. *Chinese Journal of International Law*, •••, 207–748.

Clark, H. (2019, September 11). *Rumours ExxonMobil to quit Vietnamese gas field.*, " Energy News Bulletin: https://www.energynewsbulletin.net/finance-legal/news/1371306/rumours-exxonmobil-to-quit-vietnamese-gas-field adresinden alındı

Country Profile from the Maritime Awareness Project Malaysia. (2020, September 15). Retrieved from The National Bureau of Asian Research: https://www.nbr.org/publication/malaysia/

Declaration on The Conduct of Parties in The South China Sea. (2012, May 14). Retrieved from ASEAN: https://asean.org/declaration-on-the-conduct-of-parties-in-the-south-china-sea-2/

Dolven, B., Campbell, C., & Ronald O'Rourke. (2023). *China Primer: South China Sea Disputes.* the Congressional Research Service.

Dolven, B., Elsea, J. K., Lawrence, S. V., O'Rourke, R., & Rinehart, I. E. (2015). *Chinese Land Reclamation in the South China Sea: Implications and Policy Options.* Congressional Research Service. Retrieved from https://sgp.fas.org/crs/row/R44072.pdf

Foreign Ministry Spokesperson Mao Ning's Regular Press Conference onMarch5,2024. (2024, March 5). Retrieved from Embassy of the People's Republic of China in the United States of America: http://us.china-embassy.gov.cn/eng/fyrth/202403/t20240305_11254066.htm

Gao, Z., & Jia, B. B. (2013, January). The Nine-Dash Line in the South China Sea: History, Status, and Implications. *The American Journal of International Law, 107*(1), 98–124. http://www.jstor.com/stable/10.5305/amerjintelaw.107.1.0098. DOI: 10.5305/amerjintelaw.107.1.0098

Ha, N. T. (2020). Vietnam and the South China Sea. In Buszynski, L., & Hai, D. T. (Eds.), *The South China Sea: From a Regional Maritime Dispute to Geo-Strategic Competition* (pp. 77–92). Routledge.

Hayton, B. (2017, July 21). *The Week Donald Trump Lost the South China Sea.* Foreign Policy: https://foreignpolicy.com/2017/07/31/the-week-donald-trump-lost-the-south-china-sea/ adresinden alındı

Hayton, B. (2019). The Modern Origins of China's South China Sea Claims. *Modern China, 45*(2), 127-170. doi:i.org/10.1177/0097700418771678

Heydarian, R. J. (2021, October 5). *Malaysia, China go head to head in South China Sea.* Retrieved from Asia Times: https://asiatimes.com/2021/10/malaysia-china-go-head-to-head-in-south-china-sea/

Hong, N. (2020). China and the South China Sea: continuities and adaptions. In Hai, L. B. (Ed.), *The South China Sea: From a Regional Maritime Dispute to Geo-Strategic Competition* (pp. 60–76). Routledge.

Hong, Z. (2013). The South China Sea Dispute and China-ASEAN Relations. *Asian Affairs, 44*(1), 27–43. DOI: 10.1080/03068374.2012.760785

Huysal, B. (2015, July-August). Güney Çin Denizi'nde Kriz: Çin Halk Cumhuriyeti'nin Ada İnşa/Arazi Genişletme. *Bahçeşehir Üniversitesi Hukuk Fakültesi Dergisi, 10*(131-132), pp. 53-82. Retrieved from https://www.jurix.com.tr/article/4608?u=0&c=0

Hyer, E. (1995). The South China Sea Disputes: Implications of China's Earlier Territorial Settlements. *Pacific Affairs, 68*(1), 34–54. https://www.jstor.org/stable/2759767. DOI: 10.2307/2759767

Keyvan, Ö. Z. (2017, December). Güney Çin Denizi'nde Tahkim: Çin-Filipinler Rekabeti. *ANKASAM-Bölgesel Araştırmalar Dergisi, 1*(3), 251–267.

Kuok, L. (2019, November). *How China's Action in the South China Sea Undermine the Rule of Law.* Washington: Brooking Institution. Retrieved from Global China.

Lan-Anh, N. T. (2008). *South China Sea Dispute: A Reappraisal in the Light of International Law*. University of Bristol.

Liu, F.-K. (2013). Dilemma and Domestic Uncertainty: Taiwan's Insecurity in the South China Sea. *China Report (New Delhi, India), 49*(4), 385–397. DOI: 10.1177/0009445513506635

Mahadzir, D. (2015). Malaysia's Maritime Claims in the South China Sea: Security and Military Dimensions. In *Entering Uncharted Waters* (pp. 208-222). Cambridge University Press.

Malik, M. (2013, August 30). *History the Weak Link in Beijing's Maritime Claims.* Retrieved from the Diplomat: https://thediplomat.com/2013/08/history-the-weak -link-in-beijings-maritime-claims/

Maritime Delimitation and Territorial Questions between Qatar and Bahrain (Qatar v. Bahrain) (Merits) (I.C.J March 16, 2001).

Mastro, O. S. (2021, February 17). *How China is bending the rules in the South China Sea*. Retrieved from Interpreter: https://www.lowyinstitute.org/the-interpreter/ how-china-bending-rules-south-china-sea

Mermer, C. T. (2022). *Güney Çin Denizi ABD Hegemonyasına Meydan Okuyan Çin'in Zorlu Virajı*. TASAM.

Ministry of Foreign Affairs. (2023, April 8). *Malaysia's Position on The South China Sea (Press Realese)*. Ministry of Foreign Affairs Malaysia: https://www.kln .gov.my/web/guest/-/malaysia-s-position-on-the-south-china-sea adresinden alındı

Miyoshi, M. (2012, February 10). China's "U-Shaped Line" Claim in the South China Sea: Any Validity Under International Law? *Ocean Development and International Law, 43*(1), 1–17. DOI: 10.1080/00908320.2011.619374

National People's Congress of PRC. (1992, February 25). Law on the Territorial Sea and the Contiguous Zone of 25 February 1992. UN. Retrieved from https://www.un .org/depts/los/LEGISLATIONANDTREATIES/PDFFILES/CHN_1992_Law.pdf

Nong, H. (2018). The Applicability of the Archipelagic Regime in the South China Sea: A Debate on the Rights of Continental States' Outlying Archipelagos. *Ocean Yearbook, 32*(1), 80–117. DOI: 10.1163/22116001-03201005

Quyet, L. V., & Nguyet, N. T. (2023). Sovereignty over the Paracel Islands in 1884-1945: An approach from the rivalry between France, China, and Japan. *Journal of Liberty and International Affairs*, *9*(2), 275–296. DOI: 10.47305/JLIA2392347q

Roach, J. A. (2014). *Malaysia and Brunei: An Analysis of their Claims in the South China Sea.* CNA .

Rosen, M. E. (2014, August). *Philippine Claims in the South China Sea: A Legal Analysis.* Washington: CNA. Retrieved from https://www.cna.org/archive/CNA_Files/pdf/iop-2014-u-008435.pdf

Rothwell, D. R. (2013, September 5). The 1982 UN convention on the Law of the Sea and its relevance to. (L. B. Roberts, Ed.) *National Security College Occasional Paper*, pp. 13-17.

Rowan, J. P. (2005, May- June). The U.S.-Japan Security Alliance, ASEAN, and the South China Sea Dispute. *Asian Survey*, *45*(3), 414–436. DOI: 10.1525/as.2005.45.3.414

Seo, Y. (2024). Power Shift, the South China Sea Dispute, and the Role of International Law. *Michigan Journal of International Law*, *45*(1), 93–152. DOI: 10.36642/mjil.45.1.power

Shin, W. W. (2024, July 13). *'Opportune' timing: Why the Philippines is filing a seabed bid in the South China Sea, and the likely outcome*. Channel New Asia: https://www.channelnewsasia.com/asia/philippines-south-china-sea-continental-shelf-china-malaysia-sabah-vietnam-4474626 adresinden alındı

Simpson, G. J. (2004). *Great Powers and Outlaw State: Unequal Sovereigns in the International Legal Order*. Cambridge University Press. DOI: 10.1017/CBO9780511494185

Symmons, C. R. (1979). The maritime zones of islands in international law. Hague: Martinus Nijhoff Publishers. DOI: 10.1163/9789004636170

Tanrıverdi, B. (2021). *Güney Çin Denizi'nde Güç ve Uluslararası Hukuk.* Retrieved from Hukuk ve Bilişim: https://hukukvebilisim.org/guney-cin-denizinde-guc-uluslararasi-hukuk-ve-tahkim/

Territorial and Maritime Dispute (Nicaragua v. Colombia) (Judgment) (I.C.J November 19, 2012).

Thayer, C. A. (2020). ASEAN, China, and the Code of Conduct. In Buszynski, L., & Hai, D. T. (Eds.), *The South China Sea From a Regional Maritime Dispute to Geo-Strategic Competition* (pp. 43–59). Routledge.

The South China Sea Arbitration (The Republic of Philippines v. The People's Republic of China), PCA Case N° 2013-19 (Permanent Court of Arbitration July 12, 2016). Retrieved from https://pcacases.com/web/sendAttach/2086

Tønnesson, S. (2020). Four aspects of the crisis in the South China Sea. In Buszynski, L., & Hai, D. T. (Eds.), *The South China Sea From a Regional Maritime Dispute to Geo-Strategic Competition* (pp. 9–23). Routledge Publications.

US Department of State Bureau of Oceans and International Environmental and Scientific Affairs. (2022). *People's Republic of China: Maritime Claims in the South China Sea*. U.S. Department of State.

Vu, K. (2019, August 24). *Chinese ship inches closer to Vietnam coastline amid South China Sea tensions*. Reuters: https://www.reuters.com/article/us-vietnam-china-southchinasea/chinese-ship-inches-closer-to-vietnam-coastline-amid-south-china-sea-tensions-idUSKCN1VE068. adresinden alındı

Yee, T. H. (2019, September 13). *Vietnam digs in on South China Sea oil and gas projects amid Chinese pressure*. The Strait Times: https://www.straitstimes.com/asia/se-asia/vietnam-digs-in-on-south-china-sea-oil-and-gas-projects-amid-chinese-pressure adresinden alındı

Zhao, S. (2020). East Asian Disorder China and the South China Sea Disputes. *Asian Survey*, *60*(3), 490–509. https://online.ucpress.edu/as/article/60/3/490/110498/East-Asian-DisorderChina-and-the-South-China-Sea. DOI: 10.1525/as.2020.60.3.490

ENDNOTES

1 In the latin phrase "terra dominatus maris".

2 For a case study of China's recognition of Vietnam's sovereignty, see, Quyet & Nguyet, 2023, p. 278.

3 The reef is about 100 nm from the Philippines and 500 nm from China.

4 In June 2012, the Chinese State Council declared the creation of Sansha (built in 2007), a new city located in the South China Sea. This city is China's least populous and smallest in terms of land area. According to the official Xinhua News Agency, the city """is a strong indication of China's determination to protect its maritime sovereignty in response to provocation from neighboring countries. See Zhao Hong "East Asian Disorder: China and the South China

Sea Disputes", Asian Survey, 60(3), 490–509. https://www.jstor.org/stable/48735731

5 QUAD, was initiated in 2007 and was restarted by efforts of US and Japanese Foreign Ministers in ASEAN Summit in Manila, is an informal strategic alliance composed of four nations: the United States of America (USA), India, Australia, and Japan. One of its primary goals is to promote a free, open, prosperous, and inclusive Indo-Pacific region. Through cooperation in areas such as maritime security, economic development, and technological advancement, the Quad seeks to maintain a rules-based international order and ensure the stability and security of the Indo-Pacific.

6 They are Cuarteron Reef, Fiery Cross Reef, Gaven Reef, Hughes Reef, Johnson South Reef, Mischief Reef, and Subi Reef. Large-scale reclamation that has increased the size of some land features by several times and created completely new land features that had previously been submerged reefs. These reefs are contested by China and at least one other claimant, such as the Philippines, Vietnam, Malaysia, or Taiwan. Three of these locations—Hughes Reef, Johnson South Reef, and Mischief Reef—lie within the 200-nautical mile exclusive economic zone (EEZ) claimed by the Philippines from its closest mainland, the island of Palawan. See https://sgp.fas.org/crs/row/R44072.pdf

7 It is the only country in the region to have been subjected to invasion by China.

Chapter 10
The South China Sea Politics of the Philippines

Sami Yıldırım
Independent Researcher, Turkey

ABSTRACT

The South China Sea, a critical maritime region, has been a focal point of geopolitical tensions and territorial disputes among several Southeast Asian countries, including the Philippines. This book chapter examines the intricate dynamics of the Philippines' involvement in the South China Sea politics, encompassing historical context, legal frameworks, strategic interests, and diplomatic maneuvers. The South China Sea has long been a flashpoint for regional disputes, and this situation has now escalated into a full-fledged flashpoint. China, the Philippines, Vietnam, Malaysia, Brunei, and Taiwan all assert overlapping claims over this strategically significant and resource-rich region, through which an estimated $3.37 trillion in trade passes annually. Most of these disputes date back to the mid-20th century. However, regional tensions have intensified in recent years due to China's aggressive expansion of territorial and maritime claims, and its frequent assertion of "indisputable sovereignty" over all islands and adjacent waters in the South China Sea (Singleton, 2024).

INTRODUCTION

The South China Sea, a critical maritime region, has been a focal point of geopolitical tensions and territorial disputes among several Southeast Asian countries, including the Philippines. This book chapter examines the intricate dynamics of the

DOI: 10.4018/979-8-3693-8109-0.ch010

Philippines' involvement in the South China Sea politics, encompassing historical context, legal frameworks, strategic interests, and diplomatic maneuvers.

The South China Sea has long been a flashpoint for regional disputes, and this situation has now escalated into a full-fledged flashpoint. China, the Philippines, Vietnam, Malaysia, Brunei, and Taiwan all assert overlapping claims over this strategically significant and resource-rich region, through which an estimated $3.37 trillion in trade passes annually. Most of these disputes date back to the mid-20th century. However, regional tensions have intensified in recent years due to China's aggressive expansion of territorial and maritime claims, and its frequent assertion of "indisputable sovereignty" over all islands and adjacent waters in the South China Sea (Singleton, 2024).

A pivotal moment occurred in 2016 when the Permanent Court of Arbitration (PCA) in The Hague ruled that China's claims over approximately 90% of the South China Sea were manifestly invalid, in a case brought by the Philippines. The court, which adjudicates international disputes including those arising from the United Nations Convention on the Law of the Sea, also noted that China had violated the Philippines' sovereign rights by engaging in unlawful activities within the Philippines' Exclusive Economic Zone (EEZ) and interfering with the Philippines' oil exploration activities. However, Beijing rejected this ruling outright rather than accepting it. In response to objections from the Obama administration, Beijing subsequently significantly heightened regional concerns by constructing and militarizing numerous artificial islands in the South China Sea, including Mischief Reef and Fiery Cross Reef within the internationally recognized waters of the Philippines. To this day, the long-standing tensions have led to recurring conflicts between the Chinese Coast Guard and the Philippine military (Singleton, 2024).

Philippines, island country of Southeast Asia in the western Pacific Ocean, is an archipelago consisting of more than 7,000 islands and islets lying about 500 miles (800 km) off the coast of Vietnam. Manila is the capital, but nearby Quezon City is the country's most-populous city. The Philippine archipelago is bounded by the Philippine Sea to the east, the Celebes Sea to the south, the Sulu Sea to the southwest, and the South China Sea (or West Philippines Sea) to the west and north (Britannica).[1]

The Philippines is the only country in Southeast Asia that was subjected to Western colonization before it had the opportunity to develop either a centralized government ruling over a large territory or a dominant culture.[2] In August 1896, revolts broke out in several provinces around Manila against Spanish rule. After months of fighting, severe Spanish retaliation forced the revolutionary armies to retreat to the hills. In December 1897 a truce was concluded with the Spanish. Meanwhile, the Spanish-American War had broken out between Spain and the United States (US). After the US naval victory in the Battle of Manila Bay in May 1898,

Emilio Aguinaldo[3] and his entourage returned to the Philippines with the help of Adm. George Dewey. Confident of US support, Aguinaldo reorganized his forces and soon liberated several towns south of Manila. Independence was declared on June 12 (now celebrated as Independence Day).[4]

In 1901, then the US President Theodore Roosevelt signed an executive order establishing the first military base of the U.S. in the Philippines. An area of 2,800 hectares in Subic Bay was designated as a military reserve for the US Navy. In 1903, the US declared an additional 3,420 hectares near Manila as a military reserve, later expanded and renamed as Tort Stotsenburg housing Clark Airfield by 1918. Today, Subic Naval Base serves as the headquarters for the US Seventh Fleet, and Clark Air Base hosts the US Air Force's 13th Air Force, making them the two most important US military facilities overseas. The Philippines is an ally of the US in the region (Davis, 1989). After World War II, the US established major military bases in the Philippines, which served as crucial strategic points during the Cold War. Particularly, Clark Air Base and Subic Bay Naval Base became among the largest US military facilities in Asia. Military relations between the two countries deepened with the signing of the Mutual Defense Treaty in 1951. However, in 1992, due to nationalist reactions in the Philippines, American forces were compelled to withdraw from major and enduring military bases like Subic and Clark. Following this withdrawal, regular joint military exercises since 2000 have revitalized military cooperation between the two nations (Davis, 1989).

HISTORICAL CONTEXT AND TERRITORIAL CLAIMS

The Philippines' claims in the South China Sea are primarily centered around the Spratly Islands, a group of approximately 100 small islands, reefs, and atolls. These claims are based on historical records, geographical proximity, and adherence to the United Nations Convention on the Law of the Sea (UNCLOS). The UNCLOS stipulates that coastal states have exclusive rights over resources within 200 nautical miles of their coastlines, which the Philippines argues applies to the Spratlys despite their geographical distance from its mainland. Historically, the Philippines' claims are intertwined with its colonial past, notably during the Spanish and American periods when territorial boundaries and administrative jurisdictions were established. Post-independence, the Philippines inherited these claims and has since sought to reinforce its sovereignty through legal and diplomatic channels (Çebi, 2024).

On 11 March 1976, following an extensive exploration program, the Philippines discovered the Nido oil field off the coast of Palawan Island, marking the first oil find in the Northwest Palawan Basin. This discovery occurred four years after the passage of the Oil Exploration and Development Act of 1972, which established the legal framework for the exploration and development of petroleum resources as Manila sought energy independence. Philippine Cities Service, Inc., the country's pioneering oil company, initiated drilling operations at the Nido oil field and commenced commercial production in 1979, extracting 8.8 million barrels that year (https://countrystudies.us/philippines/71.htm). By 2012, the International Monetary Fund (IMF) observed that the petroleum industry in the Philippines might possess "significant potential" in the South China Sea, which lies adjacent to the Northwest Palawan Basin (IMF, 2012).

In January 1996, three Chinese naval vessels engaged in a ninety-minute battle with a Philippine navy gunboat near Capones Island in Mischief Reef, part of the Spratly Islands claimed by Manila. This incident marked the first instance of China engaging in military confrontation with an ASEAN member state other than Vietnam. The clash triggered a crisis in Sino-Philippine relations and led to a revival of US-Philippine military cooperation. Shortly after the incident, U.S. Navy SEALs conducted a joint exercise with Philippine counterparts on Palawan Island, although then Philippine President Fidel Ramos denied any direct connection between this exercise and Manila's dispute with Beijing. By midyear, tensions over the occupation eased when the Philippines and China signed a non-binding code of conduct, which advocated for a peaceful resolution to the territorial dispute and the promotion of confidence-building measures (de Castro, 2009).

On 1 June 2011, the Philippines summoned a Chinese envoy to express escalating concerns over naval incursions into its claimed territory, following at least five reported incursions by Chinese vessels over the previous year near the Spratly Islands and the Amy Douglas Bank off the coast of Palawan Island. These incursions began in early March, when Chinese surveillance ships compelled a Philippine vessel conducting surveys in the Reed Bank to withdraw from the area. Both nations declared the incident as a breach of the 2002 ASEAN-China Declaration on the Conduct of Parties in the South China Sea, leading to a series of skirmishes between the two countries in the region. The diplomatic standoff in June coincided with Vietnam's protest against China's alleged harassment of its oil exploration ships, as Vietnam was collaborating with multinational corporations, including ExxonMobil and Chevron, to develop hydrocarbon resources. In October 2011, in response to a series of skirmishes with Chinese vessels, the Philippine government began officially referring to the South China Sea as the West Philippine Sea in all official communications (Thayer, 2016: 28).

In October 2012, the government also signed an administrative order asserting its "inherent power and right to designate its maritime areas" (Presidency of the Philippines, 2012). Additionally, U.S. Secretary of State Hillary Clinton adopted the term West Philippine Sea in her statements, and during a joint press conference with her Philippine counterpart in November 2011, she reaffirmed the "vigor" of the alliance between the two countries, particularly highlighting support "at a time when the Philippines is facing challenges to its territorial integrity" in the region (state.gov, 2011).

On 8 April 2012, diplomatic relations between Manila and Beijing deteriorated further when the Philippines deployed a warship to confront Chinese fishing boats in the Scarborough Shoal, located north of the Spratly Islands. In response, China sent surveillance vessels to protect its fishermen, leading to a two-month standoff. During this period, China imposed restrictions on the import of certain Philippine fruits and issued travel advisories against visiting the Philippines, raising concerns among regional observers that such tensions could adversely affect economic relations. In May, Philippine banana export losses were estimated at $34 million. Bilateral negotiations repeatedly faltered over the issue of withdrawing from the shoal. The Philippine government pursued multiple strategies, including seeking ASEAN involvement, exploring legal avenues under the United Nations Convention on the Law of the Sea (UNCLOS), and appealing to the United States for a security guarantee in the event of military escalation. Meanwhile, Beijing maintained regular patrols that effectively barred Philippine fishermen from accessing the contested waters (CFR).

On 22 January 2013, the Philippines initiated an international arbitration case under the United Nations Convention on the Law of the Sea (UNCLOS) concerning Chinese claims of sovereignty over the Spratly Islands and Scarborough Shoal, which stemmed from the clashes in April 2012. This move followed decades of unsuccessful attempts to resolve the dispute. China refused to participate in the arbitration process, compelling the court to proceed without its involvement. This case represents the first instance of a country bringing a claim against China under UNCLOS regarding this issue (PCA, 2013).

Due to China's increased military activities and regional claims in the South China Sea, military cooperation between the US and the Philippines has regained strength. On 28 April 2014, then the US President B. Obama, during the final leg of a four-nation tour of Asia, signed a new ten-year military agreement with the Philippines. The Enhanced Defense Cooperation Agreement (EDCA) provides for an increased rotational U.S. military presence in the Philippines[5], expanded joint training activities, and enhanced access to bases across the archipelago, including ports and airfields (Felsenthal and Spetalnick, (2014). This agreement was a central feature of Obama's first visit to the Philippines, the US' oldest ally in the region, and highlighted the administration's commitment to the Asia "pivot." While Obama expressed support for Manila's pursuit of international arbitration over the contested South China Sea islands, he emphasized that the agreement was not intended to serve as a measure to contain China (Rauhala, 2014).

On 12 July 2016, the Permanent Court of Arbitration in The Hague issued a ruling in favor of the Philippines in a case initiated in 2013 against the People's Republic of China. The tribunal determined that China's "nine-dash line" claim lacks legal foundation for asserting historic rights to resources in the South China Sea. The court further ruled that none of the maritime features in question meet the criteria under the United Nations Convention on the Law of the Sea (UNCLOS) to establish a 200-nautical-mile exclusive economic zone for China, noting that many of these features are the result of extensive Chinese land reclamation activities. The court also found that Beijing had violated its obligations under UNCLOS by damaging the marine environment through its island-building activities and by increasing navigational risks through unsafe practices of its vessels. In response, China's foreign ministry declared that it "neither accepts nor recognizes" the tribunal's award (PCA, 2016).

On 20 November 2016, then Philippine President Rodrigo Duterte announced the establishment of a no-fishing zone and marine sanctuary at a lagoon in Scarborough Shoal. This area, a focal point of tensions between the Philippines and China, saw Duterte's shift from the assertive stance of his predecessor, Benigno S. Aquino III. Duterte's administration indicated a preference for improving economic ties with China and resuming bilateral dialogue on disputed territories, signaling a potential warming of relations. Despite this, both China and the Philippines maintained their respective sovereignty claims, with leaders from both countries appearing to adopt a more reconciliatory approach (Perlez, 2016).

On 5 April 2019, R. Duterte issued a warning that he would send troops on a "suicide mission" if China continued its naval activities near Thitu Island in the Spratly chain, which the Philippines occupies. This threat followed reports of over two hundred Chinese ships being observed near the island between January and March. The Philippines had been constructing a beaching ramp on Thitu Island, also claimed by China, to facilitate the delivery of construction equipment and supplies (Westcott and Lendon, 2019).

On 9 June 2019, a Chinese fishing vessel collided with and partially sank a wooden Filipino fishing boat, the F/B Gem-Ver 1, which was anchored at Reed Bank in the South China Sea. Following the incident, the Chinese vessel reportedly turned off its signal lights and departed as the Filipino boat began to sink. The 22 Filipino fishermen were forced to abandon their vessel and remained adrift for over six hours before being rescued by a Vietnamese fishing boat in the area. This collision marked the latest and most severe incident in a series of confrontations that have strained the Philippines-China rapprochement established during Duterte's administration (de Castro, 2019).[6]

In February 2020, amid the regional struggle against the coronavirus pandemic, China intensified its assertiveness in the South China Sea. In February, a Chinese naval ship reportedly directed its weapons control system at a Philippine naval vessel in the Spratly Islands (de Castro, 2020). The following month, China established new research stations on Fiery Cross and Subi Reefs, including defense silos and military-grade runways. In April, Vietnam lodged a formal protest after a Chinese vessel collided with and sank a Vietnamese fishing boat near the Paracels. Shortly thereafter, Beijing announced the creation of two administrative districts encompassing the Paracel and Spratly Islands, prompting denunciations from the Philippines and Vietnam (Thu, 2020).

Between March 2021 and November 2022, in response to President Duterte's increasingly supportive stance on the 2016 Hague ruling, which rejected China's nine-dash line claim—a position also supported by France, Germany, and the United Kingdom—China escalated its intimidation tactics. In March 2021, China deployed two hundred ships to Whitsun Reef within the Philippines' exclusive economic zone (EEZ), which Beijing described as a "fishing fleet," while Manila alleged that the ships were manned by military personnel. In November 2022, during U.S. Vice President Kamala Harris's visit to the Philippines, the Philippine navy accused China's coast guard of seizing debris from a suspected Chinese rocket that had landed in Philippine waters (Strangio, 2020).

On 4 February 2023, less than a year after taking office, Philippine President Ferdinand Marcos Jr. welcomed an expanded U.S. military presence in the Philippines. The addition of four new military bases in northern Philippines significantly increased the U.S. footprint in the South China Sea. Chinese officials strongly objected to this expansion, while Philippine diplomats confronted their Chinese counterparts over allegations that China's navy had repeatedly used lasers to harass Philippine and Australian sailors (Gomez, 2023). The following month, as President Xi Jinping began an unprecedented third term, Beijing announced a 7.2 percent increase in military spending, citing "escalating" threats. On 11 April 2024, A trilateral summit took place shortly after US, Australian, Japanese, and Philippine forces conducted their first-ever four-way joint naval patrols within the Philippines' EEZ. In their leaders' statement, they expressed concern over China's recent aggressive maneuvers in the South China Sea and its increased patrolling in the East China Sea, where the Japan-administered Senkaku/Diaoyu Islands are situated. On April 28, China's Coast Guard confronted Japanese lawmakers conducting an inspection mission in the East China Sea (Wright, 2023).

In April 2023, the US was granted the opportunity to use four new military bases in the Philippines to deepen their longstanding alliance. This development nearly doubles the number of facilities specified under the current defense cooperation. The newly designated bases include Camilo Osias Naval Base in Sta Ana and Lal-lo in Cagayan province, Camp Melchor Dela Cruz in Isabela province, and Balabac Island near Palawan. The selection of these locations holds strategic significance: Isabela and Cagayan provide a strategic view towards Taiwan, while Palawan's proximity to the disputed Spratly Islands in the South China Sea, where China has constructed military airstrips and missile systems on artificial islands, is notable. These new military arrangements signify a significant transformation in the region's security architecture and have decisive implications for regional power balances. To strengthen its existing military presence in the Philippines, the US has committed infrastructure investments exceeding 80 million US dollars across five different regions. These regions include Antonio Bautista Air Base in Palawan, Basa Air Base in Pampanga, Fort Magsaysay in Nueva Ecija, Benito Ebuen Air Base in Cebu, and Lumbia Air Base in Mindanao. These investments aim to enhance operational capacity at these strategically important points (US Department of Defense, 2023).

President F. Marcos Jr of the Philippines announced that American troops will be stationed at four new locations across the country to enhance defense in the South China Sea. These new military bases are dispersed across various regions of the country, bringing the total number of US bases in the Philippines to nine, including the five existing bases designated under the 2014 EDCA. Marcos' administration recently announced arrangements allowing US forces to be stationed indefinitely on a rotational basis at these four new Filipino military camps (Lema, 2023).

Detailing the plans for establishing new military bases in the Philippines, F. Marcos Jr indicated that these bases would cover the eastern side of Luzon Island. Marcos emphasized that this strategic positioning would bolster the region's defense capacity, taking into account Luzon's proximity to Taiwan and its geopolitical importance as the largest island in the Philippines. However, a former Philippine military chief has stated that the United States has requested access to military bases in Isabela, Zambales, and Cagayan provinces in Luzon Island, facing Taiwan to the north and near the disputed Spratly Islands in Palawan to the southwest. In light of current tensions in the South China Sea, these requests are considered a significant development that could impact strategic balances in the region and bolster the US military presence in the Asia-Pacific (Aljazeera.com, 2023).

In response to these developments, the Chinese Embassy in Manila has expressed concerns about the increasing military cooperation between the Philippines and the United States. In their statement, the Embassy noted that such cooperation, despite economic opportunities and job creation efforts, could negatively affect regional peace and stability, push the Philippines into the center of geopolitical disputes, and potentially harm the country's long-term economic development. China's statement underscores the potential consequences of military cooperation on regional tensions and highlights the possible impacts of alliance policies and military movements (Fomenko, 2024).

LEGAL FRAMEWORKS AND INTERNATIONAL LAW

Central to the Philippines' strategy in the South China Sea is its adherence to international law, particularly UNCLOS. The country brought its territorial disputes with China to the Permanent Court of Arbitration (PCA) in The Hague in 2013. In 2016, the PCA ruled overwhelmingly in favor of the Philippines, rejecting China's expansive "nine-dash line" claim and affirming the Philippines' rights to its Exclusive Economic Zone (EEZ).

Despite the ruling, which was legally binding under international law, China refused to recognize it, asserting historical claims and continuing to assert its presence through military and infrastructural developments in the area. This defiance has posed challenges to the Philippines' efforts to assert its maritime rights and manage its territorial integrity.

Hostilities and tensions in the disputed waters have alarmingly escalated particularly between China and the Philippines over two disputed shoals since last year. Chinese coast guard ships and suspected militia vessels have used powerful water cannons and dangerous blocking maneuvers against Philippine coast guard patrol ships and navy boats that have injured Filipino navy personnel, damaged their supply boats and strained diplomatic relations between the two countries. After a tense standoff between Philippine and Chinese ships near a shoal in 2012, the Philippines brought its disputes with China the following year to international arbitration. The arbitration panel invalidated China's claim to virtually the entire South China Sea in a 2016 ruling but Beijing refused to participate in the arbitration, rejected the decision and continues to defy it.

The Philippines has asked a United Nations body to formally recognize the extent of its undersea continental seabed in the South China Sea, where it would have the exclusive right to exploit resources, the Department of Foreign Affairs said, in a move that rejects China's vast territorial claims to the region. The Philippine government submitted information to the U.N. Commission on the Limits of the Continental Shelf on the extent of its undersea shelf in the South China Sea, off western Palawan province, after more than a decade and a half of scientific research, the department said. China did not immediately comment but it will likely contest the Philippine move. The undersea region where the Philippines seeks to formally establish its sovereign rights under the U.N. Convention on the Law of the Sea, or UNCLOS, covers the Spratlys, a chain of islands, islets, reefs and atolls that has been fiercely contested over the years by China, the Philippines, Vietnam, Malaysia, Brunei and Taiwan. Indonesia has also confronted Chinese coast guard and fishing fleets in the gas-rich Natuna sea in the fringes of the South China Sea.

"Incidents in the waters tend to overshadow the importance of what lies beneath," Philippine Foreign Assistant Secretary Marshall Louis Alferez said. "The seabed and the subsoil extending from our archipelago up to the maximum extent allowed by UNCLOS hold significant potential resources that will benefit our nation and our people for generations to come. Today, we secure our future by making a manifestation of our exclusive right to explore and exploit natural resources in our extended continental shelf entitlement," Alferez said. Under the 1982 U.N. convention, a coastal state could have exclusive rights to exploit resources in its continental shelf, a vast stretch of seabed that can extend up to 350 nautical miles (648 kilometers), including the right to authorize and regulate any kind of drilling. The Philippines' undersea continental shelf could potentially overlap with those of other coastal states in the South China Sea, including that of Vietnam. Philippine officials expressed readiness to hold talks to resolve such issues based on UNCLOS. Philippine permanent representative to the U.N. Antonio Lagdameo said the move "can reinvigorate efforts of states to demonstrate their readiness to pursue UNCLOS processes in the determination of maritime entitlements and promote a rules-based international order." (Gomez, 2024).

GEOPOLITICAL STRATEGY AND DIPLOMATIC MANEUVERS

In response to China's assertiveness, the Philippines has pursued a multi-faceted geopolitical strategy. This strategy involves strengthening alliances with traditional allies such as the United States, engaging with regional partners within ASEAN (Association of Southeast Asian Nations), and enhancing its maritime capabilities through defense agreements and modernization efforts.

Diplomatically, the Philippines has navigated a delicate balance between asserting its rights under international law and maintaining economic and diplomatic relations with China. While advocating for a rules-based approach and multilateral dialogue within ASEAN, the Philippines has also pursued bilateral negotiations with China to manage tensions and promote stability in the region.

The efforts of the United States to maintain its regional power presence and protect free trade routes; China's goal to expand regional dominance and maximize national interests; and the Philippines' desire to safeguard national sovereignty and receive security support from allies are fundamental factors shaping the relationship between these two countries. These factors will determine the future political and military balance of the region.

In April 2023, there has been an increase in US military patrols and navigation operations under the name of Freedom of Navigation Operations (FONOP) in the South China Sea. the largest joint exercise in the past decade was conducted by the

United States and the Philippines. Thousands of American and Filipino troops participated in the exercises known as "Balikatan," with 12,200 Americans and 5,400 Filipinos participating in the 2023 exercise (Alaca, 2023).

Chinese Foreign Ministry Spokesperson Mao Ning has criticized US policies in the Asia-Pacific region, describing them as "selfish and futile." China perceives the increased US military presence in the region as a threat to regional stability and argues that it could have negative effects on the region. These criticisms indicate that US regional policies are a source of concern not only for the Philippines but also for all countries in the region. On the other hand, F. Marcos Jr has stated that concerns about the four newly announced military bases under defense cooperation with the US are unfounded. He emphasized that these bases would only be used for defensive purposes in the event of an attack on the Philippines. Marcos' statements underscore the Philippines' intention to maintain strategic defense cooperation with the US and reaffirm its commitment to regional security. This demonstrates that the Philippines considers the US an important partner in its regional security strategies and aims to enhance its capacity to defend itself against potential threats. These developments will play a crucial role in shaping regional power dynamics and could further escalate geopolitical tensions between the Philippines and China (Fomenko, 2024).

The events at Scarborough Shoal in January 2024 underscore the escalating geopolitical tensions in the South China Sea. It was reported that the Philippine Coast Guard vessel BRP Teresa Magbanua encountered interventions by Chinese Coast Guard vessels while conducting patrols in the region from February 2 to 9. Philippine officials stated that Chinese vessels obstructed the path of the Philippine ship 40 times and engaged in four instances of dangerous maneuvers. This situation highlights the high level of tension in the region and further emphasizes the sovereignty struggle between the two countries.

Scarborough Shoal, located 120 nautical miles north of Luzon Island, holds a strategic position with rich marine resources. It gained international attention in 2012 when the Philippine Coast Guard intervened with Chinese fishing vessels in the area, highlighting its strategic importance beyond economic considerations.

Despite efforts by the Philippines to reduce tension at Scarborough Shoal and similar strategic points, China continues its efforts to strengthen its dominance in the region. Similar incidents have occurred at Second Thomas Shoal, which is part of the Spratly Islands under Philippine control. Recent aggressive actions by the Chinese Coast Guard, such as towards Philippine supply ships, have further escalated tensions between the two countries. Such incidents are concerning for regional security and stability, drawing attention from the international community and underscoring their potential impact on regional balance.

The increasing defense cooperation between the Philippines and the US represents a significant turning point in Manila's regional security strategy, coinciding with tensions in the South China Sea. The visit of US Secretary of Defense Lloyd Austin and the granting of access to four new military bases under the Enhanced Defense Cooperation Agreement (EDCA) can be seen as responses to these concerns.

The directive by Gilberto Teodoro to enhance military presence in the Batanes Islands also reinforces the Philippines' determination to ensure regional security. These islands hold strategic importance due to their proximity to Taiwan and mainland China, making any military movements there capable of directly influencing regional dynamics.

China's response, however, has the potential to further escalate regional tensions. The warning from the Chinese Foreign Ministry spokesperson to the Philippines against "playing with fire" underscores China's sensitivity regarding the Taiwan issue and indicates close monitoring of any Philippine activities in the area. Considering Taiwan as an integral part of its territory, China perceives any military activity near this region as a potential threat.

The trilateral summit held on April 12, 2024, aimed to strengthen strategic cooperation in the Indo-Pacific region among US President Joe Biden, Japanese Prime Minister Fumio Kishida, and Philippine President Ferdinand Marcos Jr. The summit facilitated the creation of a shared vision on issues such as ensuring security and stability in the region, preserving access to free and open seas, and promoting regional development.

ECONOMIC AND ENVIRONMENTAL IMPLICATIONS

Beyond sovereignty and security concerns, the South China Sea disputes have significant economic and environmental implications for the Philippines. The region is rich in fisheries, oil and gas reserves, and strategic shipping lanes crucial to global trade. However, escalating tensions and militarization threaten maritime security, hinder resource exploration, and impact regional stability.

Furthermore, environmental degradation due to unsustainable fishing practices and reef destruction exacerbates ecological vulnerabilities in the South China Sea, affecting marine biodiversity and coastal communities reliant on marine resources.

CONCLUSION

The Philippines' involvement in the South China Sea politics reflects a complex interplay of historical claims, legal frameworks, geopolitical strategies, and economic imperatives. As the country navigates these challenges, it continues to uphold international law, pursue diplomatic solutions, and strengthen alliances to safeguard its sovereignty and promote regional stability. The resolution of the South China Sea disputes remains crucial not only for the Philippines but also for regional security and global maritime governance.

In conclusion, while the South China Sea remains a contentious geopolitical arena, the Philippines' approach underscores the importance of international cooperation, adherence to legal norms, and strategic diplomacy in addressing complex maritime disputes and promoting peace and stability in Southeast Asia.

REFERENCES

Alaca, M. (2023). *ABD ile Filipinler, Tayvan Boğazı'nın yakınındaki sularda "en büyük" savaş tatbikatına başladı,* Anatolia Agency, 11.04.2023, https://www.aa.com.tr/tr/dunya/abd-ile-filipinler-tayvan-bogazinin-yakinindaki-sularda-en-buyuk-savas-tatbikatina-basladi/2869008

Aljazeera.com. (2023). *US gets new Philippine bases with South China Sea, Taiwan in mind,* 22.03.2023, https://www.aljazeera.com/news/2023/3/22/us-gets-new-philippine-bases-with-south-china-sea-taiwan-in-mind#:~:text=The%20US%20has%20committed%20%2480,Lumbia%20Air%20Base%20in%20Mindanao

Britannica, *Philippinnes,* https://www.britannica.com/place/Philippines

Çebi, T. (2024). *Güney Çin Denizi'ndeki Amerika-Çin Rekabetinde Filipinler,* 20 April 2024 https://www.turksam.org/detay-guney-cin-denizi-ndeki-amerika-cin-rekabetinde-filipinler

Council on Foreign Relations. https://www.cfr.org/timeline/chinas-maritime-disputes#!/chinas-maritime-disputes?cid=otr-marketing_use-china_sea_InfoGuide

Davis, L. (1989). Revolutionary Struggle In The Philippines. *Palgrave Macmillan London, 1989.* Advance online publication. DOI: 10.1007/978-1-349-19862-7

de Castro, R. C. (2009). The US-Philippine Alliance: An Evolving Hedge against an Emerging China Challenge. *Contemporary Southeast Asia: A Journal of International and Strategic Affairs 31*(3), 399-423. https://www.muse.jhu.edu/article/370828

de Castro, R. C. (2019). *Incident at Reed Bank: A Crisis in the Phillipines' China Policy,* June 20, 2019, https://amti.csis.org/incident-at-reed-bank-a-crisis-in-the-philippines-china-policy/

de Castro, R. C. (2020). *Implications of the Recent Philippines-China Naval Stand-Off,* 07.05.2020, https://amti.csis.org/implications-of-the-recent-philippines-china-naval-stand-off/

Felsenthal, M., & Spetalnick, M. (2014). *Obama says U.S. commitment to defend Philippines 'ironclad',* April 29, 2014, https://www.reuters.com/article/2014/04/29/us-philippines-usa-obama-idUSBREA3S02T20140429/

Fomenko, T. (2024). *The US is cultivating an antagonist to China in Beijing's own backyard,* 25.03.2024, https://www.rt.com/news/594824-us-china-philippines-antagonist/

Gomez, J. (2023). *Philippines confronts Chinese diplomats over sea disputes,* 24.03.2023, https://apnews.com/article/china-philippines-south-china-sea-disputes-70ea7983dbf67b1f9ae5264c6ce9271a

IMF. (2012). (https://www.imf.org/external/pubs/ft/scr/2012/cr12219.pdf). August 2012 IMF Country Report No. 12/219 July 23, 2012 January 29, 2001 January 29, 2001 January 29, 2001 January 29, 2001 Philippines: Reform of the Fiscal Regimes for Mining and Petroleum

Lema, K. (2023). *Philippines reveals locations of 4 new strategic sites for U.S. military pact,* 03.04.2023, https://www.reuters.com/world/asia-pacific/philippines-reveals-locations-4-new-strategic-sites-us-military-pact-2023-04-03/

PCA-Permanent Court of Arbitration. (2013). *The South China Sea Arbitration (The Republic of Philippines v. The People's Republic of China),*https://pca-cpa.org/en/cases/7/#:~:text=On%2022%20January%202013%2C%20the,(the%20%E2%80%9CConvention%E2%80%9D)

PCA-Permanent Court of Arbitration. (2016). *The South China Sea Arbitration Award of 12 July 2016,*https://pcacases.com/web/sendAttach/2086

Perlez, J. (2016). *Rodrigo Duterte and Xi Jinping Agree to Reopen South China Sea Talks,* 20.10.2016, https://www.nytimes.com/2016/10/21/world/asia/rodrigo-duterte-philippines-china-xi-jinping.html

Presidency of the Philippines. (2012). *Administrative Order No. 29 s. 2012 "Naming the West Philippine Sea of the Republic of the Philippines",* 05.09.2021, https://www.officialgazette.gov.ph/2012/09/05/administrative-order-no-29-s-2012/

Rauhala, E. (2014). *Obama in the Philippines: 'Our Goal Is Not to Contain China'* 20.04.2014, https://time.com/78779/obama-philippines-china/

Singleton, C. (2024). *China and the U.S. Are Careening Toward a South China Sea Crisis,*https://foreignpolicy.com/2024/07/23/us-south-china-sea-philippines-crisis-military-alliance-deterrence/ (Accessed 26.07.2024).

State.gov. (2011). *Presentation of the Order of Lakandula, Signing of the Partnership for Growth and Joint Press Availability with Philippines Foreign Secretary Albert Del Rosario,* Hillary Rodham Clinton, Secretary of State, Manila, Philippines, November 16, 2011, https://2009-2017.state.gov/secretary/20092013clinton/rm/2011/11/177234.htm

Strangio, S. (2020). *In UN Speech, Duterte Stiffens Philippines' Stance on the South China Sea,* 23.09.2020, https://thediplomat.com/2020/09/in-un-speech-duterte-stiffens-philippines-stance-on-the-south-china-sea/

Thayer, C. A. (2016). In Yann-huei, S., & Zou, K. (Eds.), *China-ASEAN and the Soth China Sea: Chinese Assertiveness and South Asian Responses, Major Law and Policy Issues in the South China Sea: European and American Perspectives* (p. 28). Routledge.

Thu, H. L. (2020). *Fishing While the Water is Muddy: China's Newly Announced Administrative Districts in the South China Sea,* 06.05.2020, https://amti.csis.org/fishing-while-the-water-is-muddy-chinas-newly-announced-administrative-districts-in-the-south-china-sea/

US Department of Defense. (2023). *Philippines, U.S. Announce Locations of Four New EDCA Sites,* April 3, 2023, https://www.defense.gov/News/Releases/Release/Article/3349257/philippines-us-announce-locations-of-four-new-edca-sites/

Westcott, B., & Lendon, B. (2019). *Duterte threatens 'suicide mission' if Beijing oversteps in South China Sea,* CNN, 05.04.2019, https://edition.cnn.com/2019/04/05/asia/south-china-sea-duterte-beijing-intl/index.html

Wright, G. (2023). *China discusses military budget while warning of escalating threats,* BBC, 06.03.2023, https://www.bbc.com/news/world-asia-china-64857194

ENDNOTES

1 The islands spread out in the shape of a triangle, with those south of Palawan, the Sulu Archipelago, and the island of Mindanao outlining (from west to east, respectively) its southern base and the Batan Islands to the north of Luzon forming its apex. Historically, the total number of islands in the archipelago was held to be 7,107, but in 2016 the National Mapping and Resource Information Authority of the Philippines announced the discovery of more than 500 previously uncharted islands. The archipelago stretches about 1,150 miles (1,850 km) from north to south, and its widest east-west extent, at its southern base, is some 700 miles (1,130 km). The island of Taiwan lies north of the Batan group, the Malaysian portion of the island of Borneo is to the south of Palawan, and the eastern islands of Indonesia lie to the south and southeast of Mindanao. Only about two-fifths of the islands and islets have names, and only some 350 have areas of 1 square mile (2.6 square km) or more. The large islands fall into three groups: (1) the Luzon group in the north and west, consisting of Luzon, Mindoro, and Palawan, (2) the Visayas group in the centre, consisting of Bohol, Cebu, Leyte, Masbate, Negros, Panay, and Samar, and (3) Mindanao in the south (Britannica).

2 The Portuguese navigator and explorer Ferdinand Magellan headed the first Spanish foray to the Philippines when he made landfall on Cebu in March 1521; a short time later he met an untimely death on the nearby island of Mactan. After King Philip II (for whom the islands are named) had dispatched three further expeditions that ended in disaster, he sent out Miguel López de Legazpi, who established the first permanent Spanish settlement, in Cebu, in 1565. The Spanish city of Manila was founded in 1571, and by the end of the 16th century most of the coastal and lowland areas from Luzon to northern Mindanao were under Spanish control. Spanish rule for the first 100 years was exercised in most areas through a type of tax farming imported from the Americas and known as the *encomienda*. But abusive treatment of the local tribute payers and neglect of religious instruction by *encomenderos* (collectors of the tribute), as well as frequent withholding of revenues from the crown, caused the Spanish to abandon the system by the end of the 17th century. The governor-general, himself appointed by the king, began to appoint his own civil and military governors to rule directly. Agricultural technology changed very slowly until the late 18th century, as shifting cultivation gradually gave way to more intensive sedentary farming, partly under the guidance of the friars. The socioeconomic consequences of the Spanish policies that accompanied this shift reinforced class differences. By the late 18th century, political and economic changes in Europe were finally beginning to affect Spain and, thus, the Philippines. Important as a stimulus to trade was the gradual elimination of the monopoly enjoyed by the galleon to Acapulco. The last galleon arrived in Manila in 1815, and by the mid-1830s Manila was open to foreign merchants almost without restriction. The demand for Philippine sugar and abaca (hemp) grew apace, and the volume of exports to Europe expanded even further after the completion of the Suez Canal in 1869 (Britannica).

3 Filipino leader (of mixed Chinese and Tagalog descent) who fought for the independence of the Philippines first against Spain and then against the United States.

4 In September a constitutional congress met in Malolos, north of Manila, which drew up a fundamental law derived from European and Latin American precedents. A government was formed on the basis of that constitution in January 1899, with Aguinaldo as president of the new country, popularly known as the "Malolos Republic." Meanwhile, U.S. troops had landed in Manila and, with important Filipino help, forced the capitulation in August 1898 of the Spanish commander there. The Americans, however, would not let Filipino forces enter the city. It was soon apparent to Aguinaldo and his advisers that earlier expressions of sympathy for Filipino independence by Dewey and U.S.

consular officials in Hong Kong had little significance. They felt betrayed. U.S. commissioners to the peace negotiations in Paris had been instructed to demand from Spain the cession of the Philippines to the United States; such cession was confirmed with the signing of the Treaty of Paris on December 10, 1898. Ratification followed in the U.S. Senate in February 1899, but with only one vote more than the required two-thirds. Arguments of "manifest destiny" could not overwhelm a determined anti-imperialist minority. By the time the treaty was ratified, hostilities had already broken out between U.S. and Filipino forces. Since Filipino leaders did not recognize U.S. sovereignty over the islands and U.S. commanders gave no weight to Filipino claims of independence, the conflict was inevitable. It took two years of counterinsurgency warfare and some wise conciliatory moves in the political arena to break the back of the nationalist resistance. Aguinaldo was captured in March 1901 and shortly thereafter appealed to his countrymen to accept U.S. rule. The Filipino revolutionary movement had two goals, national and social. The first goal, independence, though realized briefly, was frustrated by the American decision to continue administering the islands. The goal of fundamental social change, manifest in the nationalization of friar lands by the Malolos Republic, was ultimately frustrated by the power and resilience of entrenched institutions. Share tenants who had rallied to Aguinaldo's cause, partly for economic reasons, merely exchanged one landlord for another. In any case, the proclamation of a republic in 1898 had marked the Filipinos as the first Asian people to try to throw off European colonial rule (Britannica).

5 EDCA granted the US rotational presence of troops in designated Philippine military facilities and allowed the US access to Philippine bases for joint training, pre-positioning of equipment, and construction of facilities such as runways, fuel storage, and military housing.

6 The Reed Bank collision follows a series of troubling incidents that have intensified domestic pressure on the Duterte administration to adopt a more assertive stance towards China. In late July 2018, the Philippine government formally conveyed its concerns to China regarding the escalation of aggressive radio warnings issued against Philippine aircraft and ships operating near Chinese-held features in the South China Sea. On August 15, 2018, President Duterte publicly criticized China for its island-building activities and urged a reduction in its provocative actions in the South China Sea. Subsequently, in early April 2019, the Philippine Department of Foreign Affairs lodged a diplomatic protest with China over the presence of over two hundred suspected militia vessels around Thitu Island (de Castro, 2019).

Chapter 11
USA Policy in the South China Sea: An Analysis From a Geopolitical Perspective

Meysune Yaşar
http://orcid.org/0000-0001-9073-6350
Istanbul Medeniyet University, Turkey

ABSTRACT

This study analyzes the US policy in the South China Sea through critical geopolitics. It emphasizes the contribution of critical geopolitics to classical geopolitical studies and evaluates this emphasis on the South China Sea. While emphasizing the impact of classical geopolitical studies on regional policies, it also highlights the contributions of critical geopolitics to the regional approaches of states. The South China Sea is one of the areas where the themes of global and regional competition are intensifying. The United States, one of the important actors in this competition, has put forward important approaches to the region, especially after the Cold War. This study examines this approach from the perspective of critical geopolitics and evaluates the US view of the region under the headings of strategic geography, diplomatic history and historical geography. Through these three topics, the study demonstrates that the geopolitical view of the region cannot be limited to geographical advantages and disadvantages and discusses the US emphasis on the long-term maritime regime.

DOI: 10.4018/979-8-3693-8109-0.ch011

INTRODUCTION

Geopolitical studies in international relations have been the subject of theoretical and field-based studies. While classical geopolitical theories mainly focused on realism, critical approaches have also taken their place in the field. While this study considers classical geopolitical theories worthy of attention, it also highlights the importance of critical geopolitics. The study argues that the interaction of geography, history, and strategy has geopolitical consequences. Also, this process as a whole is reflected in the political approaches of states. While this argument seeks an answer to how the US interaction with geographical areas transforms into a geopolitical sphere of influence, it also opens this answer to the discussion over the South China Sea. The South China Sea is one of the important areas of multidimensional competition. The geopolitical extensions of the resource competition beyond the states of the region, including strategic, political, economic and legal areas, have made the possibility of war a much debated issue. These war possibilities centre on the US and China, the two most important subjects of global competition.

China's increasing sovereignty claims over the region and its growing influence on the global arena accelerate the US involvement in the region, while increasing the emphasis on the geopolitical position of the South China Sea. This study aims to make this emphasis through a critical geopolitical reading by going beyond the classical geopolitical reading. Another important goal is to take the geopolitical perspective off the axis of realism and make it the theme of a more comprehensive research universe. While this approach breaks the dominance of the geography-based perspective in geopolitical analysis, it also paves the way for interdisciplinary analysis in geopolitics. The fact that the South China Sea is the subject of this debate is very important for this study. Since the region is the sphere of influence not only of the littoral states but also of global powers, it offers important opportunities for geopolitical analyses. The study analyses the US policy approaches to the region under three headings within the scope of critical geopolitics: historical geography, geo-strategy, and diplomatic history.

With these points emphasized, the study primarily focuses on the US presence in Southeast Asia. It seeks to answer where the political approaches it has implemented in the region stand in terms of continuity and change since the Cold War. In the second part, the political approaches, which are presented as an element of historical continuity, are geographically deeper and their regional reflections are analyzed. In the last part, the points emphasized in the first two chapters are approached from a geopolitical perspective, and it is revealed how the US handles geography as a strategic tool.

TRACES OF HISTORICAL GEOGRAPHY IN THE SOUTH CHINA SEA

The establishment of a maritime order in the Asia Pacific as a whole, and more specifically in the South China Sea, has qualities for the US that go beyond the classical meanings of geopolitics. In addition to geostrategic approaches, which are an important projection of the classical US maritime strategy, it is vital to take steps to strengthen integration in the region. In this direction, when the US presence in the region is analyzed, it is possible to go back to before the Opium Wars. The US, which acted on economic grounds in its contacts with China, has been involved in this area as a party to the competition, especially in the 20th century. In terms of sovereignty claims in the region, it is seen that a position was taken for the first time in 1907. During the Japan-China War, the assumption that Japan's possible activity on Pratas Reef could threaten the US forces in the Philippines came to the fore. With this assumption, the US remained neutral in the sovereignty claims over the Paracel and Spratly Islands before the Second World War, while opposing Japan's claims (Hayton, 2019: 3-11).

After 1945, while the region continued to be an area of strategic competition, the function of the South China Sea was also determined in the spirit of the Cold War order. While the Soviets focused on bases in regions such as Cam Ranh Bay by carefully considering their presence here against the possible US and Chinese threat, the US similarly aimed to eliminate the possible Soviet threat by building bases in the Subic Bay region of the Philippines (Harding, 2024: 1-8). Similarly, the activities of the United Kingdom, New Zealand, Australia, Singapore and Malaysia in the region under the name of the "Five Power Defense Arrangement" (1971) were noteworthy (Australian Treaty Series, 1971). In the aftermath of the Cold War, the US-China axis started to sharpen in the South China Sea competition, which will increase gradually. At this point, the US geostrategically underlined its goal of deep geostrategic influence in the region and emphasized regional integration and the strengthening of democratic regimes as important components of this influence. These two topics are not only the regional political approach of a state, but also serve to expand the geostrategic sphere of influence.

More specifically, it can be observed that after the Second World War, the United States had three main goals for the region: to build an Asia integrated into the world capitalist economy, to prevent possible Soviet influence in the region, and finally to lead revolutions that would turn Europe and the former Japanese colonial empires away from communism (Schonberger, 1985: 140). The claim that China is surrounded by the United States, which is currently frequently emphasized by China, is precisely a reference to the Cold War-era American strategy. This is because these three main objectives have been the steps taken towards the containment of Asia.

What needs to be emphasized here is the extent to which these objectives are linked to geostrategy. Geostrategically, the US has focused on points that it can quickly control and achieve effective results. The goal of improving Japan, the support given to separatist movements in China, and the emphasis on certain geographical points for the need for raw materials and markets have been indicative of geostrategic goals (Baskara, 2021: 336-338).

The most important interlocutor of the goal of establishing an economic bloc of capitalist nations was Japan in this period. In addition to the economic recovery programme, Japan was rebuilt within the framework of democratic reform steps and peace and security agreements. While this reconstruction process made Japan an important American ally in Asian waters, Japan's growth was seen as essential for the development of Southeast Asia. In this period, the Marshall Plan was considered very important for Asia, especially due to the Soviet threat (Schonberger, 1985: 147). Within the framework of the Plan, India and the Philippines were among the countries that received economic development assistance. The condition for the development aid provided in this period was tied to the agreements made with the USA, which stipulated that a common world view would be adopted (Malenbaum, 1956: 109-112). While the US believed that the more economic support it provided, the more it would protect the states in the region from the Soviet threat, the détente period, which included China in the 1970s, gave momentum to economic relations. The revival of China-Japan trade with the influence of the US and the improvement in US-China relations have been indicative of a new strategy towards the region: engagement instead of containment.

In the engagement-based political approach, the economy was taken as a driving force and the two sharp poles of the Cold War period tended to soften relatively. What is noteworthy in this period is that although economic and political relations with China have improved, military relations have remained limited. In particular, the fact that the US did not give up its arms sales to Taiwan at a time when bilateral relations tended to improve to such an extent strengthened the interpretations that concerns towards the region continued. Another important engagement-oriented development of this period was the establishment of ASEAN. Founded in 1967 as a regional intergovernmental organization against the interventions of the communist states of China and Vietnam, ASEAN has become a social network supporting economic, political, security and social integration efforts. While ASEAN has endeavored to bring the parties together and find peaceful solutions to regional problems, the support of the United States in this direction has been significant (Plummer, 2022: 70-78). In fact, ASEAN has taken steps to bring China and the regional states together on the South China Sea dispute, but China has stated that the issue should be resolved by individual states. The US support for ASEAN has been considered as an important factor in China's approach of not coming together under the ASEAN umbrella (Connolly, 2024).

Significant steps have been taken in trade, investment, technology and infrastructure co-operation with the US, especially after the Cold War. At this point, it should be emphasized that while ASEAN member states are aware that they can create a balance regarding China's presence in the region, they also endeavor not to be a part of the US strategy in the region. This balancing act has been interpreted as a tendency to preserve strategic autonomy while benefiting from the economic support of both powers (Wester and Pitakdumrongkit, 2025). The goal of economic integration, which the United States emphasized, has not slowed down in the post-Cold War period, and the inclusion of China into the international economic system has been a prominent point. While China's World Trade Organization was one of the important steps taken in this direction, the 2008 economic crisis has also created some changes in the US view of regional economic integration. In fact, China criticized the economic functioning of the international system for the first time with the crisis and stated that the institutions built on a western basis could no longer respond to the needs (Womack, 2017: 384-391; Shih, 2022: 2-6). While these statements were interpreted by the US as the failure of the goal of integrating China into the system, the need for a new vision of the region was underlined. This vision, on the other hand, expressed a process extending from engagement to the balance of power. The US stated that engagement had failed and that this failure could only be overcome by revitalizing allies in the region (Mahapatra, 2020: 207-218; Nye, 2024). While this revitalization included significant military themes, it also included the provision of economic and social support, especially to strategic point allies such as the Philippines and Taiwan.

The breakthrough in the US goal of establishing economic integration in Asia occurred under President Obama. The most important development of this period was undoubtedly the Trans-Pacific Partnership. Aiming to create an economic architecture in the Asia Pacific, the initiative envisaged building a region-wide system of trade and investment rules. Within the scope of economic relations considered as an element of rebalancing, agreements were signed with Vietnam, the Philippines, India and Brunei to facilitate financing. These initiatives were supported by steps such as export-oriented subsidies and training of economy-based personnel. In addition, the Enhanced Economic Initiative was launched to increase trade with ASEAN and ASEAN countries were aimed to prepare for the Trans-Pacific Partnership (Congressional Research Service, 2015: 3-11). The TPP, which set out with the aim of establishing regional trade rules and disciplines consistent with US interests and modern commercial realities, has witnessed the departure of the US with the era of President Trump.

Under President Trump, the US ended the TPP partnership on the grounds that it did not provide any economic benefit and that the domestic market remained vulnerable to Asian goods. In addition to withdrawing from the partnership, this period, which witnessed trade wars with China, started with the imposition of tariffs and restrictions on China on the grounds of unfair trade practices and intellectual property theft. While an agreement signed in 2020 eased trade tensions between the parties, the US balance of power approach to the region remained in place. One of the important steps taken in this direction was implemented with the Quadrilateral Security Dialogue under President Biden. Founded in 2004 and revisited in 2017 with the aim of revitalizing allies, the initiative is based on promoting democratic values, creating a rules-based order and increasing the US regional influence. The initiative, which includes topics such as climate change, clean energy development and regional infrastructure partnership, also emphasized the importance of raising maritime awareness and combating illegal fishing (Congressional Research Service, 2023: 1-3). Although these points represent the normative aspect of the Quadrilateral Security Dialogue, China's description of the initiative as a Cold War-era containment strategy has been remarkable. Indeed, when the initiative between the four states is analyzed through a map (Map 1), it is observed that the region, especially the South China Sea line, can be significantly influenced.

Figure 1. Indo Pacific initiative centered on the US, Japan, India and Australia (Welti, et al., 2018)

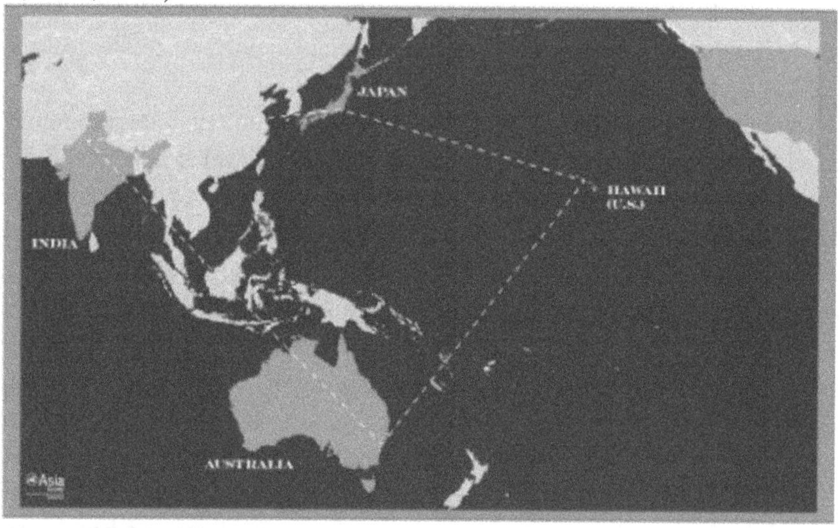

These points show that while there has been a change in the US approach to the region since the Cold War, there is a continuity in the objectives. While establishing a rules-based order in the region, strengthening the liberal economy and supporting democratization (Tanji & Lawson, 1997: 135-155) have been the main themes emphasized, the methodology has shifted from engagement to balance of power. Strategically, it is observed that the economic approach was also considered as a means to resolve regional conflicts in favor of the US, especially balancing China. In this direction, while economic relations with the states that are parties to the dispute are important, the steps taken towards states such as India and Australia are considered as another dimension of creating a balance of power. In the next section, the analysis of this process from engagement to balance of power will be discussed from a security and defense perspective.

DIPLOMATIC HISTORY IN THE REGION: THE US POSITION BETWEEN ENGAGEMENT AND BALANCE OF POWER

The previous two chapters have shown how important it is to understand the geographical characteristics of the South China Sea with its historical and physical dimensions in order to decipher the US strategy. Diplomatic contacts, which will be emphasized in this chapter, are another important topic in understanding the breadth and depth that the US strategically aims to create in the region. Moreover, it also offers opportunities to understand how the historical and physical characteristics of the region are reflected on the ground as diplomatic steps. First of all, it should be emphasized that the deterrence, balancing and power projection objectives of the US are reflected in the political, economic and military contacts with the states in the region. Undoubtedly, the meaning of the South China Sea for the US administration is strategic in nature, including international law and regional stability, and in the long run, it turns into an important gain point that includes diplomatic components. In this respect, the approach towards the states with claims in the South China Sea stands out in terms of contacts with the states in the region. Political, military and economic contacts with these states will serve three main objectives - deterrence, balancing and power projection.

In the early 1990s, the Bush administration took steps towards normalizing relations with Vietnam and supported the process with mutual visits in the 2000s (Hiebert, Nguyen and Poling, 2014: 3-8). During these talks, steps were taken towards regional cooperation, and an agreement was signed in 2005. Within the scope of the agreement, topics such as financial support and the modernization of ammunition were emphasized, while Vietnam's accession to the World Trade Organization was encouraged. As it can be understood from this point, the Bush administration acted not only to strengthen Vietnam regionally but also to make it a part of the international system globally. Following these steps, the Bilateral Political, Security, and Defence Dialogue with Vietnam was launched in 2008, and this initiative was followed by a period of progress in relations with bilateral visits. These efforts, which continued under President Obama, first manifested themselves at the ASEAN Forum in 2010, and in the same year, the two states launched the Defense Policy Dialogue (White House, 2010).

With this initiative, the Memorandum of Understanding on Advancing Bilateral Defense Cooperation was signed, which focused on maritime security, search and rescue, humanitarian assistance and disaster relief, and peacekeeping (Hiebert, Nguyen, & Poling, 2014: 4-9). In 2013, the US-Vietnam Comprehensive Partnership initiative focused on political and diplomatic cooperation, cooperation in science and technology, trade and economic ties, defense and security, and war legacy issues (Manyin, 2014: 1-7). This step signaled the creation of a mutual vision of maritime security, which is a crucial issue between the two states. In this direction, the emphasis on enhanced coastal security increased naval ammunition, and military competence came to the fore. In 2015, the Extensive Comprehensive Partnership Initiative was launched to guide military cooperation, and in 2016, the arms sales embargo on Vietnam lifted (Ball, 2019: 4-9).

Following the lifting of the embargo, improvements in ammunition, such as missile systems, intelligence systems, helicopters, and amphibious crafts have come to the agenda. The creation of regional maritime domain awareness, the development of civilian and defense capabilities of the military partnership, training activities, and the positioning of military equipment have also been prominent points. With the emphasis on maritime security, Vietnam aimed to become a crucial maritime actor in Southeast Asia while efficient cooperation with Vietnam was emphasized for the long-term interests of the US in the region (Burgess, 2020: 2-6). In line with these goals, both Vietnam and the US have advocated the protection of trade and freedom of navigation in the region and underlined international law and peaceful means to resolve sovereignty disputes.

In terms of the nature of the general alliances envisaged in the Asia Pacific strategy as a whole, including the South China Sea, Vietnam is included in the class of "countries that have expressed a desire for a closer and more comprehensive security partnership with the United States, but lack military resilience and the capacity to exert military influence beyond their immediate borders". In case direct and long-term military assistance to these countries, and thus to Vietnam, is not accepted, relations are established through topics including peacekeeping, military modernization, and capability development. Cam Ranh Bay has been another prominent point in the US contacts with bases in the region. The contact between Vietnam and the US on this point started in 2009 when Vietnam announced that it opened its commercial repair facilities to all navies (Thayer, 2017: 4-9).

The US, the first state to accept Vietnam's offer, organized expeditions to regional facilities for ship repair and renovation. Ranh Bay, which hosted four of these expeditions, consists of a military port and a civilian facility and serves the Russian-made naval fleet, including conventional submarines. While Russia has access to the port of Cam Ranh Bay due to contacts between Vietnam and Russia arising from cooperation based on naval technology, US contacts with this point have also increased, especially after the US eased its arms embargo on Vietnam in 2014 (Hiebert, Nguyen and Poling, 2014: 2-9).

An important indicator of this increase was the official establishment of the Cam Ranh International Port, a civilian facility, in 2016, followed by the visit of three US warships (Frank Cable, Mustin, and John S. McCain) in the same year (Thayer, 2017: 2-6). Another indicator that strengthens the possibility that the US may develop base-based relations with Vietnam with these steps taken is the statements in Vietnam's White Paper published in 2019 that the traditional foreign policy behavior of the Three No's can be relaxed (White Paper, 2019). Assumptions that these underlined principles could be relaxed were strengthened by the US acceptance of Vietnam's invitation to renovate its ports and the subsequent port visits of US warships to the region.

Another crucial state in the region for the US has been the Philippines. The Philippines, which is in a sovereignty dispute with China, has been one of the crucial security partners of the US since the Mutual Defense Treaty signed with the US in 1951 (Office of the Historian). Before signing the Military Basis Agreement in 1947, the two states revised this agreement in 1992 and signed the Visiting Forces Agreement in 1998. These security agreements are significant in emphasizing the importance of the US-Philippines military cooperation and partnership. Indeed, the Basing and Mutual Defense Agreements (1947 and 1952), the two agreements signed after World War II, are crucial steps to make the US presence in the region more effective after the war. In 1992 and 1998, with the agreements signed in the name of bilateral security partnership, steps were taken to strengthen the US presence in the region and military relations with the Philippines after the Cold War (Fernandez, 1976: 3-7; Arugay and Storey, 2023: 5-9).

The mentioned dates also show that the Philippines is an effective ally for the US to receive support through military cooperation at important breaking points. The fact that the three agreements signed with the US represent a historical turning point makes the agreement signed in 2014 meaningful. This is because 2014 was a crucial stage of the "pivot to Asia" strategy announced by the Obama administration, and the Philippines' perception of the threat from China increased. With China's declaration of its sovereignty in the South China Sea and the US pivot to

Asia strategy signaling that it will be more integrated into the region, the Philippines administration has entered a two-way process on the axis of threat and opportunity. In this process, with the increase in concerns about maritime security, the modernization of defense ammunition and the supply of equipment, especially the increase in military expenditures, were underlined (Hiebert, Nguyen and Poling, 2014: 9-15). The emphasis on these points is also reflected in the Bilateral Strategic Dialogue initiative launched between the US and the Philippines in 2011.

Emphasizing the vision of the Manila Declaration (Centre for International Law), the two states addressed a wide range of issues from defense to trade and human rights to law enforcement, underlining the goal of deepening and expanding maritime security cooperation. In this context, the Bilateral Strategic Dialogue initiative established in 2011 was strengthened with the Enhance Defense Cooperation Agreement in 2014 (Baviera, 2014: 4-8). Under the agreement, the topics of improving interoperability, ensuring military modernization, developing military capabilities for external defense, maritime security, maritime domain awareness, and humanitarian assistance and disaster response were emphasized. With the emphasis points, economic aid to the Philippines reached its highest level in 2011, while military support has been on the rise since then (Hundler, 2018). With these steps, the US has reached the highest level of defense contact with the Philippines as of 2015. Similar to its Asia Pacific emphasis on Vietnam, the US has also stated that the Philippines is an essential point of the Asia Pacific strategy as a whole.

The base establishment contacts between the Philippines and the US, which the US has expanded through military diplomacy, are noteworthy. Subic Bay Base, one of the areas in question, is one of the significant points addressed in line with the military agreements with the Philippines. Although US troops were withdrawn from the base in late 1992, the US naval presence in this area was revisited in 1998 with the Visiting Forces Agreement (U.S. Department of State, 1998). After these dates, the most crucial military contact between the US and the Philippines in the Subic Bay Base was the Enhanced Defense Cooperation Agreement signed in 2014.

Within the scope of the agreement, it was decided that the US Navy could dock at Subic Bay Base as a visiting force, and with these steps, the joint South China Sea exercises of the two countries were increased (Castro, 2014, 3-9). Other bases emphasized by the two states are Basa (Pampanga), Antonio Bautista (Palawan), Mactan-Benito (Cebu), Fort Magsaysay (Palayan), and Lumbia (Mindanao) air bases, where the US was authorized to store and deploy weapons. Another development that strengthened the US military presence along the coast of the South China Sea was the ratification by the Philippine Supreme Court in 2016 of the Enhanced Defense Cooperation Agreement signed between the two states in 2014 (U.S. Department of State, 2014). With this approval, the deployment of US military forces, ships, aircraft, and equipment and the use of five air bases in the Philippines were authorized. With this approval, the US naval forces have gained the opportunity to establish activities on the coast of the Spratly Islands, the most disputed area of the South China Sea, and the US naval forces have gained a crucial gain in terms of observing the artificial islands built by China in this area.

Taiwan, one of the regional states whose geopolitical importance has been emphasized by the US since the Cold War, is a party to the ongoing sovereignty dispute in the South China Sea. Considered by the US as a core element of rebalancing in the Asia Pacific (Sullivan, 2015: 3-6), relations with Taiwan encompass commercial and cultural contacts as well as maritime security. Emphasizing Taiwan's position and strategic importance, especially in the face of increasing threats to maritime security, the US believes that contacts with Taiwan provide significant advantages not only in the East and South China Seas but also in the Asia Pacific as a whole. The United States sees the consolidation of Taiwan's security in these areas as a component of its maritime order. In terms of maritime geography, it emphasizes the vital importance of Taiwan in terms of maritime security due to all these factors, underlining the geo-strategic points that extend beyond the Taiwan Strait due to its location on critical sea lanes connecting the East and its position in the South China Sea. Another factor that makes Taiwan important to the United States is its ongoing dispute with China (Congressional Research Service, 2024). More closely, China's possible intervention in Taiwan is one of the topics that the United States pays close attention to, as it could change the balance in favor of China both in the East and South China Seas and in the Asia Pacific as a whole.

While the states in the region, especially Taiwan, are satisfied with the maritime contacts with the US and moreover with the balance mechanism to be created against China; they also consider the possibility of confrontation with China. Looking at this point primarily in the case of Vietnam, the changing political approaches are noteworthy. Vietnam welcomes the US military support in particular, but also cares about maintaining the US-China balance in the region. Vietnam, which attaches particular importance to this balance due to its economic relations with China, has been one of the states in the region that has gained the most from the US-China trade wars (Ha and Phuch, 2019: 12-17). The goal of maintaining the US-China balance can also be understood from Vietnam's attitude towards the disputes with China in the South China Sea. In 2010, China and Vietnam held bilateral meetings to discuss principles for resolving maritime disputes, initiated the Strategic Defense and Security Dialogue, and in 2014 held conflict management and resolution talks under the umbrella of the Joint Steering Committee with the same objective (Evelyn, 2016: 14-16). As can be understood from the aforementioned points, Vietnam, on the one hand, tends to turn the US orientation towards the region into a strategic gain and takes steps to balance China in the region, while on the other hand, it acts in the direction of not completely confronting China in order to reduce the risks and benefit from the benefits of bordering the South China Sea.

The Philippines, on the other hand, sees approaching the US as an opportunity for strategic gain, but has endeavored to maintain a balance with China. The main motivations for this balancing tendency, which came to light especially with Rodrigo Duterte, who assumed the presidency in 2016, were attracting Chinese investments and not being sure of US assistance in a possible tension with China. In fact, the Philippines' search for balance has been labelled by some analysts as an "equilateral balancing strategy" to be formed between China and the US; it has been interpreted that the Philippines will be more lenient in implementing the decision of the Court of Arbitration on the one hand, and the US will be asked to clarify its commitment to protection against possible threats (Greitens, 2016, pp-1014). Another indication that the strategic approach of the Duterte era will be a balancing and gain-oriented approach to the US-China rivalry is the President's emphasis on the military-economic separateness of the US and the Philippines at the Philippines-China Trade and Investment Forum. With this discourse, which stands out as a clear message that the Philippines is not dependent on the US, the Philippines signalled that a pragmatic foreign policy towards China will be pursued by stating that the Arbitration Court's decision against China is insignificant (Butista, 2016: 5-8).

Similarly, Taiwan tends to observe balances in its relations with China due to both economic and strategic ties. On the one hand, Taiwan and China represent two main points of interdependence through trade partnership, investment targets and industrial exports; on the other hand, they represent two important actors in maritime security and the establishment of a long-term stable maritime order, especially the peaceful settlement of the South China Sea dispute. There are those who evaluate this interdependence and Taiwan's search for a peaceful and dialogue-based solution in terms of the cost of a possible tension between Taiwan and China. According to this view, which emphasizes China's increasingly tense policy not only in Taiwan but also in the South China Sea since 2012, even US arms support may not be sufficient in the face of a possible attack, and therefore, the only thing that can stand against the threat of a possible attack is to defend the military, economic and political costs of a Chinese step in this direction through diplomacy. The importance of the underlined elements is also recognized by Taiwan and it is moving towards seeking negotiation and peaceful solutions as much as possible in its maritime activities (Li, 2016: 3-5).

In conclusion, the US has employed a multifaceted approach to balance China's power in the South China Sea, focusing on key regional partners like Vietnam and the Philippines. By strengthening bilateral relations, promoting military cooperation, and expanding access to strategic locations, the US aims to maintain a favorable regional balance of power. However, the evolving geopolitical landscape and China's assertive behavior pose significant challenges. As the competition intensifies, the

US will need to carefully calibrate its strategies to ensure long-term stability and security in the region. At this point, in connection with the first point, it becomes clear that the political, military and economic contacts of the USA are directly linked to geopolitics. In the following section, these connections will be analyzed on a geographical basis.

STRATEGIC GEOGRAPHY IN THE SOUTH CHINA SEA: IMPLICATIONS FOR US REGIONAL STRATEGY

The transformation of geography into a strategic field and shaping state policy is one of the important parts of geopolitical theory. In this reading, the extent to which geographical characteristics affect the state's approaches reflected in the field and how they shape its long-term steps are prominent questions. The South China Sea, as a strategic area, is an important area where the aim of the extra-regional states, especially the US, to establish influence can be read through strategic geography. The maritime concepts that come to the fore in this direction are very important both in understanding the strategic nature of the region and in making sense of the US presence in the region. Looking at the region as a strategic area, as shown in Map 1, the first and second island chains, choke points and sea lines of communication are the prominent areas of action. Moreover, these areas are the points where the littoral states and extra-regional powers are most active and are discussed on Map 2 through China's nine-dash line and string of pearls. Another critical characteristic of these areas is that they have become the focus of US maritime actions as a strategic area.

Figure 2. Strategic points in the South China Sea (Nagy, 2022)

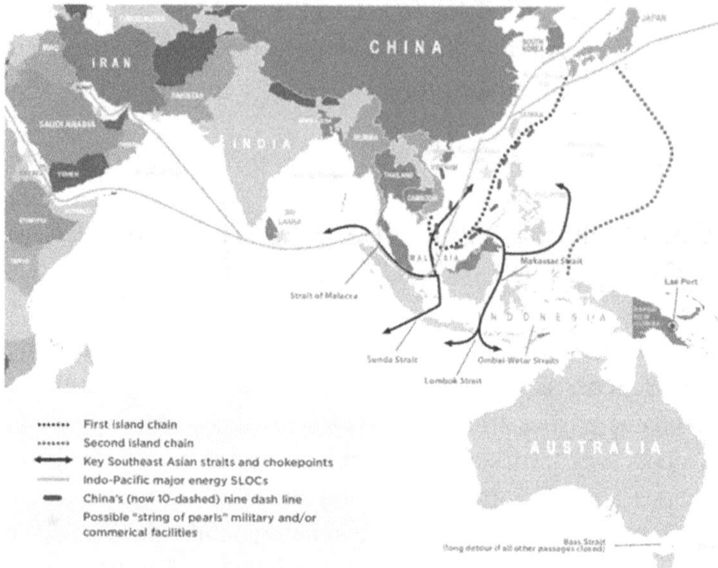

One of the most important of these focal points, the Strait of Malacca, is the main passage between the Indian Ocean and the South China Sea, narrowing as it moves eastwards to become the Singapore Strait and the Philip Channel. The Lombok Strait, the second important maritime communication line, is considered as a safe route and is used for tankers transiting between the Persian Gulf and Japan. The other maritime communication line, the Sunda Strait, is relatively less favored due to its strong currents and high water depth. The South China Sea is the largest maritime communication line, stretching from Sumatra to Taiwan, and has three major oil exploration zones. More importantly, it connects Northeast Asia to Southeast Asia and the Middle East. As can be seen in Map 1, the maritime lines of communication encompassing these four areas are not only regional geographical areas, but also promise a great deal of effectiveness to the power to exert influence. The US naval strategy not only targets effectiveness in geographical areas as a whole, but also acts on the goal of establishing a presence in a way to cover long-term conflict/war possibilities. So much so that the success of the advanced military strategy depends on the effectiveness of the navy in establishing sea lines of communication (Popescu, 2017: 1-8; Noer, 1996: 4-8).

This activity includes forces deployed in maritime lines of communication, re-inforced allies and the lines necessary for maritime trade. The most sensitive areas for the US are identified as those closest to the potential rival/enemy line. When these themes are analyzed through Map 2, we see a US naval strategy that focuses on naval effectiveness along the sea lines of communication and underlines the goal of strengthening allied navies in parallel with this focus. The line encompassing the South China Sea and extending from this region to the Asia Pacific on one side and to the Middle East on the other side is the area where the US focuses the most on surface, submarine and air activity. Undoubtedly, the emphasis on this line is directly linked to China's claims in the South China Sea and its port presence at the points expressed by the string of pearls (Map 1). Another important stage of the activity at these points is transatlantic deployment (Holmes, 2014: 2-8). This deployment, which ranges from naval personnel to multi-purpose warships, also includes the allied forces in the region and is based on the modernization of the navy and technical and equipment support.

These points show how sea control is a vital objective for the US naval strategy. The principle of free navigation of the seas is underlined as the first function of the US navy and the goal of transforming this principle into a maritime regime in the long term is emphasized. While the efficiency to be ensured along the sea lines of communication is seen as the key to the principle of free navigation, the first and second island chains are critical in making sense of the US navy's presence in the region. While the US navy's activity along these two lines (Map 2) ensures the establishment of a natural barrier in the region, it is also critical for balancing possible rivals, especially the Chinese navy. When followed along the two island chains, the Singapore and Malacca Straits stand out as the shortest route connecting the South China Sea to the Indian Ocean. These areas, which include the straits, are discussed in terms of the commercial gains they will provide to the US navy in times of peace and the privileges they will gain in times of war. The Taiwan Strait, which is one of the biggest routes of world shipping, activates the line from the Far East to the South Seas, Indian Ocean and Suez. In the US focus on the Taiwan Strait, strategic tendencies as well as commercial factors are effective (Erickson and Wuthnow, 2016: 4-13).

The Taiwan Strait crises since the Cold War and the civil war in the region represent a critical turning point for both the US and China. While for the US, protecting Taiwan is seen as the primary means of balancing China in the region, today the region has become the area where the possibility of war is most discussed. The theme of competition created by Taiwan in the eyes of the US and China shows the importance of the strategic effectiveness to be created in the region. For the US, Taiwan is an important buffer against the regional expansionism of the Chinese navy. Therefore, Taiwan maintains its importance for the US both as a transit route and in terms of restraining a possible Chinese activity in the South China Sea. However, the Verde Island Passage and the Balabac Strait represent alternative routes connecting to the Philippine Sea and the Pacific Ocean. Especially considering the Philippines' position in the South China Sea dispute, these points become even more important for the US. The Philippines is one of the regional states that have the most disputes with China in the South China Sea dispute (Popescu, 2017: 2-6; Noer, 1996: 1-7). The Philippines, one of the treaty allies of the US, has been in important contacts with the US in terms of both naval support and regional deployment due to its increasing disputes with China.

At this point, while the Verde Island Passage and the Balabac Strait gain importance for easy access to the Philippines, they are also among the lines to be considered in the event of a possible conflict in the Asia Pacific. While the transformation of geographical features into strategic lines manifests itself through these areas, easy access to allies and the physical positioning of the US navy also makes these points important. Another important strategic area of these steps taken is along the first and second island chains. Defining the island chains as protective covers, the US considers Japan as the key point in the first island chain and the Philippines as the tail of this island chain. In the light of these definitions, it is possible to see the traces of the general maritime strategy in the US approach to the first and second island chains (Erickson and Wuthnow, 2016: 2-12). From this point of view, deterrence, sea control, power design, maritime security and access to all zones of influence constitute the basic building blocks of the activities to be carried out in both areas. Especially when analyzed through Map 1, the most important goal of the steps to be taken along the lines covering the first and second island chains is the creation of deterrence.

Activities in these areas are of vital importance for the United States against potential rivals in the long term, especially China's growing navy. It is critical to create and secure in the long-term full spheres of influence, including surface, submarine and airspace, and to create effective allies along these lines. In particular, while aiming for appropriate freedom of influence in the sea, air, land, space, cyberspace and electromagnetic spectrum with access to all spheres of influence, it is envisaged to guarantee US national security in the region with all these means as a whole. From a historical point of view, these objectives and methods can be seen as a relatively more in-depth approach to the 'containment' strategy of the Cold War era.

The breaking point in these objectives promoted by the US is the Obama presidency. The 2015 National Security Strategy announced the pivot to Asia, which led to an increase in US geographic depth in the South China Sea. This depth has seen steps to expand bilateral and multilateral partnerships, promote international rules and order, and enhance US presence in the areas highlighted in Map 2 (maritime lines of communication, choke points and island chains). Within the framework of the underlined points, in the US congressional debate on the South China Sea, Admiral Dennis C. Blair presented the path followed in the past towards the region with the following statements (U.S. Policy Options in the South China Sea):

"What is happening in the South China Sea today is not conceptually new for China or the region. But what makes the situation in the region different is geography, numbers, the military incompetence of other claimants, and American history in the region. With all these elements, a new US policy to counter Chinese aggression that protects our core interests and is adapted to the new circumstances is needed. In the past, the United States has responded to this need with a two-pronged strategy: military deterrence and patient diplomacy."

Even though Admiral Blair, by referring to the US's Cold War-era relations with Taiwan and the Philippines in the South China Sea, puts forward military deterrence and patient diplomacy as important strategies, these two titles already express very critical policies for the US. From this point of view, freedom of navigation, which has an important place in the general naval strategy, expresses an important point of departure against China's increasing influence in the region and provides important indicators in terms of both military deterrence and patient diplomacy. Freedom of navigation, which is defined as the right of a ship or aircraft to cross the maritime space and to conduct operations during these transits, is addressed by the US in line with Article 87 of the UN Law of the Sea. It argues that the expression 'the high seas are open to all States' in the said article includes the freedom of the high seas and this freedom includes navigation and flight (Department of Décence, 2016).

However, it claims that the themes of freedom of navigation and freedom of overflight addressed by Article 58 on the Exclusive Economic Zone and Article 87 support the argument that 'the high seas are open to all states'. At this point, it should be emphasized that the US states that military activities carried out at sea are legitimized by these articles contained in the UN Law of the Sea and also by the details that it does not mention. In addition to these underlined points, although the US states that there is no element in the South China Sea that limits it under the UN Law of the Sea as China claims, a Chinese diplomat expresses the view of the operations carried out within the scope of freedom of navigation with the following statements (Kuok, 2016: 11).

"The difference between China and the United States is not the difference between freedom of navigation. We support freedom of navigation not only in the South China Sea but also in the rest of the world. The difference is that we think the US is using freedom of navigation as a pretext. By using these operations, the US is in fact closely monitoring China's coastline, islands and reefs with the ships and aircraft it moves around the region."

These increasing activities of the US in the region are handled from a perspective that demands the innocent passage of warships and therefore does not require coastal states to be informed about the passage. At this point, from a regional perspective, it is observed that these operations are strategically targeted towards the areas where 'extreme baselines' or 'maritime exclusion zones' are demanded. While on the one hand, the operations in the underlined areas are defended with the message that 'excessive claims in the seas are not accepted' and the theme of protection of international law, on the other hand, they remain as one of the important steps taken to balance China in the region (Burgess, 2020: 3-11). In line with the aforementioned balancing objective, the most focused areas in the US navigation operations are the areas in the region that are subject to sovereignty disputes between China and the Philippines, Taiwan and Vietnam. With the operations carried out in these areas, an effective step has been taken to support the allied pillar of the pivot to Asia strategy underlined during President Obama's term, and the function of these steps has been put forward by the spokesperson of the Ministry of Defense with the following statements (U.S. Department of State):

"The Department of Defense conducted a freedom of navigation operation in the South China Sea, specifically in the Fiery Cross Reef area in the Spratly Islands, to protect the rights and freedoms of all states under international law and to challenge the excessive maritime claims of certain claimants. These excessive maritime claims in the South China Sea are inconsistent with the Law of the Sea Convention in that they restrict the right of navigation enjoyed by the United States and all states. During the operation, a U.S. Navy surface ship used the right of innocent passage to pass within 12 nautical miles of the Fiery Cross Reef, a high-tide feature occupied by China but also claimed by Taiwan, the Philippines and Vietnam, and no claimant was notified."

In addition to the operations carried out within the framework of freedom of navigation, another important strategic approach for the US has been the patrols and exercises carried out in the region. These steps, which are also considered as important initiatives for the purpose of increasing the military presence in the region, are implemented with the aim of securing allies as well as encouraging other states to cooperate. Along with these underlined points, patrol activities and exercises are carried out in the region with amphibious assault ships (USS Wasp, USS Essex, USS Boxer), nuclear-powered attack submarines, aircraft carriers (USS Abraham Lincoln, USS Ronald Reagan, USS John C. Stennis) and strategic bombers (America's Navy, 2021). With the use of these munitions, while focusing especially on the Spratly Islands and Scarborough Beach routes, the patrol routes show that the US maintains its objectives in the South China Sea within the scope of navigation operations as a whole.

The exercises show that joint operations with the relevant states in the South China Sea and surrounding areas are intensifying. At this point, strengthening allies in the region not only provides a legitimate basis for the US presence in the disputed areas, but is also critical in balancing China. (Putz, 2019: 3-7). Another factor that should be underlined is that the areas where the exercises are held are also very important for the island chains in the region. In these areas, strategic contacts with

Japan and India, as well as the states in dispute in the region, are emphasized sensitively, and the need to establish influence in the First and Second Island Chains is emphasized by underlining the increase in China's air and naval activities. In the event of the establishment of this activity, as shown in the map below, a significant activity will be provided on the route of China's naval forces. With this underlined goal, it is seen that both the Freedom of Navigation Operations and the joint exercises and operations of the USA are indicative of a long-term strategic road map in the region (Holmes, 2014: 1-7). The main theme of the road map is the expansion and deepening of the US naval forces by strategically addressing the geography. US naval forces in the region effectively analyze geographical characteristics and act in line with the goals of deterrence, balancing and power projection. These three objectives - deterrence, stabilization and projection of power - require a discussion of US diplomatic engagement with the region.

CONCLUSION

Within the scope of the study, the South China Sea policy of the United States is discussed from a geopolitical perspective. Within the scope of the study, which focuses on strategic themes, especially geographical characteristics, it is possible to read the US view of the region and its long-term assumptions. First of all, balancing China is an important goal at the centre of the US strategic approach. This goal is reflected in the consideration of geographical characteristics, the approach to regional states and the emphasis on the long-term maritime order. The transformation of geographical features into a strategic advantage against China and guaranteeing the economic and commercial benefits of the region are among the important agendas. At this point, it is the priority of the US navy to establish effectiveness in strategic lines, especially maritime lines of communication, and to gain allies along these lines. In historical terms, China's assumption of historical rights to the region has not only been a state's claim to the seas, but also a part of the goal of creating a new maritime order. Currently, China is acting on this claim, thus talking about an alternative structure to the maritime order defended by the US. The dispute in question deepens as the US contacts with the states in the region increase, raising conflict/war predictions for the region.

In fact, although the possibility of conflict and war in the region remains, there is an important obstacle to these two developments: regional powers. The US diplomatic contacts with the states of the region show that the states of the region avoid confrontation with China. While maritime contacts with the US are important, the main focus of the regional states is not to ensure that the US becomes an important power in the region, but to create a balance between the two states. Therefore, long-term solutions to the South China Sea problem can be expected from this aspect. This is because the states in the region, especially Taiwan, offer various ways and methods of approaching the South China Sea problem, expanding their contacts with China and avoiding deep military conflicts. These issues provide a promising picture of the course of relations between China and the regional states. In the case of the United States, however, there are growing assumptions that rivalry will continue to exist in the two states' view of the South China Sea. In particular, the deepening US presence in the Asia Pacific and China's identity-based perspective, which has historically opposed foreign intervention, stand out as factors that deepen the possibility of conflict in the region.

REFERENCES

Arugay, A. A., & Storey, I. (2023). A Strategic Reset?: The Philippines - U.S. Alliance under President Marcos Jr., https://www.iseas.edu.sg/wp-content/uploads/2023/04/ISEAS_Perspective_2023_40.pdf

Australian Treaty Series. (1971). *Five Power Defence Arrangements*, https://www.austlii.edu.au/au/other/dfat/treaties/1971/21.html

Ball, J. (2019). *The U.S. and Vietnam are Expanding Areas of Military Cooperation, Defense and Security*, https://globalsecurityreview.com/u-s-vietnam-expanding-areas-military-cooperation/

Baskara, T. W. (2021). The Long Shadow of the Cold War: The Cold War Policies of the United States Towards Asia and Their Impact on Indonesia, *International Quarterly For. Asian Studies (Quezon City, Philippines)*, *52*, 331–347.

Baviera, A. S. P. (2014). *Implications of the US Philippines Enhanced Defense Cooperation Agreement, Asia Pacific Bultein*. East-West Center.

Bergsten, C. F., Tanji, M., & Lawson, S. (1997). Democratic Peace and Asian Democracy: A Universalist- Particularist Tension. *Alternatives*, *22*(1), 135–155. DOI: 10.1177/030437549702200106

Burgess, S. (2020). *Confronting China's Maritime Expansion in the South China Sea*, https://media.defense.gov/2020/Aug/31/2002488087/-1/-1/1/BURGESS.PDF

Butista, L. (2016). The Philippines and the Arbitral Tribunal's Award: A Sombre Victory and Uncertain Times Ahead. *Contemporary Southeast Asia*, *38*(2), 349–355.

Castro, R. C. D. (2019). *Incident at Reed Bank: A Crisis in the Philippines' China Policy*, https://amti.csis.org/incident-at-reed-bank-a-crisis-in-the-philippines-china-policy/

Congressional Research Service. (2015). *The Trans Pacific Partnership: Strategic Implications*, https://sgp.fas.org/crs/row/R44361.pdf

Congressional Research Service. (2023). *The "Quad": Cooperations Among the United States, Japan, India, and Australia*, https://crsreports.congress.gov/product/pdf/IF/IF11678

Congressional Research Service. (2024). *Taiwan: Background and U.S. Relations*, https://crsreports.congress.gov/product/pdf/IF/IF10275

Connoly, A. (2024). *US ASEAN Relations Grow as Tensions Rise in the South China Sea*, https://www.irinsider.org/home/3w322tz4r44s8zp-ezmt5-7223k-zrbkr-2d9wr-ww4nr

Department of Defense. (2019). *Annual Freedom of Navigation Report*, https://policy.defense.gov/Portals/11/Documents/FY19%20DoD%20FON%20Report%20FINAL.pdf?ver=2020-07-14-140514-643&timestamp=1594749943344

Erickson, A. S., & Wuthnow, J. (2016). *Why Islands Still Matter in Asia: The Enduring Significance of the Pacific Island Chains*. https://www.andrewerickson.com/2016/02/why-islands-still-matter-in-asia-the-enduring-significance-of-the-pacific-island-chains/

Evelyn, G. (2016), S*outheast Asian Strategies Toward the Great Powers: Still Hedging After All These Years*, hxp://www.theasanforum.org/southeast-asian-strategies-toward-the-great-powers-s^ll-hedging-a~er-all-these-years/

Fernandez, A. M. (1976). The Philippines and the U.S. Today, *Southeast. Asian Affairs*, •••, 269–308.

Greitens, S. C. (2016), *The US Philippines Alliance in a Year of Transition: Challenges and Opportunuties*, Center for Asian Policy Studies, Brookings Working Paper.

Ha, L. T., & Phuc, N. D. (2019). The US-China Trade War: Impact on Vietnam. *Yusof Ishak Institue, 102*(3), 2–6.

Harding, S. D. (2024). There and Back and There Again: U.S. Military Base in the Philippines, https://www.usni.org/magazines/proceedings/2024/may/there-and-back-and-there-again-us-military-bases-philippines

Hayton, B. (2019). The Modern Origins of China's South China Sea Claims: Maps, Misunderstandings, and Maritime Geobody. *Modern China, 45*(3), 127–170. DOI: 10.1177/0097700418771678

Hiebert, M., Nguyen, P., & Poling, G. B. (2015). *Building a More Robust US-Philippines Alliance*, https://csis-website-prod.s3.amazonaws.com/s3fs-public/legacy_files/files/publication/150824_Heibert_USPhilippinesAlliance_Web.pdf

Holmes, J. R. (2014). Strategic Features of the South China Sea. *Naval War College Review, 67*(2), 30–49.

Hundler, B. (2018). Duterte's Pivot to China and Prospects for Settling the South China Sea Disputes. *Contexto Internacional, 40*(2), 322–330. DOI: 10.1590/s0102-8529.2018400200005

Kuok, L. (2016), *The US FON Program in the South China Sea, Center for East Asia Policy Studies*, https://www.brookings.edu/wp-content/uploads/ 2016/07/the-us-fon-program-in-the-south-china-sea.pdf

Li, C. (2016). The South China Sea Peace Initiative in a Transitional Security Environment. *American Journal of Chinese Studies*, *23*, 119–134.

Mahapatra, C. (2010). The United States and the Emerging Balance of Power in Asia. *Indian Foreign Affairs Journal*, *5*(2), 207–218.

Malenbaum, W. (1956). U.S. Economy Policy in South and Southeast Asia. *India Quarterly*, *12*(2), 107–116. DOI: 10.1177/097492845601200203

Manyin, M. (2014). *Vietnam Among the Powers: Struggle and Cooperation*,http://www.theasanforum.org/vietnam-among-the-powers-struggle-cooperation/

Nagy, S. (2022). Taiwan and the Indo-Pacific: Defending a Global Public Good. *Commentary (New York, N.Y.)*, •••, 3.

Noer, J. H. (1996), Southeast Asian Chokepoints, https://apps.dtic.mil/dtic/tr/fulltext/u2/a394162.pdf

Nye, J. S. (2024). *What Killed US - China Engagement*, https://www.aspistrategist.org.au/what-killed-us-china-engagement/

Office of the Historian. (1951). Foreign Relations of the U.S., https://history.state.gov/historicaldocuments/frus1951v06p1/d95#:~:text=Each%20Party%20recognizes%20that%20an,accordance%20with%20its%20constitutional%20processes

Plummer, M. G. (2022). *US ASEAN Economic Relations in the Context of Asia Pacific Cooperation*, https://archivos.juridicas.unam.mx/www/bjv/libros/15/7049/5.pdf

Popescu, A. I. C. (2017). Control of Key Maritime Straits: China's Global Strategic Objective. *International Journal of Economics and Business Administration*, *5*(1), 92–119.

Putz, C. (2019), *The Art of the Balance: Japan, China and the US*, https://thediplomat.com/2019/01/the-art-of-the-balance-japan-china-and-the-united-states/

Schonberger, H. B. (1985). The Cold War and the American Empire in Asia. *Radical History Review*, *33*(33), 139–154. DOI: 10.1215/01636545-1985-33-139

Shih, V. (2022). *How China Would Like to Reshape International Economic Institutions*, https://www.atlanticcouncil.org/wp-content/uploads/2022/10/How-China-Would-Like-to-Reshape-International-Economic-Institutions.pdf

Socialist Republic of Vietnam. (2019), Vietnam National Defence, https://mod.gov.vn/en/intro/vnd/sa-en-dod-dp/sa-en-dv-mf-stqp/17493317-e8da-4830-ba9d-75d7b39df332

Sullivan, A. (2015), *Navigating the Future: US-Taiwan Maritime Cooperation and Building Order in Asia, Center for a New American Security*, https://www.files.ethz.ch/isn/191907/CNAS_Sullivan_USTaiwanMaritime_Final.pdf

Thayer, C. (2020). *Will Vietnam Lease Cam Ranh Bay to the United States?*https://thediplomat.com/2020/05/will-vietnam-lease-cam-ranh-bay-to-the-united-states/

U.S. Department of Defence. (2023). *Philippines, U.S. Announce Four New EDCA Sites*, U.S. Department of State, (1998). *Agreement Between U.S. and Philippines*, https://www.state.gov/wp-content/uploads/2019/02/12931-Philippines-Defense-Status-of-Forces-10.9.1998.pdf

Welti, P., Woker, D., & Bohn, J. (2018), Far From Geography: A Free and Open Indo Pacific, Asia Society, https://asiasociety.org/switzerland/far-geography-free-and-open-indo-pacific

Wester, S., & Pitakdumrongkit, K. (2024). On US-ASEAN Relations & Trade, https://asiasociety.org/policy-institute/us-asean-relations-trade

White House. (2010). *President Obama to Host Second U.S. - ASEAN Leaders Meeting*, https://obamawhitehouse.archives.gov/the-press-office/2010/09/03/president-obama-host-second-us-asean-leaders-meeting

Womack, B. (2017). International Crises and China's Rise: Comparing the 2008 Global Financial Crisis and the 2017 Global Political Crisis. *The Chinese Journal of International Politics*, *10*(4), 383–401. DOI: 10.1093/cjip/pox015

Chapter 12
Vietnam's Strategic Partnership Role in India's Policy to Counter China's Hegemonic Ambitions in the East Sea

Kiet Hoang Le
https://orcid.org/0009-0002-9968-1952
University of Social Sciences and Humanities, VNU Hanoi, Vietnam & Yersin University, Vietnam

Hiep Xuan Tran
https://orcid.org/0000-0002-5236-993X
University of Science and Education, The University of Danang, Vietnam

ABSTRACT

This study examines Vietnam's strategic partnership role in India's policy to counter China's hegemonic ambitions in the East Sea. Through a qualitative analysis combining policy analysis, historical methods, and document synthesis, the research explores three key factors defining this partnership: Vietnam's geostrategic position, the impact of historical conflicts with China, and Vietnam's emergence as a middle power. The findings reveal that Vietnam's critical location at the nexus of Southeast Asian maritime routes, coupled with its direct involvement in East Sea disputes, positions it as a pivotal player in regional geopolitics. The historical context of Sino-Vietnamese conflicts has profoundly shaped Vietnamese leadership perspectives, fostering a cautious yet resilient approach to regional power dynamics. Vietnam's remarkable economic growth and increasing diplomatic clout have elevated it to the

DOI: 10.4018/979-8-3693-8109-0.ch012

status of an emerging middle power, enhancing its capacity to engage in strategic partnerships.

INTRODUCTION

The 21st century is witnessing the powerful rise of India and China, two nations with the potential to become global powers (Manuel & Gates, 2016). However, these countries maintain tense relations, with historical conflicts, primarily related to border disputes and water security in Tibet. Recognizing that vital maritime routes must pass through the Indian Ocean region, an area under India's "control" - which could become a "vulnerability" for China's rise (Scott, 2017), Chinese leadership has developed the String of Pearls Strategy through the Belt and Road Initiative and China-Pakistan Economic Corridor to establish a network encompassing the entire Indian spatial domain from land to sea (Dabas, 2017). This strategy is materialized through military facilities, naval bases, and transshipment ports funded by Chinese investments in strategic locations, including Cambodia's Ream Naval Base, Myanmar's Coco Island and Kyaukpyu Port, Bangladesh's Chittagong Port, Sri Lanka's Hambantota Port, the Maldives's Male Port, Pakistan's Gwadar Port, as well as Khartoum Port and Port Sudan in Sudan by leveraging economic influence, China seeks to establish political sway in these countries (Dabas, 2017).

To counter China's String of Pearls Strategy, Indian leadership has deployed a counteroffensive strategy through the Look East Policy in 1991, which evolved into the Act East Policy in 2014. Simultaneously, India has enhanced its deterrence capability against China through the Quadrilateral Security Dialogue, promoting cooperation with Southeast Asian nations, Indian Ocean Island states, and participating in joint exercises with the United States (US), Japan, France, and Australia (Blaxland & Sharma, 2021). Within this context, Vietnam holds a strategic position in Southeast Asia and has intractable conflicts with China in the South China Sea. Moreover, the similarities in both countries' perspectives on building a peaceful and stable regional order have identified Vietnam as India's geostrategic partner in Southeast Asia, playing a vital role in the strategy to counter China's hegemony in the South China Sea and the Indo-Pacific region (Aswani et al., 2021).

The article aims to elucidate the factors defining Vietnam's strategic partnership role with India in deterring China's hegemonic ambitions in the South China Sea and Southeast Asia in general. Accordingly, the article has three specific objectives:

1. Analyze Vietnam's geostrategic position in Southeast Asia and elucidate the intractable conflicts between Vietnam and China in the South China Sea, emphasizing how these factors align with India's regional strategic interests.

2. Examine the historical factor of Vietnam-China relations, particularly the impact of past conflicts on Vietnamese leadership perspectives, and how this historical context influences Vietnam's receptiveness to strategic partnerships with India.
3. Evaluate Vietnam's rise as a middle power, highlighting the country's economic and diplomatic achievements from the late 20th century to the present day, and assess how this emergence complements India's Act East policy and its vision for the Indo-Pacific region.

This research contributes significantly to the existing literature on Indo-Pacific geopolitics by providing a comprehensive analysis of Vietnam's strategic partnership role in India's policy towards China in the South China Sea. The study's importance lies in its multifaceted approach, which combines historical analysis, contemporary policy evaluation, and future-oriented strategic assessment. By examining the factors that define Vietnam's position as India's strategic partner, this research offers valuable insights for policymakers, diplomats, and scholars engaged in Southeast Asian affairs. It sheds light on the complex dynamics of power balancing in the region and the potential for middle powers like Vietnam to play crucial roles in shaping regional security architectures.

LITERATURE REVIEW

In recent years, numerous studies have addressed the issue of strategic competition between India and China in Southeast Asia, with a particular focus on Vietnam's pivotal role in this dynamic. The study "Sino-Indian Competition in Southeast Asia" by Liem and Thao (2021) provided a comprehensive analysis of the impact of competitive strategic relations between India and China on Southeast Asian countries, emphasizing Vietnam's position and role in this relationship. The authors elucidated defense-security cooperation mechanisms between Vietnam and India, as well as Vietnam and China, offering valuable insights into the complex trilateral dynamics at play.

Building on this regional perspective, Kazuyuki's (2021) research "Future Superpowers: Redrawing the World Map in 2030" examined crucial competitive strategic relationships determining the future direction of global political dynamics. The study placed particular emphasis on the increasingly tense competitive relationship between India and China, highlighting its strong impact on the political-security situation in Vietnam and Southeast Asia. This work provides a broader geopolitical context for understanding Vietnam's strategic importance. Focusing more specifically on India's regional strategy, Nghi and Nghia's (2013) study "India's Look East Policy in the Early 21st Century: Position and Role in the South China Sea Region" analyzed the objectives and role of India's Look East Policy in the South China Sea region. The authors highlighted Vietnam's importance to India in the South China Sea and identified areas for enhanced cooperation between the two countries in face of challenges from China. This research laid the groundwork for understanding the evolution of India-Vietnam relations in the context of regional power dynamics.

More recent scholarship has further illuminated the nuances of Vietnam's strategic position. Aswani et al. (2022) in their article "Realigning India's Vietnam Policy Through Cooperative Sustainable Development: a Geostrategic Counter-balancing to China in Indo-Pacific" explore the potential for India and Vietnam to deepen their partnership through sustainable development initiatives, providing a fresh perspective on how economic cooperation can reinforce strategic alignment. Additionally, Dar's (2021) study "India-Vietnam Axis and China: The Allure of Hedging" offers a detailed examination of how Vietnam and India are navigating their relations with China through a hedging strategy. This research provides crucial context for understanding the complexities of the trilateral relationship and the strategic calculations involved.

Furthermore, Loan and Tung's (2021) article "Vietnam's Responses to India's Indo-Pacific Oceans Initiatives and Opportunities for Vietnam–India Maritime Cooperation in the South China Sea" offers a contemporary assessment of the bilateral relationship, exploring areas of convergence in maritime cooperation. Their work contributes to a more nuanced understanding of the India-Vietnam partnership within the broader context of Indo-Pacific geopolitics.In the realm of public diplomacy and its strategic implications, Nga and Quang's (2021) study "Public Diplomacy in Strengthening India: Vietnam Relations" provides valuable insights into the soft power aspects of the strategic partnership. This research highlights how public diplomacy can reinforce strategic alignment between the two nations.

While these studies have significantly contributed to our understanding of Vietnam's strategic position and its relations with India and China, there remains a gap in comprehensively assessing the factors that define Vietnam's role as India's strategic partner in deterring China's hegemonic ambitions in the South China Sea and Southeast Asia. This study aims to address this research gap by providing a multifaceted analysis that integrates historical, geopolitical, and economic perspectives.

METHODOLOGY

This study employs a qualitative research design combining policy analysis, historical method, and document synthesis method to examine Vietnam's strategic partnership role in India's policy to counter China's hegemonic ambitions in the South China Sea.

First, policy analysis: the research utilizes policy analysis to evaluate India's Act East Policy and its implications for Vietnam-India relations. This method involves a systematic examination of policy documents, official statements, and diplomatic press releases to discern the objectives, strategies, and implementation of India's engagement with Vietnam. The analysis focuses on identifying key policy drivers, assessing the alignment of interests between India and Vietnam, and evaluating the effectiveness of their partnership in countering China's influence.

Second, historical method: the historical method is employed to analyze the evolution of Vietnam-China relations and their impact on contemporary geopolitical dynamics. This approach involves examining primary and secondary historical sources to trace the development of conflicts, diplomatic relations, and strategic calculations between Vietnam and China. Particular attention is given to the 1979 Sino-Vietnamese War and its lasting effects on Vietnamese leadership perspectives. The historical analysis provides crucial context for understanding Vietnam's current strategic posture and its significance to India's regional policy.

Third, document synthesis method: this study employs a document synthesis method to integrate and analyze a diverse range of textual sources related to Vietnam's strategic partnership role in India's policy to counter China's hegemonic ambitions in the South China Sea. This approach involves systematically collecting, evaluating, and synthesizing information from various documents to construct a comprehensive understanding of the research topic.

About limitations, it is important to acknowledge certain limitations of this methodology. The reliance on publicly available information may not fully capture the nuances of closed-door diplomatic negotiations or classified strategic assessments. Additionally, the rapidly evolving nature of geopolitical dynamics in the Indo-Pacific region means that some findings may require ongoing reassessment in light of new developments. Despite these limitations, the combination of policy analysis, historical method, and document synthesis method provides a robust framework for examining Vietnam's strategic partnership role in India's policy towards China in the South China Sea. This multifaceted methodology enables a nuanced understanding of the historical, political, and strategic factors shaping this critical trilateral relationship in Southeast Asia.

VIETNAM'S GEOSTRATEGIC POSITION AND CONFLICTS WITH CHINA IN THE SOUTH CHINA SEA

Vietnam occupies a critically important geopolitical position in Southeast Asia and the Indo-Pacific region, serving as a land bridge between the largest part of the Eurasian continent and Southeast Asia (Lohman, 2020). With an area of 331,212 km^2, Vietnam is situated at the center of Southeast Asia; its land borders adjoin China to the north and Laos and Cambodia to the southwest. Vietnam's extensive maritime frontier, characterized by a 3,260 km coastline and approximately 1,000,000 km^2 of maritime jurisdiction, establishes it as a preeminent littoral state within the Indochinese peninsula (Duong & Hong, 2019). The nation's resource endowment significantly amplifies its strategic value in regional power dynamics. Vietnam's continental shelf harbors substantial hydrocarbon reserves, with geological assessments indicating approximately 10 billion tons of oil equivalent, including 2 billion tons of recoverable reserves and roughly 1000 cubic meters of natural gas deposits (Duong & Hong, 2019). The contested Paracel and Spratly archipelagos within Vietnam's maritime potentially contain significant hydrocarbon resources, particularly in the form of methane hydrates (Duong & Hong, 2019). Therefore, Vietnam's archipelagic positioning holds paramount importance in global maritime commerce. The country's territorial waters intersect with critical sea lines of communication (SLOCs) connecting the Indian and Pacific Oceans, with five major global maritime trade arteries traversing the South China Sea. Coupled with abundant continental resources and a sizable population, Vietnam has the potential to become a formidable middle power, comparable to first-tier middle powers such as Japan, India, Canada, and Brazil (Marciel, 2023). Furthermore, Vietnam's maritime territory and islands straddle vital shipping lanes between the Indian and Pacific Oceans. Studies indicate that nearly one-third of global commercial shipping passes through the South China Sea (Kiet & Tuyen, 2023). *"If the South China Sea route were obstructed, commercial vessels would need to circumnavigate the eastern side of Southeast Asian Island nations, extending voyages by thousands of nautical miles with increased weather and climate risks, as well as higher transportation costs"* (Garnier, 2012).

The South China Sea region encompasses crucial straits for global maritime commerce, with the Strait of Malacca standing as a critical strategic chokepoint. This waterway serves as the primary maritime artery through which virtually all maritime trade from Southeast and Northeast Asia must transit (Mehrotra, 2012). The strait's significance is underscored by its position as the world's second-busiest waterway in terms of vessel traffic and annual oil transport volume, with approximately 16 million barrels of oil passing through daily (EIA, 2017). For China, this maritime corridor represents a strategic vulnerability known as the "Malacca Dilemma", a term that encapsulates Beijing's deep-seated concerns about its dependence on this narrow waterway. The dilemma stems from China's heavy reliance on energy imports, with over 80% of its oil imports traversing through this strait (Paszak, 2021). This dependency creates a strategic pressure point that could be exploited by adversaries, particularly in a conflict scenario where the U.S. Navy or other powers could effectively control or blockade the strait (Shambaugh, 2022, p. 10).

India's strategic position in relation to the Malacca Strait adds another layer of complexity to this geopolitical equation. Through its military presence in the Andaman and Nicobar Islands, which sit at the western entrance of the Strait of Malacca, India maintains a strategic vantage point over this crucial maritime chokepoint. This positioning allows India to potentially influence maritime traffic and monitor Chinese naval activities in the region. India has further strengthened its strategic advantage through several key initiatives: (i) Enhanced naval capabilities in the Indian Ocean Region, including regular patrols and surveillance operations; (ii) Deepened maritime security partnerships with Southeast Asian nations, particularly Indonesia, Singapore, and Vietnam; (iii) Development of port facilities and military infrastructure in the Andaman and Nicobar Islands; and (iv) Active participation in multilateral naval exercises with regional partners. The expansion of India's maritime influence near the Malacca Strait serves as a strategic counterweight to China's growing naval presence in the Indian Ocean. By cultivating closer defense and security relationships with ASEAN nations, India has created a network of partnerships that could prove crucial in any future maritime contingency. This strategy not only enhances India's position as a regional maritime power but also provides it with significant leverage in the broader Indo-Pacific security architecture.

In Southeast Asia, Vietnam is the country most severely affected by China's "nine-dash line" policy in the South China Sea. The Beijing government imposes "regional hegemony," seeking to dominate global trade chokepoints, demonstrate power, and intimidate other countries in the region, contravening trends of globalization and internationalization in the South China Sea. Notably, the process of geopolitical movement and construction has created an asymmetry in the balance of power among countries in the region. China, with its superior national strength, has unilaterally imposed non-traditional "claims" in the South China Sea, contradicting international law, disrupting regional security structures, and escalating instability, tension, and confrontation between countries with conflicting interests with China, especially Vietnam and the Philippines. China's hegemonic actions have led to heightened tensions in the South China Sea. According to a study by Mark Raymond and David A. Welch on China's claims in the South China Sea, *"China is increasingly aggressive, as evidenced by the issuance of new biometric passports that include a map featuring the nine-dash line"* (Raymond & Welch, 2022). Consequently, if countries accept and legally stamp these passports, it would effectively recognize China's expansionist "claims" in the South China Sea.

Therefore, while promoting diplomatic relations with China, Vietnam simultaneously strengthens partnerships with countries worldwide, expands multilateral cooperation and global integration, and promotes and supports the United Nations' role as a supranational entity protecting interests, fostering peace, creating an equitable legal environment, and maintaining security and stability at regional and international levels. Concurrently, Vietnam engages in high-level exchanges and diplomatic contacts with world powers, particularly Japan, India, the US, Russia, Germany, and France, to mitigate the power imbalance in the South China Sea. This has established Vietnam as India's geostrategic partner in balancing power with China in Southeast Asia and the Indo-Pacific region.

Consequently, *"the main factors driving India's presence in the South China Sea are China's rise in the disputed waters, India's pragmatic interests in those seas, and the increasing strategic weight of the Indo-Pacific region. China's growing power has led to India's cautious stance, prompting India to engage in protecting its interests and curbing Beijing's hegemonic ambitions in Southeast Asian coastal areas"* (Sang, 2022). India, as a power that seeks to promote globalization, freedom of navigation, and actions based on international order and law, has been compelled by China's hegemonic policies to intervene in the South China Sea region to protect national interests and contain China's expansionist ambitions. India's engagement in the South China Sea represents a multifaceted approach driven by both economic necessities and strategic imperatives. As the world's fifth-largest economy and a major maritime nation, India's vital interests in these waters are shaped by several key factors:

1. India's economic security is inherently linked to the South China Sea's shipping lanes, with *"no less than 55 percent of India's total trade passes through the South China Sea"* (Singh, 2024). The region serves as a crucial corridor for India's energy imports, with significant oil and LNG shipments traversing these sea lanes (Singh, 2024). Furthermore, Indian companies have established substantial investments in Vietnam's offshore energy sector, underscoring the direct commercial interests at stake (Singh, 2024).
2. India's strategic calculation in the South China Sea extends beyond mere commercial interests. As a rising Indo-Pacific power, India seeks to: a) Maintain strategic depth beyond its immediate Indian Ocean sphere; b) Ensure that no single power dominates critical maritime chokepoints; c) Protect sea lines of communication vital for its maritime trade and energy security; and d) Counter the potential encirclement strategy through China's "String of Pearls" initiative.

In general, India's strategic objectives in the South China Sea align closely with Vietnam's security needs, creating a natural partnership based on shared concerns. Both nations prioritize: a) Maintaining freedom of navigation and overflight in accordance with UNCLOS; b) Resisting unilateral changes to the status quo in maritime territories; c) Promoting a rules-based international order in maritime affairs; d) Developing maritime domain awareness capabilities; and e) Enhancing military interoperability through joint exercises and defense cooperation. Moreover, India's current presence in the South China Sea follows a moderate trend, in contrast to China's aggression (Gill, 2021). India demonstrates support for countries in dispute with China to assert its role as a power acting on the basis of international law, aiming to build a peaceful and stable order for the Indo-Pacific region. Therefore, India and Vietnam share common strategic interests in the South China Sea. Strengthening comprehensive cooperation between the two countries, especially in the field of defense and security, is a crucial objective in deterring China's hegemonic ambitions in the South China Sea and Southeast Asia. Overall, Vietnam's geostrategic position in Southeast Asia and its conflicts with China in the South China Sea have significantly shaped regional dynamics and international relations. *"Vietnam's central location, extensive coastline, and control over critical maritime routes render it a pivotal player in the Indo-Pacific theater"* (Thanh, 2022). The country's importance is further amplified by the South China Sea's role as a global trade artery, with nearly one-third of worldwide commercial shipping traversing its waters. China's assertive "nine-dash line" policy and hegemonic ambitions in the South China Sea have created an asymmetrical power balance, directly impacting Vietnam's sovereignty and regional stability.

In response, Vietnam has adopted a multifaceted approach, balancing diplomatic relations with China while simultaneously strengthening partnerships with global powers and promoting multilateral cooperation. *"India's growing presence in the South China Sea, driven by China's expansionism and India's own strategic interests, has led to a natural alignment with Vietnam"* (Nga & Quang, 2021). Both nations share common objectives in maintaining a rules-based international order and freedom of navigation. This convergence of interests has positioned Vietnam as India's geostrategic partner in Southeast Asia, crucial for counterbalancing China's influence. The evolving trilateral dynamics between Vietnam, India, and China in the South China Sea context underscore the complex interplay of geopolitics, economic interests, and security concerns in the Indo-Pacific region (Hiep & Kiet, 2024). As tensions persist, the strengthening of the Vietnam-India comprehensive cooperation, particularly in defense and security domains, emerges as a critical factor in deterring China's hegemonic ambitions and fostering regional stability.

THE IMPACT OF WAR HISTORY WITH CHINA ON VIETNAMESE LEADERSHIP PERSPECTIVES

According to research by Stephen M. Walt and Robert A. Belfer, *"war history profoundly influences the psychology of a nation's leadership. Even the most rational leaders are affected by the power of collective memory"* (Walt & Belfer, 2017). Vietnam, a relatively small nation, shares a border with China, a country 29 times its size. Despite the diverse terrain and numerous mountain ranges along their shared border, there are many areas where China could potentially penetrate Vietnamese territory with relative ease (Marshall, 2020, p. 82). This dynamic has been evident throughout the tumultuous relationship between the two countries, from China's millennium-long domination of Vietnam from 111 BCE to 938 CE, through invasions and occupations across various dynasties prior to French colonization in 1858, to the Sino-Vietnamese Border War of 1979 and contemporary sovereignty disputes in the South China Sea (Kiet & Tuyen, 2023).

Consequently, Vietnam's collective war memories against the "northern giant" have shaped the historical diplomatic relations between the two countries and strongly influence Vietnam's current foreign policy and national security strategies. Vietnamese leadership remains cautious and vigilant regarding China's Belt and Road Initiative, despite Vietnam being China's southern neighbour and maintaining comprehensive economic cooperation, which reached $175.56 billion in 2022, making Vietnam China's largest trading partner within ASEAN (Minh, 2023). Vietnam consistently seeks to construct a peaceful, stable, and free regional order aligned with its deeply internationally integrated economy and exceptional growth rate (Thorburn, 2013).

Vietnam's strategic outlook has been profoundly shaped by its historical experiences, particularly the conflicts with China including the 1978 Southwestern Border War and the 1979 Sino-Vietnamese Border War. These confrontations, along with centuries of managing relations with larger powers, have instilled a deep understanding of the complexities of regional security dynamics (Kiet & Tuyen, 2023). However, rather than remaining constrained by historical caution, Vietnam has transformed these lessons into a sophisticated and forward-looking strategic approach. This evolution in Vietnam's strategic thinking represents a significant shift from traditional defensive isolation to proactive partnership-building. Drawing on its historical experience, Vietnam has developed a nuanced "bamboo diplomacy" - maintaining flexibility while standing firm on core interests. This approach has enabled Vietnam to: (i) Forge strategic partnerships with key regional powers while maintaining strategic autonomy; (ii) Develop multi-layered defense relationships that enhance its security position; (iii) Engage in sophisticated balancing strategies that leverage international partnerships; and (iv) Build capacity for maritime domain awareness and defense capabilities.

The India-Vietnam strategic partnership exemplifies this modern approach. Both nations share common perspectives shaped by historical experiences with regional powers, yet have evolved to embrace forward-looking strategic cooperation. This partnership is characterized by: (i) Mutual respect for territorial integrity and sovereignty; (ii) Shared commitment to international law and freedom of navigation; (iii) Complementary strategic interests in maintaining regional stability; (iv) Joint development of maritime security capabilities; and (v) Coordinated approaches to regional security challenges.

Vietnam's contemporary strategy demonstrates how historical vigilance can evolve into strategic wisdom, informing rather than limiting modern partnership choices. Through this lens, the growing Vietnam-India strategic alignment represents not just a response to current challenges, but a sophisticated application of historical lessons to modern strategic requirements, particularly in maintaining regional stability and ensuring freedom of navigation in the South China Sea. According to the Vietnam Defense Market Report 2022-2027, escalating tensions in the South China Sea necessitate military modernization. Vietnam's defense expenditure increased from $4.9 billion in 2018 to $5.8 billion in 2022, reflecting a compound annual growth rate (CAGR) of 4.5% during 2018-2022. Projections indicate that Vietnam's defense spending will increase at a CAGR of 8.5% to $8.5 billion by 2027, primarily aimed at enhancing Vietnam's defensive capabilities against Chinese hegemony in the South China Sea (Global Data, 2022).

Situated adjacent to an emerging global superpower with regional hegemonic ambitions, one that does not hesitate to employ hard power against Vietnam while simultaneously seeking influence and control over neighboring countries through military, economic, and soft power, Vietnam faces a significant threat to the political-economic structure of the region. Although Vietnam has established a particularly close, friendly, and trusting relationship with China, it continually seeks opportunities to balance power in the region. This strategic approach has led to a convergence of interests between India and Vietnam, as both nations aspire to counter Chinese hegemony in the South China Sea and promote a peaceful, stable, and free regional order (Dar, 2021).

Consequently, leveraging opportunities created by globalization trends, multilateral cooperation, and the openness of the new era, Vietnam can simultaneously engage in cooperation and struggle to develop its national economy and reduce the power disparity with China in the region. Vietnamese nationalism, deeply rooted in historical resistance against foreign domination, has evolved into a sophisticated force shaping contemporary foreign policy decisions. As Charles Dunst observes, *"China's malevolent actions in the South China Sea have ignited a resurgent nationalism within Vietnamese society"* (Dunst, 2021). This renewed nationalist sentiment manifests not merely as anti-foreign sentiment, but as a constructive force that empowers Vietnam's strategic decision-making in several key ways:

1. Popular nationalist sentiment provides domestic legitimacy for assertive foreign policy stances, particularly regarding maritime territorial claims. This public backing enables Vietnamese leadership to maintain firm positions in diplomatic negotiations and pursue robust partnerships with strategic allies like India. The widespread public support for protecting sovereign rights in the South China Sea creates a stable foundation for long-term strategic planning and international engagement.
2. Vietnamese nationalism has evolved beyond simple opposition to external pressure into a sophisticated driver of international cooperation. Rather than promoting isolation, modern Vietnamese nationalism advocates for strategic partnerships that enhance the nation's position in the international order. This has directly influenced Vietnam's approach to building relationships with India and other regional powers, where shared interests in maintaining regional stability and resisting hegemonic ambitions create natural alignments.

This nationalist-informed foreign policy stance has positioned Vietnam as an increasingly important strategic partner for India in Southeast Asia. Both nations' leadership recognize the potential for deeper cooperation, supported by strong domestic constituencies that favor robust international partnerships aimed at maintaining regional stability and protecting sovereign interests in the maritime domain. Overall, the historical context of Vietnam's conflicts with China has profoundly shaped Vietnamese leadership perspectives and strategic calculations. The collective memory of China's millennium-long domination, coupled with more recent border conflicts, has engendered a cautious and vigilant approach in Vietnam's foreign policy and national security strategies. This historical backdrop provides crucial context for understanding Vietnam's contemporary stance towards China's regional ambitions, particularly in the South China Sea. *"Vietnam's geopolitical position, adjacent to an emerging global superpower with hegemonic aspirations, presents both challenges and opportunities"* (Kiet et al., 2024). While maintaining economic cooperation with China, Vietnam simultaneously seeks to balance regional power dynamics through multilateral engagement and strategic partnerships. The convergence of interests between Vietnam and India in countering Chinese hegemony in the South China Sea exemplifies this strategic approach.

The escalating tensions in the South China Sea have catalyzed Vietnam's military modernization efforts, as evidenced by the projected increase in defense expenditure. *"This militarization trend reflects Vietnam's determination to enhance its defensive capabilities against potential threats to its sovereignty and territorial integrity"* (The

International Institute for Strategic Studies, 2023). Furthermore, the resurgence of nationalism within Vietnamese society, sparked by China's assertive actions in the South China Sea, has reinforced Vietnam's resolve to resist hegemonic pressures. This domestic sentiment aligns with Vietnam's international strategy of seeking partnerships to promote a stable, peaceful, and free regional order. In conclusion, the impact of war history on Vietnamese leadership perspectives has fostered a nuanced and multifaceted approach to regional geopolitics. By leveraging opportunities presented by globalization and multilateral cooperation, Vietnam aims to simultaneously develop its economy and reduce power disparities with China, while solidifying its position as a key strategic partner for countries like India in Southeast Asia.

VIETNAM'S RISE AS A MIDDLE POWER AND POTENTIAL FOR COOPERATION WITH INDIA

Currently, the concept of "middle power" has been defined by international relations researchers using various criteria and approaches. This research concurs with Dong-min Shin's assertion that: *"A middle power is a state actor with limited influence in determining power distribution within a specific regional system, but capable of deploying various power resources to alter the position of major powers and protect its own position in matters directly affecting its national or regional security"* (Shin, 2015). As a middle power, Vietnam exercises significant influence through multiple channels: (i) Acting as a pivotal state in ASEAN's security architecture; (ii) Maintaining strategic autonomy while engaging with major powers; (iii) Developing bilateral and multilateral security partnerships; (iv) Contributing to regional economic integration initiatives; and (v) Shaping discourse on maritime security and freedom of navigation.

A middle power must have strong or limited influence in its region and the ability to defend its stance against major powers directly influencing the region. In the 21st century, Vietnam is a country that researchers have classified as an emerging middle power on the international stage (Do, 2022). This is because Vietnam has made a remarkable breakthrough from an economy of only about 13 billion USD in 1986 (Doanh, 2021) to a scale of 409 billion USD in 2022, ranking fifth in Southeast Asia. It is projected that Vietnam's economy will rank third in Southeast Asia in 2023, with an average GDP growth rate of about 6.5-7% per year (Quynh, 2023). According to Kazuyuki (2021, p. 270): *"Currently, Vietnam is one of the most economically developed countries in Asia. At this rate, Vietnam will join the group of 20 largest economies in the world by 2048"*. This demonstrates that Vietnam has made significant progress since implementing its renovation policy and deep international integration in 1986 and has now become a country with power equivalent to middle powers in the world. This middle power position provides Vietnam with unique advantages in pursuit of its national interests. Unlike smaller states that might be more vulnerable to pressure from major powers, Vietnam's middle power status allows it to: (i) Resist unilateral actions that threaten regional stability; (ii) Pursue independent foreign policy objectives; (iii) Maintain credible deterrence capabilities; (iv) Foster meaningful security partnerships with other regional actors; and (v) Contribute substantially to regional economic development. In the context of Southeast Asian security dynamics, Vietnam's middle power status is particularly significant as it enables the country to serve as a stabilizing force, supporting a multipolar regional order that constrains hegemonic ambitions while promoting peaceful resolution of disputes through international law and established diplomatic mechanisms.

From a colony dominated by French and American imperialism, through extraordinary resilience and determination, the Vietnamese people, under the leadership of the Communist Party of Vietnam, achieved great victories in the Indochina War against France (1945-1954) and the Vietnam War against the US (1955-1975), inspiring national liberation movements worldwide. In 1978, Vietnam engaged in combat with the Khmer Rouge regime in the Southwestern Border War (1978-1989) to protect the Cambodian people from genocide. In 1979, Vietnam had to simultaneously fight in Cambodia and against China in the Sino-Vietnamese Border War (February 17, 1979 - March 16, 1979). In all these conflicts, Vietnam ultimately emerged victorious against its enemies. This demonstrates the extraordinary fighting spirit of the Vietnamese people against any threats to territorial integrity and national sovereignty.

However, the wars severely devastated the economy, making Vietnam one of the poorest countries in the world by 1986 (Dinh, 2022). But with extraordinary effort, by 2022, *"Vietnam ranks 30th among the most powerful countries in the world, with an estimated GDP of 363 billion USD and an important position in international politics"* (US News, 2022). Notably, Vietnam's economy has a high degree of openness and is increasingly deeply integrated at multiple levels with countries around the world. By the end of 2023, Vietnam had established 06 Comprehensive Strategic Partnerships, including: China (2008), Russia (2012), India (2016), South Korea (2022), the US (2023), Japan (2023); 30 Strategic Partnerships (including the 06 Comprehensive Strategic Partnerships); and established bilateral economic and diplomatic relations with 192 countries and territories worldwide (Dat, 2023). Notably, the event of the United Nations General Assembly voting to elect 5 non-permanent members of the Security Council for the 2020-2021 term with a total of 192/193 votes for Vietnam affirmed Vietnam's rising position and prestige in international politics. Therefore, considering the overall picture in Southeast Asia, Vietnam is a country with strong potential and one of the most important positions for India in this region. Vietnam's strong rise has narrowed the power gap between Vietnam and China to a certain extent. Although China is implementing "unorthodox claims" regarding Vietnam's maritime sovereignty, with its strengthening internal power, Vietnam has firmly opposed China's hegemonic actions, despite threats or China's "carrot and stick" policy. Vietnam needs support from international friends in the region and the world, especially powers with close geopolitical positions such as India, Japan, and South Korea (Ha, 2018). Therefore, the similarities in strategic interests between India and Vietnam in the South China Sea have helped both countries "find each other" in preventing China's hegemonic ambitions in the South China Sea.

Overall, Vietnam's emergence as a middle power in the 21st century represents a remarkable transformation in its geopolitical status and economic prowess. *"The country's journey from a war-torn, impoverished nation to its current position as a significant player in Southeast Asian and global affairs underscores the efficacy of its renovation policy and international integration strategies"* (Trinh & Huyen, 2024). Vietnam's economic growth, diplomatic acumen, and strategic importance have collectively contributed to its classification as an emerging middle power. This status is evidenced by its impressive GDP growth, expanding network of strategic partnerships, and increasing influence in international forums, as exemplified by its near-unanimous election to the UN Security Council.

The nation's rise has significant implications for regional power dynamics, particularly in relation to China and India (Loan & Tung, 2021). Vietnam's strengthened position has enabled it to more effectively counter China's assertive actions in the South China Sea, while simultaneously creating opportunities for enhanced cooperation with India. *"The alignment of strategic interests between Vietnam and India in the South China Sea presents a formidable counterbalance to China's hegemonic ambitions"* (Dar, 2021). However, Vietnam's ascent to middle power status also brings new challenges and responsibilities. Balancing relationships with major powers, navigating complex regional disputes, and maintaining economic growth will require continued diplomatic finesse and strategic vision. In conclusion, Vietnam's rise as a middle power not only reflects its own national achievements but also reshapes the geopolitical landscape of Southeast Asia. Its growing cooperation with India, rooted in shared strategic interests, has the potential to significantly influence regional stability and the broader Indo-Pacific power equilibrium.

CONCLUSION

This study has comprehensively analyzed the multifaceted factors defining Vietnam's strategic partnership role with India in countering China's hegemonic ambitions in the South China Sea and Southeast Asia. Through a detailed examination of Vietnam's geostrategic position, historical conflicts with China, and its emergence as a middle power, several key findings have emerged that collectively underscore the significance of this bilateral relationship in shaping regional dynamics.

Vietnam's critical location at the nexus of Southeast Asian maritime routes and its direct involvement in South China Sea disputes position it as a pivotal player in regional geopolitics, aligning closely with India's Act East policy objectives. This geostrategic significance is further amplified by the historical context of Sino-Vietnamese conflicts, which has profoundly shaped Vietnamese leadership perspectives, fostering a cautious yet resilient approach to regional power dynamics. This historical backdrop provides a crucial foundation for Vietnam's contemporary strategic calculations and its openness to partnerships that can counterbalance China's influence.

Vietnam's remarkable economic growth and increasing diplomatic clout have elevated it to the status of an emerging middle power, enhancing its capacity to engage in strategic partnerships and assert its interests on the international stage. This transformation makes Vietnam an increasingly valuable ally for India, particularly given their shared commitment to maintaining a rules-based international order, freedom of navigation, and regional stability. The alignment of these core strategic objectives forms the bedrock of their growing partnership, representing a sophisticated approach to power balancing in the Indo-Pacific region.

The evolving Vietnam-India strategic partnership carries significant implications for the broader Indo-Pacific security architecture, exemplifying the increasing importance of middle power diplomacy in shaping regional dynamics. It offers a model for constructive engagement that prioritizes stability and mutual benefit over confrontation, aiming to create a more pluralistic regional order that can mitigate the potential for unilateral dominance by any single power. However, this partnership also faces challenges, including the need to navigate complex relationships with China, balance economic interdependencies with security concerns, and maintain ASEAN centrality in regional affairs. Future research could explore the potential for expanding this bilateral relationship into broader multilateral frameworks and assess its long-term impact on regional stability and economic integration.

In conclusion, Vietnam's role as a strategic partner for India in Southeast Asia is defined by a synergy of geographic necessity, historical experience, and emerging capabilities. As both nations continue to deepen their cooperation, particularly in defense and economic spheres, this partnership has the potential to significantly influence the strategic landscape of the Indo-Pacific region. The success of this relationship could offer valuable insights into effective strategies for managing great power competition and promoting a more balanced and stable regional order, ultimately contributing to the broader goal of peace, prosperity, and stability in Southeast Asia and beyond.

REFERENCES

Aswani, R. S., Sajith, S., & Bhat, M. Y. (2022). Realigning India's Vietnam Policy Through Cooperative Sustainable Development: A Geostrategic Counterbalancing to China in Indo-Pacific. *East Asia (Piscataway, N.J.), 39*(2), 97–115. DOI: 10.1007/s12140-021-09371-0 PMID: 34276182

Blaxland, J., & Sharma, A. (2021). *Bolstering the Quad beyond its military dimensions.*https://www.eastasiaforum.org/2021/04/30/bolstering-the-quad-beyond-its-military-dimensions/, accessed on March 5, 2024.

Dabas, M. (2017). *Here Is All You Should Know About 'String Of Pearls', China's Policy To Encircle India.*https://www.indiatimes.com/news/india/here-is-all-you-should-know-about-string-of-pearls-china-s-policy-to-encircle-india-324315.html, accessed on March 12, 2024.

Dar, A. I. (2021). India-Vietnam Axis and China: The Allure of Hedging. *India Quarterly, 77*(2), 252–268. DOI: 10.1177/09749284211005011

Dat, T. D. (2023). *Vietnam establishes diplomatic relations with the 192nd country.* https://thanhnien.vn/viet-nam-thiet-lap-quan-he-ngoai-giao-voi-quoc-gia-thu-192-185230202163546862.htm, accessed on March 15, 2024

Dinh, Q. D. (2022). *Great achievements of the country after 35 years of implementing the renovation policy initiated and led by the Party.*http://dukcqtw.dcs.vn/nhung-thanh-tuu-to-lon-cua-dat-nuoc-sau-35-nam-thuc-hien-duong-loi-doi-moi-do-dang-khoi-xuong-va-lanh-dao-duk15671.aspx, accessed on March 19, 2024

Do, T. T. (2022). Vietnam's Emergence as a Middle Power in Asia: Unfolding the Power-Knowledge Nexus. *Journal of Current Southeast Asian Affairs, 41*(2), 279–302. DOI: 10.1177/18681034221081146

Doanh, L. D. (2021). *Clarifying the path forward.*https://tuoitre.vn/vach-ro-con-duong-di-toi-20210826114737271.htm, accessed on March 5, 2024.

Dunst, C. (2021). *Chinese aggression pushes Vietnam ever closer to Washington.* https://asia.nikkei.com/Opinion/Chinese-aggression-pushes-Vietnam-ever-closer-to-Washington, accessed on March 15, 2024

Duong, L. H., & Hong, D. T. M. (2019). South China Sea - Natural Resources in Vietnam. *European Journal of Engineering and Technology Research, 4*(9), 65–69.

EIA. (2017). *The Strait of Malacca, a key oil trade chokepoint, links the Indian and Pacific Oceans.*https://www.eia.gov/todayinenergy/detail.php?id=32452, accessed on January 13, 2025.

Garnier, L. (2012). *Multilateral resolution of disputes in the South China Sea.*https://vietnamnet.vn/giai-quyet-da-phuong-tranh-chap-bien-dong-72659.html, accessed on June 12, 2024.

Gill, D. M. (2021). *India is sailing into the South China Sea with more than China on its mind.*https://www.scmp.com/comment/opinion/article/3144544/india-sailing-south-china-sea-more-china-its-mind, accessed on June 22, 2024.

Global Data. (2022). Vietnam Defense Market. https://www.globaldata.com/reports/vietnam-defense-market-2022-free-report/, accessed on May 12, 2024.

Ha, N. T. T. (2018). Improving the effectiveness of Vietnam's relations with major countries in the current period. *Journal of Theoretical Education, 272*, 25–34.

Hiep, T. X., & Kiet, L. H. (2024). India's competitive strategy with China in Southeast Asia: An analysis of the case of Vietnam. *Journal of Chinese Studies, 2*(270), 68–80.

Kazuyuki, H. (2021). *Future superpower: Redrawing the world map in 2030 (translated version).* The World Publishers.

Kiet, L. H., Hiep, T. X., Minh, N. A., & Phuc, N. H. (2024). The soft power impact of China in strategic competition with the US in Vietnam. In Zreik, M. (Ed.), *Soft power and diplomatic strategies in Asia and the Middle East* (pp. 314–331). IGI Global., DOI: 10.4018/979-8-3693-2444-8.ch018

Kurlantzick, J. (2022). *China goes all in with support for Myanmar's military regime.* https://www.japantimes.co.jp/opinion/2022/04/14/commentary/world-commentary/china-backs-myanmar/, accessed on July 17, 2024.

Loan, H. T., & Tung, N. D. (2021). Vietnam's Responses to India's Indo-Pacific Oceans Initiatives and Opportunities for Vietnam–India Maritime Cooperation in the South China Sea. *India Quarterly, 77*(2), 185–199. DOI: 10.1177/09749284211005035

Lohman, W. (2020). *Vietnam's place in the U.S.-China great power competition.* https://www.gisreportsonline.com/r/us-china-rivalry-vietnam/, accessed on June 23, 2024.

Manuel, A., & Gates, R. (2016). *India And China, The New Superpowers.*https://iis.berkeley.edu/india-and-china-new-superpowers, accessed on June 24, 2024.

Marciel, S. (2023). *From Foe to Friend: Explaining the Development of US-Vietnam Relations.*https://aparc.fsi.stanford.edu/news/foe-friend-explaining-development-us-vietnam-relations, accessed on June 29, 2024.

Marshall, T. (2020). *Prisoners of Geography (translated version).* Vietnam Writers' Association Publishing House.

Mehrotra, L. (2012). India's Look East Policy: Its Origin and Development. *Indian Foreign Affairs Journal,* 7(1), 75-85. https://www.jstor.org/stable/45341805

Minh, T. (2023). *Vietnam - China relationship maintains development trend.*https://en.nhandan.vn/vietnam-china-relationship-maintains-development-trend-post126731.html, accessed on June 12, 2024.

Nga, L. T. H., & Quang, T. H. (2021). Public Diplomacy in Strengthening India: Vietnam Relations. *India Quarterly, 77*(2), 289–303. DOI: 10.1177/09749284211005012

Paszak, P. (2021). *China and the "Malacca Dilemma".*https://warsawinstitute.org/china-malacca-dilemma/, accessed on January 11, 2025.

Quynh, T. (2023). *What is Vietnam's GDP ranking in the world in 2022?*https://cafef.vn/gdp-viet-nam-dung-thu-bao-nhieu-the-gioi-nam-2022-20230320092746924.chn, accessed on June 12, 2024.

Raymond, M., & Welch, D. A. (2022). What's Really Going On in the South China Sea? *Journal of Current Southeast Asian Affairs, 41*(2), 214–239. DOI: 10.1177/18681034221086291

Sang, T. M. (2022). *The Growing Importance of Vietnam to India's South China Sea Policy.*https://www.airuniversity.af.edu/JIPA/Display/Article/2980923/the-growing-importance-of-vietnam-to-indias-south-china-sea-policy/, accessed on June 2, 2024.

Scott, D. (2017). *Chinese Maritime Strategy For The Indian Ocean.*https://cimsec.org/chinese-maritime-strategy-indian-ocean/, accessed on May 24, 2024.

Shambaugh, D. (2022). *Southeast Asia: Convergence of US-China superpowers (translated version).* National Political Publishing House.

Shin, D. M. (2015). *A Critical Review of the Concept of Middle Power.*https://www.e-ir.info/2015/12/04/a-critical-review-of-the-concept-of-middle-power/, accessed on June 13, 2024.

Singh, A. (2024). *Rethinking the South China Sea in Indian Maritime Security Strategy.*https://thediplomat.com/2024/06/rethinking-the-south-china-sea-in-indian-maritime-security-strategy/, accessed on January 10, 2025.

Thanh, P.Q. (2022). Great power strategic competition and Vietnam's countermeasures. *Journal of Political Theory,* 534.

The International Institute for Strategic Studies. (2023). *Arming Vietnam: Widened International-security Relations in Support of Military-capability Development.* https://www.iiss.org/globalassets/global-content---content--migration/arming-vietnam-widened-internationalsecurity-relations-in-support-of-militarycapability-development.pdf, accessed on June 18, 2024.

Thorburn, J. (2013). Vietnam as a Role Model for Development. *Journal of Oxford Academic*, *53*(2), 99–118. DOI: 10.1093/acprof:oso/9780199671557.003.0005

Trinh, V. D., & Huyen, H. D. (2024). Vietnam's Response to the US Indo-Pacific Strategy in the Context of a Rising China. *Journal of Current Southeast Asian Affairs*, *43*(1), 120–147. DOI: 10.1177/18681034241237813

US News. (2022). Best Countries: Power. https://www.usnews.com/news/best-countries/rankings/power, accessed on June 12, 2024.

Walt, S. M., & Belfer, R. A. (2017). *Great Powers Are Defined by Their Great Wars.* https://foreignpolicy.com/2017/09/21/great-powers-are-defined-by-their-great-wars/, accessed on June 12, 2024.

Chapter 13
Taiwan's Policy Regarding the South China Sea

Göktuğ Çalışkan
https://orcid.org/0000-0003-2189-7550
International University of Rabat, Morocco

ABSTRACT

This chapter analyzes Taiwan's SCS policies by examining their historical, legal, security, economic, and diplomatic dimensions. The historical context will explore the origins and evolution of Taiwan's territorial claims, while the legal section will analyze how international law influences its maritime strategy. The security section will focus on Taiwan's asymmetric defense measures and their implications for regional stability. The economic section will highlight Taiwan's reliance on the SCS for trade and resource security, illustrating how its economic strategy aligns with its broader policy objectives. Finally, the diplomatic section will evaluate Taiwan's efforts to overcome international isolation through soft power initiatives and strategic partnerships. By integrating these perspectives, this chapter aims to provide a nuanced understanding of Taiwan's multifaceted SCS policies and their implications for regional geopolitics.

INTRODUCTION

With its strategic importance and abundant natural resources, the South China Sea (SCS) is a vital maritime area with geopolitical tensions (U.S. Energy Information Administration, 2024). Taiwan's approach to this region reflects a complex interplay of historical claims, national security concerns, and economic interests.

DOI: 10.4018/979-8-3693-8109-0.ch013

Grounded in neoclassical realism, this chapter argues that Taiwan's SCS policy prioritizes safeguarding its sovereignty, ensuring maritime security, and maintaining economic engagement while navigating the diplomatic constraints imposed by its unique international status (Kuok, 2015). To achieve these objectives, Taiwan employs a multifaceted strategy that integrates historical claims, legal arguments, and pragmatic diplomacy to protect its interests in a region characterized by increasing militarization, primarily driven by China's assertive actions (Grossman, 2024).

Taiwan's historical claims to the SCS date back to the post-World War II era when the Republic of China (ROC) government demarcated the "Eleven-Dash Line" or "U-shaped line," asserting sovereignty over key islands and maritime zones (Hossain, 2013). These claims persist despite Taiwan's ambiguous political status, which complicates its ability to participate in international forums like the United Nations (Chuang, 2023). The legal basis of Taiwan's maritime claims rests on its interpretation of the United Nations Convention on the Law of the Sea (UNCLOS). However, its limited international recognition prevents it from formally participating in UNCLOS mechanisms (Ginanjar et al., 2023). Taiwan was notably absent from the Philippines' legal challenge against China's "Nine-Dash Line" at the Permanent Court of Arbitration in 2016 despite having overlapping claims to features like Itu Aba Island (Napang et al., 2019). Taiwan's strategy involves balancing the assertion of its territorial claims with diplomatic efforts to prevent escalation and maintain regional stability (Chong, 2023).

Taiwan's rivalry with China is a critical factor shaping its SCS policy. Beijing's militarization of the region, including artificial island construction and the deployment of military assets, directly challenges Taiwan's security interests (Chong, 2023). The construction of military facilities on the Spratly Islands and deploying advanced fighter jets like the J-20 to the Paracel Islands exemplify this militarization, significantly increasing security risks for Taiwan (Asia Maritime Transparency Initiative, 2024). Taiwan has adopted an asymmetric defense strategy to deter potential aggression without engaging in direct conflict (Lee & Lee, 2020; Gomez, 2023). Taiwan has also invested in advanced missile systems designed to counter China's superior military capabilities, reflecting a defensive posture to safeguard its sovereignty (Anderson, 2024; Missile Threat, 2021). The deployment of the domestically developed Tien Kung III (Sky Bow III) air defense system underscores Taiwan's commitment to protecting its airspace and maritime claims (Kajal, 2024). This defensive approach emphasizes resilience and aligns with the United States' strategic objective of balancing Beijing's growing regional power (U.S. Department of Defense, 2022).

Economically, the SCS is vital to Taiwan's global trade network, with a significant portion of its trade passing through these waters (Ministry of Economic Affairs, Taiwan (ROC), 2023). The region also provides access to essential fisheries and potential hydrocarbon resources, which are crucial for Taiwan's economic sustainability (Wu et al., 2024). However, Taiwan's limited international recognition restricts its ability to formalize resource-sharing agreements with other claimants (Royoux, 2018; Chong, 2023). Taiwan's fisheries disputes with the Philippines remain unresolved due to its exclusion from regional mechanisms like the Association of Southeast Asian Nations (ASEAN) (Chang, 2020; Royoux, 2018). Instead, Taiwan relies on informal economic cooperation and environmental initiatives to promote regional stability while securing resource access (Cain, 2021; Ho et al. 2023). Taiwan's promotion of sustainable fisheries practices through informal dialogues with Vietnam exemplifies its efforts to balance environmental conservation with economic interests (Huynh, 2023; United Nations Development Programme, 2023). This pragmatic economic diplomacy highlights Taiwan's adaptability in navigating the SCS's complex financial and geopolitical challenges.

Diplomatically, Taiwan leverages informal partnerships to compensate for its exclusion from multilateral platforms such as ASEAN (Jing, 2016). For instance, Taiwan's collaboration with Southeast Asian states on shared security concerns reflects its strategic use of soft power, including humanitarian aid and cultural exchanges, to enhance its regional influence (Lee & Chan, 2023). Some regional actors, such as the Philippines and Vietnam, view Taiwan's presence in the SCS as a potential counterbalance to China's growing assertiveness. However, they remain cautious due to their economic ties with Beijing (Smith & Lin, 2023). The United States (US) remains a crucial ally, providing strategic and military support that bolsters Taiwan's position in the SCS (U.S. Department of Defense, 2023). Through initiatives like the Global Cooperation and Training Framework (GCTF), Taiwan and the U.S. jointly address regional challenges, such as maritime security and humanitarian assistance, further enhancing Taiwan's strategic relevance (Ministry of Foreign Affairs of Japan et al., 2023). These partnerships underscore Taiwan's ability to navigate diplomatic isolation while contributing to regional security and stability.

Taiwan's policies in the SCS have broader implications for regional stability. While Taiwan's defensive posture aims to prevent escalation, its territorial claims partially overlap with China's, creating friction with other Southeast Asian nations (South China Morning Post, 2019). Conversely, Taiwan's adherence to international law and its cooperative approach to resource management contribute to de-escalation efforts. The delicate balance between these competing dynamics highlights Taiwan's role in maintaining a stable regional order.

This chapter analyzes Taiwan's SCS policies by examining their historical, legal, security, economic, and diplomatic dimensions. The historical context will explore the origins and evolution of Taiwan's territorial claims, while the legal section will analyze how international law influences its maritime strategy. The security section will focus on Taiwan's asymmetric defense measures and their implications for regional stability. The economic section will highlight Taiwan's reliance on the SCS for trade and resource security, illustrating how its economic strategy aligns with its broader policy objectives. Finally, the diplomatic section will evaluate Taiwan's efforts to overcome international isolation through soft power initiatives and strategic partnerships. By integrating these perspectives, this chapter aims to provide a nuanced understanding of Taiwan's multifaceted SCS policies and their implications for regional geopolitics.

HISTORICAL CONTEXT

Taiwan's strategic interests in the SCS are deeply rooted in the post-World War II era, which witnessed significant shifts in East Asia's territorial claims and maritime boundaries (Lin, 1997). In 1947, the ROC government formally asserted its territorial claims by introducing the "Eleven-Dash Line," encompassing the Spratly and Paracel Islands (Hossain, 2013). This demarcation, later adopted and modified by the People's Republic of China (PRC), represented the ROC's initial central assertion of sovereignty over the resource-rich and strategically vital SCS (U.S. Department of State, 2014; Perlez, 2016). The ROC's territorial claims were supported by historical documents, such as the 1935 Map of Chinese Islands in the SCS which aimed to demonstrate historical continuity and legitimacy (Zheng & Wu, 2020).

Taiwan's territorial claims were further solidified following World War II and the 1943 Cairo Declaration, which emphasized the return of territories seized by Japan, including islands in the SCS, to the ROC (China Diaoyu Dao, 2015). The 1945 Potsdam Declaration reaffirmed these provisions, legitimizing the ROC's reclamation of key islands, including Taiping (Itu Aba), which remains Taiwan's most important outpost in the Spratly Islands (U.S. Department of State, 1945). Despite the region's evolving geopolitical landscape, these developments played a crucial role in shaping Taiwan's maritime policies and assertion of historical sovereignty.

The Chinese Civil War and the subsequent establishment of the PRC in 1949 marked a turning point in maritime disputes. With the ROC government's retreat to Taiwan, its ability to effectively assert its claims in the SCS was significantly diminished (Chong, 2013). Nevertheless, Taiwan retained control of Itu Aba Island, which it fortified in the 1950s to protect its regional strategic interests (Hammer, 2020). The ROC's continued presence in Itu Aba has served as a tangible manifestation of its territorial claims despite its exclusion from international negotiations on the SCS, including those led by ASEAN (Kuok, 2015).

Figure 1. Spratly Islands and Itu Aba (Source: VOA, 2016)

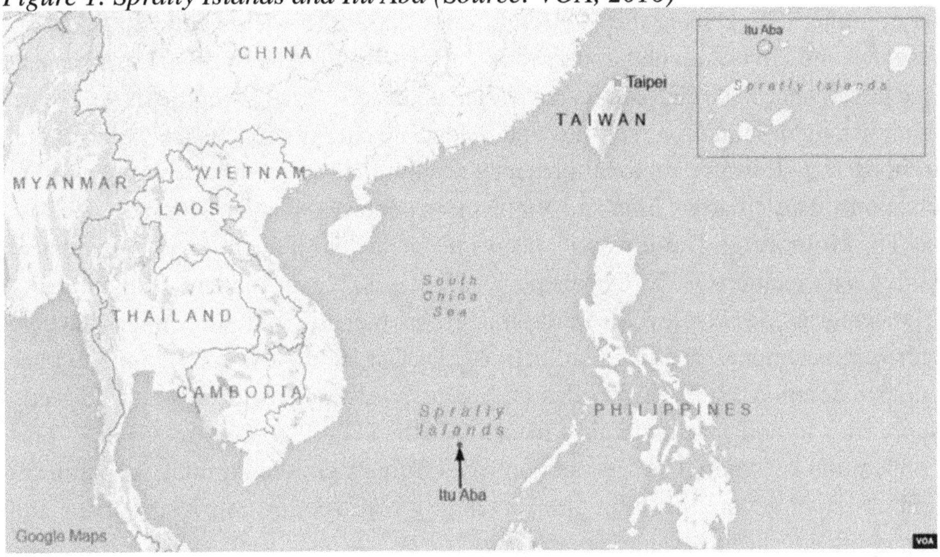

The geopolitical dynamics of the Cold War further complicated Taiwan's position in the SCS. In the 1970s, Taiwan faced diplomatic setbacks when the PRC was recognized as the legitimate representative of China in the United Nations, effectively excluding Taiwan from international legal frameworks, including UNCLOS. In 1971, United Nations General Assembly Resolution 2758 recognized the PRC as the only legitimate representative of China to the United Nations, resulting in the expulsion of Taiwan's representatives (Winkler, 2012). Despite this, Taiwan enacted domestic laws, such as the 1998 Territorial Sea and Contiguous Zone Act, to align its maritime policies with international standards, maintaining the legal consistency of its claims even without formal recognition (Taiwan Laws & Regulations Database, 1998).

The Philippines' initiation of arbitration proceedings against China at the Permanent Court of Arbitration in 2013 presented new challenges to Taiwan's legal and historical claims. Although Taiwan was not a party to the case, the tribunal's 2016 ruling indirectly affected Taiwan's interests, particularly concerning Itu Aba Island. The tribunal classified Itu Aba as a "rock," thereby denying it an Exclusive Economic Zone (EEZ) (Permanent Court of Arbitration, 2016). Taiwan rejected this classification, arguing that Itu Aba meets the criteria for an island under UNCLOS because it can sustain human habitation and economic life (Ministry of Foreign Affairs Taiwan, 2016; Song, 2015). This legal dispute highlighted Taiwan's challenges in reconciling its historical claims with contemporary international maritime law.

Taiwan's historical claims have influenced its approach to resource management in the SCS. During the 1990s and early 2000s, Taiwan conducted scientific research and environmental conservation efforts on Itu Aba to demonstrate effective governance and reinforce its territorial claims (Global Taiwan Institute, 2020). Establishing desalination facilities and renewable energy projects has been crucial in bolstering Taiwan's regional presence despite the increasing activities of other claimants, particularly China and Vietnam, in contested waters (Honrada, 2024).

The evolution of Taiwan's policies is intertwined with the broader dynamics of U.S.-China relations (U.S. Department of State, 2022). In the late 20th and early 21st centuries, Taiwan leveraged its strategic partnership with the United States to enhance its regional standing (Zulkifli, 2021). The 1979 Taiwan Relations Act has enabled continued U.S. arms sales and security assurances to Taiwan, indirectly supporting its ability to maintain a presence in the SCS (U.S. Congress, 1979). This cooperation is essential as Taiwan confronts China's growing military capabilities and assertive actions in the region, including constructing artificial islands and deploying advanced naval assets (Huang, 2022).

Taiwan's historical claims have shaped its regional strategy in recent decades, characterized by firmness and pragmatism. Taiwan has strengthened its military and civilian infrastructure on Itu Aba while pursuing dialogue and confidence-building measures with other claimants (Rapp-Hooper, 2015). It has also proposed joint resource management agreements and emphasized the peaceful resolution of disputes while upholding its sovereignty claims. These actions demonstrate Taiwan's dual emphasis on safeguarding its historical claims and promoting regional stability.

As Taiwan's position in the SCS continues to evolve, its historical claims remain a cornerstone of its policy framework. Taiwan's approach to the contested waters reflects a complex interplay of historical legitimacy, international law, and strategic considerations. By balancing the assertion of its rights with engagement and cooperation with regional stakeholders, Taiwan navigates the challenges and opportunities presented by the complex maritime disputes in a dynamic geopolitical environment.

LEGAL FRAMEWORK AND INTERNATIONAL LAW

Taiwan's territorial claims in the SCS are closely linked to international legal frameworks, particularly UNCLOS. Due to its unique political status, Taiwan is not a signatory to UNCLOS but has committed to adhering to its principles (Huyhn, 2022). This alignment with UNCLOS demonstrates Taiwan's respect for international norms and desire to be responsible in regional maritime disputes. By aligning its domestic legislation and policy actions with UNCLOS principles, Taiwan seeks to enhance the legitimacy of its claims while navigating the constraints imposed by its limited international recognition.

Figure 2. Nine-Dash line (Source: Gator Prints, 2023)

The 2016 arbitral tribunal ruling in the case brought by the Philippines against China significantly impacted the legal landscape of the SCS disputes. The tribunal concluded that Beijing's claims to historic rights within the "Nine-Dash Line" were incompatible with the Convention and invalid (Permanent Court of Arbitration, 2016). Although Taiwan was not a party to the arbitration due to its non-state status in international legal institutions, the ruling indirectly affected its claims, particularly regarding Itu Aba (Taiping Island), which was classified as a rock incapable of generating an EEZ. Taiwan rejected this classification, asserting that Itu Aba meets the criteria for an island under UNCLOS because it can sustain human habitation and economic life. Taiwan has implemented various governance measures on Itu Aba to substantiate this claim, such as installing renewable energy systems, maintaining a permanent civilian presence, and engaging in sustainable agricultural practices.

In response to these legal challenges, Taiwan has taken concrete steps to reinforce its claims while adhering to international legal norms. For instance, in 2016, Taiwan's Ministry of Foreign Affairs issued a comprehensive statement reaffirming its sovereignty over the islands in the SCS and their adjacent waters, emphasizing that its claims are based on international law and historical rights (Ministry of Foreign Affairs, ROC (Taiwan), 2016). This statement also underscored Taiwan's commitment to resolving disputes peacefully, positioning itself as a constructive actor in regional maritime affairs. Furthermore, Taiwan has engaged in environmental diplomacy by conducting marine biodiversity research and promoting sustainable fisheries management in the SCS, demonstrating its capacity for responsible governance (Luo & Chi, 2022).

Taiwan's legal framework for maritime claims is supported by its domestic legislation. The enactment of the Territorial Sea and Contiguous Zone Act and the EEZ and Continental Shelf Act reflects Taiwan's proactive approach to aligning its national laws with UNCLOS principles (Taiwan Laws & Regulations Database, 1998). These laws define Taiwan's maritime zones and provide a legal basis for managing marine resources, reinforcing its compliance with international standards. Taiwan has leveraged these laws to regulate its fishing activities and protect its marine environment, demonstrating effective governance (Luo & Chi, 2022).

Despite these efforts, Taiwan faces significant challenges due to its exclusion from international organizations like the United Nations and its associated legal mechanisms. The "One China" policy that most countries adopt limits Taiwan's ability to participate in multilateral discussions on maritime law, such as ASEAN-led dialogues on a Code of Conduct for the SCS (Tsai, 2022). To overcome these obstacles, Taiwan has engaged in informal mechanisms, such as track-two diplomacy and academic exchanges, to assert its legal position and contribute to regional discussions on maritime governance (Pertiwi, Kabinawa & Elias, 2018). For instance, Taiwan's participation in the East and South China Seas International Conference exemplifies its efforts to engage in dialogue despite formal diplomatic constraints (Lang, 2015).

Regional reactions to Taiwan's legal assertions are mixed. Some countries, like the Philippines and Vietnam, acknowledge Taiwan's claims to certain features but remain cautious due to potential overlaps with their interests (Asia Pacific Foundation of Canada, 2023). At the same time, Taiwan's adherence to international norms and commitment to peaceful dispute resolution has garnered some tacit support among ASEAN members concerned about China's increasingly assertive behaviour in the SCS.

TAIWAN'S SECURITY AND DEFENSE POLICIES IN THE SOUTH CHINA SEA

Its strategic priorities shape Taiwan's security policies in the SCS amid escalating regional tensions, particularly with the PRC (Mazza, 2023). As a globally significant maritime region with immense economic and military value, the SCS is strategically crucial to Taiwan. Located at the intersection of territorial sovereignty and regional geopolitics, Taiwan's defense policies reflect its efforts to assert sovereignty while navigating the complexities of regional dynamics. Itu Aba, Taiwan's largest outpost in the Spratly Islands, is central to this strategy. It is a cornerstone of its territorial claims and a symbol of its commitment to regional stability and national sovereignty (Sioco, 2020).

Taiwan's defense of Itu Aba is emblematic of its broader strategy in the SCS. This island, covering 46 hectares, is the largest naturally formed feature in the Spratly Islands under Taiwan's control (Perlez, 2018). The upgraded infrastructure on the island, including an expanded wharf capable of accommodating larger naval vessels and an extended airstrip for both military and humanitarian operations, underscores Taiwan's commitment to maintaining a robust presence in the region (Taipei Times, 2024). Taiwan has installed advanced radar systems that enable continuous surveillance of the surrounding waters, providing an early warning mechanism against the PRC's or other claimants' potential incursions. These measures signal Taiwan's determination to defend its sovereignty while seeking peaceful coexistence with regional actors.

Taiwan's recent investments underscore its ability to integrate military and civilian functions in Itu Aba. For example, establishing renewable energy systems, such as solar panels, has decreased reliance on external energy sources and improved the island's sustainability (Global Nation Inquirer, 2015). Taipei has built facilities like hospitals and desalination plants, enhancing the living conditions of personnel stationed on the island. These projects reinforce Taiwan's claim to Itu Aba by showcasing effective administration and a commitment to the island's long-term sustainability. This strategy sets Taiwan's activities apart from the PRC's militarized outposts in the region.

Taiwan has adopted an asymmetric defense strategy emphasizing agility, precision, and cost-efficiency because of the PRC's overwhelming military capabilities. Rooted in neoclassical realism, asymmetric warfare allows Taiwan to maximize its limited resources while deterring aggression from larger adversaries (Ripsman, Taliaferro, & Lobell, 2016). This approach, often called the "porcupine strategy," focuses on making any potential invasion costly and challenging for the aggressor (China Observers in Central and Eastern Europe, 2023). The deployment of domestically developed Hsiung Feng II and III anti-ship missiles exemplifies this strategy. These missile systems, capable of striking naval targets with high accuracy, provide Taiwan with a credible deterrent against potential threats in the SCS (O'Hanlon, 2021).

Moreover, Taiwan's focus on mobile air defense units and fast-attack vessels aligns with its broader strategy of countering the PRC's naval expansion without seeking confrontation (The Defense Post, 2023). In recent years, Taiwan has increased its production of these assets, ensuring rapid deployment capabilities in times of crisis. Taiwan has mass-produced its short-range air defense system, the Sky Sword II, to enhance its defensive capabilities (The Defense Post, 2023). Also, Taiwan plans to build six new Harpoon anti-ship missile bases to strengthen its coastal defenses (Army Recognition, 2023). This approach allows Taiwan to maintain a credible defense posture while underscoring the importance of avoiding unnecessary escalation, highlighting the sophistication of its strategic planning in response to a growing military imbalance.

Taiwan's exclusion from formal diplomatic frameworks such as ASEAN challenges its regional engagement. However, Taiwan has compensated for this isolation by establishing informal networks and participating in cooperative security dialogues. Taipei has engaged in track-two diplomacy with countries like the Philippines, Vietnam, and Malaysia, focusing on shared concerns such as maritime security and freedom of navigation. Notably, in September 2024, Vietnam and the Philippines agreed to deepen defense and military relations and collaborate on maritime security (Strangio, 2024).

Taiwan's diplomatic strategy also emphasizes confidence-building measures to foster trust among regional actors. In 2021, Taiwan initiated a series of unofficial maritime security dialogues with Southeast Asian nations, underscoring its commitment to international norms and regional stability (Ministry of Foreign Affairs, Republic of China (Taiwan), 2021). Such initiatives have helped portray Taiwan as a responsible participant in the SCS, garnering tacit support from countries wary of the PRC's assertive behavior. These efforts carefully balance advancing Taiwan's interests and contributing to regional stability.

Beyond its military and diplomatic strategies, Taiwan has integrated environmental stewardship into its approach to the SCS (Sato et al., 2023). This strategy strengthens Taiwan's claims and enhances its image as a responsible actor. For example, Taiwan has implemented a solar-powered desalination system on Itu Aba, addressing water scarcity issues while minimizing the environmental impact of its operations. Besides, agricultural projects and waste management systems have been introduced to improve self-sufficiency and sustainability on the island. Taiwan's emphasis on environmental conservation starkly contrasts with the PRC's environmentally damaging activities in the region, such as large-scale land reclamation and ecological degradation. By promoting sustainability, Taiwan differentiates itself as a claimant committed to the long-term health of the SCS's ecosystem. These environmental initiatives bolster Taiwan's claims under international law and project an image of responsible governance to the global community.

The U.S. remains a crucial security partner for Taiwan, especially in the context of heightened tensions in the SCS. Under the Taiwan Relations Act, the U.S. has provided Taiwan with advanced defensive weaponry, including maritime patrol aircraft and missile systems. In 2023 alone, U.S. arms sales to Taiwan amounted to $2.1 billion, reflecting the deepening security partnership between the two sides (Mistreanu, 2024). Likewise, regular U.S. freedom of navigation operations (FONOPs) in the SCS indirectly support Taiwan by reinforcing international maritime norms and challenging the PRC's expansive territorial claims. While Taiwan values its partnership with the U.S., it carefully manages this relationship to avoid unnecessary provocation of the PRC. This delicate balancing act underscores Taiwan's nuanced approach to regional security, which seeks to maximize strategic benefits while minimizing the risk of escalation (Liu, 2024).

Taiwan's multi-dimensional approach to security and defense in the SCS demonstrates its resilience and adaptability in a complex geopolitical environment. Taiwan asserts its sovereignty by integrating military preparedness, diplomatic engagement, and environmental stewardship while contributing to regional peace and stability. This balanced strategy highlights Taiwan's ability to navigate the challenges of the SCS disputes while maintaining a non-escalatory stance. Taiwan's ability to sustain this approach will be critical in ensuring its long-term security and role as a responsible regional actor.

TAIWAN'S DIPLOMATIC, REGIONAL RELATIONS, AND ECONOMIC INTERESTS

Taiwan's diplomatic and economic strategies are critical for its survival and prosperity in a region marked by complex alliances, economic interdependencies, and strategic tensions, particularly with China. Taipei faces significant obstacles in achieving diplomatic recognition and establishing formal regional relationships due to China's One China policy, which limits Taiwan's formal engagement with most countries (Huynh & Truong, 2024; Rich, 2023; Maizland, 2023). Nevertheless, Taiwan has adopted resilient strategies, cultivating unofficial relationships, engaging in economic diplomacy, and securing a robust presence in international trade networks. Taiwan's proactive efforts in fostering regional partnerships prove its commitment to stability and influence within the Asia-Pacific's dynamic political and economic landscape.

Taiwan has developed informal relations with over 60 countries, positioning itself as a valuable partner for democratic cooperation and regional stability. Its success in building these unofficial partnerships is evident in its strong relations with key players like the U.S., Japan, and the European Union. As highlighted in a 2023 report by Taiwan's Ministry of Foreign Affairs, these partnerships have facilitated over 1,700 informal agreements globally, covering areas ranging from economic cooperation to educational exchanges. These informal agreements allow Taiwan to circumvent diplomatic isolation while maintaining its global relevance (MOFA, 2023).

The Taiwan-U.S. relationship remains robust, underpinned by the 1979 Taiwan Relations Act, which ensures continued U.S. support for Taiwan's self-defense. In 2022, the U.S. Congress approved a $1.1 billion arms package for Taiwan, which included advanced radar systems, Harpoon missiles, and Stinger air defense systems, directly enhancing Taiwan's defense capabilities against potential Chinese aggression (France 24, 2022). The 2018 Taiwan Travel Act further strengthened bilateral ties by enabling high-level security, trade, and culture exchanges, aligning Taiwan more closely with U.S.-led regional strategies to balance China's influence.

In addition to its close relationship with the U.S., Taiwan's growing partnership with Japan has become a cornerstone of its regional strategy. As Taiwan's third-largest trading partner, Japan has deepened economic ties and increased cooperation on maritime security. The trade volume between Taiwan and the U.S. reached a significant milestone of $160 billion in 2022, with American exports to Taiwan amounting to $54.5 billion and imports from Taiwan reaching $105.5 billion (Office of the United States Trade Representative, 2023). By 2023, trade dynamics improved as Taiwan's exports to the United States grew by 17%, while U.S. imports from Taiwan increased by 21.3%, reflecting the resilience and expansion of bilateral trade amidst global economic uncertainties (United States International Trade Commission, 2023). Collaboration in technology, particularly in the semiconductor industry, has further cemented this partnership, with Japan relying heavily on Taiwan's expertise in advanced chip manufacturing. Moreover, Japan has supported Taiwan's informal participation in regional maritime security dialogues, including coast guard collaboration and joint surveillance efforts in the contested East China Sea (Yano, 2020). These initiatives underscore Japan's strategic alignment with Taiwan as a key partner in countering China's growing assertiveness in the region.

Taiwan's efforts to diversify its economic partnerships, primarily through the New Southbound Policy (NSP), have been instrumental in reducing its economic reliance on China. Launched in 2016, the NSP aims to foster deeper trade, investment, and people-to-people ties with countries in South and Southeast Asia, Australia, and

New Zealand. By 2023, Taiwan's trade with the NSP target countries increased to approximately $90.16 billion in exports, marking a significant rise since the policy's inception, thereby demonstrating its effectiveness in expanding Taiwan's economic reach (Statista, 2023). One notable success of the NSP is the Taiwan-Vietnam Technology Development Partnership, which has led to the establishment of five research and development centers in Hanoi and Ho Chi Minh City since 2022, focusing on intelligent manufacturing and renewable energy solutions. Furthermore, Taiwan's flagship initiative, the Taiwan Excellence Program, has promoted Taiwanese products to over 2.5 million consumers across Southeast Asia, enhancing Taiwan's regional brand visibility and bolstering its economic resilience.

Taiwan's semiconductor industry, a critical component of its economic strategy, underscores its global technological leadership. The Taiwan Semiconductor Manufacturing Company (TSMC) dominates the worldwide semiconductor foundry market, accounting for approximately 61.7% of the market share in the first quarter of 2024 (Statista, 2024). This significant share underscores TSMC's pivotal role in the semiconductor industry. In 2022, TSMC announced a $40 billion investment in two chip manufacturing plants in Arizona, USA, to begin production in 2024 (Taiwan Semiconductor Manufacturing Company, 2022). This investment strengthens Taiwan's economic leverage within global supply chains. It solidifies its strategic partnership with the U.S.

Despite these achievements, Taiwan faces significant challenges from China's ongoing economic and diplomatic campaigns to isolate it. China's substantial investments in the Solomon Islands and Central America have influenced several nations to re-evaluate and sometimes sever formal diplomatic ties with Taiwan. Between 2019 and 2022, the Solomon Islands received over $500 million in infrastructure loans from China, enhancing Beijing's regional influence (Habru, 2023). Taiwan has effectively utilized soft power initiatives to counter diplomatic challenges, notably through its "Mask Diplomacy" during the COVID-19 pandemic. By July 2020, Taiwan had donated over 51 million masks to more than 80 countries, showcasing its commitment to global health and solidarity (Business Wire, 2020). Such efforts have significantly enhanced Taiwan's international reputation and highlighted the stark contrast between its democratic governance model and China's authoritarian system.

Taiwan's soft power extends beyond humanitarian aid to encompass cultural diplomacy, academic exchanges, and the promotion of democratic values. In 2022, Taiwan hosted approximately 103,700 international students, reflecting its status as a hub for educational excellence (Statista, 2023). These efforts reinforce Taiwan's image as a beacon of democracy in Asia, countering China's narrative and fostering informal support networks globally.

Despite these successes, Taiwan's economic and diplomatic strategies remain constrained by its unresolved political status and China's persistent efforts to limit its international space. By 2023, numerous Taiwanese firms had relocated parts of their operations to Southeast Asian countries such as Vietnam, Thailand, and Malaysia, aiming to diversify their manufacturing bases and reduce reliance on China. This strategic shift decreased Taiwan's export dependency on China, with exports to China and Hong Kong dropping from 43.9% in 2020 to 35.2% in 2023 (I-Connect, 2023). These efforts highlight Taiwan's determination to enhance its economic resilience while navigating the complexities of cross-strait relations.

Looking ahead, Taiwan's ability to sustain its current strategies in the face of China's growing assertiveness will depend on its capacity for adaptation and continued innovation. Taiwan's partnerships with the U.S., Japan, and Southeast Asia will likely deepen, focusing on defense collaboration, economic diversification, and sustainability initiatives. Taiwan's role in the evolving geopolitical landscape of the Asia-Pacific underscores its resilience as a constructive and indispensable actor adeptly navigating the region's complexities.

CHALLENGES AND STRATEGIC ADAPTATION

Taiwan faces a complex and dynamic environment that necessitates ongoing adaptation and innovation to safeguard its interests and maintain its de facto independence. One of Taiwan's most persistent challenges is China's diplomatic isolation campaign, which has successfully reduced the number of countries formally recognizing Taiwan from 30 in the 1980s to just 13 as of 2023 (Freedom House, 2023). This tactic and China's influence over international organizations such as the United Nations limit Taiwan's ability to participate in global governance frameworks and multilateral dialogues. Taiwan has responded to these diplomatic constraints in recent years by cultivating informal alliances and leveraging public diplomacy to maintain its international visibility. Taiwan has secured over 1,700 informal agreements with countries worldwide, spanning various areas such as economics, culture, and science (MOFA, 2023). This enables it to remain engaged in global conversations despite its exclusion from formal platforms.

Taiwan's economy is crucial in bolstering its international standing amid these diplomatic challenges. Although Taiwan remains heavily reliant on trade with China—with 40% of its exports directed to mainland China and Hong Kong—recent policies have sought to mitigate this dependency. Taiwan's NSP has expanded trade relations with Southeast Asian nations. Beyond trade relations, Taiwan has strategically partnered with Vietnam and Thailand to establish joint research centers for technology development, focusing on sectors such as artificial intelligence and renewable energy. These initiatives exemplify Taiwan's proactive approach to diversifying its economic partnerships and reducing its vulnerability to geopolitical pressures.

In the realm of security, Taiwan faces a direct military threat from the PRC, which has escalated its military activities around Taiwan. In 2023, Taiwan recorded over 1,703 incursions into its Air Defense Identification Zone (ADIZ), marking a significant increase from previous years. This escalation reflects heightened military tensions in the region (McCartney, 2023). This persistent military pressure has compelled Taiwan to adopt an asymmetric defense strategy, focusing on mobility, precision, and cost-effectiveness. These measures highlight Taiwan's commitment to maintaining a robust deterrent posture while minimizing the risk of full-scale conflict.

Taiwan's efforts to address its vulnerabilities extend beyond military upgrades to encompass a range of soft power initiatives. Cultural exchanges and academic collaborations have complemented these humanitarian efforts. Furthermore, Taiwan's health assistance programs in Latin America and Africa have fostered goodwill and strengthened its informal alliances in these regions, demonstrating its ability to project influence through non-coercive means.

Environmental sustainability has also become a cornerstone of Taiwan's strategic planning. Taiwan has committed to generating 20% of its electricity from renewable sources by 2025. It plans to install 20 GW of photovoltaic capacity and exceed 5.7 GW in offshore wind power (Ministry of Economic Affairs, 2023). A significant milestone in this endeavor is the Formosa 2 Offshore Wind Farm, which, by May 2023, achieved an installed capacity of 376 MW, supplying power to approximately 380,000 households annually (Formosa 2, 2023). These initiatives contribute to Taiwan's energy independence and align its policies with global sustainability goals, strengthening its partnerships with environmentally conscious nations like the European Union.

While Taiwan's international efforts are commendable, domestic challenges further complicate its strategic environment. Political polarization within Taiwan occasionally hinders consensus on critical issues such as defense spending and cross-strait relations. Taiwan's limited military resources necessitate careful prioritization, often requiring difficult trade-offs between maintaining current capabilities and investing in emerging technologies. These internal dynamics underscore the need for Taiwan to balance its domestic constraints with its external ambitions.

The evolving geopolitical landscape of the Asia-Pacific region significantly influences Taiwan's strategic calculations. As China intensifies its efforts to undermine Taiwan's sovereignty, various international actors have increasingly rallied in support of Taiwan, recognizing it as a symbol of democracy and resilience in the region. The European Parliament passed a resolution in 2023 calling for stronger EU-Taiwan ties, particularly in technology, green energy, and education (European

Parliament, 2023). Such developments underscore the growing recognition of Taiwan's strategic importance, even as it faces significant challenges.

Taiwan's ability to navigate these complexities effectively rests on its proactive approach to diplomacy, economic diversification, and defense modernization. Taiwan safeguards its autonomy by aligning its domestic policies with international trends and fostering robust partnerships with like-minded nations. It also positions itself as a primary contributor to regional stability. As the strategic competition between the U.S. and China intensifies, Taiwan's role as a critical player in global supply chains and a champion of democratic values will remain crucial.

CONCLUSION

Taiwan's multifaceted and dynamic strategies demonstrate its resilience in navigating one of the most complex geopolitical environments of the 21st century. Taiwan has applied adaptability, innovation, and proactive diplomacy to counter various challenges, including diplomatic isolation, economic dependencies, and escalating security risks from the PRC. Taiwan's ability to effectively balance these pressures while pursuing its strategic objectives highlights the sophistication of its approach to maintaining its de facto independence and enhancing its regional and global role.

Central to Taiwan's success has been its ability to forge and strengthen alliances with countries that share its democratic values and strategic goals. The deepening partnership with the U.S., exemplified by robust defense agreements and collaborative semiconductor projects, underscores Taiwan's importance as a crucial node in global supply chains and a bulwark against authoritarianism. Meanwhile, Japan's alignment with Taiwan on issues of maritime security and trade diversification demonstrates the potential for broader regional cooperation to counterbalance China's growing influence.

Taiwan could pursue advanced trade agreements with like-minded nations to solidify its partnerships further. These agreements could focus on green technology, artificial intelligence, and supply chain resilience. Such contracts would reinforce Taiwan's position in global value chains, especially as technology and sustainability become increasingly central to international economic agendas.

Taiwan's adoption of asymmetric defense strategies has proven both pragmatic and practical in security. By prioritizing mobile defense systems, precision weaponry, and intelligence gathering, Taiwan has strengthened its deterrence against a more powerful adversary while showcasing a model of cost-efficient defense modernization. Future strategies might include closer collaboration with members of the Quad – Japan, the U.S., India, and Australia – on cybersecurity, intelligence sharing, and joint military exercises. These initiatives would enhance Taiwan's national security while contributing to broader regional stability.

Economically, Taiwan's strategic diversification efforts are reshaping its global economic footprint. The NSP, which has significantly expanded trade and investment ties with Southeast Asia, demonstrates Taiwan's ability to reduce its financial dependence on China while opening new markets for its advanced manufacturing capabilities. The semiconductor sector, where Taiwan holds a dominant global position, remains a pillar of its economic strength. However, the intensifying U.S.-China technology competition may necessitate further localization of chip production or diversification of export markets to mitigate geopolitical risks. A forward-looking approach could involve expanding semiconductor partnerships with the European Union and increasing investment in emerging technologies like quantum computing and artificial intelligence.

Taiwan's environmental initiatives highlight its commitment to global sustainability goals, adding a unique dimension to its geopolitical strategies. As one of Asia's offshore wind energy development leaders, Taiwan's renewable energy projects have strengthened its energy independence and bolstered its image as a responsible global citizen. In the future, Taiwan could further enhance its regional influence by exporting renewable energy expertise and collaborating on clean energy projects with developing nations in Southeast Asia. Such initiatives would address global climate challenges while reinforcing Taiwan's soft power in a region increasingly impacted by environmental concerns.

Taiwan's challenges, however, require both external engagement and internal consolidation. Domestic political polarization and resource constraints could hinder its effective implementation of long-term strategies. Strengthening bipartisan support for key policies, such as defense spending and energy independence, will be crucial for maintaining Taiwan's strategic momentum. Investing in workforce development, particularly in the high-tech and green energy sectors, is essential to ensure Taiwan remains competitive in the global economy. Likewise, strengthening social cohesion through education reforms and public awareness campaigns could further reinforce the unity needed to counter external pressures.

Taiwan's future will depend significantly on its ability to navigate the U.S.-China rivalry without becoming overly entangled in their strategic competition. As Beijing continues its diplomatic campaign to isolate Taiwan, soft power initiatives such as global health diplomacy, humanitarian assistance, and educational exchanges will become increasingly important. Taiwan's participation in informal multilateral frameworks, such as track-two diplomacy and regional think tank dialogues, could enable it to shape narratives and policy discussions that align with its strategic objectives.

Taiwan's approach to regional stability and global cooperation offers valuable lessons for other countries facing diplomatic constraints. By integrating economic, security, and environmental strategies into a cohesive framework, Taiwan has demonstrated the ability of small states to exert influence on more significant geopolitical dynamics. Its emphasis on innovation, resilience, and sustainability provides a roadmap for how nations can align domestic priorities with international cooperation. Taiwan's measured but resolute stance ensures that it remains a stabilizing force in the Indo-Pacific, a region grappling with growing uncertainties amid shifting power dynamics.

In conclusion, Taiwan's strategic evolution is a testament to its ability to adapt and thrive under pressure. By leveraging its technological prowess, forging robust partnerships, and upholding a rules-based international order, Taiwan has positioned itself as a regional leader and a global innovator. The coming years will undoubtedly test Taiwan's capacity to sustain this trajectory, particularly as geopolitical tensions escalate. However, if Taiwan continues to align its domestic policies with international trends and proactively engages with the global community, its role as a resilient and indispensable actor in international affairs will only strengthen.

REFERENCES

Anderson, C. (2024, November 10). *Taiwan Receives US ATACMS Missiles to Counter China Threat*. Defense Feeds. Retrieved from https://defensefeeds.com/taiwan-receives-us-atacms-missiles/

Army Recognition. (2023, October 15). Taiwan Enhances Defense Capabilities with New Harpoon Missile Bases. Retrieved from https://www.armyrecognition.com/news/army-news/army-news-2023/taiwan-enhances-defense-capabilities-with-new-harpoon-missile-bases

Asia Maritime Transparency Initiative. (n.d.). *Chinese Power Projection Capabilities in the South China Sea*. Center for Strategic and International Studies. Retrieved December 4, 2024, from https://amti.csis.org/chinese-power-projection/

Asia Pacific Foundation of Canada. (2023). *Philippines and Vietnam discuss overlapping South China Sea claims*. Retrieved from https://www.asiapacific.ca/asia-watch/philippines-vietnam-discuss-overlapping-south-china-sea

Business Wire. (2020, July 22). *Taiwan Donates Over 51 Million Masks to Countries Worldwide*. Retrieved from https://www.businesswire.com/news/home/20200722005405/en/Taiwan-Donates-Over-51-Million-Masks-to-Countries-Worldwide

Cain, B. (2021). To Deepen and Broaden Our Presence: Taiwan's Strategies for Participating in the International System. China Research Center. Retrieved from https://www.chinacenter.net/2021/china-currents/20-1/to-deepen-and-broaden-our-presence-taiwans-strategies-for-participating-in-the-international-system/

China Diaoyu Dao. (2015, January 25). *The Cairo Declaration and its implications for the Diaoyu Dao issue*. Retrieved from https://www.diaoyudao.org.cn/en/2015-01/25/content_34649421.htm

China Observers in Central and Eastern Europe. (2023). The porcupine strategy: Taiwan's road to self-defense. Retrieved from https://chinaobservers.eu/the-porcupine-strategy-taiwans-road-to-self-defense/

Chong, A. (2023). *Still waters run deep: Taiwan's South China Sea strategy*. Clingendael Spectator. Retrieved December 4, 2024, from https://spectator.clingendael.org/en/publication/still-waters-run-deep-taiwans-south-china-sea-strategy

Chong, J. (2013). The South China Sea Disputes: some documentary context. chinese Law & Government, 46(3-4), 3-9. DOI: 10.2753/CLG0009-4609460300

Chuang, S. (2023). The Taiwan problem. *International Journal of Arts Humanities & Social Science, 04*(03), 27–30. DOI: 10.56734/ijahss.v4n3a3

European Parliament. (2023, April 20). Resolution on EU-Taiwan political relations and cooperation. https://www.europarl.europa.eu/doceo/document/TA-9-2023-0139_EN.html

Formosa 2. (2023, May 16). *Formosa 2 marks the first Round 2 offshore wind farm completed in Taiwan and continues to build a greener future*. Retrieved from https://formosa2windpower.com/en/formosa-2-marks-the-first-round-2-offshore-wind-farm-completed-in-taiwan-and-continues-to-build-a-greener-future/

France 24. (2022, September 3). *US approves $1.1 billion arms package for Taiwan, angering China*. Retrieved from https://www.france24.com/en/asia-pacific/20220903-us-approves-1-1-billion-arms-package-for-taiwan-angering-china

Freedom House. (2023). Taiwan: Freedom in the World 2023 Country Report. Retrieved from https://freedomhouse.org/country/taiwan/freedom-world/2023

Ginanjar, W., Pramono, B., & Priyanto, P. (2023). Overviewing the context of the balance of power to the South China Sea issue in ASEAN. *International Journal of Humanities Education and Social Sciences (Ijhess), 2*(4). Advance online publication. DOI: 10.55227/ijhess.v2i4.372

Global Nation Inquirer. (2015, June 30). *Taiwan promotes its island claim in South China Sea*. Retrieved from https://globalnation.inquirer.net/126376/taiwan-promotes-its-island-claim-in-south-china-sea

Global Taiwan Institute. (2020, July 15). *Taiwan's South China Sea Policy: Sovereignty and Pragmatism*. Retrieved from https://globaltaiwan.org/2020/07/vol-5-issue-14/

Gomez, E. (2023). *Taiwan's Urgent Need for Asymmetric Defense* (Policy Analysis No. 965). Cato Institute. Retrieved December 4, 2024, from https://www.cato.org/policy-analysis/taiwans-urgent-need-asymmetric-defense

Grossman, D. (2024). How to Respond to China's Tactics in the South China Sea. RAND Corporation. https://www.rand.org/pubs/commentary/2024/06/how-to-respond-to-chinas-tactics-in-the-south-china.html

Habru, P. (2023, April 17). *China's influence weighs heavily on Solomon Islands election*. 360info. Retrieved from https://360info.org/chinas-influence-weighs-heavily-on-solomon-islands-election/

Hammer, L. (2020). Taiwan and Itu Aba (Taiping): Creating an 'Island for All' in the South China Sea. International Journal of Taiwan Studies.

Ho, C. H., & Lee, K. (2023). Sustainable fisheries under net-zero emissions: A case study of the Taiwan Fishery Administration. In H. H. Wu, W. Y. Liu, & M. C. Huang (Eds.), Moving toward net-zero carbon society (pp. 91–105). Springer Climate. Springer, Cham. DOI: 10.1007/978-3-031-24545-9_6

Honrada, G. (2024, October 20). *Vietnam imitating China's island-making in South China Sea.* Asia Times. Retrieved from https://asiatimes.com/2024/10/vietnam-imitating-chinas-island-making-in-south-china-sea/

Hossain, K. (2013). The unclos and the us-china hegemonic competition over the South China Sea. *Journal of East Asia and International Law*, *6*(1). Advance online publication. https://www.usitc.gov/publications/332/executive_briefings/ebot_us_taiwan_trade.pdf. DOI: 10.14330/jeail.2013.6.1.05

Huang, K. (2022, November 7). *Fortified South China Sea artificial islands project Beijing's military reach and power, say observers.* South China Morning Post. Retrieved from https://www.scmp.com/news/china/diplomacy/article/3198504/fortified-south-china-sea-artificial-islands-project-beijings-military-reach-and-power-say-observers

Huynh, N. T. T. (2023). *Taiwan-Vietnam Cooperation in the Blue Economy.* Taiwan-Asia Exchange Foundation. Retrieved from https://www.taef.org/doc/1314

Huynh, T. S. (2022, October 4). *UNCLOS's relevance to Taiwan amid a raging storm.* Fulcrum. Retrieved from https://fulcrum.sg/uncloss-relevance-to-taiwan-amid-a-raging-storm/

Huynh, T. S., & Truong, T. T. K. (2024, November 9). *Taiwan's Struggle to Retain Diplomatic Allies.* The Diplomat. Retrieved from https://thediplomat.com/2024/11/taiwans-struggle-to-retain-diplomatic-allies/

I-Connect. (2023, August 15). Taiwan Imports and Exports: Trade Insights. Retrieved from https://www.i-connectweb.com/blog/taiwan-imports-and-exports-trade-insights

Kajal, K. (2024). *Taiwan deploys Sky Bow III air defence systems.* Janes. Retrieved December 4, 2024, from https://www.janes.com/osint-insights/defence-news/defence/taiwan-deploys-sky-bow-iii-air-defence-systems

Kuok, L. (2015). Tides of Change: Taiwan's Evolving Position in the South China Sea. Brookings Institution. https://www.brookings.edu/wp-content/uploads/2016/06/taiwan-south-china-sea-kuok-paper.pdf

Kuok, L. (2021). Taiwan's Evolving Position in the South China Sea—And Why Other Actors Should Take Notice. Center for Strategic and International Studies. Asia Maritime Transparency Initiative. https://amti.csis.org/taiwans-evolving-position-in-the-south-china-sea-and-why-other-actors-should-take-notice/

Lang, B. (2015). Off the beaten track: Taiwan's changing 'track-two diplomacy' after democratisation – and its pitfalls. *European Journal of East Asian Studies, 14*(1), 75–102. https://www.academia.edu/11885584/Off_the_beaten_track_Taiwans_changing_track_two_diplomacy_after_democratisation_and_its_pitfalls

Laws & Regulations Database of The Republic of China. (1998). *Law on the Territorial Sea and the Contiguous Zone*. Retrieved from https://law.moj.gov.tw/ENG/LawClass/LawAll.aspx?pcode=A0000009

Lee, H., & Lee, E. (2020). *Taiwan's Overall Defense Concept Explained*. The Diplomat. Retrieved December 4, 2024, from https://thediplomat.com/2020/11/taiwans-overall-defense-concept-explained/

Lee, K. C. L., & Chan, Y.-K. (Eds.). (2023). *Taiwan and Southeast Asia: Soft Power and Hard Truths Facing China's Ascendancy* (1st ed.). Routledge., DOI: 10.4324/9781003320463

Lin, C. (1997). Taiwan's South China Sea Policy. *Asian Survey, 37*(4), 323–339. DOI: 10.2307/2645651

Liu, I.-C. (2024, November 16). *The Risks of Oversimplifying Taiwan's Defense Needs*. The Diplomat. Retrieved from https://thediplomat.com/2024/11/the-risks-of-oversimplifying-taiwans-defense-needs/

Luo, G., & Chi, Z. (2022). Conflicts and challenges of sustainable fisheries governance cooperation under the securitization of the maritime commons. *Fishes, 8*(1), 1. DOI: 10.3390/fishes8010001

Maizland, L. (2023, January 24). *Why China-Taiwan Relations Are So Tense*. Council on Foreign Relations. Retrieved from https://www.cfr.org/backgrounder/china-taiwan-relations-tension-us-policy-biden

Mazza, M. (2023, October 4). *Beijing's aggressive moves in the South China Sea and the potential for a Taiwan crisis*. Global Taiwan Institute. Retrieved from https://globaltaiwan.org/2023/10/beijings-aggressive-moves-in-the-south-china-sea-and-the-potential-for-a-taiwan-crisis/

McCartney, M. (2023, December 1). *China Deployed Over 1,700 Military Planes Around Taiwan in 2023*. Newsweek. Retrieved from https://www.newsweek.com/china-military-aircraft-taiwan-strait-2023-1858106

Ministry of Economic Affairs. Republic of China (Taiwan). (2023). Taiwan's Trade Statistics. https://www.moea.gov.tw/MNS/dos/home/Home.aspx

Ministry of Economic Affairs. (2023). *Important Policies - Policies & Programs.* Retrieved from https://www.moea.gov.tw/MNS/english/Policy/Policy.aspx?menu_id=32904&policy_id=19

Ministry of Foreign Affairs. Republic of China (Taiwan). (2016, July 12). *ROC government reiterates its position on South China Sea issues.* Retrieved from https://en.mofa.gov.tw/News_Content.aspx?n=1EADDCFD4C6EC567&s=F5170FE043DADE98

Ministry of Foreign Affairs. Republic of China (Taiwan). (2016, July 14). *ROC position on the South China Sea Arbitration.* Retrieved from https://www.mofa.gov.tw/en/News_Content.aspx?n=1EADDCFD4C6EC567&s=5B5A9134709EB875

Ministry of Foreign Affairs. Republic of China (Taiwan). (2021, August 20). *Ketagalan Forum—2021 Asia-Pacific Security Dialogue to discuss regional security issues in the postpandemic era.* Retrieved from https://en.mofa.gov.tw/News_Content.aspx?n=1328&s=96298&sms=273

Ministry of Foreign Affairs. American Institute in Taiwan, Japan-Taiwan Exchange Association, & Australian Office. (2023, December 6). Joint Statement on the 2023 Global Cooperation and Training Framework (GCTF) Joint Committee Meeting. https://www.koryu.or.jp/Portals/0/taipei/2023/1207/2023-12-06%20Joint%20Statement%20on%20the%202023%20GCTF.pdf

Ministry of Foreign Affairs. Republic of China (Taiwan). (2023). Taiwan's International Cooperation and Development. [REMOVED HYPERLINK FIELD] https://www.moea.gov.tw/Mns/english/home/English.aspx

Missile Threat. (2021, April 28). *Missiles of Taiwan.* Center for Strategic and International Studies. Retrieved from https://missilethreat.csis.org/country/taiwan/

Mistreanu, S. (2024, October 26). *US approves $2 billion in arms sales to Taiwan including advanced missile defense system.* Associated Press. Retrieved from https://apnews.com/article/us-taiwan-china-arms-sale-missile-defense-bd14986ada9cfc894c5b1168aea27d02

Napang, M., Patittingi, F., Aspan, Z., Ruslan, A., Latief, B., Hambali, R., & Hendrapati, M. (2019). Contesting views of the philippines and china over the nine-dash line in the south china sea. *Journal of East Asia and International Law, 12*(1), 180–192. DOI: 10.14330/jeail.2019.12.1.10

O'Hanlon, M. E. (2021, October 13). *An asymmetric defense of Taiwan*. Brookings Institution. Retrieved from https://www.brookings.edu/articles/an-asymmetric-defense-of-taiwan/

Office of the United States Trade Representative. (2023). Taiwan. Retrieved from https://ustr.gov/countries-regions/china/taiwan

Perlez, J. (2016, July 12). Tribunal Rejects Beijing's Claims in South China Sea. The New York Times. https://www.nytimes.com/2016/07/13/world/asia/south-china-sea-hague-ruling-philippines.html

Perlez, J. (2018, May 20). *On a Tiny Island in the South China Sea, Taiwan Stakes Its Claim*. The New York Times. Retrieved from https://www.nytimes.com/2018/05/20/world/asia/china-taiwan-island-south-sea.html

Permanent Court of Arbitration. (2016). The South China Sea Arbitration Award. https://pca-cpa.org/en/cases/7/

Permanent Court of Arbitration. (2016, July 12). *Press Release: The South China Sea Arbitration (The Republic of the Philippines v. The People's Republic of China)*. Retrieved from https://docs.pca-cpa.org/2016/07/PH-CN-20160712-Press-Release-No-11-English.pdf

Pertiwi, S. B., Kabinawa, L. N. R. W., & Elias, R. A. (2018). The diplomacy of quasi-state in territorial disputes: Taiwan in the South China Sea. *Jurnal Hubungan Internasional, 8*(2), 153–166. Retrieved from https://www.academia.edu/86585224/The_Diplomacy_of_Quasi_State_in_Territorial_Disputes_Taiwan_in_the_South_China_Sea

Rapp-Hooper, M. (2015, February 18). *Before and After: The South China Sea Transformed*. Asia Maritime Transparency Initiative. Retrieved from https://amti.csis.org/before-and-after-the-south-china-sea-transformed/

Rich, T. S. (2023, July 12). *Rethinking Taiwan's Diplomatic Relations: Beyond the Term "Diplomatic Allies"*. Global Taiwan Institute. Retrieved from https://globaltaiwan.org/2023/07/rethinking-taiwans-diplomatic-relations-beyond-the-term-diplomatic-allies/

Ripsman, N. M., Taliaferro, J. W., & Lobell, S. E. (2016). *Neoclassical realist theory of international politics*. Academic., DOI: 10.1093/acprof:oso/9780199899234.001.0001

Royoux, D. (2018). Compte rendu de [MOTTET, Éric, LASSERRE, Frédéric et COURMONT, Barthélémy (dir.) (2017) Géopolitique de la mer de Chine méridionale. Eaux troubles en Asie du Sud-Est. Québec, Presses de l'Université du Québec, 202 p. (ISBN 978-2-76054-805-3)]. *Cahiers de Geographie de Quebec*, *62*(177), 472–473. DOI: 10.7202/1068753ar

Sato, M., Prétat, H., Mallory, T., Chen, H., & Poling, G. (2023, December 18). *Deep Blue Scars: Environmental Threats to the South China Sea*. Center for Strategic and International Studies. Retrieved from https://features.csis.org/environmental-threats-to-the-south-china-sea/

Sioco, M. A. (2020). *Taiwan's strategic role in the Spratly Islands and the significance of Itu Aba*. Radio Taiwan International. Retrieved from https://en.rti.org.tw/news/view/id/2010876

Song, Y. H. (2015, May 7). *Taiping Island: An Island or a Rock under UNCLOS*. Asia Maritime Transparency Initiative. Retrieved from https://amti.csis.org/taiping-island-an-island-or-a-rock-under-unclos/

South China Morning Post. (2019, February 18). *Explained: South China Sea dispute*. Retrieved from https://www.scmp.com/week-asia/article/2186449/explained-south-china-sea-dispute

Statista. (2023). *Taiwan's exports to New Southbound Policy countries from 2013 to 2023*. Retrieved from https://www.statista.com/statistics/1271612/taiwan-exports-to-new-southbound-policy-countries/

Statista. (2024). *Top semiconductor foundries market share 2024*. Retrieved from https://www.statista.com/statistics/867223/worldwide-semiconductor-foundries-by-market-share/

Taipei Times. (2024, January 30). *Itu Aba dredging completed, CGA says*. Retrieved from https://www.taipeitimes.com/News/front/archives/2024/01/30/2003812822

Taiwan Semiconductor Manufacturing Company. (2022, December 6). *TSMC Announces Updates for TSMC Arizona*. Retrieved from https://pr.tsmc.com/english/news/2977

The Defense Post. (2023, November 30). Taiwan Begins Mass Production of Indigenous Air Defense System. Retrieved from https://thedefensepost.com/2023/11/30/taiwan-air-defense-system/

Tsai, C.-T. (2022). *Taiwan's South China Sea policy evolution and its exclusion from regional dialogues*. Asia Maritime Transparency Initiative. Retrieved from https://amti.csis.org/taiwan-scs-policy-evolution/

United Nations Development Programme. (2023, December 8). *Dialogue between the Minister of Agriculture and Rural Development and Fishermen and Associations: Promoting Co-management for Sustainable Fisheries*. Retrieved from https://www.undp.org/vietnam/press-releases/dialogue-between-minister-agriculture-and-rural-development-and-fishermen-and-associations-promoting-co-management-sustainable

United States International Trade Commission. (2023). Executive Briefings on Trade: U.S.-Taiwan Trade. Retrieved from Winkler, S. (2012). *Taiwan's UN Dilemma: To Be or Not To Be*. Brookings. Retrieved from https://www.brookings.edu/articles/taiwans-un-dilemma-to-be-or-not-to-be/

U.S. Congress. (1979). *Taiwan Relations Act*. Retrieved from https://www.congress.gov/bill/96th-congress/house-bill/2479

U.S. Department of Defense. (2022). *Military and Security Developments Involving the People's Republic of China 2022*. Retrieved from https://media.defense.gov/2022/Nov/29/2003122279/-1/-1/1/2022-MILITARY-AND-SECURITY-DEVELOPMENTS-INVOLVING-THE-PEOPLES-REPUBLIC-OF-CHINA.PDF

U.S. Department of Defense. (2023, September 14). U.S. Strengthening Deterrence in Taiwan Strait. https://www.defense.gov/News/News-Stories/Article/Article/3531094/us-strengthening-deterrence-in-taiwan-strait/

U.S. Department of State. (2014). China: Maritime Claims in the South China Sea. Limits in the Seas, No. 143. https://www.state.gov/wp-content/uploads/2019/10/LIS-143.pdf

U.S. Department of State. (2022, May 28). *U.S. Relations With Taiwan*. Retrieved from https://www.state.gov/u-s-relations-with-taiwan/

U.S. Energy Information Administration. (2024). Regional Analysis Brief: South China Sea. https://www.eia.gov/international/content/analysis/regions_of_interest/South_China_Sea/south_china_sea.pdf

Wu, Y., Lim, I. C. L., Li, L., Chen, L., Hsiao, P., Lee, W., & Lan, K. (2024). The evolution of resource management in Taiwanese fisheries: Coastal and offshore perspectives. *PeerJ*, *12*, e18434. DOI: 10.7717/peerj.18434 PMID: 39619187

Yano, K. (2020, November 20). Maritime Security Involving Japan and Taiwan. Security Strategy Research Institute of Japan. Retrieved from https://www.ssri-j.com/Taiwan/Strategic%20dialogue/taiwanS/yanokazu-2-20201120.pdf

Zheng, Z., & Wu, J. (2020, July 13). Legal implications of the map of the South China Sea Islands of China under international law. South China Sea Strategic Situation Probing Initiative (SCSPI). Retrieved from https://ssrn.com/abstract=3995467

Zulkifli, N. (2021). *The United States (US)-Taiwan Strategic Partnership*. Retrieved from https://www.academia.edu/50194003/The_United_States_US_Taiwan_Strategic_Partnership U.S. Department of State. (1945, July 26). *Potsdam Declaration*. In *Foreign Relations of the United States: Diplomatic Papers, The Conference of Berlin (The Potsdam Conference), 1945, Volume II*. Retrieved from https://history.state.gov/historicaldocuments/frus1945Berlinv02/d1382

Compilation of References

Abdullah, S. (2013). Effect of Malay-China Trade Relations During the Malacca Sultanate on the Emergence of Chinese Peranakan Community. *World Journal of Islamic History and Civilization*, *3*(4), 143–149. DOI: 10.5829/idosi.wjihc.2013.3.4.3401

Acharya, A. (2001). *Constructing a Security Community in Southeast Asia: ASEAN and the Problem of Regional Order*. Routledge.

Ahmed, G. G. J. W., Nasrin, M. I., & Abdullah, M. M. A. (2022). Study on Significance of Shura in Islam and its Practice in Contemporary Muslim Family Affairs. *Al-Bukhari Journal of Arabic and Islamic Studies*, *2*(1), 38–49.

Al-Aboudi, N.K.M. (2021). The Islamic Sultanate of Malacca: a study of its inception and the factors of its development into a global trade center in the first half of the 15th century. *PalArch's Journal of Archaeology of Egypt/Egyptology* 18(5), 491-510.

Alaca, M. (2023). *ABD ile Filipinler, Tayvan Boğazı'nın yakınındaki sularda "en büyük" savaş tatbikatına başladı,* Anatolia Agency, 11.04.2023, https://www.aa.com.tr/tr/dunya/abd-ile-filipinler-tayvan-bogazinin-yakinindaki-sularda-en-buyuk-savas-tatbikatina-basladi/2869008

Alden, C. (2012, September). China and Africa: The Relationship Matures. Strategic Analysis. Retrieved from DOI: 10.1080/09700161.2012.712365

Alden, C. (2008). China and africa: A new development partnership. *Strategic Analysis*, *32*(2), 297–304. DOI: 10.1080/09700160801994902

Al-Haj, T. A. P. (1969, January 8). Statement by the Prime Minister, Tunku Abdul Rahman Putra Al-haj, at the Commonwealth Prime Ministers' Meeting in London. *Foreign Affairs Malaysia*, 2 (1), 2-4. https://www.kln.gov.my/documents/8390448/8418517/VOLUME+2.pdf/148bc9c1-a73e-429f-be86-9477db7a3c35?version=1.0&download=true

Aljazeera (2021, October 5). Malaysia summons China envoy over South China Sea 'encroachment'. https://www.aljazeera.com/news/2021/10/5/malaysia-summons-china-ambassador-over-south-china-sea-incursion

Aljazeera (2023, August 31). Malaysia rejects new China map claiming entire South China Sea. https://www.aljazeera.com/news/2023/8/31/malaysia-rejects-new-china-map-claiming-entire-south-china-sea

Aljazeera.com. (2023). *US gets new Philippine bases with South China Sea, Taiwan in mind,* 22.03.2023, https://www.aljazeera.com/news/2023/3/22/us-gets-new-philippine-bases-with-south-china-sea-taiwan-in-mind#:~:text=The%20US%20has%20committed%20%2480,Lumbia%20Air%20Base%20in%20Mindanao

Anderson, C. (2024, November 10). *Taiwan Receives US ATACMS Missiles to Counter China Threat.* Defense Feeds. Retrieved from https://defensefeeds.com/taiwan-receives-us-atacms-missiles/

Anna, K. (2017). Strategic Narratives of Public Diplomacy and the Enactment of Soft Power: An Exploratory Study. *Dissertation.* Retrieved from https://hdl.handle.net/11244/51905

Army Recognition. (2023, October 15). Taiwan Enhances Defense Capabilities with New Harpoon Missile Bases. Retrieved from https://www.armyrecognition.com/news/army-news/army-news-2023/taiwan-enhances-defense-capabilities-with-new-harpoon-missile-bases

Arrighi, G. (2007). *Adam Smith in Beijing : lineages of the twenty-first century.* Verso.

Arrighi, G. (2009). *Adam Smith in Beijing: Lineages of the 21st Century.* Verso Books.

Arrighi, G. (2010). *The long twentieth century : money, power, and the origins of our times.* Verso.

Arrighi, G., & Silver, B. J. (2001). Capitalism and world (dis)order. Source[[]. Retrieved from]. *Review of International Studies, 27*(5), 257–279. https://about.jstor.org/terms. DOI: 10.1017/S0260210501008117

Arugay, A. A., & Storey, I. (2023). A Strategic Reset?: The Philippines - U.S. Alliance under President Marcos Jr., https://www.iseas.edu.sg/wp-content/uploads/2023/04/ISEAS_Perspective_2023_40.pdf

ASEAN & UNCTAD. (2023). A Special ASEAN Investment Report 2023 International investment trends: Key issues and policy options. https://asean.org/wp-content/uploads/2023/12/AIR-Special-2023.pdf

ASEAN. (2011). Guidelines for the Implementation of the DOC. https://www.asean.org/wp-content/uploads/images/archive/documents/20185-DOC.pdf

ASEAN. (2012, May 14). Declaration on the Conduct of Parties in the South China Sea. https://asean.org/declaration-on-the-conduct-of-parties-in-the-south-china-sea-2/

ASEAN. (2012, May 14). Declaration on the conduct of parties in the South China Sea. https://asean.org/declaration-on-the-conduct-of-parties-in-the-south-china-sea-2/

ASEAN. (2014). Chairman's Statement of the 17th ASEAN-China Summit. Retrieved from https://www.asean.org/wp-content/uploads/images/Chairmans_statement_of_17th_ASEAN-China_Summit.pdf

ASEAN. (n.d.). The Regional Comprehensive Economic Partnership (RCEP). https://asean.org/our-communities/economic-community/integration-with-global-economy/the-regional-comprehensive-economic-partnership-rcep/

Asia Financial (2023, December 19). Red Sea Attacks Disrupt Key Asia-Europe Sea Trade Route. https://www.asiafinancial.com/red-sea-attacks-disrupt-key-asia-europe-sea-trade-route

Asia Maritime Transparency Initiative. (n.d.). *Chinese Power Projection Capabilities in the South China Sea*. Center for Strategic and International Studies. Retrieved December 4, 2024, from https://amti.csis.org/chinese-power-projection/

Asia Pacific Foundation of Canada. (2023). *Philippines and Vietnam discuss overlapping South China Sea claims*. Retrieved from https://www.asiapacific.ca/asia-watch/philippines-vietnam-discuss-overlapping-south-china-sea

Association of Southeast Asian Nations – ASEAN. (2012). "Declaration On The Conduct Of Parties In The South China Sea". https://asean.org/declaration-on-the-conduct-of-parties-in-the-south-china-sea-2/.

Association of Southeast Asian Nations (ASEAN). (1967). The ASEAN Declaration (Bangkok Declaration). Retrieved from https://agreement.asean.org/media/download/20140117154159.pdf

Association of Southeast Asian Nations (ASEAN). (1976). The Declaration of ASEAN Concord, Bali, Indonesia, 24 February 1976. ASEAN Main Portal. Retrieved from https://asean.org

Association of Southeast Asian Nations. (1992). ASEAN Declaration on the South China Sea. Retrieved from https://asean.org/asean-declaration-south-china-sea/

Association of Southeast Asian Nations. (2002). Declaration on the conduct of parties in the South China Sea. Retrieved from https://cil.nus.edu.sg/wp-content/uploads/2017/07/2002-Declaration-on-the-Conduct-of-Parties-in-the-South-China-Sea.pdf

Association of Southeast Asian Nations. (2011). Guidelines for the Implementation of the DOC. Retrieved from https://asean.org/guidelines-implementation-doc

Association of Southeast Asian Nations. (2012). Statement of the ASEAN foreign ministers on the six-point principles on the South China Sea. Retrieved from https://www.asean.org/wpcontent/uploads/images/AFMs%20Statement%20on%206%20Principles%20on%20SCS.pdf

Association of Southeast Asian Nations. (2017). Declaration for a decade of coastal and marine environmental protection in the South China Sea (2017-2027). Retrieved from https://asean.org/wp-content/uploads/2017/11/Declaration-for-a-Decade-of-Coastal-and-Marine-Environmental-Protection-in-the-South-China-Sea-2017-2027.pdf

Aswani, R. S., Sajith, S., & Bhat, M. Y. (2022). Realigning India's Vietnam Policy Through Cooperative Sustainable Development: A Geostrategic Counterbalancing to China in Indo-Pacific. *East Asia (Piscataway, N.J.)*, *39*(2), 97–115. DOI: 10.1007/s12140-021-09371-0 PMID: 34276182

Attali, J. (2018). *Denizin Tarihi*. Kırmızı Kedi Yayınevi.

Australian Government. (2017). *2017 Foreign Policy White Paper.* Canberra: Australian Government. 1-124.

Australian Government-Department of Defence. (2020). *2020 Defence Strategic Update*. Department of Defence.

Australian Government-Department of Defence. (2023). *National Defence-Defence Strategic Review 2023*. Department of Defence.

Australian Government-Department of Defence. (2024). *National Defence Strategy 2024*. Department of Defence.

Australian Treaty Series. (1971). *Five Power Defence Arrangements*, https://www.austlii.edu.au/au/other/dfat/treaties/1971/21.html

Ayyub, R. (2016, April 13). A primer on the complicated battle for the South China Sea. *National Public Radio-NPR*. Retrieved from https://www.npr.org/sections/parallels/2016/04/13/472711435/a-primer-on-the-complicated-battle-for-the-south-china-sea

Aziz, R., Ali, A., Liaqat, B. B., & Arslan, M. (2024). ASEAN's diplomatic and strategic engagement in the South China Sea dispute: An analysis. *Journal of Social & Organizational Matters*, *3*(2), 204–224. DOI: 10.56976/jsom.v3i2.82

Baabood, A. (2024) "The Geopolitics of Economic Development in the Middle East", February 15, Carnegie Middle East Center, https://carnegie-mec.org/2024/02/15/geopolitics-of-economic-development-in-middle-east-pub-91650

Bailey, M. (2017). Supporting the wartime economy: Imperial maritime trade and the globalised maritime trade system, 1914–1916. *Journal for Maritime Research*, *19*(1), 23–45. DOI: 10.1080/21533369.2017.1331617

Baldino, D. & Bloomfield, A. (2018). The rise of the 'Indo-Pacific' in Australian grand-strategic discourse. *Indo-Pacific Insight Series*, 13, Crawley: Australia: Perth USAsia Centre.

Ball, J. (2019). *The U.S. and Vietnam are Expanding Areas of Military Cooperation, Defense and Security*, https://globalsecurityreview.com/u-s-vietnam-expanding-areas-military-cooperation/

Baskara, T. W. (2021). The Long Shadow of the Cold War: The Cold War Policies of the United States Towards Asia and Their Impact on Indonesia, *International Quarterly For. Asian Studies (Quezon City, Philippines)*, *52*, 331–347.

Basrur, R. M. (2010). Global Quest and Regional Reversal: Rising India and South Asia. *International Studies*, *47*(2-4), 267–284. DOI: 10.1177/002088171104700412

Baviera, A. S. P. (2014). *Implications of the US Philippines Enhanced Defense Cooperation Agreement, Asia Pacific Bultein*. East-West Center.

BBC (2021, June 2). South China Sea dispute: Malaysia accuses China of breaching airspace. https://www.bbc.com/news/world-asia-57328868

BBC. (2016, July 12). *South China Sea: Tribunal backs case against China brought by Philippines*. Retrieved from https://www.bbc.com/news/world-asia-china-36771749

BBC. (July 7, 2023). What is the South China Sea dispute? https://www.bbc.com/news/world-asia-pacific-13748349

Beckman, R., & Dang, V. H. (2023). ASEAN and peaceful management of maritime disputes in the South China Sea. In J. Kraska, R. Long, & M. H. Nordquist (Eds.), Peaceful maritime engagement in East Asia and the Pacific region (pp. 342-358). Brill | Nijhoff.

Beckman, R. (2013, January). The UN Convention on the Law of the Sea and the Maritime Disputes in the South China Sea. *The American Journal of International Law, 107*(1), 142–163. https://www.jstor.org/stable/10.5305/amerjintelaw.107.1.0142. DOI: 10.5305/amerjintelaw.107.1.0142

Beech, H. (2016). ''Just Where Exactly Did China Get the South China Sea Nine-Dash Line From?'', *Time*, https://time.com/4412191/nine-dash-line-9-south-china-sea/.

Bergsten, C. F., Tanji, M., & Lawson, S. (1997). Democratic Peace and Asian Democracy: A Universalist- Particularist Tension. *Alternatives, 22*(1), 135–155. DOI: 10.1177/030437549702200106

Bernama (2024, July 28). Malaysia has applied to join BRICS-Ibrahim. https://www.bernama.com/en/news.php?id=2322706#:~:text=BRICS%2C%20which%20initially%20included%20Brazil,and%20the%20United%20Arab%20Emirates

Biber, A. B., & Ateş, H. Y. (2021, March 3). *Güney Çin Denizi'nde ABD ve Çin'in güç mücadelesi*. Retrieved from TRT Haber: https://www.trthaber.com/haber/dunya/guney-cin-denizinde-abd-ve-cinin-guc-mucadelesi-566452.html

Bin Hussein, T. A. R. (1969, September 23). Text of speech by the Acting Prime Minister and Director of Operations, Tun Abdul Razak bin Hussein, at the opening of the Soviet Trade and Industrial Exhibition at Dewan Bahasa dan Pustaka, Kuala Lumpur, at 4.00 p.m. September 23, 1969. *Foreign Affairs Malaysia*, 2 (1), 22-25. https://www.kln.gov.my/documents/8390448/8418517/VOLUME+2.pdf/148bc9c1-a73e-429f-be86-9477db7a3c35?version=1.0&download=true

Bisht, I. S. (2023). Vietnam Negotiating BrahMos Missile Purchase With India: Report, The Defense Post, https://www.thedefensepost.com/2023/06/14/vietnam-brahmos-missile-india/#google_vignette

Bisley, N. (2023). Australia's Indo-Pacific Strategy: From Optimism to Hard Balancing. *Asia Policy, 18*(3), 35–45. DOI: 10.1353/asp.2023.a903862

Blarel, N. (2012) India: the next superpower?: India's soft power: from potential to reality? IDEAS reports - special reports, Kitchen, Nicholas (ed.) SR010. LSE IDEAS, London School of Economics and Political Science, London, UK.

Blaxland, J., & Sharma, A. (2021). *Bolstering the Quad beyond its military dimensions.*https://www.eastasiaforum.org/2021/04/30/bolstering-the-quad-beyond-its-military-dimensions/, accessed on March 5, 2024.

Bonesh, F. R. (2024). India-Malaysia Economic Partnership: Challenges, Prospects, and Strategic Collaborations, *India Briefing*, https://www.india-briefing.com/news/india-malaysia-economic-partnership-challenges-prospects-and-strategic-collaborations-30687.html/

BRIA. (2018). ''The Dispute Over The SCS'', https://teachdemocracy.org /images/pdf/members/bria_33_2.pdf.

Britannica (n.d.(a)). Peranakan. https://www.britannica.com/topic/Peranakan

Britannica (n.d.(b)). Sultanate of Malacca. https://www.britannica.com/place/sultanate-of-Malacca

Britannica (The Editors of Encyclopedia Britannica) (2024, June 4). Strait of Malacca. https://www.britannica.com/place/Strait-of-Malacca

Britannica, *Philippinnes,* https://www.britannica.com/place/Philippines

Brodie, B. (1965). *A Guide To Naval Strategy*. Praeger.

Brunnstrom, D., & Blanchard, B. (2016, July 13). South China Sea ruling will 'intensify conflict', says Chinese envoy. *Malaysiakini.* https://www.malaysiakini.com/news/348366

Bueger, C. (2015). What is maritime security? *Marine Policy*, *53*, 159–164. DOI: 10.1016/j.marpol.2014.12.005

Bueger, C., & Edmunds, T. (2017). Beyond seablindness: A new agenda for maritime security studies. *International Affairs*, *93*(6), 1293–1311. DOI: 10.1093/ia/iix174

Burgess, S. (2020). *Confronting China's Maritime Expansion in the South China Sea*, https://media.defense.gov/2020/Aug/31/2002488087/-1/-1/1/BURGESS.PDF

Burgess, H., & Burgess, G. (2010). *Conducting Track II peacemaking*. United States Institute of Peace.

Burgess, J. P. (2003, March). The Politics of the South China Sea: Territoriality and International Law. *Security Dialogue*, *34*(1), 7–10. DOI: 10.1177/09670106030341002

Busbarat, P., Camba, A., Pratiwi, F. I., Po, S., Đ , H., Sengkhamkhoutlavong, B., Yean, T. S., & Thuzar, M. (2023, December 5). How Has China's Belt and Road Initiative Impacted Southeast Asian Countries? https://carnegieendowment.org/posts/2023/12/how-has-chinas-belt-and-road-initiative-impacted-southeast-asian-countries?lang=en

Business Wire. (2020, July 22). *Taiwan Donates Over 51 Million Masks to Countries Worldwide*. Retrieved from https://www.businesswire.com/news/home/20200722005405/en/Taiwan-Donates-Over-51-Million-Masks-to-Countries-Worldwide

Buszynski, L. (2013). The development of the South China Sea Maritime Dispute. In L. Buszynski & C. Roberts (Eds.), The South China Sea Security Environment (pp. 3-7). National Security College Occasional Paper No. 5.

Buszynski, L. (2013, September 5). The development of the South China Sea maritime dispute. (L. Buszynski, & L. Buszynski-, Eds.) *National Security College Occasional Paper*, pp. 3-7.

Buszynski, L. (2010). Rising Tensions in the South China Sea: Prospects for a Resolution of the Issue. *Security Challenges*, *6*(2), 85–104.

Buszynski, L. (2020). The Development of South China Sea Disputes. In Buszynski, L., & Hai, D. T. (Eds.), *The South China Sea: From a Regional Maritime Dispute to Geo-strategic Competition* (pp. 1–8). Routledge.

Butista, L. (2016). The Philippines and the Arbitral Tribunal's Award: A Sombre Victory and Uncertain Times Ahead. *Contemporary Southeast Asia*, *38*(2), 349–355.

Caballero-Anthony, M. (2005). *Regional security in Southeast Asia: Beyond the ASEAN way*. Institute of Southeast Asian Studies. DOI: 10.1355/9789812307095

Cain, B. (2021). To Deepen and Broaden Our Presence: Taiwan's Strategies for Participating in the International System. China Research Center. Retrieved from https://www.chinacenter.net/2021/china-currents/20-1/to-deepen-and-broaden-our-presence-taiwans-strategies-for-participating-in-the-international-system/

Campling, L., & Colas, A. (2021). *Capitalism and the Sea: The Maritime Factor in the Making of the Modern World*. Verso.

Carauna, A. (2023). ''Maritime Affairs Program (MAP) Handbill Spotlight'', ICAS, https://chinaus-icas.org/research/map-spotlight-nine-dash-line/.

Caşın, M. H. (2022). In Caşın, M. H., Kısacık, S., & Donduran, C. (Eds.), *"Yükselen Çin Deniz Gücünün Küresel Güç Dengelerine Yansıması", in 21. Yüzyılda Bütün Boyutlarıyla Çin Halk Cumhuriyeti 1. Cilt* (pp. 278–340). Nobel Akademik Yayıncılık.

Castro, R. C. D. (2019). *Incident at Reed Bank: A Crisis in the Philippines' China Policy*, https://amti.csis.org/incident-at-reed-bank-a-crisis-in-the-philippines-china-policy/

Çebi, T. (2024). *Güney Çin Denizi'ndeki Amerika-Çin Rekabetinde Filipinler,* 20 April 2024 https://www.turksam.org/detay-guney-cin-denizi-ndeki-amerika-cin-rekabetinde-filipinler

Center for Preventive Action. (May, 2024). Territorial Disputes in South China Sea, *CFR,*https://www.cfr.org/global-conflict-tracker/conflict/territorial-disputes-south-china-sea

Chang, I.-J. (2020, July 15). *Taiwan's Delicate Balancing Act in the South China Sea.* Retrieved from Global Taiwan Institute: https://globaltaiwan.org/2020/07/taiwans-delicate-balancing-act-in-the-south-china-sea/

Chang, T. K. (1991). China's Claim of Sovereignty over Spratly and Paracel Islands: A Historical and Legal Perspective. *Case Western Reserve Journal of International Law, 23*(3), 399–420.

Chang, Y.-Y. (2021). The post-pandemic world: Between constitutionalized and authoritarian orders–China's narrative-power play in the pandemic era. *Journal of Chinese Political Science, 26*(1), 27–65. DOI: 10.1007/s11366-020-09695-3 PMID: 33071536

Charter, A. S. E. A. N. (1967). The ASEAN Charter. Retrieved from https://asean.org

Cheeppensook, K. (2020). ASEAN in the South China Sea Conflict, 2012–2018: A lesson in conflict transformation from normative power Europe. *International Economics and Economic Policy, 17*(3), 747–764. DOI: 10.1007/s10368-020-00477-z

Chellaney, B. (2023). The Sino-Indian Rivalry is Reshaping Asia, *Project Syndicate,* https://www.project-syndicate.org/commentary/china-cannot-win-india-himalayan-border-dispute-by-brahma-chellaney-2023-04

Chen, W. C., Ou, C. H., Yang, M. H., Shih, Y. C. (2024). "China's gray zone actions in the East China Sea, Taiwan Strait, and South China Sea: A comparative study and impact on fisheries", *Marine Policy* (167): 1-12, https://doi.org/.DOI: 10.1016/j.marpol.2024.106246

Chen, H.-Y. (2016, August). Republic of China's Decision-Making Process in Regards to Drawing a U-shaped Line on the Map of the South China Seaand Its Implications. *Pacific Focus, 31*(2), 283–306. DOI: 10.1111/pafo.12074

Chiang, H.-c. (2015, April 2). *Itu Aba claim a distracting waste.* Retrieved from Taipei Times: https://www.taipeitimes.com/News/editorials/archives/2015/04/02/2003614945

China Daily. (2022, December 21). *Xi says China ready to advance relations with Australia based on mutual respect, win-win principles*. Retrieved from http://www.chinadaily.com.cn/a/202212/21/WS63a29bb8a31057c47eba57c1.html

China Diaoyu Dao. (2015, January 25). *The Cairo Declaration and its implications for the Diaoyu Dao issue*. Retrieved from https://www.diaoyudao.org.cn/en/2015-01/25/content_34649421.htm

China Observers in Central and Eastern Europe. (2023). The porcupine strategy: Taiwan's road to self-defense. Retrieved from https://chinaobservers.eu/the-porcupine-strategy-taiwans-road-to-self-defense/

China Power. (n.d.), "How Much Trade Transits the South China Sea?", https://chinapower.csis.org/much-trade-transits-south-china-sea/.

Chinese Society of International Law. (2018). The South China Sea Arbitration Awards: A Critical Study. [Retrieved from Chinese Society of International Law.]. *Chinese Journal of International Law*, •••, 207–748.

Chong, A. (2023). *Still waters run deep: Taiwan's South China Sea strategy*. Clingendael Spectator. Retrieved December 4, 2024, from https://spectator.clingendael.org/en/publication/still-waters-run-deep-taiwans-south-china-sea-strategy

Chong, J. (2013). The South China Sea Disputes: some documentary context. chinese Law & Government, 46(3-4), 3-9. DOI: 10.2753/CLG0009-4609460300

Chuang, S. (2023). The Taiwan problem. *International Journal of Arts Humanities & Social Science*, *04*(03), 27–30. DOI: 10.56734/ijahss.v4n3a3

Chung, L. (2016, July 13). *Tsai Ing-wen tells warship crew to defend Taiwan's interests as they set off for island in South China Sea.* Retrieved from South China Morning Post: https://www.scmp.com/news/china/diplomacy-defence/article/1989282/tsai-ing-wen-tells-warship-crew-defend-taiwans

Clark, H. (2019, September 11). *Rumours ExxonMobil to quit Vietnamese gas field.*, " Energy News Bulletin: https://www.energynewsbulletin.net/finance-legal/news/1371306/rumours-exxonmobil-to-quit-vietnamese-gas-field adresinden alındı

Clayman, T. (2023, December 22). *China's New Map: The 10-Dash Line*. Retrieved from Boston Political Review: https://www.bostonpoliticalreview.org/post/china-s-new-map-the-10-dash-line

Clayman, T. (2023, December 22). China's New Map: The 10-Dash Line. *The Boston Political Review.*https://www.bostonpoliticalreview.org/post/china-s-new-map-the-10-dash-line

Congressional Research Service. (2015). *The Trans Pacific Partnership: Strategic Implications*, https://sgp.fas.org/crs/row/R44361.pdf

Congressional Research Service. (2023). *The "Quad": Cooperations Among the United States, Japan, India, and Australia*, https://crsreports.congress.gov/product/pdf/IF/IF11678

Congressional Research Service. (2024). *Taiwan: Background and U.S. Relations*, https://crsreports.congress.gov/product/pdf/IF/IF10275

Connoly, A. (2024). *US ASEAN Relations Grow as Tensions Rise in the South China Sea*, https://www.irinsider.org/home/3w322tz4r44s8zp-ezmt5-7223k-zrbkr-2d9wr-ww4nr

Conrad, M. P. B. (2017). China's Access to Gwadar Port: Strategic Implications and Options for India. *Maritime Affairs*, *13*(1), 55–62. DOI: 10.1080/09733159.2017.1317123

Cook, M. (2021). *Australia's South China Sea challenges*. Sydney: The Lowy Institute-. *Policy Brief*, •••, 1–22.

Cordesman, A. H. (2022). The Other Side of Chinese Sea Power: 'White Area Warfare'.

Cordesman, A. H., Burke, A. A., & Molot, M. (2019). The Critical Role of Chinese Trade in the South China Sea. Report by Center for Strategic and International Studies (CSIS). http://www.jstor.com/stable/resrep22586.30

Council on Foreign Relations. (2024). *Timeline: China's Maritime Disputes*. Retrieved from https://www.cfr.org/timeline/chinas-maritime-disputes

Council on Foreign Relations. https://www.cfr.org/timeline/chinas-maritime-disputes#!/chinas-maritime-disputes?cid=otr-marketing_use-china_sea_InfoGuide

Country Profile from the Maritime Awareness Project Malaysia. (2020, September 15). Retrieved from The National Bureau of Asian Research: https://www.nbr.org/publication/malaysia/

Dabas, M. (2017). *Here Is All You Should Know About 'String Of Pearls', China's Policy To Encircle India*.https://www.indiatimes.com/news/india/here-is-all-you-should-know-about-string-of-pearls-china-s-policy-to-encircle-india-324315.html, accessed on March 12, 2024.

Dar, K. B. (2023). "The South China Sea dispute and Sino-Vietnamese reconciliation", *Journal of International Studies* 19(1): 37-59. https://doi.org/.DOI: 10.32890/jis2023.19.1.2

Dar, A. I. (2021). India-Vietnam Axis and China: The Allure of Hedging. *India Quarterly*, *77*(2), 252–268. DOI: 10.1177/09749284211005011

Darmawan, A. B. (2020). Japan's Balanced Strategy to Face China's Threat in South China Sea Dispute. *Jurnal Ilmu Sosial*, *19*(2), 137–159. DOI: 10.14710/jis.19.2.2020.137-159

Das, D. (2024). Revisiting the contours of the evolving Middle Eastern order through the India-Middle East-EU Corridor: Mapping India's scopes and limitations. *Asian Journal of Political Science*, *32*(1), 1–22. DOI: 10.1080/02185377.2024.2322498

Dat, T. D. (2023). *Vietnam establishes diplomatic relations with the 192nd country.* https://thanhnien.vn/viet-nam-thiet-lap-quan-he-ngoai-giao-voi-quoc-gia-thu-192-185230202163546862.htm, accessed on March 15, 2024

Davis, L. (1989). Revolutionary Struggle In The Philippines. *Palgrave Macmillan London*, *1989*. Advance online publication. DOI: 10.1007/978-1-349-19862-7

de Castro, R. C. (2009). The US-Philippine Alliance: An Evolving Hedge against an Emerging China Challenge. *Contemporary Southeast Asia: A Journal of International and Strategic Affairs 31*(3), 399-423. https://www.muse.jhu.edu/article/370828

de Castro, R. C. (2019). *Incident at Reed Bank: A Crisis in the Phillipines' China Policy,* June 20, 2019, https://amti.csis.org/incident-at-reed-bank-a-crisis-in-the-philippines-china-policy/

de Castro, R. C. (2020). *Implications of the Recent Philippines-China Naval Stand-Off,* 07.05.2020, https://amti.csis.org/implications-of-the-recent-philippines-china-naval-stand-off/

Debates, R. (2020). India's 'Act East' Policy and Regional Cooperation, *Observer Research Foundation (ORF),* https://www.orfonline.org/expert-speak/indias-act-east-policy-and-regional-cooperation-61375

Declaration on The Conduct of Parties in The South China Sea. (2012, May 14). Retrieved from ASEAN: https://asean.org/declaration-on-the-conduct-of-parties-in-the-south-china-sea-2/

Department of Defense. (2019). *Annual Freedom of Navigation Report*, https://policy.defense.gov/Portals/11/Documents/FY19%20DoD%20FON%20Report%20FINAL.pdf?ver=2020-07-14-140514-643&timestamp=1594749943344

Department of Foreign Affairs of the Philippines. (2013, November 14). PHL embassy expresses gratitude for assistance from the Malaysian government and, general public for Yolanda victims. https://dfa.gov.ph/authentication-functions/148-typhoon-yolanda/1281-phl-embassy-expresses-gratitude-for-assistance-from-malaysian-government-general-public-for-yolanda-victims

Dewi, I. F., & Dewi, K. U. (2019, October). Strategi Pemerintahan Xi Jinping terhadap Taiwan dalam Mengamankan Kedaulatan Tiongkok. *Jurnal Hubungan International*, *7*(2), 161–168.

Dinh, Q. D. (2022). *Great achievements of the country after 35 years of implementing the renovation policy initiated and led by the Party.*http://dukcqtw.dcs.vn/nhung-thanh-tuu-to-lon-cua-dat-nuoc-sau-35-nam-thuc-hien-duong-loi-doi-moi-do-dang-khoi-xuong-va-lanh-dao-duk15671.aspx, accessed on March 19, 2024

Doanh, L. D. (2021). *Clarifying the path forward.*https://tuoitre.vn/vach-ro-con-duong-di-toi-20210826114737271.htm, accessed on March 5, 2024.

Dolven, B., Campbell, C., & Ronald O'Rourke. (2023). *China Primer: South China Sea Disputes.* the Congressional Research Service.

Dolven, B., Elsea, J. K., Lawrence, S. V., O'Rourke, R., & Rinehart, I. E. (2015). *Chinese Land Reclamation in the South China Sea: Implications and Policy Options.* Congressional Research Service. Retrieved from https://sgp.fas.org/crs/row/R44072.pdf

Donnellon-May, G. (2023). India and China's rivalry is reshaping South Asia, *ASPI The Strategist*, https://www.aspistrategist.org.au/india-and-chinas-rivalry-is-reshaping-south-asia/

Do, T. T. (2022). Vietnam's Emergence as a Middle Power in Asia: Unfolding the Power-Knowledge Nexus. *Journal of Current Southeast Asian Affairs*, *41*(2), 279–302. DOI: 10.1177/18681034221081146

Dugin, A. G. (1997). *Foundations of Geopolitics*. Arktogeja.

Dunst, C. (2021). *Chinese aggression pushes Vietnam ever closer to Washington.* https://asia.nikkei.com/Opinion/Chinese-aggression-pushes-Vietnam-ever-closer-to-Washington, accessed on March 15, 2024

Duong, L. H., & Hong, D. T. M. (2019). South China Sea - Natural Resources in Vietnam. *European Journal of Engineering and Technology Research*, *4*(9), 65–69.

Eco-Business. (2013), "South China Sea energy profile: critical world trade route and potential source of hydrocarbons", 12 February 2013, https://www.eco-business.com/news/south-china-sea-energy-profile-critical-world-trade-route-and-potential-source-of-hydrocarbons/.

Edmonstone, G. (2024, April 2). China's trade restrictions on Australian exports. *USSC*. Retrieved from https://www.ussc.edu.au/chinas-trade-restrictions-on-australian-exports

EIA. (2017). *The Strait of Malacca, a key oil trade chokepoint, links the Indian and Pacific Oceans*.https://www.eia.gov/todayinenergy/detail.php?id=32452, accessed on January 13, 2025.

EIA. (2024). ''Regional Analysis Brief: SCS'', https://www.eia.gov/international/analysis/regions-of-interest/South_China_Sea.

Elmali, B. (2023) "Unrest in the Middle East Is Bad for Both CPEC and IMEC", Retrieved from The Diplomat: https://thediplomat.com/2023/11/unrest-in-the-middle-east-is-bad-for-both-cpec-and-imec/

Embassy of Malaysia. Beijing (2023). Important announcement on visa exemptions for Chinese passport holders. https://www.kln.gov.my/web/chn_beijing/news-from-mission/-/blogs/visa-exemptions-for-chinese-passport-holders?_33_redirect=%2Fweb%2Fchn_beijing%2Farchives

Embassy of Malaysia. Beijing (2024, January 30). Ambassador of Malaysia Presents Letter of Credence to President Xi Jinping. https://www.kln.gov.my/web/chn_beijing/home/-/asset_publisher/uilwCm9JrwYv/blog/ambassador-of-malaysia-presents-letter-of-credence-to-president-xi-jinping?inheritRedirect=false&redirect=https%3A%2F%2Fwww.kln.gov.my%2Fweb%2Fchn_beijing%2Fhome%3Fp_p_id%3D101_INSTANCE_uilwCm9JrwYv%26p_p_lifecycle%3D0%26p_p_state%3Dnormal%26p_p_mode%3Dview%26p_p_col_id%3D_118_INSTANCE_NF5xaQSGH7fe__column-2%26p_p_col_count%3D2

Emmers, R. (2010). "The changing power distribution in the South China Sea: Implications for conflict management and avoidance", *Political Science* 62 (2): 118-131, https://doi.org/.DOI: 10.1177/0032318710381519

Emmerson, D. K. (2017). ASEAN between China and America: Is it time to try horsing the cow? TRaNS: Trans-Regional and -National Studies of Southeast Asia, 5(1), 1–23. DOI: 10.1017/trn.2016.31

Emmers, R. (2003). *Cooperative Security and the Balance of Power in ASEAN and the ARF*. Routledge Curzon Taylor & Francis Group. DOI: 10.4324/9780203401064

Emmers, R. (2010). *Geopolitics and Maritime Territorial Disputes in East Asia.* Routledge.

Erickson, A. S., & Wuthnow, J. (2016). *Why Islands Still Matter in Asia: The Enduring Significance of the Pacific Island Chains*. https://www.andrewerickson.com/2016/02/why-islands-still-matter-in-asia-the-enduring-significance-of-the-pacific-island-chains/

Eurasia Review. (2024). "South China Sea Energy Profile: Critical World Trade Route – Analysis", 25 March 2024, https://www.eurasiareview.com/25032024-south-china-sea-energy-profile-critical-world-trade-route-analysis/.

European Commision. (2021) "EU trade relations – India", Retrieved from European Commission, https://policy.trade.ec.europa.eu/eu-trade-relationships-country-and-region/countries-and-regions/india_en

European Parliament. (2023, April 20). Resolution on EU-Taiwan political relations and cooperation. https://www.europarl.europa.eu/doceo/document/TA-9-2023-0139_EN.html

Evelyn, G. (2016), *Southeast Asian Strategies Toward the Great Powers: Still Hedging After All These Years*, hxp://www.theasanforum.org/southeast-asian-strategies-toward-the-great-powers-s^ll-hedging-a~er-all-these-years/

Evers, H. D. (2014). Nusantara: Malaysia and the Governance of the South China Sea. The 9th International Malaysian Studies Conference (MSC9) Malaysia's Development: 2020 and Beyond. 18 –20 August 2014. Universiti Malaysia Terengganu. https://www.researchgate.net/publication/265057806

Feith, H. (1962). *The Decline of Constitutional Democracy in Indonesia.* Cornell University Press.

Feldman, N., Eiran, E., & Rubin, A. (2021). Naval Power and Effects of Third-Party Trade on Conflict. *The Journal of Conflict Resolution*, *65*(2–3), 342–371. DOI: 10.1177/0022002720958180

Feldt, L., Roell, P., & Thiele, R. D. (2013). ISPSW Strategy Series: Focus on Defense and International Security Maritime Security-Perspectives for a Comprehensive Approach Maritime Security-Perspectives for a Comprehensive Approach. Retrieved from http://www.ispsw.de

Felsenthal, M., & Spetalnick, M. (2014). *Obama says U.S. commitment to defend Philippines 'ironclad',* April 29, 2014, https://www.reuters.com/article/2014/04/29/us-philippines-usa-obama-idUSBREA3S02T20140429/

Fernandez, A. M. (1976). The Philippines and the U.S. Today, *Southeast. Asian Affairs*, •••, 269–308.

Flemming, T. (2023, September 1). *The South China Sea has been contested for decades, so what does China's new map mean?* Retrieved from ABC News: https://www.abc.net.au/news/2023-09-01/why-chinas-latest-map-is-causing-new-south-china-sea-conflict/102803902

Fomenko, T. (2024). *The US is cultivating an antagonist to China in Beijing's own backyard,* 25.03.2024, https://www.rt.com/news/594824-us-china-philippines-antagonist/

Foreign Ministry Spokesperson Mao Ning's Regular Press Conference on-March5,2024. (2024, March 5). Retrieved from Embassy of the People's Republic of China in the United States of America: http://us.china-embassy.gov.cn/eng/fyrth/202403/t20240305_11254066.htm

Formosa 2. (2023, May 16). *Formosa 2 marks the first Round 2 offshore wind farm completed in Taiwan and continues to build a greener future*. Retrieved from https://formosa2windpower.com/en/formosa-2-marks-the-first-round-2-offshore-wind-farm-completed-in-taiwan-and-continues-to-build-a-greener-future/

France 24. (2022, September 3). *US approves $1.1 billion arms package for Taiwan, angering China*. Retrieved from https://www.france24.com/en/asia-pacific/20220903-us-approves-1-1-billion-arms-package-for-taiwan-angering-china

Freedom House. (2023). Taiwan: Freedom in the World 2023 Country Report. Retrieved from https://freedomhouse.org/country/taiwan/freedom-world/2023

Freeman, C. P. (2018). China's 'regionalism foreign policy' and China-India relations in South Asia. *Contemporary Politics, 24*(1), 81–97. DOI: 10.1080/13569775.2017.1408168

Galvez, D. (2023, March 1). Malaysia vows continuing support for Mindanao peace, aid to Bangsamoro. https://globalnation.inquirer.net/211584/malaysia-vows-continued-support-for-mindanao-peace-process-continued-aid-to-bangsamoro-people

Gao, Z., & Jia, B. B. (2013). The nine-dash line in the South China Sea: History,status, and implications. *The American Journal of International Law, 107*(1), 98–124. DOI: 10.5305/amerjintelaw.107.1.0098

Garnier, L. (2012). *Multilateral resolution of disputes in the South China Sea.*https://vietnamnet.vn/giai-quyet-da-phuong-tranh-chap-bien-dong-72659.html, accessed on June 12, 2024.

Gerace, M. P. (1991). Between Mackinder and Spykman: Geopolitics, containment, and after. *Comparative Strategy*, *10*(4), 347–364. DOI: 10.1080/01495939108402855

Gill, D. M. (2021). *India is sailing into the South China Sea with more than China on its mind.* https://www.scmp.com/comment/opinion/article/3144544/india-sailing-south-china-sea-more-china-its-mind, accessed on June 22, 2024.

Gilpin, R. (1987). The Political Economy of International Relations.

Ginanjar, W., Pramono, B., & Priyanto, P. (2023). Overviewing the context of the balance of power to the South China Sea issue in ASEAN. *International Journal of Humanities Education and Social Sciences (Ijhess)*, *2*(4). Advance online publication. DOI: 10.55227/ijhess.v2i4.372

Global Data. (2022). Vietnam Defense Market. https://www.globaldata.com/reports/vietnam-defense-market-2022-free-report/, accessed on May 12, 2024.

Global Nation Inquirer. (2015, June 30). *Taiwan promotes its island claim in South China Sea*. Retrieved from https://globalnation.inquirer.net/126376/taiwan-promotes-its-island-claim-in-south-china-sea

Global Taiwan Institute. (2020, July 15). *Taiwan's South China Sea Policy: Sovereignty and Pragmatism.* Retrieved from https://globaltaiwan.org/2020/07/vol-5-issue-14/

Global Times (2024a, February 26). Malaysian PM's remarks reveal US' self-entertaining hegemonic diplomacy. https://www.globaltimes.cn/page/202402/1307708.shtml

Global Times (2024b, April 26). China willing to cooperate with Malaysia in standing up for justice on intl stage, opposing unilateralism: official. https://www.globaltimes.cn/page/202404/1311325.shtml

Global Times (2024c, June 23). US profits from confrontations it provokes in Ukraine, South China Sea: Mahathir. https://www.globaltimes.cn/page/202406/1314662.shtml

Global Times. (2023, May 9). Exclusive: GT's interview with former Prime Minister of Malaysia Mahathir bin Mohamad. https://www.globaltimes.cn/page/202305/1290398.shtml

Gomez, E. (2023). *Taiwan's Urgent Need for Asymmetric Defense* (Policy Analysis No. 965). Cato Institute. Retrieved December 4, 2024, from https://www.cato.org/policy-analysis/taiwans-urgent-need-asymmetric-defense

Gomez, J. (2023). *Philippines confronts Chinese diplomats over sea disputes,* 24.03.2023, https://apnews.com/article/china-philippines-south-china-sea-disputes-70ea7983dbf67b1f9ae5264c6ce9271a

Gong, X. (2019). The Belt & Road Initiative and China's influence in Southeast Asia. *The Pacific Review*, *32*(4), 635–665. DOI: 10.1080/09512748.2018.1513950

Government of Malaysia. (n.d.). Summary Of Malaysia's History. https://www.malaysia.gov.my/portal/content/30120

Gragnani, L. (2022). *Assessing Tsai Ying-wen's strategy in the South China Sea* (Unpublished master thesis). Charles University-Faculty of Social Sciences, Prague.

Greitens, S. C. (2016), *The US Philippines Alliance in a Year of Transition: Challenges and Opportunuties*, Center for Asian Policy Studies, Brookings Working Paper.

Gresh, F., G. (. (2017). A Vital Maritime Pinch Point: China, the Bab al-Mandeb, and the Middle East. *Asian Journal of Middle Eastern and Islamic Studies*, *11*(1), 37–46. DOI: 10.1080/25765949.2017.12023324

Grossman, D. (2024). How to Respond to China's Tactics in the South China Sea. RAND Corporation. https://www.rand.org/pubs/commentary/2024/06/how-to-respond-to-chinas-tactics-in-the-south-china.html

Groten, D. (2019). *How Sentiment Matters in International Relations: China and the South China Sea Dispute*. Verlag Barbara Budrich. DOI: 10.2307/j.ctvmd84bx

Guoqiang, L. (2015). ''China Sea Oil and Gas Resources'', CIIS, https://www.ciis.org.cn/english/COMMENTARIES/202007/t20200715_2762.html.

Gupta, A. (2020). Global Strike vs. Globalization: The US-China Rivalry and the BRI. In Leandro, F. J. B. S., & Duarte, P. A. B. (Eds.), *The Belt and Road Initiative: An Old Archetype of a New Development Model*. Palgrave Macmillan. DOI: 10.1007/978-981-15-2564-3_3

Guzman, C. (2023). Philippines Coast Guard Accuses China of Blinding Crew With 'Military-Grade' Laser, *Time*, https://time.com/6255012/philippines-laser-south-china-sea-tensions-escalate/

Habru, P. (2023, April 17). *China's influence weighs heavily on Solomon Islands election*. 360info. Retrieved from https://360info.org/chinas-influence-weighs-heavily-on-solomon-islands-election/

Hagström, L., & Gustafsson, K. (2019). Narrative power: How storytelling shapes East Asian international politics. *Cambridge Review of International Affairs*, *32*(4), 387–406. DOI: 10.1080/09557571.2019.1623498

Hahn, L. C. (2024, April 18). Revitalising US relations with Southeast Asia through public diplomacy. https://eastasiaforum.org/2024/04/18/revitalising-us-relations-with-southeast-asia-through-public-diplomacy/

Haidar, S. (2023). India supports Philippines' sovereignty, says Jaishankar, sparking response from China, *The Hindu*, https://www.thehindu.com/news/national/india-supports-philippines-in-upholding-its-national-sovereignty-eam-jaishankar/article67993485.ece

Ha, L. T., & Phuc, N. D. (2019). The US-China Trade War: Impact on Vietnam. *Yusof Ishak Institue, 102*(3), 2–6.

Hall, I., & Ganguly, Š. (2022). Introduction: Narendra Modi and India's foreign policy. *International Politics, 59*(1), 1–8. DOI: 10.1057/s41311-021-00363-8

Hammer, L. (2020). Taiwan and Itu Aba (Taiping): Creating an 'Island for All' in the South China Sea. International Journal of Taiwan Studies.

Ha, N. T. T. (2018). Improving the effectiveness of Vietnam's relations with major countries in the current period. *Journal of Theoretical Education, 272*, 25–34.

Harding, S. D. (2024). There and Back and There Again: U.S. Military Base in the Philippines, https://www.usni.org/magazines/proceedings/2024/may/there-and-back-and-there-again-us-military-bases-philippines

Hayton, B. (2017, July 21). *The Week Donald Trump Lost the South China Sea.* Foreign Policy: https://foreignpolicy.com/2017/07/31/the-week-donald-trump-lost-the-south-china-sea/ adresinden alındı

Hayton, B. (2019). The Modern Origins of China's South China Sea Claims. *Modern China, 45*(2), 127-170. doi:i.org/10.1177/0097700418771678

Hayton, B. (2014). *The South China Sea: The struggle for power in Asia.* Yale University Press.

Hayton, B. (2019). The Modern Origins of China's South China Sea Claims: Maps, Misunderstandings, and Maritime Geobody. *Modern China, 45*(3), 127–170. DOI: 10.1177/0097700418771678

Hazarika, O. B., & Mishra, V. (2016). South Asia As A Battleground: Soft Power Contestation between India and China. *World Affairs: The Journal of International Issues, 20*(3), 112–129. https://www.jstor.org/stable/48505297

He, B. (2018). Security Regionalism: A New Form of Strategic Competition or Cooperation between the United States and China in the South China Sea? In Feng, H., & He, K. (Eds.), *US-China Competition and the South China Sea Disputes* (pp. 151–169). Routledge. DOI: 10.4324/9781351214308-10

He, K., & Feng, H. (2023). *After Hedging: Hard Choices for the Indo-Pacific States Between the United States and China*. Cambridge University Press. DOI: 10.1017/9781009420570

Hernik, J. (2022, April 22). Australia's Role in the Indo-Pacific Strategy of the United States. *Warsaw Institute*. Retrieved from https://warsawinstitute.org/australias-role-indo-pacific-strategy-united-states/

Herscovitch, B. (2017). *A Balanced Threat Assessment of China's South China Sea Policy.* Cato Institute. Retrieved from http://www.jstor.com/stable/resrep04873

Herscovitch, B. (2023, March 15). China's sound and fury over Aukus will mean little for ties with Australia. *The Guardian*. Retrieved from https://t.ly/D1qT3

Heydarian, R. J. (2021, October 5). *Malaysia, China go head to head in South China Sea*. Retrieved from Asia Times: https://asiatimes.com/2021/10/malaysia-china-go-head-to-head-in-south-china-sea/

Hiebert, M., Nguyen, P., & Poling, G. B. (2015). *Building a More Robust US-Philippines Alliance*, https://csis-website-prod.s3.amazonaws.com/s3fs-public/legacy_files/files/publication/150824_Heibert_USPhilippinesAlliance_Web.pdf

Hiep, T. X., & Kiet, L. H. (2024). India's competitive strategy with China in Southeast Asia: An analysis of the case of Vietnam. *Journal of Chinese Studies*, *2*(270), 68–80.

Ho, C. H., & Lee, K. (2023). Sustainable fisheries under net-zero emissions: A case study of the Taiwan Fishery Administration. In H. H. Wu, W. Y. Liu, & M. C. Huang (Eds.), Moving toward net-zero carbon society (pp. 91–105). Springer Climate. Springer, Cham. DOI: 10.1007/978-3-031-24545-9_6

Holmes, J. R. (2014). Strategic Features of the South China Sea. *Naval War College Review*, *67*(2), 30–49.

Holsti, K. J. (1970). National role conceptions in the study of foreign policy. *International Studies Quarterly*, *14*(3), 233–309. DOI: 10.2307/3013584

Hongbin, D., & Ullah, I. (2022). The South China Sea's Nine-Dash Line: Key Disputes Andchina's Historical Rights Claims. [JPCS]. *Journal of Pakistan-China Studies*, *3*(1), 67–86. DOI: 10.55733/jpcs.v3i1.53

Hong, Z. (2013). The South China Sea Dispute and China-ASEAN Relations. *Asian Affairs*, *44*(1), 27–43. DOI: 10.1080/03068374.2012.760785

Honrada, G. (2024, October 20). *Vietnam imitating China's island-making in South China Sea*. Asia Times. Retrieved from https://asiatimes.com/2024/10/vietnam-imitating-chinas-island-making-in-south-china-sea/

Hossain, K. (2013). The unclos and the us-china hegemonic competition over the South China Sea. *Journal of East Asia and International Law*, *6*(1). Advance online publication. https://www.usitc.gov/publications/332/executive_briefings/ebot_us_taiwan_trade.pdf. DOI: 10.14330/jeail.2013.6.1.05

Hostetler, L. (2024). China's Nine-Dash Line: Cartographic Science and the Adoption of New Map Languages in the Transition from Empire to Nation State. In *Reimagining the Globe and Cultural Exchange* (pp. 293–320). Brill., DOI: 10.1163/9789004684782_012

Hsiung, J. C. (1995). "China's Omni-Directional Diplomacy: Realignment to Cope with Monopolar U.S. Power", *Asian Survey* 35 (6): 573-586. https://doi.org/10.2307/2645710.

Huang, K. (2022, November 7). *Fortified South China Sea artificial islands project Beijing's military reach and power, say observers*. South China Morning Post. Retrieved from https://www.scmp.com/news/china/diplomacy/article/3198504/fortified-south-china-sea-artificial-islands-project-beijings-military-reach-and-power-say-observers

Huang, Q.-z., Wang, W.-z., Li, Y. S., & Li, C. W. (1994). Current Characteristics Of The South China Sea. In *Oceanology of China Seas* (pp. 39-47).

Huang, Y. (2016). Understanding China's Belt & Road Initiative: Motivation, framework and assessment. *China Economic Review*, *40*, 314–321. DOI: 10.1016/j.chieco.2016.07.007

Hundler, B. (2018). Duterte's Pivot to China and Prospects for Settling the South China Sea Disputes. *Contexto Internacional*, *40*(2), 322–330. DOI: 10.1590/s0102-8529.2018400200005

Huynh, N. T. T. (2023). *Taiwan-Vietnam Cooperation in the Blue Economy*. Taiwan-Asia Exchange Foundation. Retrieved from https://www.taef.org/doc/1314

Huynh, T. S. (2022, October 4). *UNCLOS's relevance to Taiwan amid a raging storm*. Fulcrum. Retrieved from https://fulcrum.sg/uncloss-relevance-to-taiwan-amid-a-raging-storm/

Huynh, T. S., & Truong, T. T. K. (2024, November 9). *Taiwan's Struggle to Retain Diplomatic Allies*. The Diplomat. Retrieved from https://thediplomat.com/2024/11/taiwans-struggle-to-retain-diplomatic-allies/

Huysal, B. (2015, July-August). Güney Çin Denizi'nde Kriz: Çin Halk Cumhuriyeti'nin Ada İnşa/Arazi Genişletme. *Bahçeşehir Üniversitesi Hukuk Fakültesi Dergisi, 10*(131-132), pp. 53-82. Retrieved from https://www.jurix.com.tr/article/4608?u=0&c=0

Hwang, Y. J., & Frettingham, E. (2021). *Maritime and Territorial Disputes in the South China Sea: Faces of Power and Law in the Age of China's Rise*. Routledge. DOI: 10.4324/9781003035855

Hyer, E. (1995). The South China Sea Disputes: Implications of China's Earlier Territorial Settlements. *Pacific Affairs*, *68*(1), 34–54. https://www.jstor.org/stable/2759767. DOI: 10.2307/2759767

Ian, C. J. (2023). "Still waters run deep: Taiwan's South China Sea strategy", *Clingendael Spectator*, 19 October 2023, https://spectator.clingendael.org/en/publication/still-waters-run-deep-taiwans-south-china-sea-strategy.

Ibrahim, A. (2023, September 22). National Statement by the Honourable Mr. Anwar Ibrahim Prime Minister of Malaysia at the General Debate of the 78th Session of the United Nations General Assembly New York, 22 September 2023. https://gadebate.un.org/sites/default/files/gastatements/78/my_en.pdf

I-Connect. (2023, August 15). Taiwan Imports and Exports: Trade Insights. Retrieved from https://www.i-connectweb.com/blog/taiwan-imports-and-exports-trade-insights

Idrus, P. G. (2024). "Nearly 80% of Indonesians see Beijing's South China Sea actions as threat", *Benar News*, 21 March 2024, https://www.benarnews.org/english/news/indonesian/80-percent-indonesians-see-china-threatens-sovereignty-03212024143829.html.

Ikenberry, G. J. (2014, August 18). *Book Review: Liberal Internationalism: Theory, History, Practice By Beate Jahn*. Retrieved from Foreign Affairs: https://www.foreignaffairs.com/reviews/capsule-review/2014-08-18/liberal-internationalism-theory-history-practice

Ikenberry, G. J. (2015). Between the Eagle and the Dragon: America, China, and Middle State Strategies in East Asia. *Political Science Quarterly*, *XX*(XX), 1–35.

IMF. (2012). (https://www.imf.org/external/pubs/ft/scr/2012/cr12219.pdf). August 2012 IMF Country Report No. 12/219 July 23, 2012 January 29, 2001 January 29, 2001 January 29, 2001 January 29, 2001 Philippines: Reform of the Fiscal Regimes for Mining and Petroleum

IMF. (n.d.). Malaysia. https://www.imf.org/en/Countries/MYS

India Times. (August 30, 2020). Post-Galwan clash, Indian Navy quietly deployed warship in South China Sea. *Indian Times,*https://timesofindia.indiatimes.com/articleshow/77834259.cms?utm_source=contentofinterest&utm_medium=text&utm_campaign=cppst

International Crisis Group. (2021). ‘‘Vietnam Tacks Between Cooperation and Struggle in The SCS’’, https://www.crisisgroup.org/asia/north-east-asia/china/318-vietnam-tacks-between-cooperation-and-struggle-south-china-sea.

Jawli, N. (2016). South China Sea and India’s Geopolitical Interests. *Indian Journal of Asian Affairs, 29*(1/2), 85–100.

Jian, S. (1997). “Multinational oil companies and the Spratly dispute”, *Journal of Contemporary China* 6(16): 591-601, https://doi.org/.DOI: 10.1080/10670569708724298

Jianren, Z. (2019). Power Transition and Paradigm Shift in Diplomacy: Why China and the US March towards Strategic Competition? *The Chinese Journal of International Politics, 12*(1), 1–34. DOI: 10.1093/cjip/poy019

Jones, M. J., & Smith, M. L. R. (2006). *ASEAN and East Asian International Relations: Regional Delusion*. Edward Elgar Publishing. DOI: 10.4337/9781845428921

Joshi, Y. (2019). China and India’s maritime rivalry has a new flashpoint: the Andaman Sea, *South China Morning Post*, https://www.scmp.com/week-asia/opinion/article/3042032/china-and-indias-maritime-rivalry-has-new-flashpoint-andaman-sea

Juutinen, M. (2018). Kautilyan foreign policy analysis: Sino-Indian dynamics in South Asia and the Indian Ocean region. *Journal of the Indian Ocean Region, 14*(2), 206–226. DOI: 10.1080/19480881.2018.1472859

Kajal, K. (2024). *Taiwan deploys Sky Bow III air defence systems*. Janes. Retrieved December 4, 2024, from https://www.janes.com/osint-insights/defence-news/defence/taiwan-deploys-sky-bow-iii-air-defence-systems

Kashif, H. K., & Koch, H. (2024) “‘INSTC and Chabahar Port’: An Introduction, Edited Kashif Hasan Khan, India’s Economic Corridor Initiatives”, March, Routledg, New York, pp. 3-19. DOI: DOI: 10.4324/9781003454540-2

Kasım, K., (2024). “Güney Çin Denizi Sorunlarının Bölgesel ve Uluslararası Güvenliğe Etkileri,” *International Journal of Politics and Security (IJPS)* 6(1): 22-37. DOI: .DOI: 10.53451/ijps.1413751

Katsumata, H. (2009). *ASEAN’s cooperative security enterprise: Norms and interests in the ASEAN Regional Forum*. Palgrave Macmillan. DOI: 10.1057/9780230277038

Kavas, M., Jarzabkowski, P., & Nigam, A. (2020). Islamic Family Business: The Constitutive Role of Religion in Business. *Journal of Business Ethics, 163*(4), 689–700. DOI: 10.1007/s10551-019-04384-5

Kaya, E. (2024). ABD Hegemonyasına Karşı Orta Ölçekli Güçlerin Stratejik Özerklik Arayışı, *Gumushane University. The Social Science Journal, 15*(1), 220–236.

Kaygusuz, B. (2023) “Hindistan’ı Avrupa’ya bağlayacak koridor hakkında bilinenler”, Independent Turkish, Sebtember *12,*https://www.indyturk.com/node/660456/dünya/hindistanı-avrupaya-bağlayacak-koridor-hakkında-bilinenler

Kazuyuki, H. (2021). *Future superpower: Redrawing the world map in 2030 (translated version).* The World Publishers.

Keck, Z. (2014). India Wades Into South China Sea Dispute, *The Diplomat,*https://thediplomat.com/2014/03/india-wades-into-south-china-sea-dispute/

Keling, M. F., Som, H. M., Saludin, M. N., Shuib, M. S., & Ajis, M. N. (2011). The Development of ASEAN from Historical Approach. *Asian Social Science*, *7*(7), 169–189. DOI: 10.5539/ass.v7n7p169

Keyvan, Ö. Z. (2017, December). Güney Çin Denizi’nde Tahkim: Çin-Filipinler Rekabeti. *ANKASAM-Bölgesel Araştırmalar Dergisi*, *1*(3), 251–267.

Khalid, M. (2019). Littoral States Conflicts in the South China Sea: a Constant Danger to Regional Peace. *South China Sea: Emerging Scenario*, 193. https://www.researchgate.net/publication/340174502_Littoral_States_Conflicts_in_the_South_China_Sea_A_constant_danger_to_regional_peace

Khaliq, R. U. (2021, February 25). '3 reasons' China tries to control South China Sea. *AA*.https://www.aa.com.tr/en/asia-pacific/3-reasons-china-tries-to-control-south-china-sea/2157110

Khan, K. H., Bastanifar, I., & Omidi, A.. (2024). Integrating gravity models and network analysis in logistical strategic planning: A case of the India Middle-East Europe Economic Corridor (IMEC). *Maritime Economics & Logistics*, *26*(2). Advance online publication. DOI: 10.1057/s41278-024-00289-x

Khikmatov, F. K. (2022). Geopolıtıcal Power In The 21st Century Clash Of Tellurocracy And Thalassocracy. *British Journal of Global Ecology and Sustainable Development*, *10*, 53–64.

Khilnani, S., Kumar, R., Mehta, P. B., Menon, P., Nilekani, N., Raghavan, S., Saran, S., & Varadarajan, S. (2014). *NonAlignment 2.0: A foreign and strategic policy for India in the 21st century*. Penguin Publications.

Kiet, L. H., Hiep, T. X., Minh, N. A., & Phuc, N. H. (2024). The soft power impact of China in strategic competition with the US in Vietnam. In Zreik, M. (Ed.), *Soft power and diplomatic strategies in Asia and the Middle East* (pp. 314–331). IGI Global., DOI: 10.4018/979-8-3693-2444-8.ch018

Kim, J. (2016, May 7). *Where Does Taiwan Stand on the South China Sea?* Retrieved from The National Interest: https://nationalinterest.org/blog/the-buzz/where-does-taiwan-stand-the-south-china-sea-16099

Kim, J. (2015). Territorial Disputes in The SCS: Implications for Security in Asia and Beyond. *Strategic Studies Quarterly*, *9*(2), 107–141.

Kin, S. E., & Ryan, Z. (2023). "Malaysia: Securing sovereignty in the South China Sea through ASEAN centrality", *Yale Journal of International Affairs*, 15 May 2023, https://www.yalejournal.org/publications/malaysia-securing-sovereignty-in-the-south-china-sea-through-asean-centrality.

Kipgen, N. (2020). *The Politics of South China Sea Disputes*. Routledge. DOI: 10.4324/9781003026334

Kızılay, Ş. (2023). A Possible Scenario for 2023 India: Opportunities and Challenges, *ANKASAM,* https://www.ankasam.org/a-possible-scenario-for-2023-india-opportunities-and-challenges/?lang=en

Kocadal, Ö. (2022). Asya-Pasifik'te ABD-Çin Rekabeti: Tukidides'in Tuzağı ve Liberal Uluslararası Düzen. In Al, A., & Kaya, H. (Eds.), *Uluslararası Politik Ekonomide Avrasya* (pp. 105–123). Nobel Akademik Yayıncılık.

Kocka, J. (2016). *Capitalism: A Short History*. Princeton University Press. DOI: 10.2307/j.ctvc77kv8

Koga, K. (2020). *Managing Great Power Politics: ASEAN, Institutional Strategy, and the South China Sea*. Palgrave Macmillan.

Koh, C. S. L. (2018). *Inaugural ASEAN-China maritime exercise: What to expect (RSIS Commentaries, No. 131). RSIS Commentaries*. Nanyang Technological University.

Korkmaz, H. (2024) İsrail'deki Savaş IMEC Projesini Rafa Kaldırabilir, Tasam, September 14, https://tasam.org/tr-TR/Icerik/72436/israildeki_savas_imec_projesini_rafa_kaldirabilir

Kraft, H. J. S. (2012). Driving East Asian Regionalism: The Reconstruction of ASEAN's Identity. In Emmers, R. (Ed.), *ASEAN and the Institutionalization of East Asia* (pp. 61–74). Routledge.

Krishnan, U., & Boudreau, J. (2014). Vietnam Seeks India Role in China Sea as Dung Meets Modi, *BBC,* https://www.bloomberg.com/news/articles/2014-10-28/vietnam-seeks-india-role-in-china-sea-spat-as-dung-meets-modi

Ku, J. (2014). "Can International Law Be an Obstacle to Peace? Some Thoughts on Taiwan's East China Sea Peace Initiative", *Opinio Juris*, 05 August 2014, https://opiniojuris.org/2014/08/05/just-long-can-shelve-sovereignty-disputes-thoughts-taiwans-east-china-sea-peace-initiative/.

Kucharski, J. (2022, September 13). *Taiwan's Greatest Vulnerability Is Its Energy Supply*. Retrieved from The Diplomat: https://thediplomat.com/2022/09/taiwans-greatest-vulnerability-is-its-energy-supply/

Küçükdeğirmenci, O. & Zandamela, A. C. (2020). "From Balancing to Accommodation: Understanding the Philippines's Relations with the US and China in Post-Arbitration Period", *The International Journal of Humanities & Social Studies* 8 (12): 66-74, DOI No.: .DOI: 10.24940/theijhss/2020/v8/i12/HS2012-024

Küçükdeğirmenci, O. (2024). Security Architecture in Indo-Pacific from the Past to Present: Bilateral Alliances and Multilateral Structures. In Güçyetmez, F., & Doğan, D. (Eds.), *Emerging Power in Indo-Pacific Geopolitics* (pp. 335–400). İdeal Kültür Yayıncılık.

Kugelman, M. (2022) Another Quad Rises, Foreign Policy, July 14. https://foreignpolicy.com/2022/07/14/i2u2-quad-india-israel-uae-us-south-asia/#fn:2

Kuik, C. C. (2008). The Essence of Hedging Malaysia and Singapore's Response to a Rising China. *Contemporary Southeast Asia, 30*(2), 159–185. DOI: 10.1355/CS30-2A

Kuik, C. C. (2024). Explaining Hedging. *Contemporary Southeast Asia, 46*(1), 43–76. DOI: 10.1355/CS46-1c

Kuisong, Y. (2009). "The theory and implementation of the People's Republic of China's revolutionary diplomacy", *Journal of Modern Chinese History* 3 (2): 276–309, DOI: .DOI: 10.1080/17535650903345346

Kuok, L. (2015). Tides of Change: Taiwan's Evolving Position in the South China Sea. Brookings Institution. https://www.brookings.edu/wp-content/uploads/2016/06/taiwan-south-china-sea-kuok-paper.pdf

Kuok, L. (2015, May 22). *Taiwan's Evolving Position in the South China Sea—And Why Other Actors Should Take Notice*. Retrieved from Asia Maritime Transparency Initiative: https://amti.csis.org/taiwans-evolving-position-in-the-south-china-sea-and-why-other-actors-should-take-notice/

Kuok, L. (2015, May 7). *Tides of change: Taiwan's evolving position in the South China Sea*. Retrieved from Brookings: https://www.brookings.edu/articles/tides-of-change-taiwans-evolving-position-in-the-south-china-sea/

Kuok, L. (2016), *The US FON Program in the South China Sea, Center for East Asia Policy Studies*, https://www.brookings.edu/wp-content/uploads/ 2016/07/the-us-fon-program-in-the-south-china-sea.pdf

Kuok, L. (2019, November). *How China's Action in the South China Sea Undermine the Rule of Law.* Washington: Brooking Institution. Retrieved from Global China.

Kuok, L. (2021). Taiwan's Evolving Position in the South China Sea—And Why Other Actors Should Take Notice. Center for Strategic and International Studies. Asia Maritime Transparency Initiative. https://amti.csis.org/taiwans-evolving-position-in-the-south-china-sea-and-why-other-actors-should-take-notice/

Kurlantzick, J. (2022). *China goes all in with support for Myanmar's military regime.* https://www.japantimes.co.jp/opinion/2022/04/14/commentary/world-commentary/china-backs-myanmar/, accessed on July 17, 2024.

Kusuma, W., Kurnia, A., & Agustian, R. A. (2021). *South China Sea: Conflict, Challenge, and Solution.* Lampung Journal of International Law., DOI: 10.25041/lajil.v3i1.2266

Lai, Y. M., & Kuik, C. C. (2021). Structural sources of Malaysia's South China Sea policy: Power uncertainties and small-state hedging. *Australian Journal of International Affairs, 75*(3), 277–304. DOI: 10.1080/10357718.2020.1856329

Lan-Anh, N. T. (2008). *South China Sea Dispute: A Reappraisal in the Light of International Law.* University of Bristol.

Lang, B. (2015). Off the beaten track: Taiwan's changing 'track-two diplomacy' after democratisation – and its pitfalls. *European Journal of East Asian Studies, 14*(1), 75–102. https://www.academia.edu/11885584/Off_the_beaten_track_Taiwans_changing_track_two_diplomacy_after_democratisation_and_its_pitfalls

Larsen, J. (2024). Maritime security: How geopolitics hardens threat patterns at sea and challenges known solutions.

Larsson, O. L. (2024). Sea blindness in grey zone preparations. *Defence Studies, 24*(3), 399–420. Advance online publication. DOI: 10.1080/14702436.2024.2359913

Laws & Regulations Database of The Republic of China. (1998). *Law on the Territorial Sea and the Contiguous Zone.* Retrieved from https://law.moj.gov.tw/ENG/LawClass/LawAll.aspx?pcode=A0000009

Lee, H., & Lee, E. (2020). *Taiwan's Overall Defense Concept Explained.* The Diplomat. Retrieved December 4, 2024, from https://thediplomat.com/2020/11/taiwans-overall-defense-concept-explained/

Lee, H. (2023). The legality of militarization of the South China Sea and its legal implications. *KMI International Journal of Maritime Affairs and Fisheries*, *15*(1), 1–24. DOI: 10.54007/ijmaf.2023.15.1.1

Lee, K. C. L., & Chan, Y.-K. (Eds.). (2023). *Taiwan and Southeast Asia: Soft Power and Hard Truths Facing China's Ascendancy* (1st ed.). Routledge., DOI: 10.4324/9781003320463

Lee, W. (2017). Taiwan, the South China Sea Dispute, and the 2016 Arbitration Decision. *Journal of Chinese Political Science*, *22*(2), 229–250. DOI: 10.1007/s11366-017-9470-2

Lefebvre, H. (1991). *The Production of Space*. Blackwell Publishing.

Le, H. (2021). Examining ASEAN's effectiveness in managing South China Sea disputes. *The Pacific Review*. Advance online publication. DOI: 10.1080/09512748.2021.1934519

Leifer, M. (1999, April 24-26). Stalemate in the South China Sea. Paper presented at aWworkshop on the Conflict in the South China Sea, Oslo.

Lema, K. (2023). *Philippines reveals locations of 4 new strategic sites for U.S. military pact,* 03.04.2023, https://www.reuters.com/world/asia-pacific/philippines-reveals-locations-4-new-strategic-sites-us-military-pact-2023-04-03/

Lema, K., Blanchard, B., Lee, L., & Vu, K. (2023, August 31). *Philippines, Taiwan, Malaysia reject China's latest South China Sea map*. (M. Petty, & F. Kerry, Editors) Retrieved August 2024, from Reuters: https://www.reuters.com/world/asia-pacific/philippines-taiwan-malaysia-reject-chinas-latest-south-china-sea-map-2023-08-31/

Li, C. (2016). The South China Sea Peace Initiative in a Transitional Security Environment. *American Journal of Chinese Studies*, *23*, 119–134.

Li, L. (2018). *China's Policy Towards the South China Sea: When Geopolitics Meets the Law of the Sea*. Routledge. DOI: 10.4324/9781315158709

Lin, C.-y. (1997, April). Taiwan's South China Sea Policy. *Asian Survey*, *37*(4), 323–339. DOI: 10.2307/2645651

Liu, I.-C. (2024, November 16). *The Risks of Oversimplifying Taiwan's Defense Needs*. The Diplomat. Retrieved from https://thediplomat.com/2024/11/the-risks-of-oversimplifying-taiwans-defense-needs/

Liu, F.-K. (2013). Dilemma and Domestic Uncertainty: Taiwan's Insecurity in the South China Sea. *China Report (New Delhi, India)*, *49*(4), 385–397. DOI: 10.1177/0009445513506635

Liu, F.-k. (2021). Mainland China-Taiwan interplay in the South China Sea. In *K.-Y. Zou, Routledge Handbook of the South China Sea* (pp. 376–391). Routledge. DOI: 10.4324/9780367822217-26

Liu, R., & Yang, S. (2023). China and the liberal international order: A pragmatic and dynamic approach. *International Affairs, 99*(4), 1383–1400. DOI: 10.1093/ia/iiad169

Loan, H. T., & Tung, N. D. (2021). Vietnam's Responses to India's Indo-Pacific Oceans Initiatives and Opportunities for Vietnam–India Maritime Cooperation in the South China Sea. *India Quarterly, 77*(2), 185–199. DOI: 10.1177/09749284211005035

Lohman, W. (2020). *Vietnam's place in the U.S.-China great power competition.* https://www.gisreportsonline.com/r/us-china-rivalry-vietnam/, accessed on June 23, 2024.

Luo, G., & Chi, Z. (2022). Conflicts and challenges of sustainable fisheries governance cooperation under the securitization of the maritime commons. *Fishes, 8*(1), 1. DOI: 10.3390/fishes8010001

Ma, Y.-j. (2015, June 11). *A Plan for Peace in the South China Sea.* Retrieved from Wall Street Journal: https://www.wsj.com/articles/a-plan-for-peace-in-the-south-china-sea-1434040267

Macaraig, C. E., & Fenton, A. J. (2021). "Analyzing the Causes and Effects of the South China Sea Dispute", *The Journal of Territorial and Maritime Studies* 8(2): 42-58, https://www.jstor.org/stable/10.2307/48617340.

Mackinder, H. J. (1904). The Geographical Pivot of History. Source. *The Geographical Journal, 23*(4), 421. DOI: 10.2307/1775498

Madan, T. (2022). India and the QUAD. In T. Huxley & L. Kuok (Eds.), *Asia-Pacific regional security assessment 2022-Key developments and trends* (pp.198-221). London, UK: The International Institute for Strategic Studies (IISS).

Magramo, K. (2023) Tensions are flaring once more in the South China Sea. Here's why it matters for the world, *CNN,*https://edition.cnn.com/2023/09/29/asia/south-china-sea-tensions-philippines-china-us-explainer-intl-hnk/index.html

Mahadzir, D. (2015). Malaysia's Maritime Claims in the South China Sea: Security and Military Dimensions. In *Entering Uncharted Waters* (pp. 208-222). Cambridge University Press.

Mahadzir, D. (2022, June 7). China denies harassing Canadian, Australian patrol aircraft in the Western Pacific. *USNİ*. Retrieved from https://news.usni.org/2022/06/07/china-denies-harassing-canadian-australian-patrol-aircraft-in-the-western-pacific

Mahadzir, D. (2014). Malaysia's maritime claims in the South China Sea: security and military dimensions. In Chachavalpongpun, P. (Ed.), *Entering unchartered waters: ASEAN and the South China Sea* (pp. 208–222). Institute of Southeast Asian Studies.

Mahan, A. T. (1987). *The Influence of Sea Power Upon History, 1660-1783*. Dover Publications.

Mahapatra, C. (2010). The United States and the Emerging Balance of Power in Asia. *Indian Foreign Affairs Journal*, *5*(2), 207–218.

Maizland, L. (2023, January 24). *Why China-Taiwan Relations Are So Tense*. Council on Foreign Relations. Retrieved from https://www.cfr.org/backgrounder/china-taiwan-relations-tension-us-policy-biden

Malaysia Ministry of Foreign Affairs. (2023). "Malaysia's Position On The South China Sea", 08 April 2023, https://www.kln.gov.my/web/guest/-/malaysia-s-position-on-the-south-china-sea.

Malaysian Investment Development Authority. (2024, August 1). PM Anwar: Strong Malaysia-Japan ties key to sustainable economic growth. https://www.mida.gov.my/mida-news/pm-anwar-strong-malaysia-japan-ties-key-to-sustainable-economic-growth/

Malaysian Ministry of Defence. (2020). Defence White Paper: A secure, sovereign and prosperous Malaysia. https://www.mod.gov.my/images/mindef/article/kertas_putih/KPP2.pdf

Malenbaum, W. (1956). U.S. Economy Policy in South and Southeast Asia. *India Quarterly*, *12*(2), 107–116. DOI: 10.1177/097492845601200203

Malik, M. (2013, August 30). *History the Weak Link in Beijing's Maritime Claims.* Retrieved from the Diplomat: https://thediplomat.com/2013/08/history-the-weak-link-in-beijings-maritime-claims/

Manuel, A., & Gates, R. (2016). *India And China, The New Superpowers*.https://iis.berkeley.edu/india-and-china-new-superpowers, accessed on June 24, 2024.

Manyin, M. (2014). *Vietnam Among the Powers: Struggle and Cooperation*,http://www.theasanforum.org/vietnam-among-the-powers-struggle-cooperation/

Marciel, S. (2023). *From Foe to Friend: Explaining the Development of US-Vietnam Relations*. https://aparc.fsi.stanford.edu/news/foe-friend-explaining-development-us-vietnam-relations, accessed on June 29, 2024.

Maritime Delimitation and Territorial Questions between Qatar and Bahrain (Qatar v. Bahrain) (Merits) (I.C.J March 16, 2001).

Marshall, T. (2020). *Prisoners of Geography (translated version)*. Vietnam Writers' Association Publishing House.

Marston, H. (2023). The Struggle for Autonomy amidst Great Power Rivalry in Southeast Asia. In The National Institute for Defense Studies, Japan. *NIDS ASEAN Workshop 2023 The Era of Great Power Competition in the Indo-Pacific Region*, pp. 22-34.

Marvel, M. J. C. (2024). The South China Sea Arbitration: Navigating Compliance Strategies through the Lens of Raya and the Last Dragon. In Voigt, C., & Foster, C. (Eds.), *International Courts versus Non-Compliance Mechanisms: Comparative Advantages in Strengthening Treaty Implementation* (pp. 471–488). Cambridge University Press. DOI: 10.1017/9781009373913.029

Mastro, O. S. (2021, February 17). *How China is bending the rules in the South China Sea*. Retrieved from Interpreter: https://www.lowyinstitute.org/the-interpreter/how-china-bending-rules-south-china-sea

Ma, X. (2016). The SCS dispute. *Atlantisch Perspectief, 40*(3), 39–41.

Mazza, M. (2023, October 4). *Beijing's aggressive moves in the South China Sea and the potential for a Taiwan crisis*. Global Taiwan Institute. Retrieved from https://globaltaiwan.org/2023/10/beijings-aggressive-moves-in-the-south-china-sea-and-the-potential-for-a-taiwan-crisis/

McCartney, M. (2023, December 1). *China Deployed Over 1,700 Military Planes Around Taiwan in 2023*. Newsweek. Retrieved from https://www.newsweek.com/china-military-aircraft-taiwan-strait-2023-1858106

McGillis, J. (2021, December 15). *Taiwan's Energy Security and the Threat of a PRC Blockade*. Retrieved from Global Taiwan Institute: https://globaltaiwan.org/2021/12/taiwans-energy-security-and-the-threat-of-a-prc-blockade/

Mearsheimer, J. J. (2021). The inevitable rivalry: America, China, and the tragedy of great-power politics, *Foreign Affairs,* 100(48). Pdf available: https://www.foreignaffairs.com/articles/china/2021-10-19/inevitable-rivalry-cold-war

Mehrotra, L. (2012). India's Look East Policy: Its Origin and Development. *Indian Foreign Affairs Journal,* 7(1), 75-85. https://www.jstor.org/stable/45341805

Mehrotra, L. (2012). India's Look East Policy: Its Origin and Development. *Indian Foreign Affairs Journal, 7*(1), 75–85.

Mermer, C. T. (2022). *Güney Çin Denizi ABD Hegemonyasına Meydan Okuyan Çin'in Zorlu Virajı*. TASAM.

Ming, O. K. (2016, July 14). What the decision on South China Sea means to Malaysia. *Malaysiakini*. https://m.malaysiakini.com/news/348469

Minh, T. (2023). *Vietnam - China relationship maintains development trend.* https://en.nhandan.vn/vietnam-china-relationship-maintains-development-trend-post126731.html, accessed on June 12, 2024.

Ministry of Economic Affairs. (2023). *Important Policies - Policies & Programs*. Retrieved from https://www.moea.gov.tw/MNS/english/Policy/Policy.aspx?menu_id=32904&policy_id=19

Ministry of Economic Affairs. Republic of China (Taiwan). (2023). Taiwan's Trade Statistics. https://www.moea.gov.tw/MNS/dos/home/Home.aspx

Ministry of External Affairs Government of India. Joint Statement on the 5th India-Philippines Joint Commission on Bilateral Cooperation, Ministry of External Affairs Government of India, https://www.mea.gov.in/bilateral-documents.htm?dtl/36743/Joint+Statement+on+the+5th+IndiaPhilippines+Joint+Commission+on+Bilateral+Cooperation

Ministry of Foreign Affair of the People's Republic of China. (2020). China's initiation of the five principles of peaceful. *Co-Existence (Glasgow, Scotland), 29*(June). http://ir.china-embassy.gov.cn/eng/dtxw/201407/t20140702_1894012.htm

Ministry of Foreign Affairs Brunei Darussalam. (2013). "Joint Statement between Brunei Darussalam and the People's Republic of China", 11 October 2013, https://www.mfa.gov.bn/Lists/Press%20Releases/NDispForm.aspx?ID=106&ContentTypeId=0x0100DE0D91A42F563640A6718A29AE56AE67.

Ministry of Foreign Affairs of PRC. (2024, January 31). Xi Jinping Sends Message of Congratulation to Malaysia's New King Sultan Ibrahim Sultan Iskandar. https://www.fmprc.gov.cn/eng/zxxx_662805/202402/t20240201_11237752.html

Ministry of Foreign Affairs. (2023, April 8). *Malaysia's Position on The South China Sea (Press Realese)*. Ministry of Foreign Affairs Malaysia: https://www.kln.gov.my/web/guest/-/malaysia-s-position-on-the-south-china-sea adresinden alındı

Ministry of Foreign Affairs. American Institute in Taiwan, Japan-Taiwan Exchange Association, & Australian Office. (2023, December 6). Joint Statement on the 2023 Global Cooperation and Training Framework (GCTF) Joint Committee Meeting. https://www.koryu.or.jp/Portals/0/taipei/2023/1207/2023-12-06%20Joint%20 Statement%20on%20the%202023%20GCTF.pdf

Ministry of Foreign Affairs. Republic of China (Taiwan). (2016, July 12). *ROC government reiterates its position on South China Sea issues*. Retrieved from https://en.mofa .gov.tw/News_Content.aspx?n=1EADDCFD4C6EC567&s=F5170FE043DADE98

Ministry of Foreign Affairs. Republic of China (Taiwan). (2016, July 14). *ROC position on the South China Sea Arbitration*. Retrieved from https://www.mofa.gov .tw/en/News_Content.aspx?n=1EADDCFD4C6EC567&s=5B5A9134709EB875

Ministry of Foreign Affairs. Republic of China (Taiwan). (2021, August 20). *Ketagalan Forum—2021 Asia-Pacific Security Dialogue to discuss regional security issues in the postpandemic era*. Retrieved from https://en.mofa.gov.tw/News_Content.aspx ?n=1328&s=96298&sms=273

Ministry of Foreign Affairs. Republic of China (Taiwan). (2023). Taiwan's International Cooperation and Development. [REMOVED HYPERLINK FIELD] https:// www.moea.gov.tw/Mns/english/home/English.aspx

Miskimmon, A., O'Loughlin, B., & Roselle, L. (2018). Strategic Narrative: 21st Century Diplomatic Statecraft. *Revista Mexicana de Política Exterior, 113*. Retrieved from https://pure.qub.ac.uk/en/publications/strategic-narrative-21st-century -diplomatic-statecraft-narrativa-

Miskimmon, A., O'loughlin, B., & Roselle, L. (2014). *Strategic narratives: Communication power and the new world order*. Routledge. DOI: 10.4324/9781315871264

Miskimmon, A., O'Loughlin, B., & Roselle, L. (2015). Strategic Narratives: A response. *Critical Studies on Security, 3*(3), 341–344. DOI: 10.1080/21624887.2015.1103023

Miskimmon, A., O'Loughlin, B., & Roselle, L. (2017). *Forging The World: Strategic Narratives and International Relations*. University of Michigan Press. DOI: 10.3998/mpub.6504652

Missile Threat. (2021, April 28). *Missiles of Taiwan*. Center for Strategic and International Studies. Retrieved from https://missilethreat.csis.org/country/taiwan/

Mistreanu, S. (2024, October 26). *US approves $2 billion in arms sales to Taiwan including advanced missile defense system*. Associated Press. Retrieved from https:// apnews.com/article/us-taiwan-china-arms-sale-missile-defense-bd14986ada9c fc894c5b1168aea27d02

Mitchell, M. D. (2016). The South China Sea: A Geopolitical Analysis. *Journal of Geography and Geology*, *8*(3), 14–25. DOI: 10.5539/jgg.v8n3p14

Miyoshi, M. (2012, February 10). China's "U-Shaped Line" Claim in the South China Sea: Any Validity Under International Law? *Ocean Development and International Law*, *43*(1), 1–17. DOI: 10.1080/00908320.2011.619374

Modelski, G. (1978). The Long Cycle of Global Politics and the Nation-State (Vol. 20). Retrieved from https://about.jstor.org/terms

MOFAM (Ministry of Foreign Affairs of Malaysia). (2023, April 8). Malaysia's Position on The South China Sea. https://www.kln.gov.my/web/guest/-/malaysia-s-position-on-the-south-china-sea

MOFAM (Ministry of Foreign Affairs of Malaysia). (2024a, March 4). Joint Statement for the 2nd Australia-Malaysia Annual Leaders' Meeting Monday 4 March 2024. https://www.kln.gov.my/web/guest/speeches-statements/-/asset_publisher/statement/content/joint-statement-for-the-2nd-australia-malaysia-annual-leaders-meeting-monday-4-march-2024?inheritRedirect=false&redirect=https%3A%2F%2Fwww.kln.gov.my%2Fweb%2Fguest%2Fspeeches-statements%3Fp_p_id%3D101_INSTANCE_statement%26p_p_lifecycle%3D0%26p_p_state%3Dnormal%26p_p_mode%3Dview%26p_p_col_id%3Dcolumn-2%26p_p_col_count%3D1

MOFAM (Ministry of Foreign Affairs of Malaysia). (2024b, June 20). Joint Statement between the People's Republic of China and Malaysia on Deepening the Comprehensive Strategic Partnership towards China-Malaysia Community with a Shared Future. https://www.kln.gov.my/web/guest/speeches-statements/-/asset_publisher/statement/content/joint-statement-between-the-people-s-republic-of-china-and-malaysia-on-deepening-the-comprehensive-strategic-partnership-towards-china-malaysia-commun?inheritRedirect=false&redirect=https%3A%2F%2Fwww.kln.gov.my%2Fweb%2Fguest%2Fspeeches-statements%3Fp_p_id%3D101_INSTANCE_statement%26p_p_lifecycle%3D0%26p_p_state%3Dnormal%26p_p_mode%3Dview%26p_p_col_id%3Dcolumn-2%26p_p_col_count%3D1

Munir, T., & Sajjad, N. (2022). Strategic rebalancing: SinoUSs interplay in the South China Sea. *International Journal of Applied Research in Social Sciences*, *4*(7), 221–236. DOI: 10.51594/ijarss.v4i7.371

Myers, L. (2023, March 22). China's Economic Security Challenge: Difficulties Overcoming the Malacca Dilemma. Georgetown *Journal of International Affairs*. https://gjia.georgetown.edu/2023/03/22/chinas-economic-security-challenge-difficulties-overcoming-the-malacca-dilemma/

Nagy, S. (2022). Taiwan and the Indo-Pacific: Defending a Global Public Good. *Commentary (New York, N.Y.)*, •••, 3.

Nambiar, S. (2024, August 2). Will Malaysia build ASEAN with BRICS? (The Lowy Institute). https://www.lowyinstitute.org/the-interpreter/will-malaysia-build-asean-brics

Napang, M., Patittingi, F., Aspan, Z., Ruslan, A., Latief, B., Hambali, R., & Hendrapati, M. (2019). Contesting views of the philippines and china over the nine-dash line in the south china sea. *Journal of East Asia and International Law*, *12*(1), 180–192. DOI: 10.14330/jeail.2019.12.1.10

Narine, S. (2018). *The New ASEAN in Asia Pacific and Beyond*. Lynne Rienner Publishers. DOI: 10.1515/9781626377097

Narramore, T. (2008). China and Europe: Engagement, multipolarity and strategy. *The Pacific Review*, *21*(1), 87–108. DOI: 10.1080/09512740701868930

National People's Congress of PRC. (1992, February 25). Law on the Territorial Sea and the Contiguous Zone of 25 February 1992. UN. Retrieved from https://www.un.org/depts/los/LEGISLATIONANDTREATIES/PDFFILES/CHN_1992_Law.pdf

News. (2023, March 10). *Albanese defends nuclear subs plan after Beijing accuses AUKUS of stirring up an arms race*. Retrieved from https://bit.ly/3TT612e

Nga, L. T. H., & Quang, T. H. (2021). Public Diplomacy in Strengthening India: Vietnam Relations. *India Quarterly*, *77*(2), 289–303. DOI: 10.1177/09749284211005012

Nguyen, N. L. (2023). "Vietnam and China: Conflicting neighbors stuck in nationalism and memory", *Harvard International Review*, 03 May 2023, https://hir.harvard.edu/vietnam-and-china-conflicting-neighbors-stuck-in-nationalism-and-memory/.

Nguy n, A. C., Ph m, M. T., Nguy n, V. H., & Tr n, B. H. (2024). Kennedy, P. S. J. (2022). Explaining the Increase of China's Power in The South China Sea Through International Relation Theories. *Cogent Arts & Humanities*, *11*(1), 1–16. DOI: 10.1080/23311983.2024.2383107

Nischalke, T. I. (2000). Insights from ASEAN's Foreign Policy Cooperation: The "ASEAN Way," a Real Spirit or a Phantom? *Contemporary Southeast Asia*, *22*(1), 89–112. DOI: 10.1355/CS22-1D

Noer, J. H. (1996), Southeast Asian Chokepoints, https://apps.dtic.mil/dtic/tr/fulltext/u2/a394162.pdf

Nong, H. (2018). The Applicability of the Archipelagic Regime in the South China Sea: A Debate on the Rights of Continental States' Outlying Archipelagos. *Ocean Yearbook, 32*(1), 80–117. DOI: 10.1163/22116001-03201005

Nordin, N. A. B. M. (2020, October 20). Maritime Security-Malaysia and South China Sea. https://midas.mod.gov.my/gallery/publication/midas-commentaries/219-maritime-security-malaysia-and-south-china-sea-by-nor-aini-binti-mohd-nordin

Nye, J. S. (1990). *Soft Power,* Foreign Policy, *No. 80*. JSTOR., Retrieved October 14, 2024, from, DOI: 10.2307/1148580

Nye, J. S. (2004) Soft Power, New York, Public Affairs.

Nye, J. S. (2024). *What Killed US - China Engagement*, https://www.aspistrategist.org.au/what-killed-us-china-engagement/

Nye, J. S., & Goldsmith, J. L. (2011). The Future of Power. *Bulletin - American Academy of Arts and Sciences. American Academy of Arts and Sciences, 64*(3), 45–52. https://www.jstor.org/stable/41149419.#

O'Hanlon, M. E. (2021, October 13). *An asymmetric defense of Taiwan*. Brookings Institution. Retrieved from https://www.brookings.edu/articles/an-asymmetric-defense-of-taiwan/

Office of the Historian. (1951). Foreign Relations of the U.S., https://history.state.gov/historicaldocuments/frus1951v06p1/d95#:~:text=Each%20Party%20recognizes%20that%20an,accordance%20with%20its%20constitutional%20processes

Office of the President Republic of China (Taiwan). (2016, January 28). *Remarks by President Ma on Taiping Island*. Retrieved from https://english.president.gov.tw/NEWS/4832/Remarks%20by%20President%20Ma%20on%20Taiping%20Island

Office of the United States Trade Representative. (2023). Taiwan. Retrieved from https://ustr.gov/countries-regions/china/taiwan

Ogden, C., & Jones, C. (2023). "Chapter: 17 Chinese conceptions of the Indo-Pacific The impact of identity and history", in *Handbook of Indo-Pacific Studies*, edited by Barbara Kratiuk, Jeroen J. J. Van den Bosch, Aleksandra Jaskólska ve Yoichiro Sato, 343-365, New York: Routledge.

Osiewicz, P. (2023). "Chapter 14: International conflicts in the Indo-Pacific region", in *Handbook of Indo-Pacific Studies*, edited by Barbara Kratiuk, Jeroen J. J. Van den Bosch, Aleksandra Jaskólska ve Yoichiro Sato, 290-305, New York: Routledge.

Özdemir, G. S., & Yıldız, A. K. (2024). Bringing Diplomacy to the Digital Age: The Implementation and Impact of Digital Diplomacy in the USA. In Akıllı, E., Güneş, B., & Güner, O. (Eds.), *Digital Diplomacy in the OSCE Region* (pp. 113–123). Spronger., DOI: 10.1007/978-3-031-50966-7_11

Pant, H. V. (2018) "The future of India's ties with ASEAN", The Diplomat, January, 26, Retrieved from, https://thediplomat.com/2018/01/the-future-of-indias-ties-with-asean/

Pant, H. V. (2018). India and Vietnam: A "Strategic Partnership" in the Making, *RSIS*, https://www.rsis.edu.sg/wp-content/uploads/2018/04/PB180409_-India-and-Vietnam.pdf

Pant, H. V., & Basu, P. (2024). India's nuanced approach in the South China Sea, *The Hindu*, https://www.thehindu.com/opinion/op-ed/indias-nuanced-approach-in-the-south-china-sea/article68080577.ece

Pape, R. A. (2005). Soft Balancing against the United States. *International Security*, *30*(1), 7–45. https://www.jstor.org/stable/4137457. DOI: 10.1162/0162288054894607

Paraskova, T. (2024). "CNOOC Begins Oil Production at South China Sea Field", Oil Price, 27 June 2024, https://oilprice.com/Latest-Energy-News/World-News/CNOOC-Begins-Oil-Production-at-South-China-Sea-Field.html.

Partha, S. G. (2013). An Enigma that is South Asia: India versus the Region. *Asia-Pacific Review*, *20*(1), 100–120. DOI: 10.1080/13439006.2013.788336

Pascal, C. (2018, December 7). Australia and New Zealand Must Rethink Their Approach to Pacific Trade. *Chatham House*. Retrieved from https://www.chathamhouse.org/2018/10/australia-and-new-zealand-must-rethink-their-approach-pacific-trade

Paszak, P. (2021). *China and the "Malacca Dilemma"*. https://warsawinstitute.org/china-malacca-dilemma/, accessed on January 11, 2025.

PCA-Permanent Court of Arbitration. (2013). *The South China Sea Arbitration (The Republic of Philippines v. The People's Republic of China),* https://pca-cpa.org/en/cases/7/#:~:text=On%2022%20January%202013%2C%20the,(the%20%E2%80%9CConvention%E2%80%9D)

PCA-Permanent Court of Arbitration. (2016). *The South China Sea Arbitration Award of 12 July 2016,* https://pcacases.com/web/sendAttach/2086

Peace Palace Library. (2024, June 24). *South China Sea territorial disputes*. Retrieved from https://peacepalacelibrary.nl/research-guide/south-china-sea-territorial-disputes

Pearsall, A. W. H. (1986). The royal navy and trade protection 1688–1714. *Renaissance and Modern Studies*, *30*(1), 109–123. DOI: 10.1080/14735788609366499

Pemmaraju, S. R. (2016). The South China Sea arbitration (The Philippines v. China): Assessment of the award on jurisdiction and admissibility. *Chinese Journal of International Law*, *15*(2), 265–307. DOI: 10.1093/chinesejil/jmw019

Peng, N. & Ngeow, C. B. (2022). "Managing the South China Sea Dispute: Multilateral and Bilateral Approaches, *Ocean Development & International Law* 1-23, https://doi.org/.DOI: 10.1080/00908320.2022.2034555

Peng, N. (2023). India's Growing Involvement in the South China Sea Disputes, *The Diplomat,* https://thediplomat.com/2023/11/indias-growing-involvement-in-the-south-china-sea-disputes/

Perlez, J. (2016). *Rodrigo Duterte and Xi Jinping Agree to Reopen South China Sea Talks,* 20.10.2016, https://www.nytimes.com/2016/10/21/world/asia/rodrigo-duterte-philippines-china-xi-jinping.html

Perlez, J. (2016, July 12). Tribunal Rejects Beijing's Claims in South China Sea. The New York Times. https://www.nytimes.com/2016/07/13/world/asia/south-china-sea-hague-ruling-philippines.html

Perlez, J. (2018, May 20). *On a Tiny Island in the South China Sea, Taiwan Stakes Its Claim*. The New York Times. Retrieved from https://www.nytimes.com/2018/05/20/world/asia/china-taiwan-island-south-sea.html

Permanent Court of Arbitration. (2013, August 27). PCA Press Release: Arbitration between the Republic of the Philippines and the People's Republic of China: Arbitral Tribunal Establishes Rules of Procedure and Initial Timetable. https://www.pcacases.com/web/sendAttach/227

Permanent Court of Arbitration. (2016). The South China Sea Arbitration Award. https://pca-cpa.org/en/cases/7/

Permanent Court of Arbitration. (2016, July 12). Award: PCA Case No 2013-19, in the matter of the South China Sea arbitration before an arbitral tribunal constituted under annex vii to the 1982 united nations convention on the Law Of The Sea between the Republic of the Philippines and the People's Republic of China. https://pcacases.com/web/sendAttach/2086

Permanent Court of Arbitration. (2016, July 12). *Press Release: The South China Sea Arbitration (The Republic of the Philippines v. The People's Republic of China).* Retrieved from https://docs.pca-cpa.org/2016/07/PH-CN-20160712-Press-Release-No-11-English.pdf

Permanent Mission of PRC to UN. (2009, May 7). Submission No. CML/17/2009. https://www.un.org/Depts/los/clcs_new/submissions_files/mysvnm33_09/chn_2009re_mys_vnm_e.pdf

Pertiwi, S. B., Kabinawa, L. N. R. W., & Elias, R. A. (2018). The diplomacy of quasi-state in territorial disputes: Taiwan in the South China Sea. *Jurnal Hubungan Internasional, 8*(2), 153–166. Retrieved from https://www.academia.edu/86585224/The_Diplomacy_of_Quasi_State_in_Territorial_Disputes_Taiwan_in_the_South_China_Sea

Pigafetta, A., & Stanley, H. E. J. (Eds.). (2010). *The First Voyage Round the World by Magellan: Translated from the Accounts of Pigafetta and Other Contemporary Writers*. Cambridge University Press. DOI: 10.1017/CBO9780511708046

Plummer, M. G. (2022). *US ASEAN Economic Relations in the Context of Asia Pacific Cooperation*, https://archivos.juridicas.unam.mx/www/bjv/libros/15/7049/5.pdf

Political-Security Community Blueprint, A. S. E. A. N. (2009). ASEAN Political-Security Community Blueprint 2009. ASEAN Secretariat. Retrieved from https://asean.org/wp-content/uploads/2021/03/APSC_BluePrint.pdf

Popescu, A. I. C. (2017). Control of Key Maritime Straits: China's Global Strategic Objective. *International Journal of Economics and Business Administration, 5*(1), 92–119.

Porter, E. (2010). Women, Political Decision-making, and Peace-building. *Global Change, Peace & Security, 15*(3), 245–262. DOI: 10.1080/0951274032000124965

Prabhakar, W. L. S. (2007). The regional dimension of territorial and maritime disputes in Southeast Asia: Actors, disagreements, and dynamics. In Guan, K. C., & Skogan, J. K. (Eds.), *Maritime security in Southeast Asia* (pp. 34–47). Routledge.

Presidency of the Philippines. (2012). *Administrative Order No. 29 s. 2012 "Naming the West Philippine Sea of the Republic of the Philippines"*, 05.09.2021, https://www.officialgazette.gov.ph/2012/09/05/administrative-order-no-29-s-2012/

Putra, B. A. (2024). "Brunei's silent claims in the South China Sea: a case for the theory of trade expectations", *Cogent Social Sciences*, 10(1): 1-14, https://doi.org/. DOI: 10.1080/23311886.2024.2317533

Putz, C. (2019), *The Art of the Balance: Japan, China and the US*, https://thediplomat.com/2019/01/the-art-of-the-balance-japan-china-and-the-united-states/

Quyet, L. V., & Nguyet, N. T. A. (2023). Sovereignty Over The Paracel Islands in 1884-1945: An Approach From The Rivalry Between France, China and, Japan. *Journal of Liberty and International Affairs*, *9*(2), 275–296. DOI: 10.47305/JLIA2392347q

Quynh, T. (2023). *What is Vietnam's GDP ranking in the world in 2022?*https://cafef.vn/gdp-viet-nam-dung-thu-bao-nhieu-the-gioi-nam-2022-20230320092746924.chn, accessed on June 12, 2024.

Raditio, K. H. (2018). *Understanding China's Behaviour in the South China Sea: A Defensive Realist Perspective*. Springer.

Rahmanillah, A. R., Bastian, T. P., & Ihsan, R. (2023). Indonesia's South China Sea Policy: The Limits of Hedging. *Edunity*, *2*(11), 1279–1291. DOI: 10.57096/edunity.v2i11.177

Raine, S., & Mière, L. C. (2013). *Regional Disorder: The South China Sea Disputes*. Routledge.

Ramcharan, R. (2003). ASEAN and non-interference. In Siddique, S., & Kumar, S. (Eds.), *The 2nd ASEAN reader* (pp. 52–57). Institute of Southeast Asian Studies.

Ranade, J. (2014). "China's New Policy of Peripheral Diplomacy", *Centre For China Analysis & Strategy (CCAS)*, May 2014, Https://Ccasindia.Org/Article_Details.Php?Aid=14.

Ranjan, A. (2019). India's South Asia Policy: Changes, Continuity or Continuity with Changes. *The Round Table*, *108*(3), 259–274. DOI: 10.1080/00358533.2019.1618611

Rapp-Hooper, M. (2015, February 18). *Before and After: The South China Sea Transformed*. Asia Maritime Transparency Initiative. Retrieved from https://amti.csis.org/before-and-after-the-south-china-sea-transformed/

Rauhala, E. (2014). *Obama in the Philippines: 'Our Goal Is Not to Contain China'* 20.04.2014, https://time.com/78779/obama-philippines-china/

Raymond, M., & Welch, D. A. (2022). What's really going on in the South China Sea? *Journal of Current Southeast Asian Affairs*, *4*(2), 214–239. DOI: 10.1177/18681034221086291

Reuters. (2023, August 25). *Australia says it will conduct more joint patrols with Philippines in South China Sea*. Retrieved from https://www.reuters.com/world/australia-says-it-will-conduct-more-joint-patrols-with-philippines-south-china-2023-08-25/

Rich, T. S. (2023, July 12). *Rethinking Taiwan's Diplomatic Relations: Beyond the Term "Diplomatic Allies"*. Global Taiwan Institute. Retrieved from https://globaltaiwan.org/2023/07/rethinking-taiwans-diplomatic-relations-beyond-the-term-diplomatic-allies/

Ripsman, N. M., Taliaferro, J. W., & Lobell, S. E. (2016). *Neoclassical realist theory of international politics*. Academic., DOI: 10.1093/acprof:oso/9780199899234.001.0001

Rizvi, O. (2023) "From India to Europe: What Opportunities and Challenges will the New Corridor Bring?", December 12, https://www.euronews.com/business/2023/12/15/from-india-to-europe-economic-corridor-to-offer-new-trade-opportunities

Roach, J. A. (2014). *Malaysia and Brunei: An Analysis of their Claims in the South China Sea.* CNA .

Roberts, C. B. (2012). *ASEAN regionalism: Cooperation, values and institutionalization*. Routledge. DOI: 10.4324/9780203181041

Rolland, N. (2017). China's "Belt and Road Initiative": Underwhelming or Game-Changer? *The Washington Quarterly*, *40*(1), 127–142. DOI: 10.1080/0163660X.2017.1302743

Roselle, L., Miskimmon, A., & O'Loughlin, B. (2014). Strategic narrative: A new means to understand soft power. *Media, War & Conflict*, *7*(1), 70–84. DOI: 10.1177/1750635213516696

Rosen, M. E. (2014, August). *Philippine Claims in the South China Sea: A Legal Analysis.* Washington: CNA. Retrieved from https://www.cna.org/archive/CNA_Files/pdf/iop-2014-u-008435.pdf

Rossi, E. (2023) "How IMEC (and Italy) can reshape trade and ties. A conversation with Soliman", Decode 39, September 12, https://decode39.com/7712/imec-italy-reshape-trade-ties-soliman/

Rossiana, Y. S. (2022). The South China Sea Dispute: Code of Conduct Implementation as the Dispute Settlement. *Jurnal Diplomasi Pertahanan*, *8*(1), 15–30. DOI: 10.33172/jdp.v8i1.884

Rothwell, D. R. (2013, September 5). The 1982 UN convention on the Law of the Sea and its relevance to. (L. B. Roberts, Ed.) *National Security College Occasional Paper*, pp. 13-17.

Rowan, J. P. (2005, May- June). The U.S.-Japan Security Alliance, ASEAN, and the South China Sea Dispute. *Asian Survey*, *45*(3), 414–436. DOI: 10.1525/as.2005.45.3.414

Royoux, D. (2018). Compte rendu de [MOTTET, Éric, LASSERRE, Frédéric et COURMONT, Barthélémy (dir.) (2017) Géopolitique de la mer de Chine méridionale. Eaux troubles en Asie du Sud-Est. Québec, Presses de l'Université du Québec, 202 p. (ISBN 978-2-76054-805-3)]. *Cahiers de Geographie de Quebec*, *62*(177), 472–473. DOI: 10.7202/1068753ar

Russett, B. (2016). Liberalism. In Dunne, T., Kurki, M., & Smith, S. (Eds.), *International Relations Theories: Discipline and Diversity*. Oxford University Press. DOI: 10.1093/hepl/9780198707561.003.0005

Ryan, S. E. K. Z. (2023). Malaysia: Securing sovereignty in the South China Sea through ASEAN centrality. *Yale Journal of International Affairs*. (March 15). https://www.yalejournal.org/publications/malaysia-securing-sovereignty-in-the-south-china-sea-through-asean-centrality

Sacks, B. J. (2022). The Political Geography of the South China Sea Disputes. Perspective: Expert Insights on a Timely Policy Issue, 1-32.

Saha, P. (2021). India Calibrates its South China Sea Approach, *Observer Research Foundation (ORF)*, https://www.orfonline.org/research/india-calibrates-its-south-china-sea-approach

Sang, H. T. (2022). The Growing Importance of Vietnam to India's South China Sea Policy, *Journal of Indo-Pacific Affairs*, 133-150.

Sang, T. M. (2022). *The Growing Importance of Vietnam to India's South China Sea Policy*.https://www.airuniversity.af.edu/JIPA/Display/Article/2980923/the-growing-importance-of-vietnam-to-indias-south-china-sea-policy/, accessed on June 2, 2024.

Sang, H. T. (2017). Australia's engagement in the South China Sea under the prospect theory approach and implications for Australia-Vietnam relations. *Asian Culture and History*, *9*(2), 60–70. DOI: 10.5539/ach.v9n2p60

Sato, M., Prétat, H., Mallory, T., Chen, H., & Poling, G. (2023, December 18). *Deep Blue Scars: Environmental Threats to the South China Sea*. Center for Strategic and International Studies. Retrieved from https://features.csis.org/environmental-threats-to-the-south-china-sea/

Saw, S., Sheng, L., & Chin, K. W. (2005). *ASEAN-China Relations: Realities and Prospects*. ISEAS. DOI: 10.1355/9789812306364

Schofield, C. (2014). Adrift on complex waters: geographical, geopolitical and legal dimensions to the South China Sea disputes. In Roberts, C. B., & Buszynski, L. (Eds.), *The South China Sea Maritime Dispute: Political, Legal and Regional Perspectives* (pp. 24–45). Routledge. DOI: 10.4324/9781315858029-2

Schonberger, H. B. (1985). The Cold War and the American Empire in Asia. *Radical History Review, 33*(33), 139–154. DOI: 10.1215/01636545-1985-33-139

Scott, D. (2017). *Chinese Maritime Strategy For The Indian Ocean.*https://cimsec.org/chinese-maritime-strategy-indian-ocean/, accessed on May 24, 2024.

Scott, D. (2013). India's role in the South China Sea: Geopolitics and Geoeconomics in Play. *India Review, 12*(2), 51–69. DOI: 10.1080/14736489.2013.786965

Senkyr, J., & Merkle, D. (2023). *Geopolitics in the South China Sea. Konrad-Adenauer-Stiftung e.* V. Monitor Security.

Senkyr, J., & Merkle, D. (2023). *Geopolitics in the South China Sea.* Konrad-Adenauer-Stiftung Monitör Security.

Seo, Y. (2024). Power Shift, the South China Sea Dispute, and the Role of International Law. *Michigan Journal of International Law, 45*(1), 93–152. DOI: 10.36642/mjil.45.1.power

Severino, R. C. (2006). *Southeast Asia: ASEAN community in search of an identity.* Institute of Southeast Asian Studies. DOI: 10.1355/9789812305671

Severino, R. C. (2010). ASEAN and the South China Sea. *Security Challenges, 6*(2), 37–47.

Severino, R. C. (2016). Global Issues and National Interests in the South China Sea. In Jenner, C. J., & Thuy, T. T. (Eds.), *The South China Sea: A Crucible of Regional Cooperation or Conflict-making SovereigntyClaims?* (pp. 31–42). Cambridge University Press. DOI: 10.1017/CBO9781139963084.003

Shambaugh, D. (2014). The Illusion of Chinese Power. *National Interest, 132*, 39–48. https://www.jstor.org/stable/44151213

Shambaugh, D. (2022). *Southeast Asia: Convergence of US-China superpowers (translated version).* National Political Publishing House.

Sharma, R. (2024). India's Plan To Develop "China Chokepoint" At Strategic Andaman & Nicobar Islands, In The Eye Of Storm, *Eurasian Times*, https://www.eurasiantimes.com/indias-plan-to-develop-china-chokepoint-at-strategic-andaman-nicobar-islands-in-the-eye-of-storm/

Shattuck, T. J. (2021, October 25). *A New Type of Diplomacy: Taiwan 50 Years after UN Expulsion*. Retrieved from Foreign Policy Research Institute: https://www.fpri.org/article/2021/10/a-new-type-of-diplomacy-taiwan-50-years-after-un-expulsion/

Shelton, G. (2001). China and Africa: Building an economic partnership. *The South African Journal of International Affairs*, *8*(2), 111–119. DOI: 10.1080/10220460109545365

Shih, V. (2022). *How China Would Like to Reshape International Economic Institutions*, https://www.atlanticcouncil.org/wp-content/uploads/2022/10/How-China-Would-Like-to-Reshape-International-Economic-Institutions.pdf

Shih, Y.-C. (2020, January). Taiwan's progress towards becoming an ocean country. *Marine Policy*, *111*, 1–7. DOI: 10.1016/j.marpol.2019.103725

Shin, D. M. (2015). *A Critical Review of the Concept of Middle Power*.https://www.e-ir.info/2015/12/04/a-critical-review-of-the-concept-of-middle-power/, accessed on June 13, 2024.

Shin, W. W. (2024, July 13). *'Opportune' timing: Why the Philippines is filing a seabed bid in the South China Sea, and the likely outcome*. Channel New Asia: https://www.channelnewsasia.com/asia/philippines-south-china-sea-continental-shelf-china-malaysia-sabah-vietnam-4474626 adresinden alındı

Shinde, V. (2023) "History Repeats: A new (old) Economic Corridor Emerges", Lowy Institute, November 1, https://www.lowyinstitute.org/the-interpreter/history-repeats-new-old-economic-corridor-emerges

Shorbagy, M. (2024). Triangular Dymamics: US Response to China's Assertivenes in the Middle East. *Arab Studies Quarterly*, *46*(2), 137–161. DOI: 10.13169/arabstudquar.46.2.0137

Shuib, M. S., Keling, M. F., & Ajis, M. N. (2009). The Implications of Cold War on Malaysia State Building Process. *Asian Culture and History*, *1*(2), 89–98. DOI: 10.5539/ach.v1n2p89

Siddiqa, A. (2023). Corridor Politics IMEC vs. BRI: Another Geopolitical Face-off in U.S.-China Rivalry. *Journal of Pakistan-China Studies*, *4*(1), 1–22. DOI: 10.55733/jpcs.v4i1.69

Signature states of ASEAN (Indonesia, Malaysia, Philippines, Singapore, Thailand) (1971, November 27). Zone of Peace, Freedom and Neutrality Declaration. https://www.pmo.gov.my/wp-content/uploads/2019/07/ZOPFAN.pdf

Simpson, G. J. (2004). *Great Powers and Outlaw State: Unequal Sovereigns in the International Legal Order*. Cambridge University Press. DOI: 10.1017/CBO9780511494185

Singh, A. (2022). ''Securing Sea Lines of Communication in Asia'', ORF, https://www.orfonline.org/public/uploads/posts/pdf/20230717144443.pdf.

Singh, A. (2023). Despite the excitement, India's South China Sea policy remains unchanged, https://www.lowyinstitute.org/the-interpreter/despite-excitement-india-s-south-china-sea-policy-remains-unchanged

Singh, A. (2024). *Rethinking the South China Sea in Indian Maritime Security Strategy.*https://thediplomat.com/2024/06/rethinking-the-south-china-sea-in-indian-maritime-security-strategy/, accessed on January 10, 2025.

Singh, M. (2024). India, Vietnam deepen defense partnership to confront regional challenges, *Indo-Pasific Defence Forum*, https://ipdefenseforum.com/2024/04/india-vietnam-deepen-defense-partnership-to-confront-regional-challenges/

Singleton, C. (2024). *China and the U.S. Are Careening Toward a South China Sea Crisis,*https://foreignpolicy.com/2024/07/23/us-south-china-sea-philippines-crisis-military-alliance-deterrence/ (Accessed 26.07.2024).

Sioco, M. A. (2020). *Taiwan's strategic role in the Spratly Islands and the significance of Itu Aba*. Radio Taiwan International. Retrieved from https://en.rti.org.tw/news/view/id/2010876

Sładkowski, A., Bošnjak, R., Kezić, D. and Krile, S. (2024) BRI Project: Are There Alternatives? Transactions on Maritime Science. Split, Croatia, 13(1). .DOI: 10.7225/toms.v13.n01.018

Smith, A. (2005). An Inquıry Into The Nature and Causes of The Wealth of Natıons.

Smith, N. (2019, January 5). *Taiwan president signals support for UK base in South China Sea*. Retrieved from The Telegraph: https://www.telegraph.co.uk/news/2019/01/05/taiwan-president-calls-international-support-defend-democracy/

Socialist Republic of Vietnam. (2019), Vietnam National Defence, https://mod.gov.vn/en/intro/vnd/sa-en-dod-dp/sa-en-dv-mf-stqp/17493317-e8da-4830-ba9d-75d7b39df332

Song, V. S., Don, N. T., & Khoi, N. L. H. (2020, June 16). Examining the "historical evidence" for China's sovereignty over the South China Sea islands (Part 1). https://usvietnam.uoregon.edu/en/examining-chinese-historical-evidences-of-sovereignty-over-the-south-china-sea-islands-part-1-china-was-the-first-to-discover-and-name-the-nansha-islands/

Song, Y. H. (2015, May 7). *Taiping Island: An Island or a Rock under UNCLOS.* Asia Maritime Transparency Initiative. Retrieved from https://amti.csis.org/taiping-island-an-island-or-a-rock-under-unclos/

Song, Y.-h. (2013). The South China Sea Workshop Process and Taiwan's Participation. In *N.-T. A. Hu, & T. L. McDorman, Maritime Issues in the South China Sea: Troubled Waters or A Sea of Opportunity* (pp. 70–86). Routledge.

Song, Y.-h., & Zou, K. (2016). *Major Law and Policy Issues in the South China Sea: European and American Perspectives.* Routledge. DOI: 10.4324/9781315593210

South China Morning Post (2024, June 15). Anwar Ibrahim on navigating Malaysia through China-US tensions- Talking Post with Yonden Lhatoo. *Youtube.* https://www.youtube.com/watch?v=xtM-wPrgl6k&list=LL

South China Morning Post (SCMP). (August, 2023). South China Sea: Malaysia joins India in rejecting new Chinese map over land claim ahead of G20 summit, *SCMP,* https://www.scmp.com/news/asia/southeast-asia/article/3232887/south-china-sea-malaysia-joins-india-rejecting-new-chinese-map-over-land-claim-ahead-g20-summit

South China Morning Post. (2019, February 18). *Explained: South China Sea dispute.* Retrieved from https://www.scmp.com/week-asia/article/2186449/explained-south-china-sea-dispute

Southgate, L. (2019). *ASEAN Resistance to Sovereignty Violation: Interests, Balancing and the Role of the Vanguard State.* Bristol University Press.

Spykman, N. J. (1944). THE Geography of the Peace. New York: HARCOURT, BRACE AND COMPANY. Retrieved from www.questia.com

State.gov. (2011). *Presentation of the Order of Lakandula, Signing of the Partnership for Growth and Joint Press Availability with Philippines Foreign Secretary Albert Del Rosario,* Hillary Rodham Clinton, Secretary of State, Manila, Philippines, November 16, 2011, https://2009-2017.state.gov/secretary/20092013clinton/rm/2011/11/177234.htm

Statista. (2023). *Taiwan's exports to New Southbound Policy countries from 2013 to 2023*. Retrieved from https://www.statista.com/statistics/1271612/taiwan-exports-to-new-southbound-policy-countries/

Statista. (2024). *Top semiconductor foundries market share 2024*. Retrieved from https://www.statista.com/statistics/867223/worldwide-semiconductor-foundries-by-market-share/

Stevens, P. (2004). Resource curse and investment in energy industries. In C. Cleveland (Ed.) *Encyclopedia of Energy 5*, pp. 451-9. DOI: 10.1016/B0-12-176480-X/00548-9

Stewart, S., & Reininger, B. (2016). Executive Summary. In Fung, E. & Loong, A. (Eds.). *Assessing the Obama Administration's Pivot to Asia*. Jackson School of International Studies, University of Washington. https://digital.lib.washington.edu/researchworks/bitstreams/e3fe0493-a6c6-4787-b5ea-2a62465ccc33/download

Stopford, M. (2008). *MARITIME ECONOMICS* (3rd ed.). DOI: 10.4324/9780203891742

Storey, I. (2024). "Commentary: Malaysia and the South China Sea dispute - a sea change under PM Anwar Ibrahim?", *Channel News Asia*, 31 August 2024, https://www.channelnewsasia.com/commentary/south-china-sea-malaysia-anwar-dispute-policy-4575821.

Storey, I. (2016). The South China Sea dispute: Navigating diplomatic and strategic tensions. In Storey, I., & Cheng-Yi, L. (Eds.), *ASEAN and the South China Sea: Maintaining peace in the Asia-Pacific* (pp. 134–160). Routledge. DOI: 10.1355/9789814695565

Strangio, S. (2020). *In UN Speech, Duterte Stiffens Philippines' Stance on the South China Sea,* 23.09.2020, https://thediplomat.com/2020/09/in-un-speech-duterte-stiffens-philippines-stance-on-the-south-china-sea/

Strangio, S. (2023, April 11). Malaysia Clarifies South China Sea Policy Following PM's Comments. *The Diplomat*. https://thediplomat.com/2023/04/malaysia-clarifies-south-china-sea-policy-following-pms-comments/

Strating, R. (2019). *Australia's approach to the South China Sea disputes* (Number 485). Washington: East West Center-Asia Pacific Bulletin. 1-2.

Sullivan, A. (2015), *Navigating the Future: US-Taiwan Maritime Cooperation and Building Order in Asia, Center for a New American Security*, https://www.files.ethz.ch/isn/191907/CNAS_Sullivan_USTaiwanMaritime_Final.pdf

Sunariyanto, B. P., & Hanan, A. (2022). The Importance of the South China Sea Energy Perspective. *Purnomo Yusgiantoro Center (PYC),* https://www.purnomoyusgiantorocenter.org/the-importance-of-the-south-china-sea-energy-perspective/

Sundaram, R. (2024). China Factor in India-Vietnam Strategic Relations, *India Defence Review*, https://www.indiandefencereview.com/news/china-factor-in-india-vietnam-strategic-relations/

Supriyanto, R. A. (2016). "Out of Its Comfort Zone: Indonesia and the South China Sea", *Asia Policy* (21): 21-28, https://www.jstor.org/stable/24905085.

Symmons, C. R. (1979). The maritime zones of islands in international law. Hague: Martinus Nijhoff Publishers. DOI: 10.1163/9789004636170

Taipei Times. (2024, January 30). *Itu Aba dredging completed, CGA says*. Retrieved from https://www.taipeitimes.com/News/front/archives/2024/01/30/2003812822

Taiwan Semiconductor Manufacturing Company. (2022, December 6). *TSMC Announces Updates for TSMC Arizona*. Retrieved from https://pr.tsmc.com/english/news/2977

Taiwan Today. (2013). "Caution needed in promoting East China Sea peace initiative", 06 January 2013, https://taiwantoday.tw/news_amp.php?unit=2&post=2776&unitname= Politics-Top-News&postname=Caution-needed-in-promoting-East-China-Sea-peace-initiative.

Taiwan Today. (2017, September 08). *Taiping Island visited for 1st time by international science group*. Retrieved from https://nspp.mofa.gov.tw/nsppe/news.php?post=121166&unit=390

Taiwan, M. O. F. A. (2015, May 26). *South China Sea Peace Initiative*. Retrieved from https://www.mofa.gov.tw/News_Content.aspx?n=604CBAA3DB3DDA11&sms=69594088D2AB9C50&s=4589151C339E71C5

Taiwan, M. O. F. A. (2016, July 19). *Sustainable Governance and Enduring Peace in the South China Sea*. Retrieved from https://en.mofa.gov.tw/theme.aspx?n=1462&s=40&sms=294

Taiwan, M. O. F. A. (2022, July 7). *Foreign Policy Guidelines*. Retrieved March 25, 2024, from https://en.mofa.gov.tw/cp.aspx?n=1302

Tambi, R. (2023) "India pushes back against China's economic influence" September 9, https://eastasiaforum.org/2023/09/09/india-pushes-back-against-chinas-economic-influence/

Tamer, C. (2022) "The 'I2U2' Alliance in West Asia: A New 'QUAD'", July 25, ANKASAM, https://www.ankasam.org/the-i2u2-alliance-in-west-asia-a-new-quad/?lang=en

Tan, R. (2024). Malaysia's appetite for oil and gas puts it on collision course with China, *The Washington Post,*https://www.washingtonpost.com/world/2024/05/11/china-malaysia-south-china-sea/

Tanrıverdi, B. (2021). *Güney Çin Denizi'nde Güç ve Uluslararası Hukuk.* Retrieved from Hukuk ve Bilişim: https://hukukvebilisim.org/guney-cin-denizinde-guc-uluslararasi-hukuk-ve-tahkim/

Territorial and Maritime Dispute (Nicaragua v. Colombia) (Judgment) (I.C.J November 19, 2012).

Thaliyakkattil, S. (2019). *China's Achilles' Heel: The Belt and Road Initiative and Its Indian Discontents.* Palgrave Macmillan. DOI: 10.1007/978-981-13-8425-7

Thanh, P.Q. (2022). Great power strategic competition and Vietnam's countermeasures. *Journal of Political Theory,* 534.

Thao, N. H. (2003). "The 2002 Declaration On The Conduct Of Parties In The South China Sea: A Note", *Ocean Development & International Law* 34 (3-4): 279-285, Https://Doi.Org/10.1080/00908320390221849.

Thayer, C. (2014). 'Speak Softly and Carry a Big Stick': What is Malaysia Playing At? *The Diplomat.* https://thediplomat.com/2014/03/speak-softly-and-carry-a-big-stick-what-is-malaysia-playing-at/

Thayer, C. (2020). *Will Vietnam Lease Cam Ranh Bay to the United States?*https://thediplomat.com/2020/05/will-vietnam-lease-cam-ranh-bay-to-the-united-states/

Thayer, C. A. (2013). ASEAN, China and the code of conduct in the South China Sea. *SAIS Review (Paul H. Nitze School of Advanced International Studies), 33*(2), 75–84. DOI: 10.1353/sais.2013.0022

Thayer, C. A. (2016). In Yann-huei, S., & Zou, K. (Eds.), *China-ASEAN and the Soth China Sea: Chinese Assertiveness and South Asian Responses, Major Law and Policy Issues in the South China Sea: European and American Perspectives* (p. 28). Routledge.

Thayer, C. A. (2020). ASEAN, China, and the Code of Conduct. In Buszynski, L., & Hai, D. T. (Eds.), *The South China Sea From a Regional Maritime Dispute to Geo-Strategic Competition* (pp. 43–59). Routledge.

The America Times. (2023, March 14). *China's reaction to AUKUS agreement*. Retrieved from https://www.america-times.com/chinas-reaction-to-aukus-agreement/

The Australian Government-Department of Foreign Affairs and Trade. (2023, December 12). *Australian Government concerns about recent actions in the South China Sea*. Retrieved from https://www.dfat.gov.au/news/media-release/australian-government-concerns-about-recent-actions-south-china-sea

The Defense Post. (2023, November 30). Taiwan Begins Mass Production of Indigenous Air Defense System. Retrieved from https://thedefensepost.com/2023/11/30/taiwan-air-defense-system/

The Economic Times. (2023, July 29). *US, Australia to cooperate with India to ensure security and stability of Indo-Pacific*. Retrieved from https://economictimes.indiatimes.com/news/defence/us-australia-to-cooperate-with-india-to-ensure-security-and-stability-of-indo-pacific/articleshow/102231936.cms?from=mdr

The Guardian. (2022, June 7). *China accuses Australia and Canada of 'disinformation' over jet encounters*. Retrieved from https://www.theguardian.com/world/2022/jun/07/china-accuses-australia-canada-jet-encounters

The Guardian. (2023, March 19). *Australia has 'absolutely not' committed to join US in event of war over Taiwan, Marles says*. Retrieved from https://www.theguardian.com/world/2023/mar/19/australia-has-absolutely-not-committed-to-join-us-in-event-of-war-over-taiwan-marles-says

The Guardian. (2024). ''Asean leaders cite 1982 UN treaty in SCS dispute'', https://www.theguardian.com/world/2020/jun/27/asean-leaders-cite-1982-un-treaty-in-south-china-sea-dispute.

The International Institute for Strategic Studies. (2023). *Arming Vietnam: Widened International-security Relations in Support of Military-capability Development.* https://www.iiss.org/globalassets/global-content---content--migration/arming-vietnam-widened-internationalsecurity-relations-in-support-of-militarycapability-development.pdf, accessed on June 18, 2024.

The South China Sea Arbitration (The Republic of Philippines v. The People's Republic of China), PCA Case N° 2013-19 (Permanent Court of Arbitration July 12, 2016). Retrieved from https://pcacases.com/web/sendAttach/2086

The U.S. Energy Information Administration. (2024). *Regional analysis brief: South China Sea*. U.S. Department of Energy.

The US Department of Defense. (2023, July 29). *Joint statement on Australia-U.S. Ministerial Consultations (AUSMIN)2023*. Retrieved from https://www.defense.gov/News/Releases/Release/Article/3476104/joint-statement-on-australia-us-ministerial-consultations-ausmin-2023/

Thorburn, J. (2013). Vietnam as a Role Model for Development. *Journal of Oxford Academic*, *53*(2), 99–118. DOI: 10.1093/acprof:oso/9780199671557.003.0005

Thu, H. L. (2020). *Fishing While the Water is Muddy: China's Newly Announced Administrative Districts in the South China Sea,* 06.05.2020, https://amti.csis.org/fishing-while-the-water-is-muddy-chinas-newly-announced-administrative-districts-in-the-south-china-sea/

Tien, H.-M., & Cheng, T.-j. (2016). *The Security Environment in the Asia-Pacific*. Routledge. DOI: 10.4324/9781315292090

Tiezzi, S. (2016, January 28). *Taiwan's President Ma to Visit Disputed South China Sea Island*. Retrieved from https://thediplomat.com/2016/01/taiwans-president-ma-to-visit-disputed-south-china-sea-island/

Till, G. (2016). The Global Gignificance of the South China Sea Disputes. In Jenner, C. J., & Thuy, T. T. (Eds.), *The South China Sea: A Crucible of Regional Cooperation or Conflict-making Sovereignty Claims?* (pp. 13–30). Cambridge University Press. DOI: 10.1017/CBO9781139963084.002

Tkachenko, B. I. (2014). Territorial disputes in the South China Sea. The Spratly Archipelago. *Asia-Pacific Journal of Marine Science & Education*, *4*(2), 56–94.

Tønnesson, S. (2002). "The Paracels: The "Other" South China Sea Dispute", *Asian Perspective Special Issue on China-ASEAN Relations* 26(4):145-169, https://www.jstor.org/stable/42704389.

Tønnesson, S. (2020). Four aspects of the crisis in the South China Sea. In Buszynski, L., & Hai, D. T. (Eds.), *The South China Sea: From a Regional Maritime Dispute to Geo-Strategic Competition* (pp. 9–23). Routledge.

Tonnesson, S. (2021). The SCS: Historical Developments. In Zou, K. (Ed.), *Routledge Handbook of The SCS* (pp. 31–45). Routledge.

Townsend-Gault, I. (1998). Preventive Diplomacy and Pro-activity in the South China Sea. *Contemporary Southeast Asia*, *20*(2), 171–190. DOI: 10.1355/CS20-2D

Treaty of Amity and Cooperation in Southeast Asia. (1976). Treaty of Amity and Cooperation in Southeast Asia (TAC). Retrieved from https://asean-aipr.org/treaty-of-amity-and-cooperation-in-southeast-asia-1976-tac

Trinh, V. D., & Huyen, H. D. (2024). Vietnam's Response to the US Indo-Pacific Strategy in the Context of a Rising China. *Journal of Current Southeast Asian Affairs, 43*(1), 120–147. DOI: 10.1177/18681034241237813

Tsai, C.-T. (2022). *Taiwan's South China Sea policy evolution and its exclusion from regional dialogues*. Asia Maritime Transparency Initiative. Retrieved from https://amti.csis.org/taiwan-scs-policy-evolution/

Tuan, H. A. (1996). ASEAN Dispute Management: Implications for Vietnam and an Expanded ASEAN. *Contemporary Southeast Asia, 18*(1), 61–80. DOI: 10.1355/CS18-1D

Tuan, H. A. (2016). The South China Sea Dispute: Navigating Diplomatic and Strategic Tensions. In Storey, I., & Cheng-Yi, L. (Eds.), *The South China Sea dispute: Navigating Diplomatic and Strategic Tensions* (pp. 186–204). Yusof Ishak Institute.

Turcsány, R. Q. (2017). *Chinese Assertiveness in the South China Sea: Power Sources, Domestic Politics, and Reactive Foreign Policy*. Springer.

Turker, H. (2023). "Maritime Chessboard: The Geopolitical Dynamics of the South China Sea", *Geopolitical Monitor*, 24 August 2023, https://www.geopoliticalmonitor.com/maritime-chessboard-the-geopolitical-dynamics-of-the-south-china-sea/.

Türkeş, H. (2018). "South China Sea 'major' trade route for crude oil", *Anatolian Agency (AA) Energy Terminal*, 28 August 2018, https://www.aa.com.tr/en/energy/general/south-china-sea-major-trade-route-for-crude-oil-/21401

Tüter, M. (2022). "Vietnam's Policy over South China Sea: Potential for Conflict Escalation?", *International Journal of Political Studies* 8 (2): 63-74, Doi: , https://dergipark.org.tr/en/download/article-file/2544043.DOI: 10.25272/icps.1145238

Tzeng, W. F. (2023). "The Anatomy of Diplomatic Work among China's Top Leaders", *China Review Special Issue: External and Internal Factors Shaping the Outcomes of 2024 Elections in Taiwan* 23(4): 229-258, https://www.jstor.org/stable/10.2307/48750787.

U.S. Congress. (1979). *Taiwan Relations Act*. Retrieved from https://www.congress.gov/bill/96th-congress/house-bill/2479

U.S. Defence Secretary. (2023) AUKUS: The Trilateral Security Partnership Between Australia, U.K. and U.S., September 12, https://www.defense.gov/Spotlights/AUKUS/

U.S. Department of Defence. (2023). *Philippines, U.S. Announce Four New EDCA Sites*, U.S. Department of State, (1998). *Agreement Between U.S. and Philippines*, https://www.state.gov/wp-content/uploads/2019/02/12931-Philippines-Defense-Status-of-Forces-10.9.1998.pdf

U.S. Department of Defense. (2022). *Military and Security Developments Involving the People's Republic of China 2022*. Retrieved from https://media.defense.gov/2022/Nov/29/2003122279/-1/-1/1/2022-MILITARY-AND-SECURITY-DEVELOPMENTS-INVOLVING-THE-PEOPLES-REPUBLIC-OF-CHINA.PDF

U.S. Department of Defense. (2023, September 14). U.S. Strengthening Deterrence in Taiwan Strait. https://www.defense.gov/News/News-Stories/Article/Article/3531094/us-strengthening-deterrence-in-taiwan-strait/

U.S. Department of State. (2014). China: Maritime Claims in the South China Sea. Limits in the Seas, No. 143. https://www.state.gov/wp-content/uploads/2019/10/LIS-143.pdf

U.S. Department of State. (2022, May 28). *U.S. Relations With Taiwan*. Retrieved from https://www.state.gov/u-s-relations-with-taiwan/

U.S. Energy Information Administration. (2024). Regional Analysis Brief: South China Sea. https://www.eia.gov/international/content/analysis/regions_of_interest/South_China_Sea/south_china_sea.pdf

UN. (2024, April 11). Commission on the Limits of the Continental Shelf (CLCS) Outer limits of the continental shelf beyond 200 nautical miles from the baselines: Submissions to the Commission: Joint submission by Malaysia and the Socialist Republic of Viet Nam. https://www.un.org/Depts/los/clcs_new/submissions_files/submission_mysvnm_33_2009.htm

United Nations Development Programme. (2023, December 8). *Dialogue between the Minister of Agriculture and Rural Development and Fishermen and Associations: Promoting Co-management for Sustainable Fisheries*. Retrieved from https://www.undp.org/vietnam/press-releases/dialogue-between-minister-agriculture-and-rural-development-and-fishermen-and-associations-promoting-co-management-sustainable

United Nations. (1945). Charter of the United Nations and Statute of the International Court of Justice. Retrieved from https://treaties.un.org/doc/publication/ctc/uncharter.pdf

United Nations. (1983). United Nations Convention on the Law of the Sea. Retrieved from https://www.un.org/depts/los/convention_agreements/texts/unclos/unclos_e.pdf

United States International Trade Commission. (2023). Executive Briefings on Trade: U.S.-Taiwan Trade. Retrieved from Winkler, S. (2012). *Taiwan's UN Dilemma: To Be or Not To Be*. Brookings. Retrieved from https://www.brookings.edu/articles/taiwans-un-dilemma-to-be-or-not-to-be/

US Department of Defense. (2023). *Philippines, U.S. Announce Locations of Four New EDCA Sites,* April 3, 2023, https://www.defense.gov/News/Releases/Release/Article/3349257/philippines-us-announce-locations-of-four-new-edca-sites/

US Department of State Bureau of Oceans and International Environmental and Scientific Affairs. (2022). *People's Republic of China: Maritime Claims in the South China Sea*. U.S. Department of State.

US Department of State. (2022). Limits in the Seas No. 150: People's Republic of China: Maritime Claims in the South China Sea. United States Department of State Bureau of Oceans and International Environmental and Scientific Affairs. https://www.state.gov/wp-content/uploads/2022/01/LIS150-SCS.pdf

US Energy Information Administration. (2024, last updated on March 21). South China Sea: Overview. https://www.eia.gov/international/content/analysis/regions_of_interest/South_China_Sea/south_china_sea.pdf

US Energy Information Administration. (2024, March 21). *South China Sea*. Retrieved from US Energy Information Administration: https://www.eia.gov/international/analysis/regions-of-interest/South_China_Sea

US News. (2022). Best Countries: Power. https://www.usnews.com/news/best-countries/rankings/power, accessed on June 12, 2024.

Valencia, M. (1988). Spratley Islands: Dangerous ground in the South China Sea. *The Pacific Review, 1*(4), 443–448. DOI: 10.1080/09512748808718792

Villaruel, J. J. C. (2015). India's Interests in the South China Sea, *Center for International RElations & Strategic Studies (CIRSS), Vol 2 No. 8*, https://fsi.gov.ph/indias-interests-in-the-south-china-sea-by-jemimah-joanne-c-villaruel-vol-ii-no-8-march-2015/

Vu, K. (2019, August 24). *Chinese ship inches closer to Vietnam coastline amid South China Sea tensions*. Reuters: https://www.reuters.com/article/us-vietnam-china-southchinasea/chinese-ship-inches-closer-to-vietnam-coastline-amid-south-china-sea-tensions-idUSKCN1VE068. adresinden alındı

Vu, K. (2024). "Why Vietnam Cannot Copy the Philippines' China Policy", *The Diplomat*, 14 February 2024, https://thediplomat.com/2024/02/why-vietnam-cannot-copy-the-philippines-china-policy/.

Wade, R. H. (2020). Rethinking the world economy as a two bloc hierarchy. *Real-World Economics Review*, Issue no. 92. https://www.paecon.net/PAEReview/issue92/Wade92.pdf

Wade, R. H. (2003). What strategies are viable for developing countries today? The World Trade Organization and the shrinking of 'development space'. *Review of International Political Economy, 10*(4), 621–644. DOI: 10.1080/09692290310001601902

Wagner, C. (2005) From Hard Power to Soft Power? Ideas, Interaction, Institutions, and Images in India's South Asia Policy, Heidelber Papers in South Asian and Comparative Politics. Working Paper No. 26.

Wagner, C. (2016). The Role of India and China in South Asia. *Strategic Analysis, 40*(4), 307–320. DOI: 10.1080/09700161.2016.1184790

Wallerstein, I. (1991). *Geopolitics and Geoculture: Essays on the Changing World-System*. Cambridge University Press.

Walt, S. M., & Belfer, R. A. (2017). *Great Powers Are Defined by Their Great Wars*.https://foreignpolicy.com/2017/09/21/great-powers-are-defined-by-their-great-wars/, accessed on June 12, 2024.

Waltz, K. N. (2014). Anarchic orders and balance of power. In Elman, C., & Jensen, M. A. (Eds.), *Realism Reader* (pp. 104–123). Routledge.

Wang, Z. (2015). Chinese Discourse on the "Nine-Dashed Line": Rights, Interests, and Nationalism. *Asian Survey, 55*(3), 502–524. DOI: 10.1525/as.2015.55.3.502

Weatherbee, D. E. (2009). *International relations in Southeast Asia: The struggle for autonomy*. Rowman & Littlefield Publishers, Inc.

Wee, L. Z. (2022). ''What is Nanyang art?'', Think China, https://www.Thinkchina.sg /culture/what-Nanyang-art.

Wei, S. T. (2024). "YL Blog #60 – Caught in the Middle: The Measured Voice of Brunei's Foreign Policy Amidst the South China Sea Disputes", *Pacific Forum*, 29 February 2024, https://pacforum.org/publications/yl-blog-60-caught-in-the-middle-the-measured-voice-of-bruneis-foreign-policy-amidst-the-south-china-sea-disputes/.

Weiss, J. C., & Wallace, J. L. (2021). omestic politics, China's rise, and the future of the liberal international order. *International Organization, 75*(2), 635–664. DOI: 10.1017/S002081832000048X

Welti, P., Woker, D., & Bohn, J. (2018), Far From Geography: A Free and Open Indo Pacific, Asia Society, https://asiasociety.org/switzerland/far-geography-free-and-open-indo-pacific

Wen, W., & Xiaochen, C. (2016). Who Supports China in the South China Sea and Why, *The Diplomat,*https://thediplomat.com/2016/07/who-supports-china-in-the-south-china-sea-and-why/

Westcott, B., & Lendon, B. (2019). *Duterte threatens 'suicide mission' if Beijing oversteps in South China Sea,* CNN, 05.04.2019, https://edition.cnn.com/2019/04/05/asia/south-china-sea-duterte-beijing-intl/index.html

Wester, S., & Pitakdumrongkit, K. (2024). On US-ASEAN Relations & Trade, https://asiasociety.org/policy-institute/us-asean-relations-trade

White House. (2010). *President Obama to Host Second U.S. - ASEAN Leaders Meeting*, https://obamawhitehouse.archives.gov/the-press-office/2010/09/03/president-obama-host-second-us-asean-leaders-meeting

Womack, B. (2017). International Crises and China's Rise: Comparing the 2008 Global Financial Crisis and the 2017 Global Political Crisis. *The Chinese Journal of International Politics*, *10*(4), 383–401. DOI: 10.1093/cjip/pox015

Wong, A. C. (2024). "The 2012 Scarborough Shoal Standoff: Analyzing China in Crisis with the Philippines," Encounters and Escalations in the Indo-Pacific Perspectives on China's Military and Implications for Regional Security. In Mastro, O. S. (Ed.), *The National Bureau of Asian Research* (pp. 75–90).

Woods, S. (2016, July). The Sino-Philippine South China Sea Dispute. *American Journal of Chinese Studies*, *23*(1), 159–171.

World Population Review. (2024) world population by country 2024, https://worldpopulationreview.com/countries/by-gdp

Wright, G. (2023). *China discusses military budget while warning of escalating threats,* BBC, 06.03.2023, https://www.bbc.com/news/world-asia-china-64857194

Wu, S. (2013). *Solving disputes for regional cooperation and development in the South China Sea: A Chinese perspective*. Chandos Publishing. DOI: 10.1533/9781780633558

Wu, Y., Lim, I. C. L., Li, L., Chen, L., Hsiao, P., Lee, W., & Lan, K. (2024). The evolution of resource management in Taiwanese fisheries: Coastal and offshore perspectives. *PeerJ*, *12*, e18434. DOI: 10.7717/peerj.18434 PMID: 39619187

Yano, K. (2020, November 20). Maritime Security Involving Japan and Taiwan. Security Strategy Research Institute of Japan. Retrieved from https://www.ssri-j.com/Taiwan/Strategic%20dialogue/taiwanS/yanokazu-2-20201120.pdf

Yee, T. H. (2019, September 13). *Vietnam digs in on South China Sea oil and gas projects amid Chinese pressure*. The Strait Times: https://www.straitstimes.com/asia/se-asia/vietnam-digs-in-on-south-china-sea-oil-and-gas-projects-amid-chinese-pressure adresinden alındı

Yi, S. W. (2024, January 04). *Navigating South China Sea Security in2024*. Retrieved from The Diplomat: https://thediplomat.com/2024/01/navigating-south-china-sea-security-in-2024/

Yi, W. (2024, April 26) Written Interview with Al Jazeera Media Network by Foreign Minister Wang Yi. https://www.fmprc.gov.cn/eng/wjb_663304/wjbz_663308/2461_663310/202404/t20240426_11289693.html

Yuan, Z., & Fu, Q. (2020). Narrative Framing and the United States' Threat Construction of Rivals. *The Chinese Journal of International Politics*, *13*(13), 419–453. DOI: 10.1093/cjip/poaa008

Yuying, Z., & Jingyi, C. (2024, May 7). China extends visa exemption for 12 countries to 2025 year-end. *Global Times*. https://www.globaltimes.cn/page/202405/1311838.shtml

Zha, D., & Valencia, M. J. (2001). Mischief Reef: Geopolitics and implications. *Journal of Contemporary Asia*, *31*(1), 86–103. DOI: 10.1080/00472330180000061

Zhang, R. (2021). "Explainer | South China Sea: what are rival claimants building on islands and reefs?", *South China Morning Post*, 07 March 2021, https://www.scmp.com/news/china/diplomacy/article/3124309/south-china-sea-what-are-rival-claimants-building-islands-and.

Zhang, D. (2018). The Concept of 'Community of Common Destiny' in China's Diplomacy: Meaning, Motives and Implications. *Asia & the Pacific Policy Studies*, *5*(2), 196–207. https://onlinelibrary.wiley.com/doi/epdf/10.1002/app5.231. DOI: 10.1002/app5.231

Zhang, Y., & Buzan, B. (2012). The tributary system as international society in theory and practice. *The Chinese Journal of International Politics*, *5*(1), 3–36. DOI: 10.1093/cjip/pos001

Zhao, M. (2024). The belt & road initiative and U.S.-China competition over the global South. *China Economic Journal*, *17*(2), 166–181. DOI: 10.1080/17538963.2024.2344270

Zhao, S. (2020). East Asian Disorder China and the South China Sea Disputes. *Asian Survey, 60*(3), 490–509. https://online.ucpress.edu/as/article/60/3/490/110498/East-Asian-DisorderChina-and-the-South-China-Sea. DOI: 10.1525/as.2020.60.3.490

Zheng, Z., & Wu, J. (2020, July 13). Legal implications of the map of the South China Sea Islands of China under international law. South China Sea Strategic Situation Probing Initiative (SCSPI). Retrieved from https://ssrn.com/abstract=3995467

Zhou, L. (2020, November 12). What is RCEP and what does an Indo-Pacific free-trade deal offer China? *South China Morning Post.* https://www.scmp.com/news/china/diplomacy/article/3109436/what-rcep-and-what-does-indo-pacific-free-trade-deal-offer

Zhou, O. (2024). "CNOOC discovers Kaiping South oilfield in South China Sea with over 100 mil mt proven volume", *S&P Global*, 08 March 2024, https://www.spglobal.com/commodityinsights/en/market-insights/latest-news/oil/030824-cnooc-discovers-kaiping-south-oilfield-in-south-china-sea-with-over-100-mil-mt-proven-volume.

Zhou, W., & Esteban, M. (2018). Beyond Balancing: China's approach towards the Belt and Road Initiative. *Journal of Contemporary China, 27*(112), 487–501. DOI: 10.1080/10670564.2018.1433476

Zone of Peace, Freedom and Neutrality Declaration (ZOPFAN). (1971). Zone of Peace, Freedom and Neutrality Declaration (ZOPFAN). Retrieved from https://pmo.gov.my

Zou, Y. (2023). "China and Indonesia's responses to maritime disputes in the South China Sea: forming a tacit understanding on security", *Marine Policy* (149): 1-8, https://doi.org/.DOI: 10.1016/j.marpol.2023.105502

Zou, L., Shen, J. H., Zhang, J., & Lee, C. C. (2021). What is the rationale behind China's infrastructure investment under the Belt and Road Initiative. *Journal of Economic Surveys, 36*(3), 605–633. DOI: 10.1111/joes.12427

Zulkifli, N. (2021). *The United States (US)-Taiwan Strategic Partnership.* Retrieved from https://www.academia.edu/50194003/The_United_States_US_Taiwan_Strategic_Partnership U.S. Department of State. (1945, July 26). *Potsdam Declaration.* In *Foreign Relations of the United States: Diplomatic Papers, The Conference of Berlin (The Potsdam Conference), 1945, Volume II.* Retrieved from https://history.state.gov/historicaldocuments/frus1945Berlinv02/d1382

About the Contributors

Ferdi Güçyetmez studied international relations and political science at the University of Zurich and the University of Geneva. He completed his master's degree in political science at the University of Bern, Switzerland. He worked as a visiting researcher at Oxford University, one of the world's leading universities, and conducted research on European Politics with a Swiss scientific team. He is currently pursuing his PhD on "Geopolitics and Politics in International Relations" in Switzerland. He has spoken and presented papers at the United Nations, the World Trade Organization, the UN High Commissioner for Refugees, the International Organization for Migration and the European Parliament. He lectures on the European Union, Security and Geopolitics at University chairs and institutes. He has scientific articles and books in the fields of geopolitics."

Aybala Lale Kahraman earned her Ph.D. in 2023 from Ankara Hacı Bayram Veli University with a dissertation titled "Strategic Communication Approach in the Context of (Digital) Propaganda and (Digital) Public Diplomacy: The Cases of North and South Korea." She has been continuing her studies in the Department of Korean Language and Literature at Ankara University's Faculty of Language, History, and Geography since 2018. She began her academic career as a Research Assistant in 2019 and currently serves as an Assistant Professor at Bursa Technical University. Additionally, she holds the position of Women and Family Coordinator at the university. Her research primarily focuses on East Asian countries, with a particular emphasis on Korean Studies. She is proficient in English and Korean and has published numerous book chapters and academic articles.

***

Göktuğ Çalışkan earned his bachelor's degree in Political Science and Public Administration from Ankara Yıldırım Beyazıt University. Simultaneously, he pursued a double major program in the Faculty of Political Science, specializing in International Relations. After completing his undergraduate studies in 2017, he pursued a master's degree in International Relations at Ankara Hacı Bayram Veli University, successfully graduating in 2020 with his thesis titled "Indian Shiism and the Evaluation of Iran's India Policy within the Framework of Soft Power: A Constructivist Perspective." In 2018, he also obtained his second bachelor's degree in International Relations through the double major program. As part of the Milli Eğitim Bakanlığı Yurtdışı Seçme ve Yerleştirme (YLSY) scholarship program, Çalışkan underwent language training in France before continuing his academic journey at the Université Internationale de Rabat in Morocco. He completed his second master's degree in 2022 with a thesis entitled "La Présence Chinoise En Afrique Et L'évaluation De La Politique Africaine De La Chine Dans Le Contexte Du Projet « La Ceinture Et La Route »: Les Cas du Kenya et de l'Ouganda" (China's Presence in Africa and the Evaluation of China's African Policy in the Context of the Belt and Road Initiative: The Cases of Kenya and Uganda). In addition to his studies in international relations, Çalışkan also holds a bachelor's degree in Law from Erciyes University. He is currently pursuing a Ph.D. in International Relations at Ankara Hacı Bayram Veli University. Additionally, as part of the YLSY program, he has commenced another Ph.D. at the Université Internationale de Rabat in Morocco. As an international relations expert at ANKASAM (Ankara Center for Crisis and Policy Studies), Çalışkan has conducted interviews and published analyses on a range of geopolitical topics. His academic contributions include book chapters, articles, and book reviews. Fluent in English and French, his research primarily focuses on China-Africa Relations, the Sahel Region, Religion and Security in the Sahel, Iran, Shiism, India, Food Security, Climate Change in Africa, Insurgencies and Terrorism, African Geopolitics, the Belt and Road Initiative, and Central Asia.

Halil Deligöz completed his Ph.D. in International Relations in 2023 at Ankara Yildirim Beyazit University with a dissertation titled "US Economic Statecraft Towards China: The Case of Technological Sanctions", and published scholarly articles and book chapters. He studies on the interface between geopolitical/geoeconomic context and development, and "technological statecraft" in international politics. Currently, he works at the Ministry of Energy and Natural Resources, Turkiye.

Sina Kısacık is an assistant professor doctor at the Department of International Relations in Cyprus Science University, in Ozanköy-Girne (Kyrenia)-Turkish Republic of Northern Cyprus. He holds a PhD in political science and international relations from Yeditepe University. He got his M.A. degree on European Union studies from Galatasaray University and B.A. on international relations from Bilgi

University. He has authored/co-authored several academic publications in various national and international academic journals in English and Turkish. His research interests include: energy geopolitics, Turkish foreign policy, Russian foreign policy, Eurasia geopolitics.

Şeyma Kızılay continues her PhD education at Uludağ University, Department of International Relations. In 2016, she graduated from Erciyes University, Faculty of Economics and Administrative Sciences, Department of International Relations. She received her master's degree from Kırşehir Ahi Evran University, Institute of Social Sciences, Department of International Relations in 2019 with her thesis titled "The Case of Iraq in the Context of Nation Building in International Relations". She has published numerous analyses on global politics on various platforms. She continues her academic contributions with book chapters, articles and analyses. His main research interests are ontological security, Middle East Studies, but she also focuses on terrorism, South Asia and global crises and conflicts. She speaks fluent English and intermediate Arabic.

Kiet Le Hoang has a Master's degree in Public Policy and is a PhD candidate in International Relations. Hoang works at the Thai Binh Duong University and University of Social Sciences and Humanities (Hanoi). Hoang has research experience in international relations and public policy with published research in Vietnam and some internationally. Additionally, Hoang often participates in and collaborates on international projects by governmental organizations in Southeast Asia. Hoang's research interests focus on Europe and the Indo-Pacific. It focuses on issues of power competition between great powers.

Cenk Tamer graduated from Sakarya University, Department of International Relations in 2014. In the same year, he started his master's degree at Gazi University, Department of Middle Eastern and African Studies. In 2016, Tamer completed his master's degree with his thesis titled "Iran's Iraq Policy after 1990", started working as a Research Assistant at ANKASAM in 2017 and was accepted to Gazi University International Relations PhD Program in the same year. Tamer, whose areas of specialization are Iran, Sects, Sufism, Mahdism, Identity Politics and Asia-Pacific and who speaks English fluently, completed his PhD education at Gazi University in 2022 with his thesis titled "Identity Construction Process and Mahdism in the Islamic Republic of Iran within the Framework of Social Constructionism Theory and Securitization Approach". He is currently working as an Asia-Pacific Specialist at ANKASAM.

Tran Xuan Hiep is a scholar and researcher currently working at Falcuty of History, University of Science and Education, University of Da Nang, Vietnam. He is a leading International Relations researcher in Vietnam. With a prolific academic record, he has published over 160 scholarly works including books, book chapters, and articles, with nearly 40 publications indexed in SCOPUS/ISI databases.

Murat Yorulmaz is an Assistant Professor in Havsa Vocational Collegue at Trakya University. He holds a PhD. in the Department of International Relations at Trakya University in 2014 and a M.Sc. in the department of International Relations at London School of Economics in 2004. Bachelor in ELT at Dokuz Eylul University. Before joining Trakya University, he was an English teacher in state schools in Turkey. His research interests include: National and International Security, Concepts and Theories of International Security, Security Dilemma, Energy Security, Foreign and Security Policies of U.S., the Russian Federation and China.

Index

A

C

D

E

G

H

I

L

M

P

R

S

T

X

www.ingramcontent.com/pod-product-compliance
Lightning Source LLC
LaVergne TN
LVHW080604300926
849162LV00005B/1043